Tama Mitsuboshi

I Call the Name of the Night I

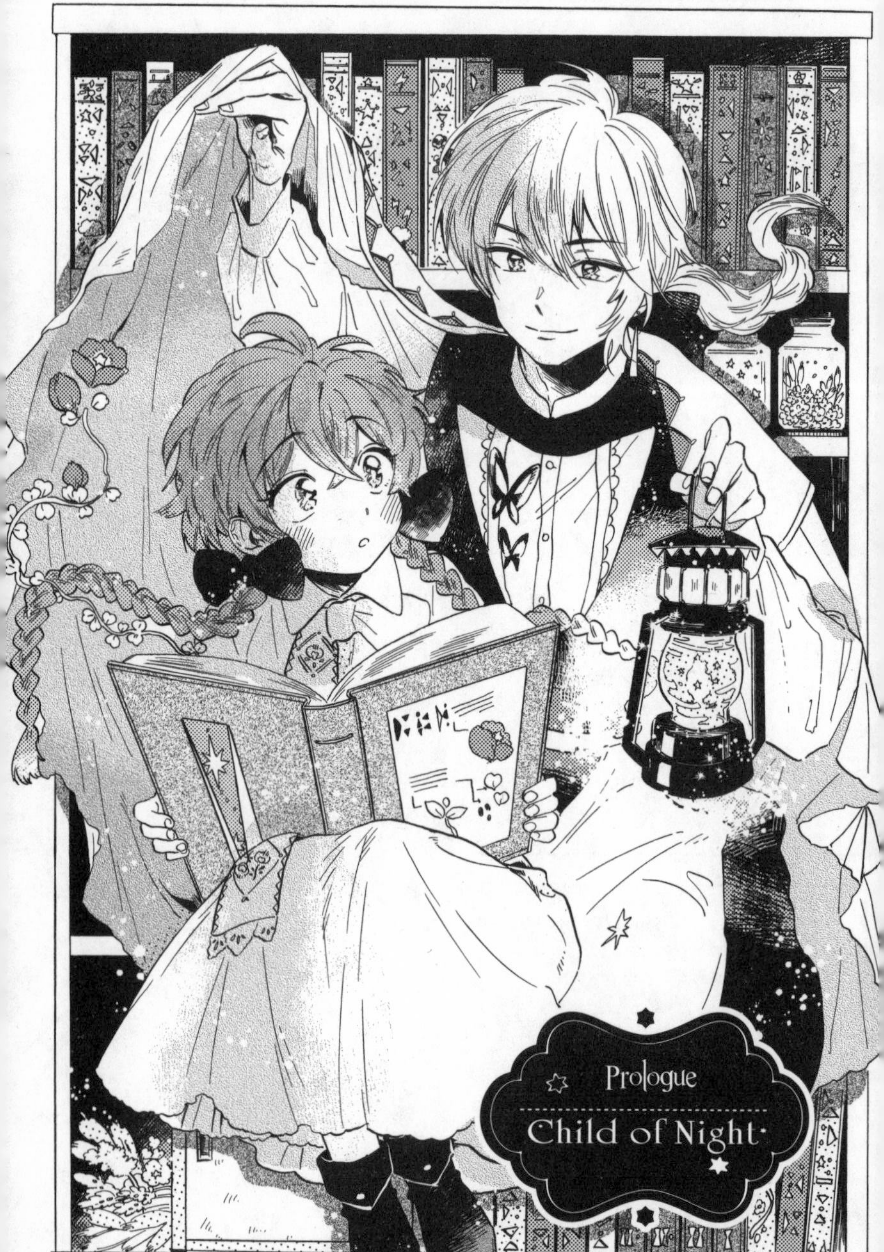
Prologue
Child of Night

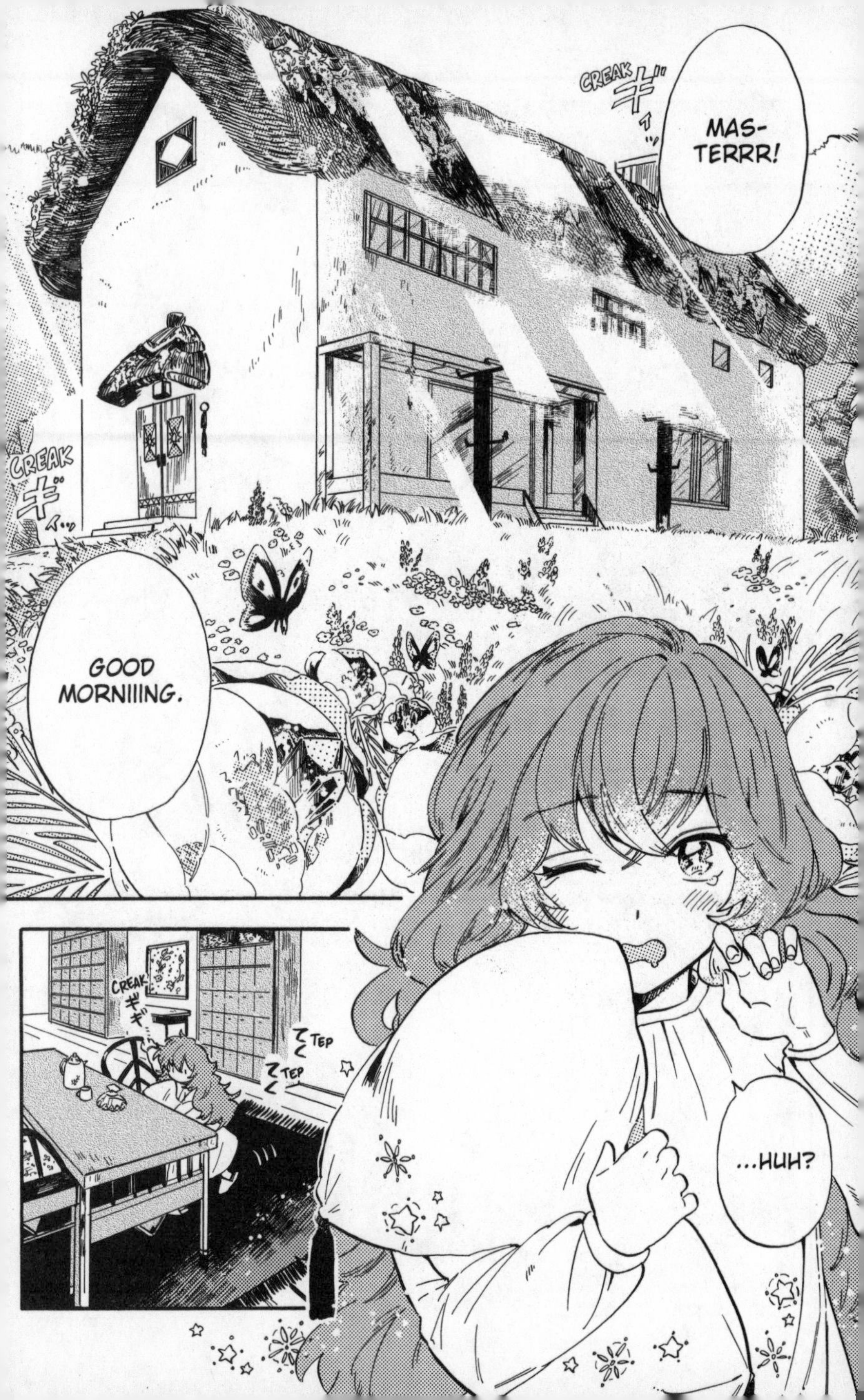
CREAK
MAS-TERRR!
CREAK
GOOD MORNIIING.
...HUH?
CREAK
TEP
TEP

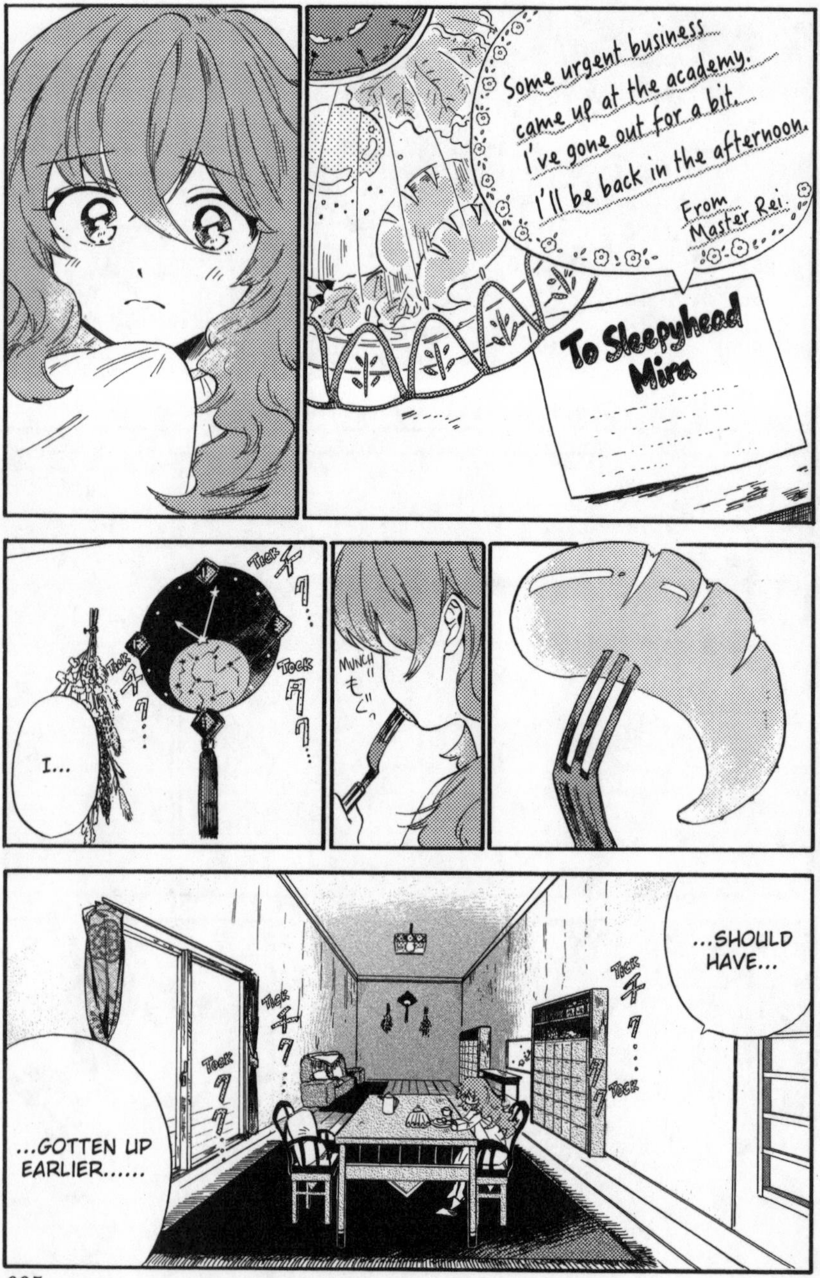
Some urgent business came up at the academy. I've gone out for a bit. I'll be back in the afternoon.
From Master Rei
To Sleepyhead Mira
MUNCH
TOCK
TICK
TICK
I...
...SHOULD HAVE...
TICK
TOCK
TICK
TOCK
...GOTTEN UP EARLIER......

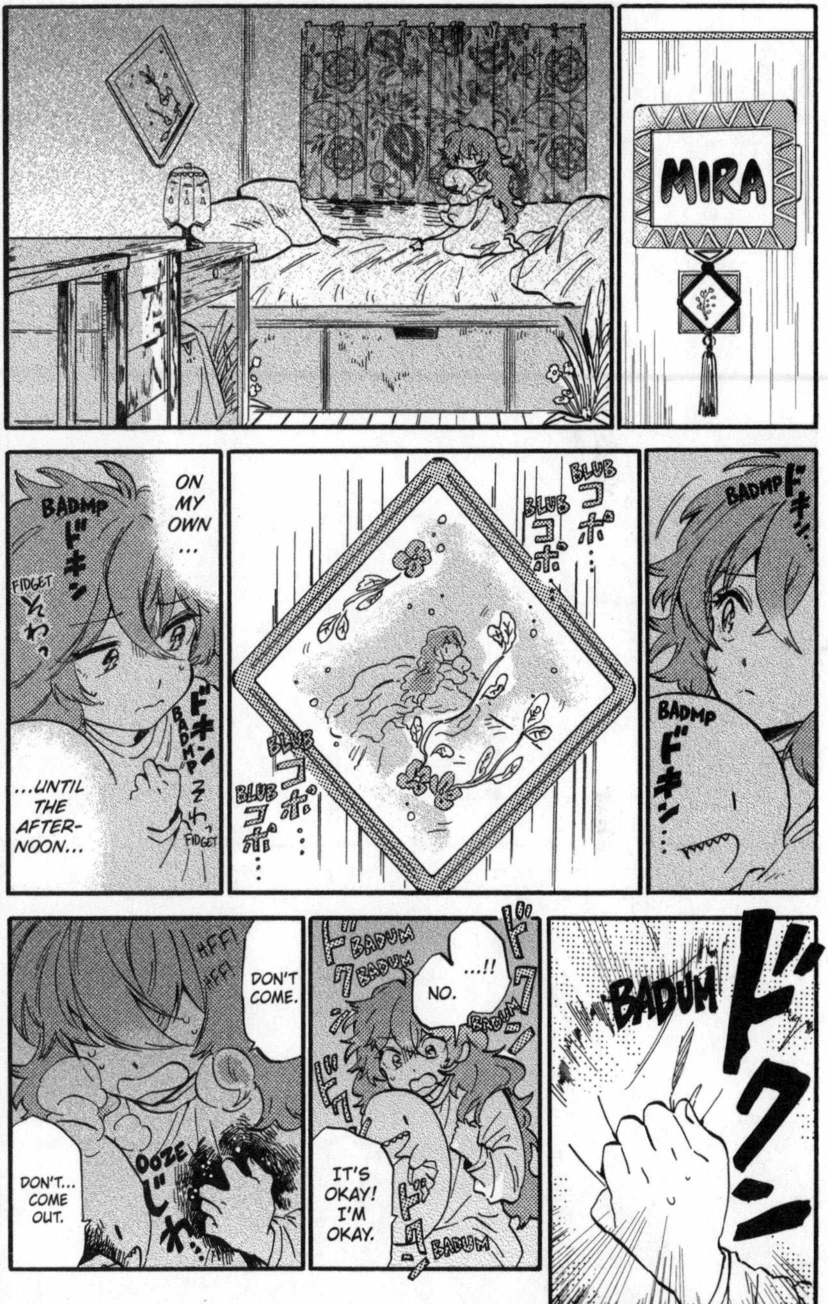
MIRA
BADMP ドキ…
BADMP ドキン…
BLUB コポ…
BLUB コポ…
BLUB コポ…
BLUB コポ…
ON MY OWN…
BADMP ドキン
FIDGET そわっ
…UNTIL THE AFTER-NOON…
ドキン BADMP
そわっ FIDGET
BADUM ドクン
…!!
NO.
BADUM ドク
BADUM ドク
IT'S OKAY! I'M OKAY.
BADUM ドク
HFF! HFF!
DON'T COME.
DOZE じわ…
DON'T… COME OUT.

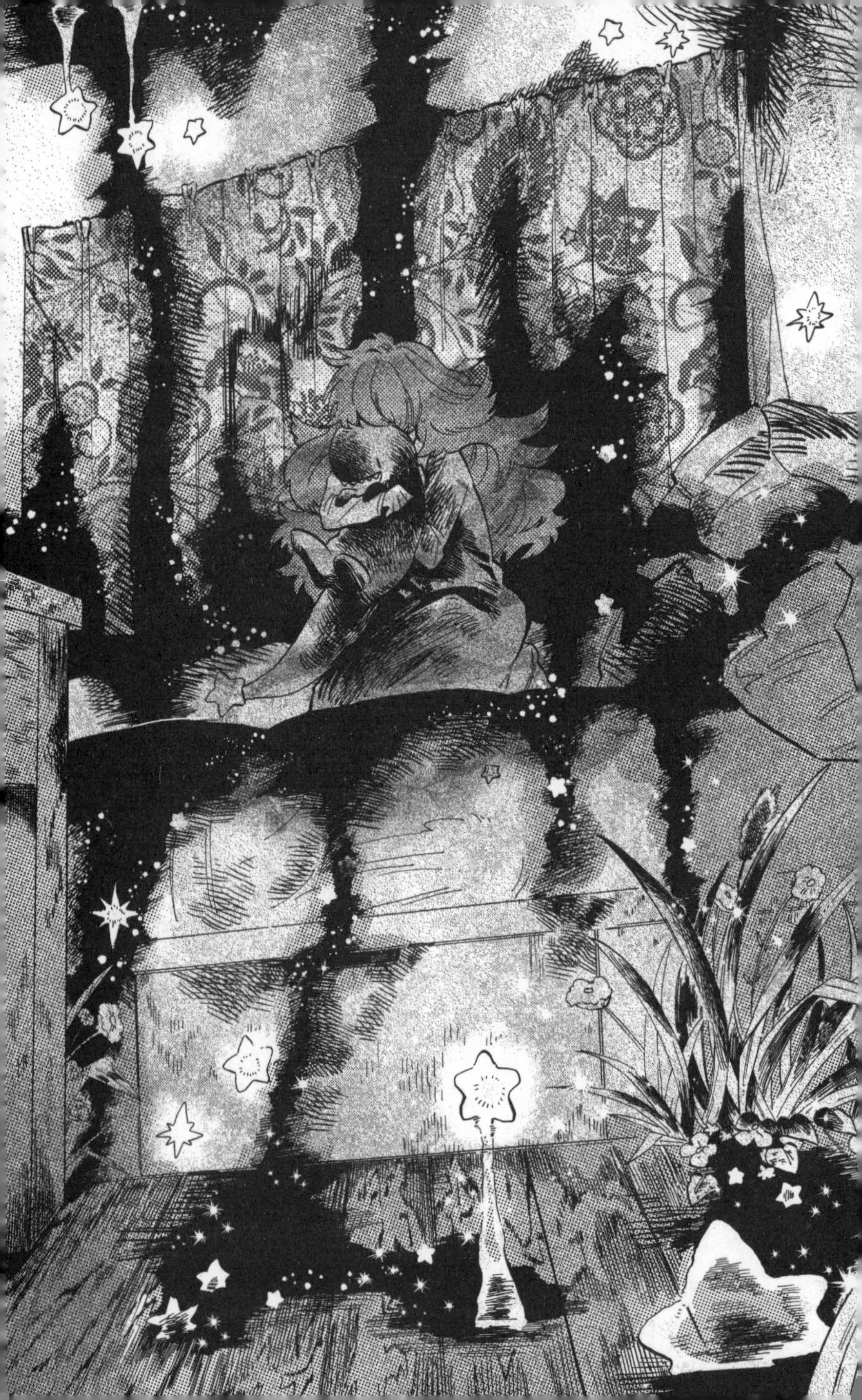

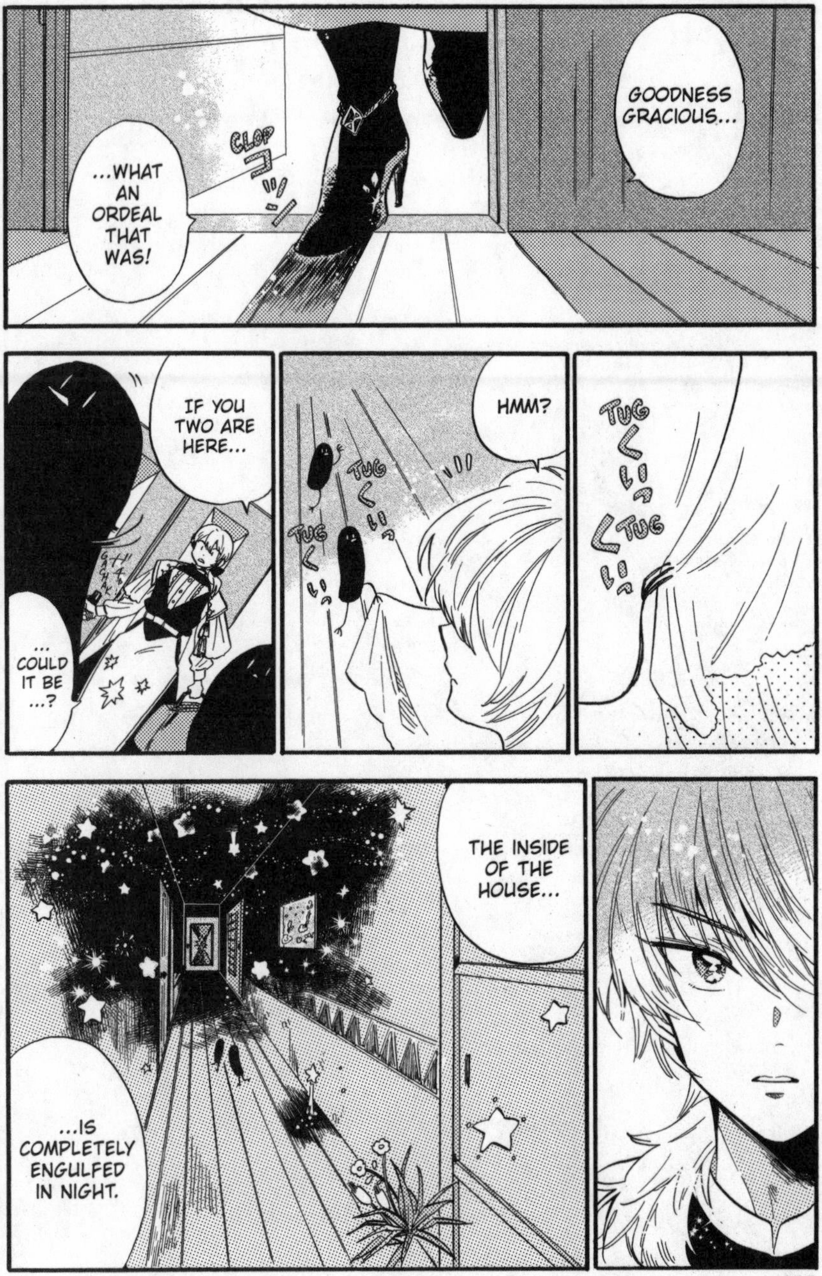
GOODNESS GRACIOUS...
CLOP
...WHAT AN ORDEAL THAT WAS!
TUG
TUG
HMM?
TUG
TUG
IF YOU TWO ARE HERE...
...COULD IT BE ...?
THE INSIDE OF THE HOUSE...
...IS COMPLETELY ENGULFED IN NIGHT.

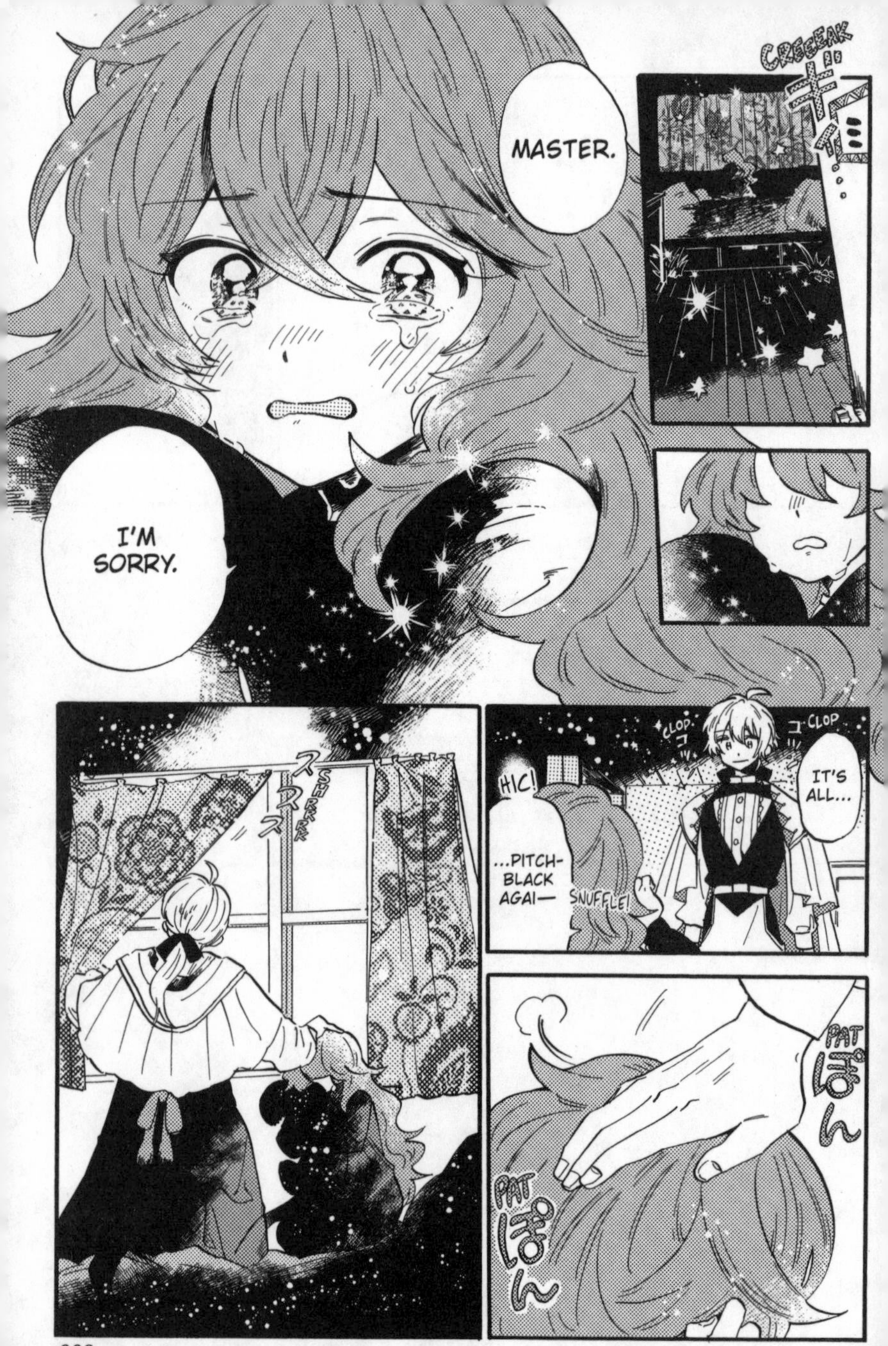
CREEEAK
MASTER.
I'M SORRY.
CLOP
IT'S ALL...
CLOP
HIC!
...PITCH-BLACK AGAI—
SNUFFLE!
PAT
ぽん
PAT
ぽん
SHRRRR

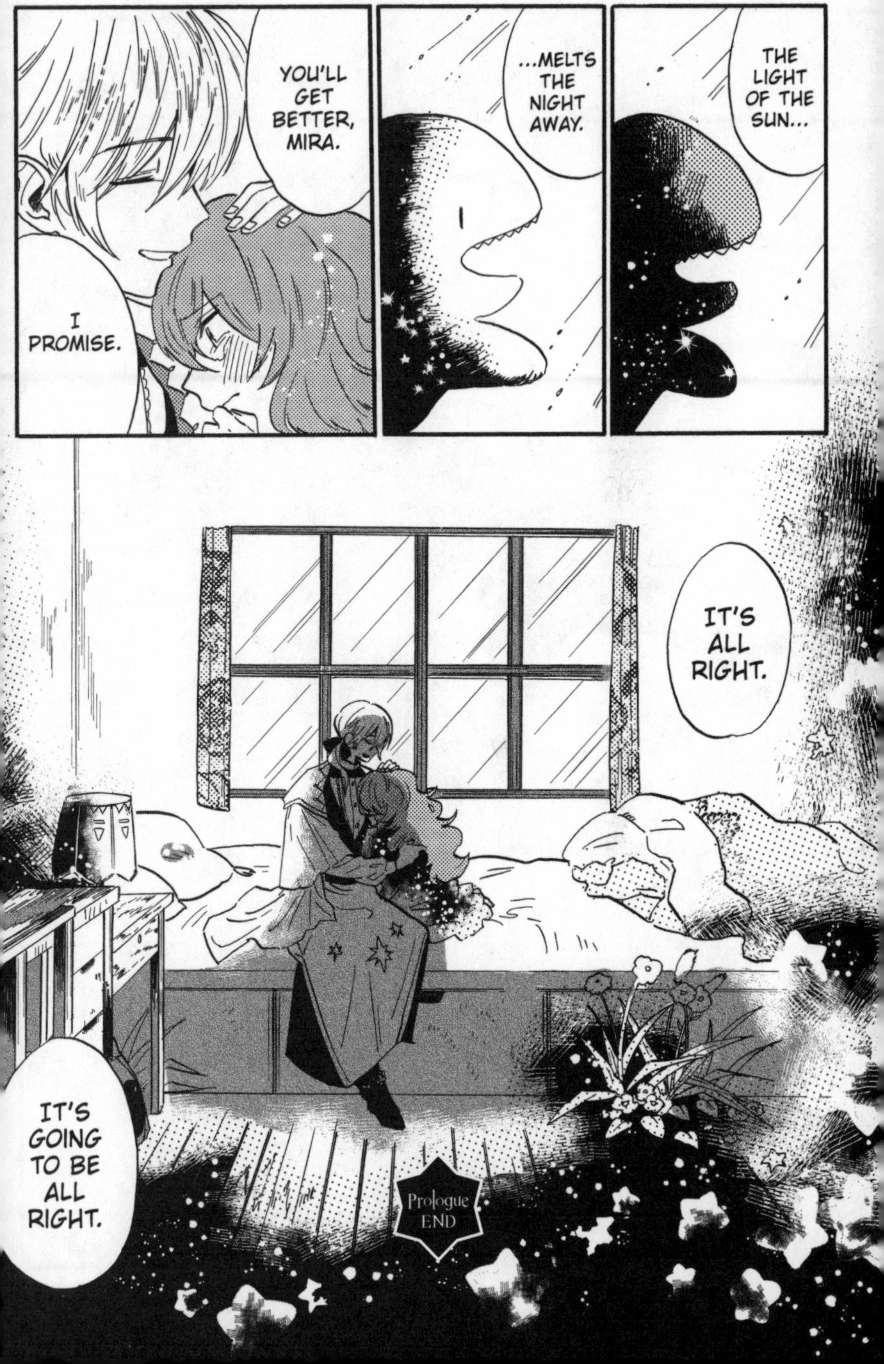
THE LIGHT OF THE SUN...
...MELTS THE NIGHT AWAY.
YOU'LL GET BETTER, MIRA.
I PROMISE.
IT'S ALL RIGHT.
IT'S GOING TO BE ALL RIGHT.
Prologue END

Call the Name of the Night

1

Tama Mitsuboshi

Call the Name of the Night

CONTENTS

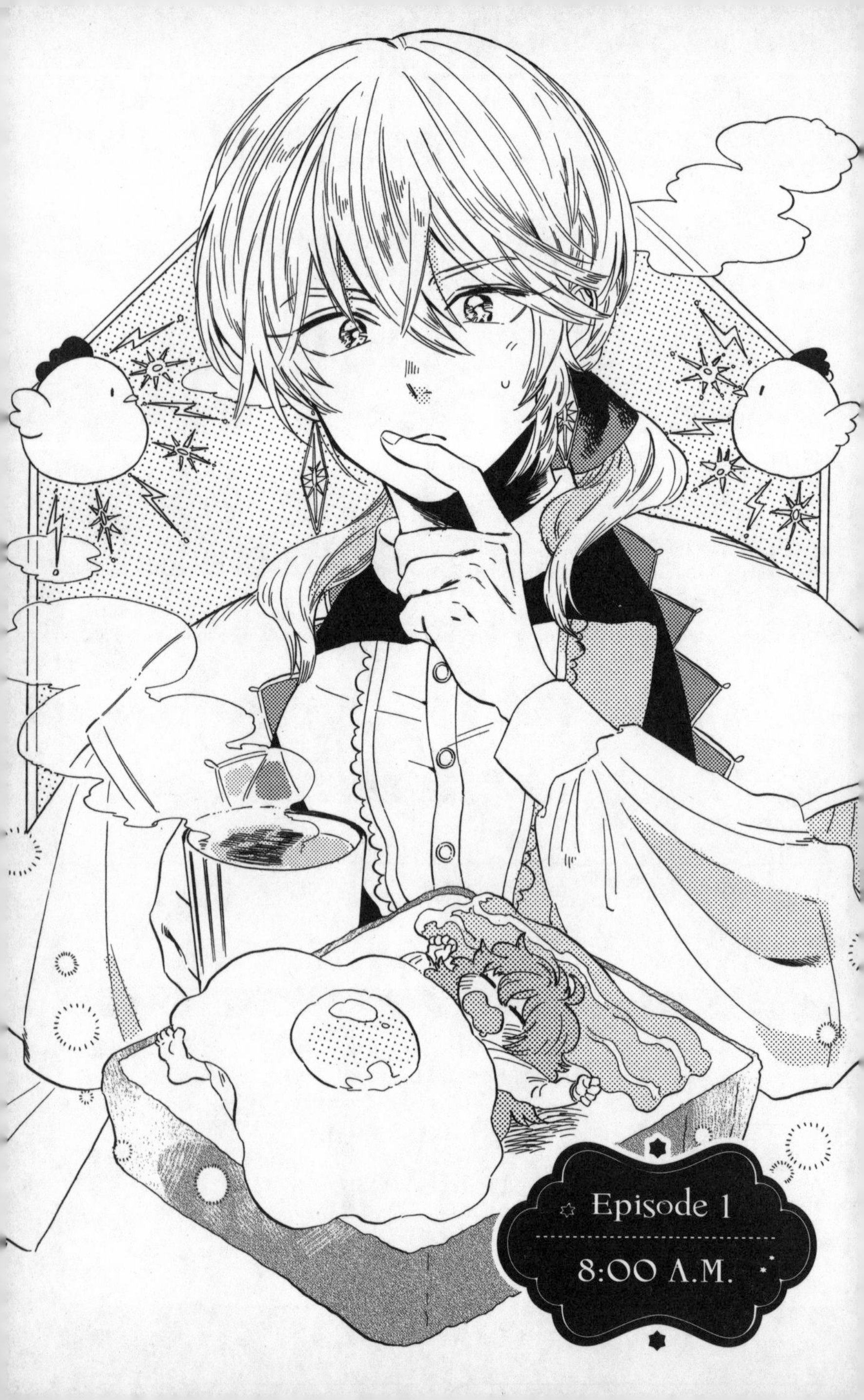
Episode 1
8:00 A.M.

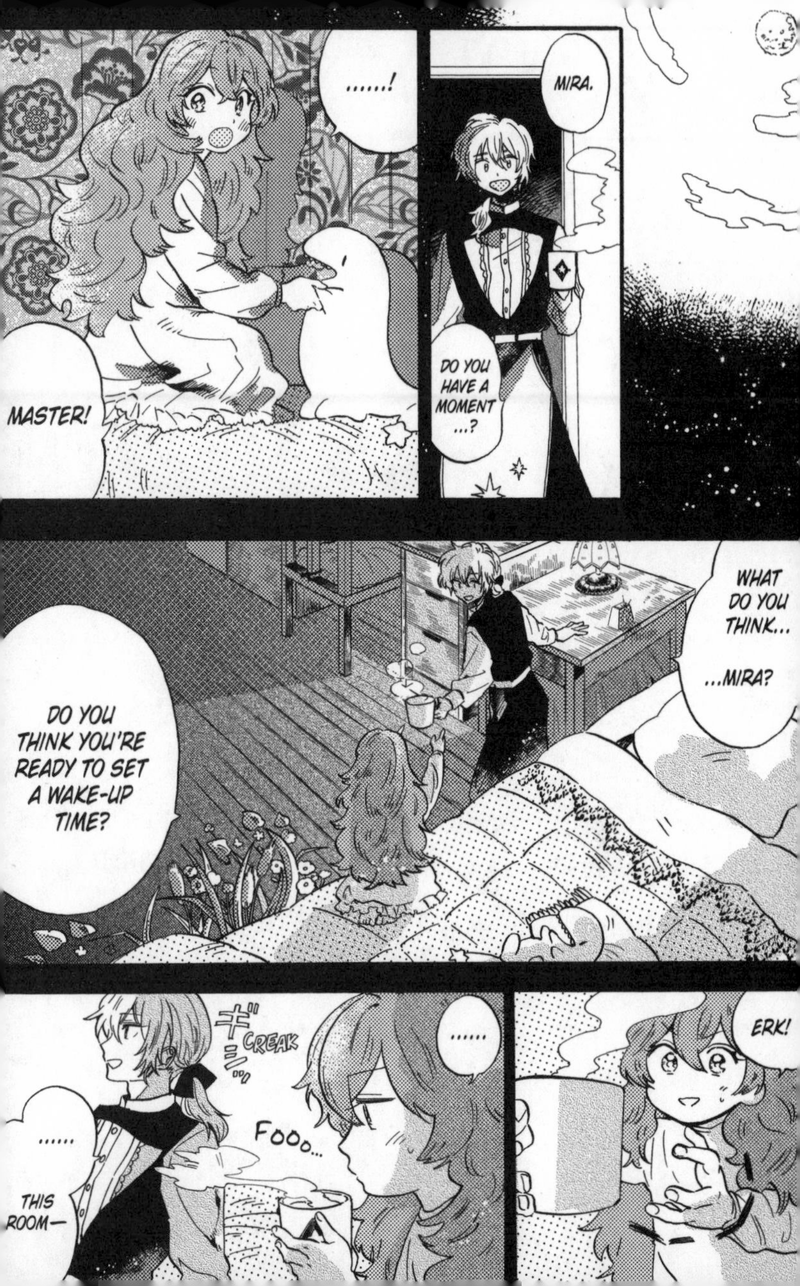
MIRA.
DO YOU HAVE A MOMENT ...?
......!
MASTER!
WHAT DO YOU THINK...
...MIRA?
DO YOU THINK YOU'RE READY TO SET A WAKE-UP TIME?
ERK!
......
ギシッ CREAK
FOOo...
......
THIS ROOM—

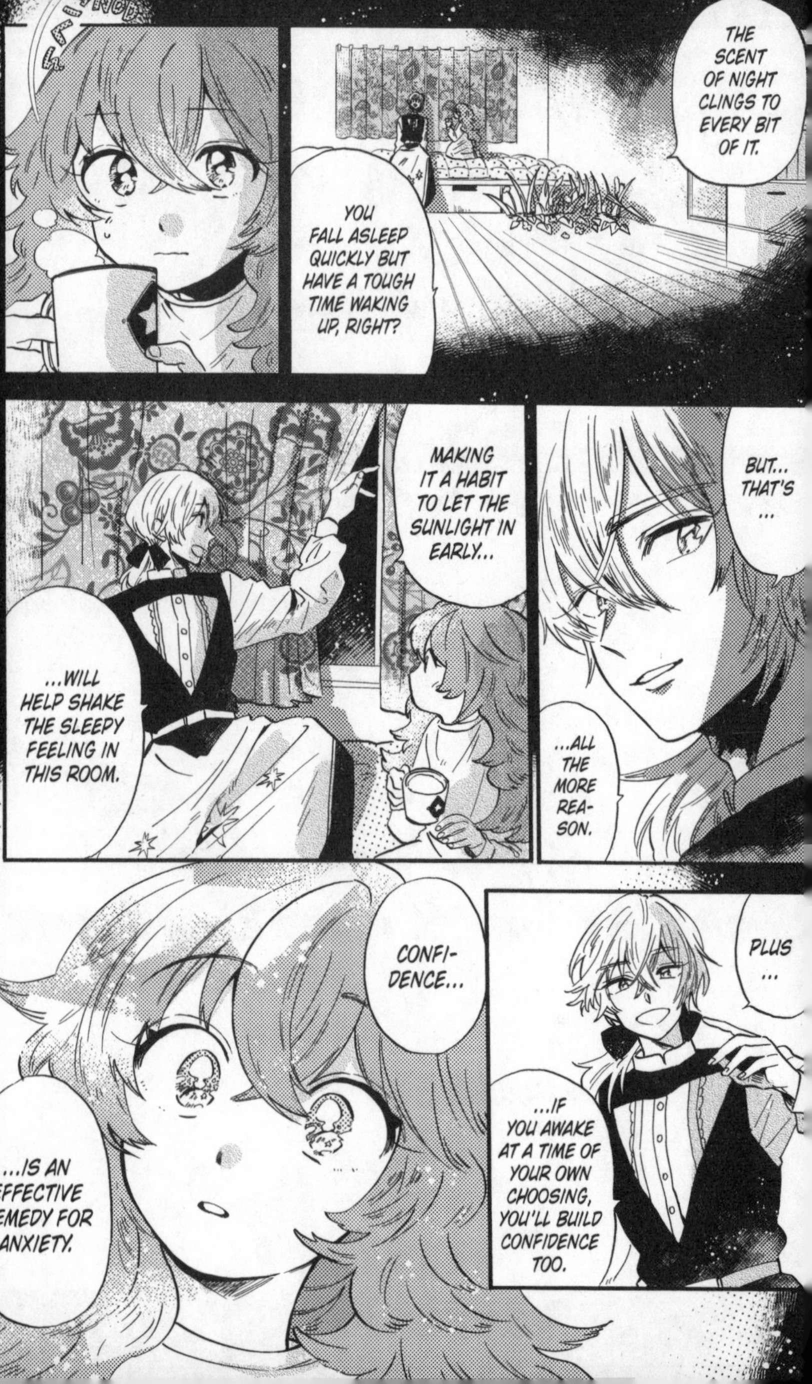
THE SCENT OF NIGHT CLINGS TO EVERY BIT OF IT.
YOU FALL ASLEEP QUICKLY BUT HAVE A TOUGH TIME WAKING UP, RIGHT?
NOD
BUT... THAT'S ...
...ALL THE MORE REA-SON.
MAKING IT A HABIT TO LET THE SUNLIGHT IN EARLY...
...WILL HELP SHAKE THE SLEEPY FEELING IN THIS ROOM.
PLUS ...
...IF YOU AWAKE AT A TIME OF YOUR OWN CHOOSING, YOU'LL BUILD CONFIDENCE TOO.
CONFI-DENCE...
...IS AN EFFECTIVE REMEDY FOR ANXIETY.

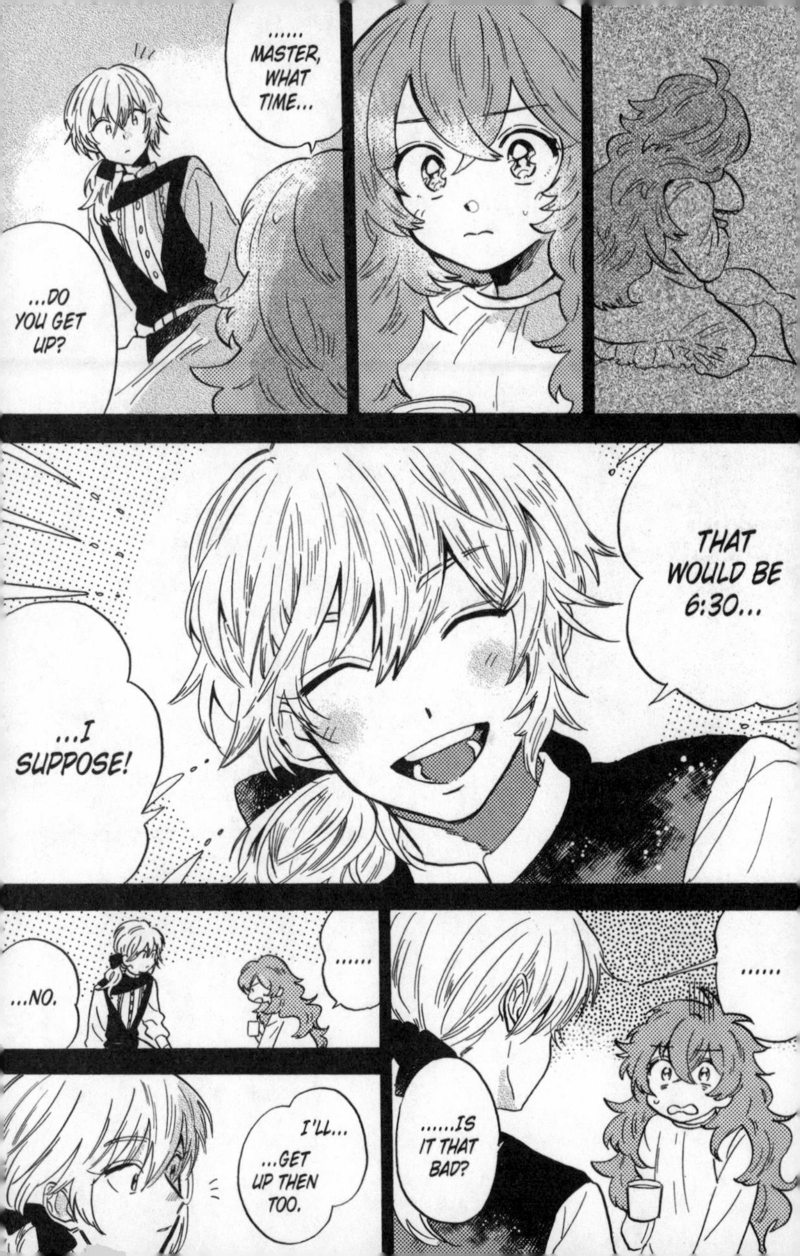
......MASTER, WHAT TIME...
...DO YOU GET UP?
THAT WOULD BE 6:30...
...I SUPPOSE!
......
......IS IT THAT BAD?
......
...NO.
I'LL... ...GET UP THEN TOO.

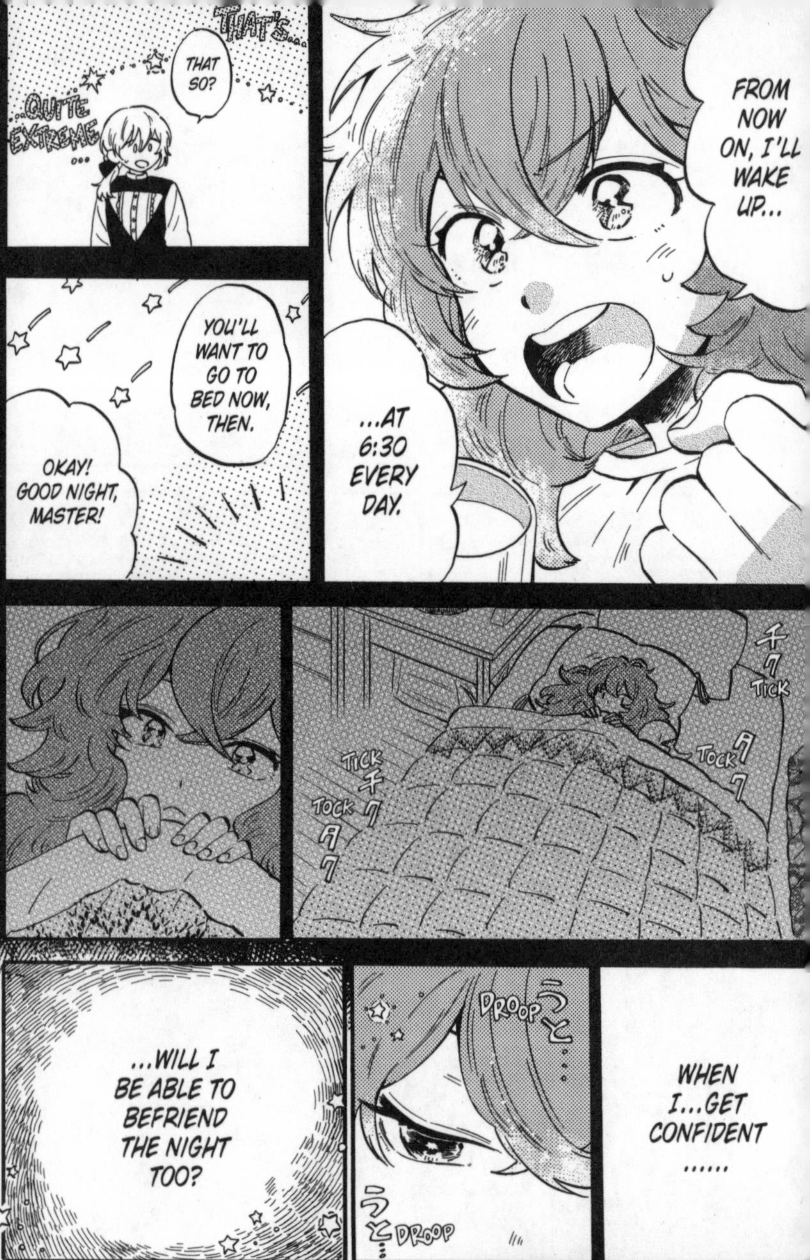
FROM NOW ON, I'LL WAKE UP...
...AT 6:30 EVERY DAY.
THAT'S...
THAT SO?
...QUITE EXTREME...
YOU'LL WANT TO GO TO BED NOW, THEN.
OKAY! GOOD NIGHT, MASTER!
チク TICK
タク TOCK
TICK チク
TOCK タク
WHEN I...GET CONFIDENT ......
DROOP うと
うと DROOP
...WILL I BE ABLE TO BEFRIEND THE NIGHT TOO?

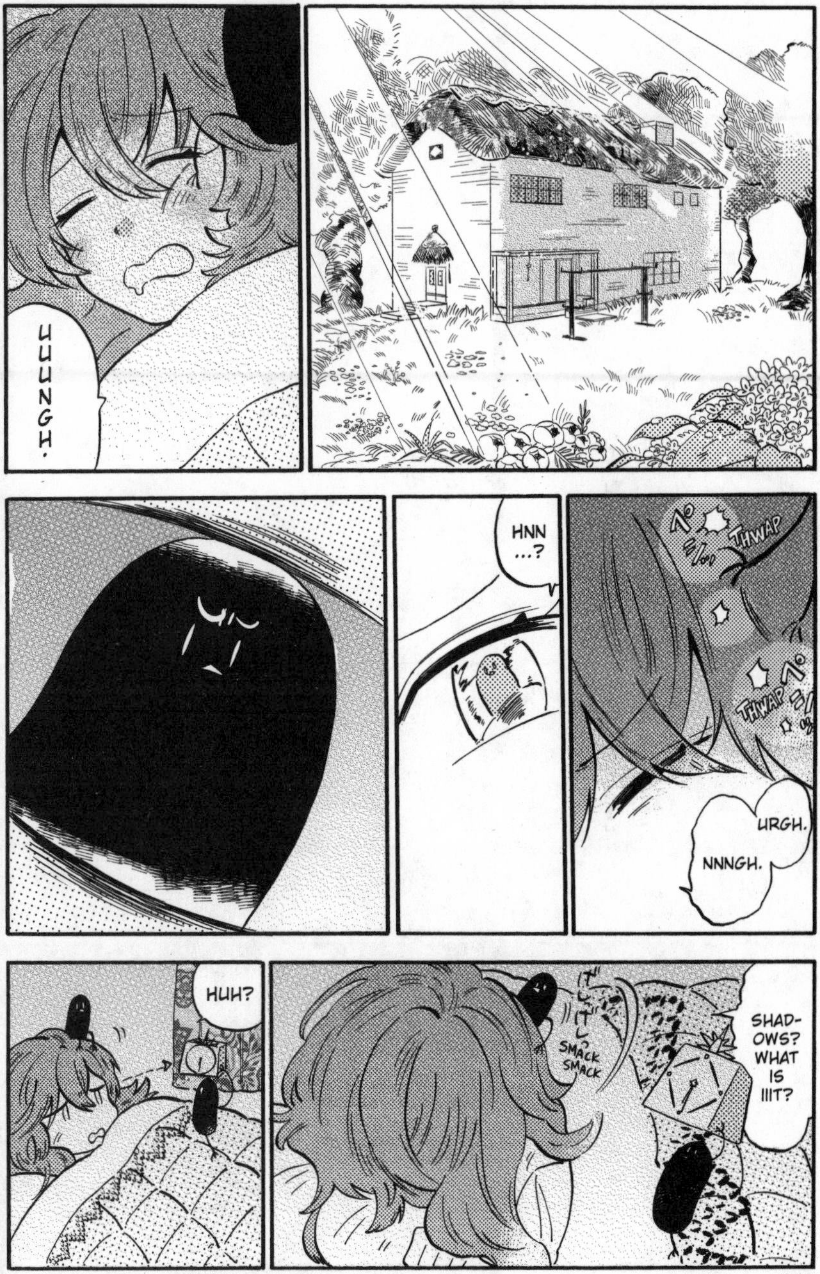
UUUNGH.
THWAP
THWAP
URGH.
NNNGH.
HNN ...?
SMACK SMACK
SHAD-OWS? WHAT IS IIIT?
HUH?

IT'S ONLY 6:30!

ROLL

FWAAH!!

LURCH

THAT'S RIGHT!!

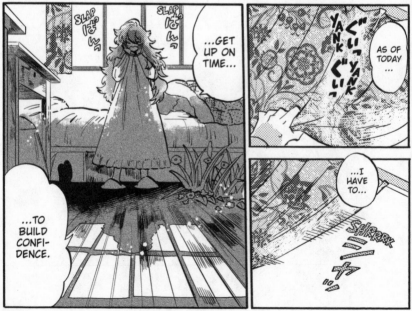

...GET UP ON TIME...

SLAP SLAP

AS OF TODAY...

YANK YANK

...TO BUILD CONFIDENCE.

...I HAVE TO...

SHRKK

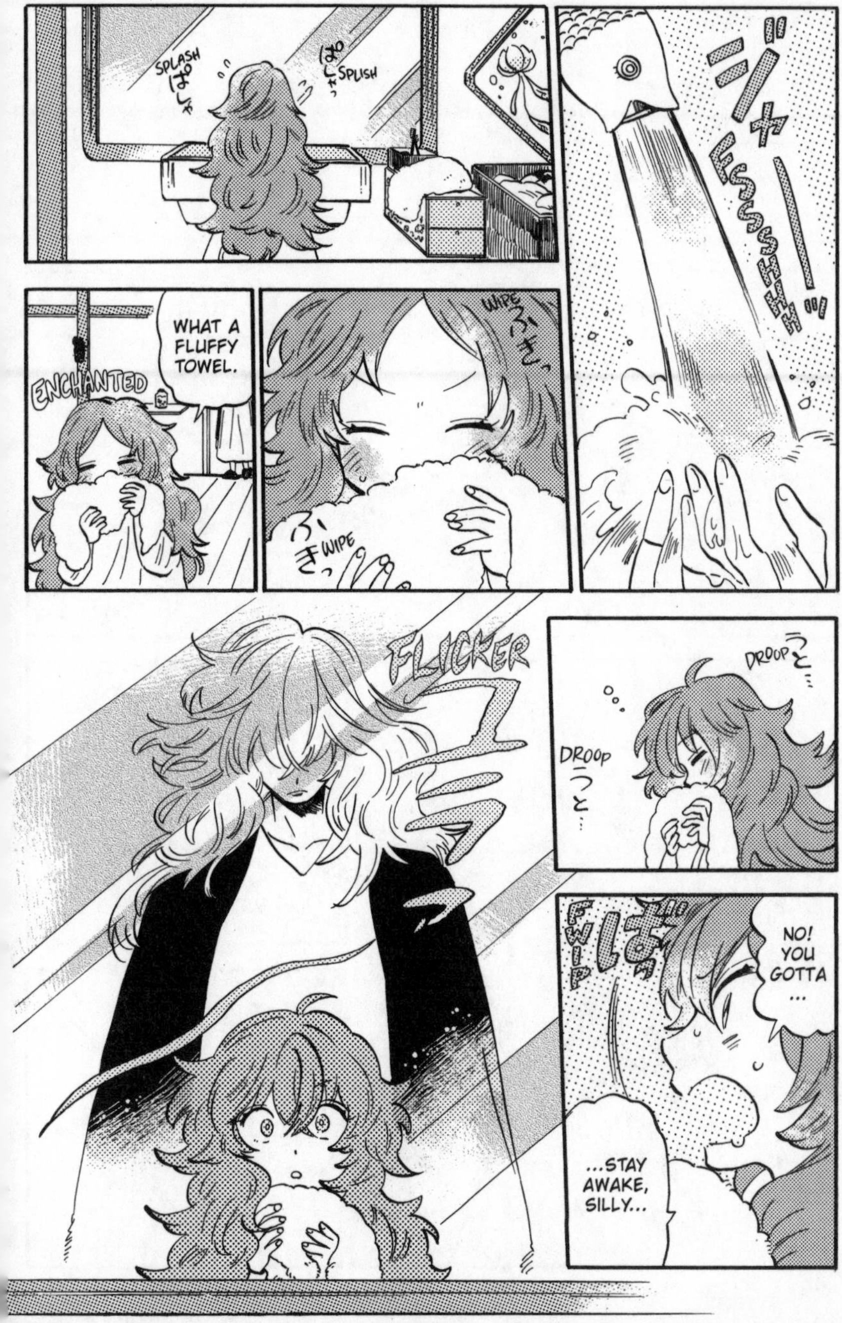
ジャー
ESSSHHHH!!!
SPLASH
ぱしゃ
ぱしゃっ
SPLISH
WIPE
ふきっ
ふきっ
WIPE
WHAT A FLUFFY TOWEL.
ENCHANTED
DROOP
うと…
DROOP
うと…
FWIP
はっ
NO! YOU GOTTA…
…STAY AWAKE, SILLY…
FLICKER

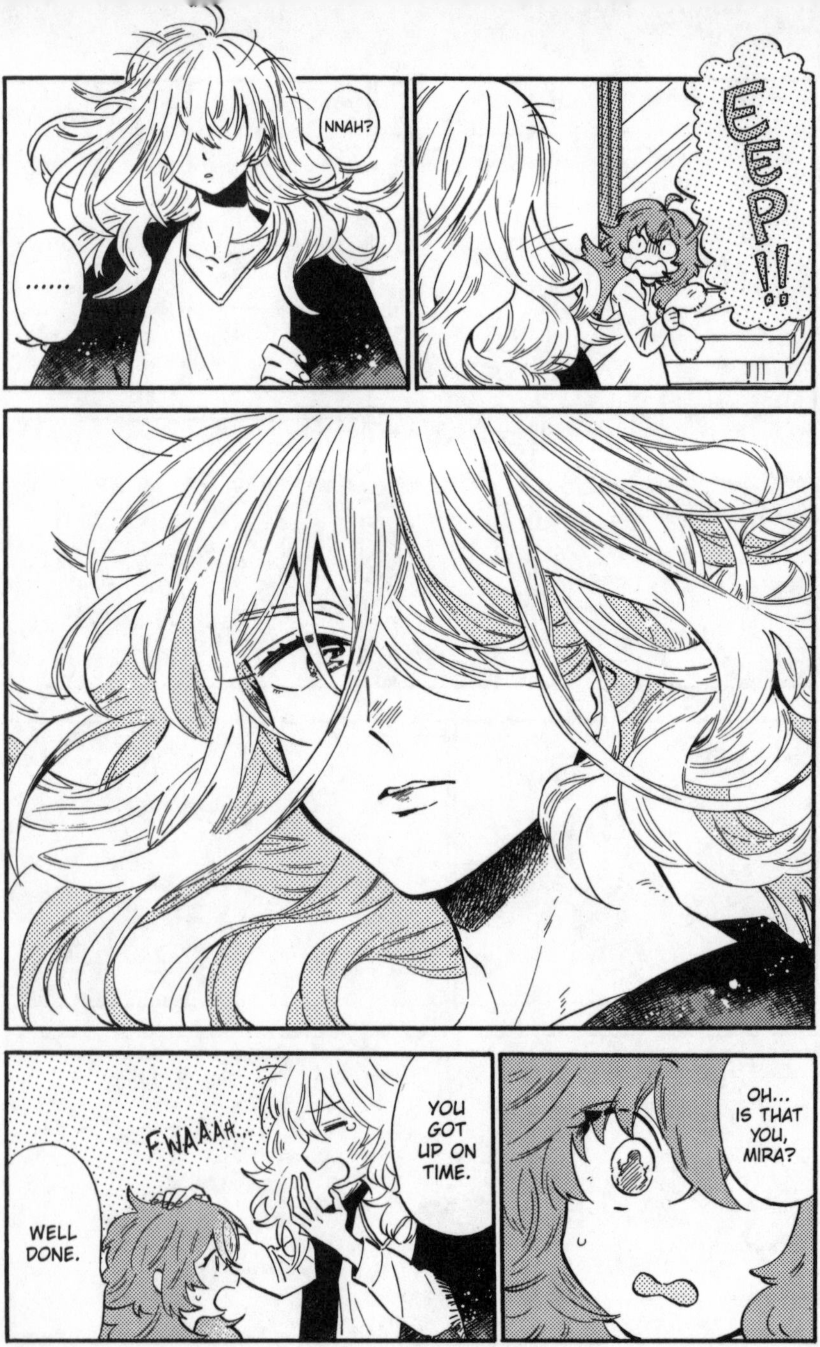
EEP!!
NNAH?
......
OH... IS THAT YOU, MIRA?
YOU GOT UP ON TIME.
FWAAAH...
WELL DONE.

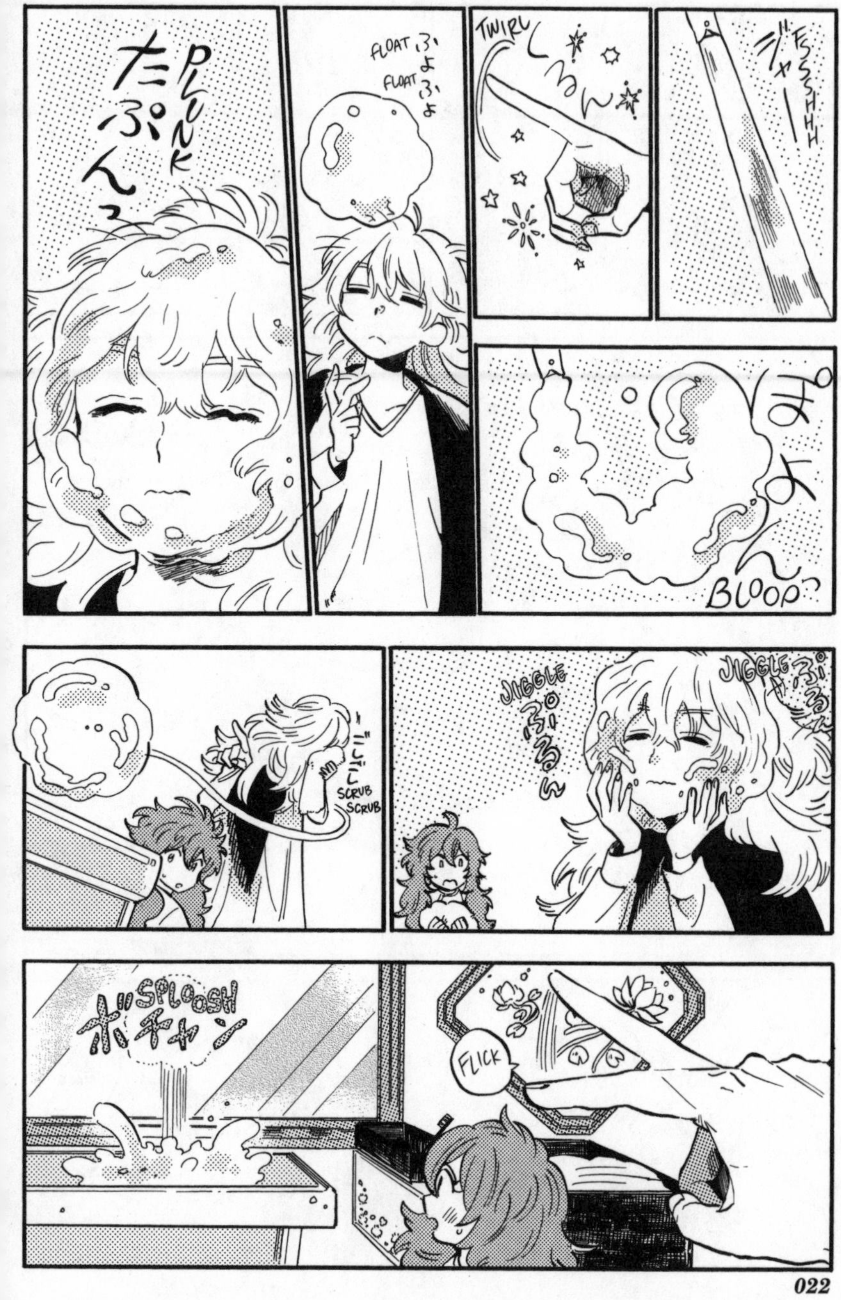
FSSHHH
ジャー
TWIRL
くるん
BLOOP
ぽよん
FLOAT ふよ
FLOAT ふよ
PLUNK
たぷんっ
JIGGLE ぷるん
JIGGLE ぷるん
ごしごし SCRUB SCRUB
FLICK
SPLOOSH
ボチャン

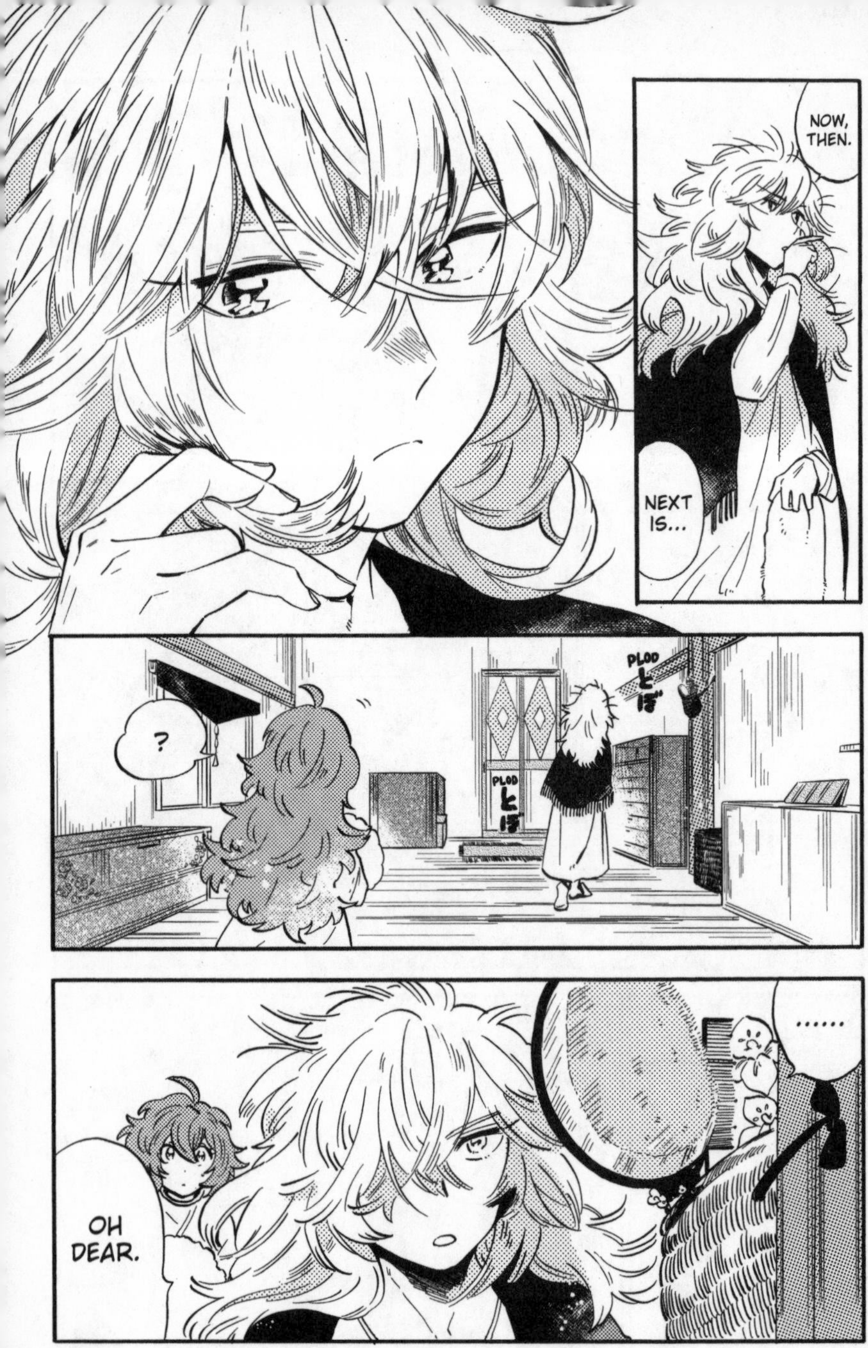
NOW, THEN.
NEXT IS...
PLOD とぼ
PLOD とぼ
?
......
OH DEAR.

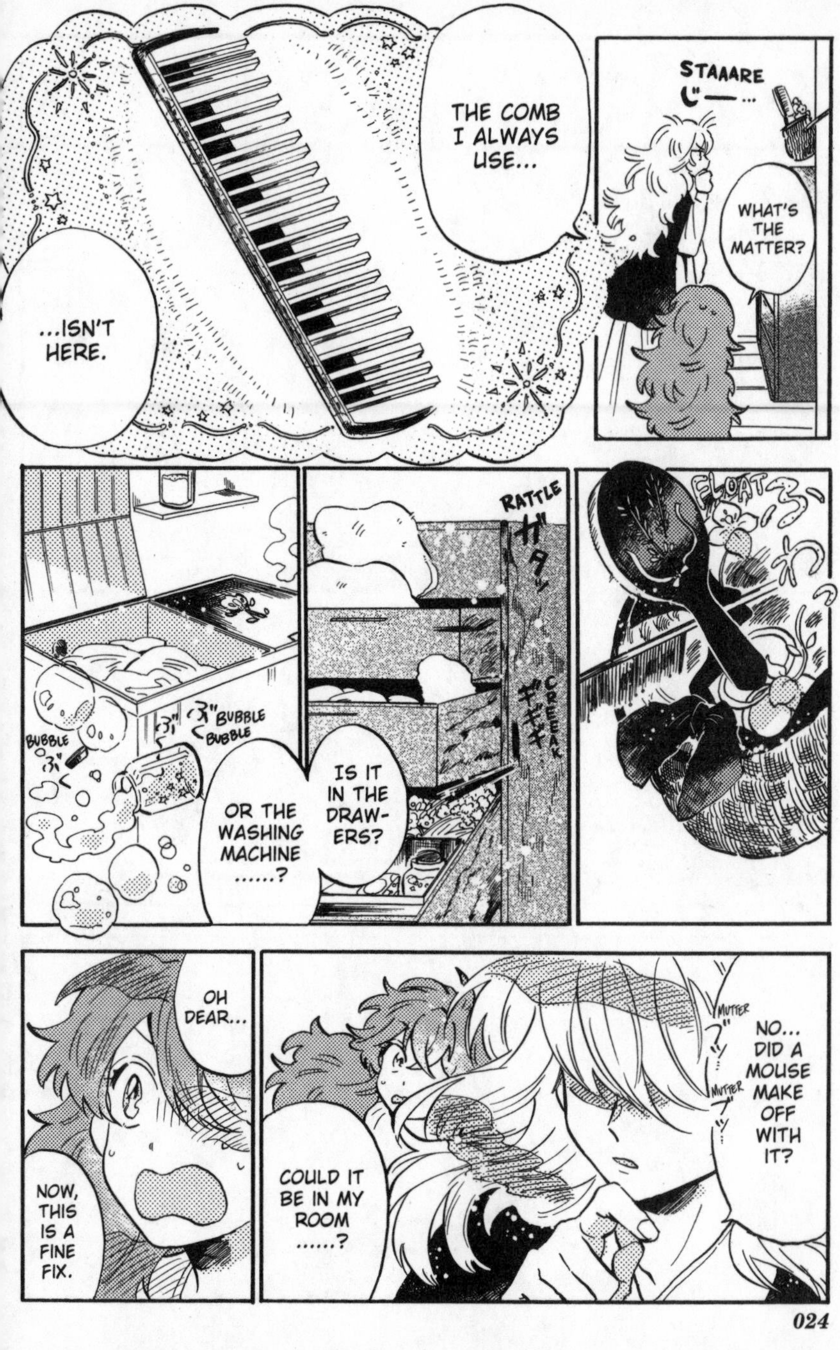
STAAARE
WHAT'S THE MATTER?
THE COMB I ALWAYS USE...
...ISN'T HERE.
FLOAT
RATTLE
IS IT IN THE DRAW-ERS?
CREEAK
OR THE WASHING MACHINE ......?
BUBBLE BUBBLE
BUBBLE
MUTTER
MUTTER
NO... DID A MOUSE MAKE OFF WITH IT?
COULD IT BE IN MY ROOM ......?
OH DEAR...
NOW, THIS IS A FINE FIX.

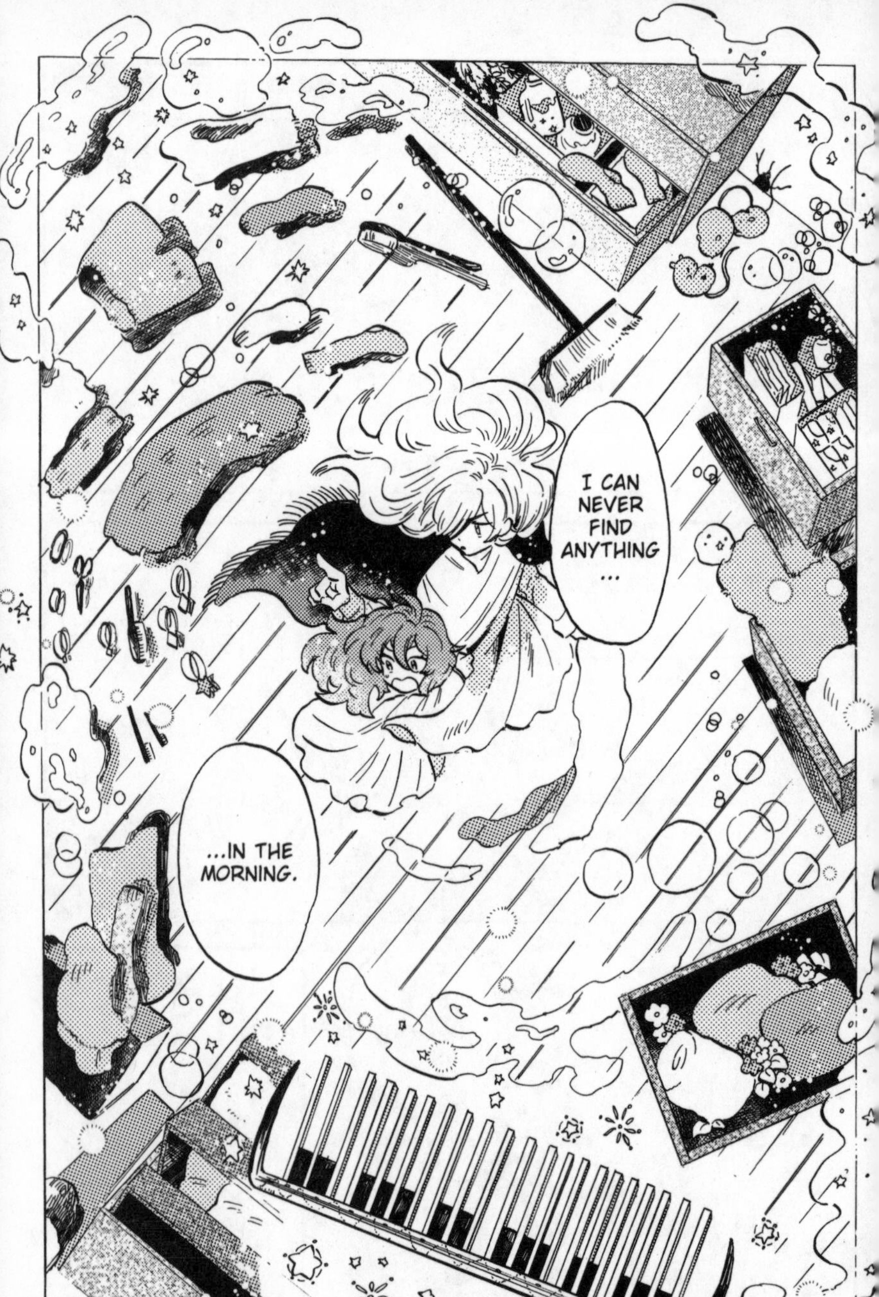
I CAN NEVER FIND ANYTHING ...
...IN THE MORNING.

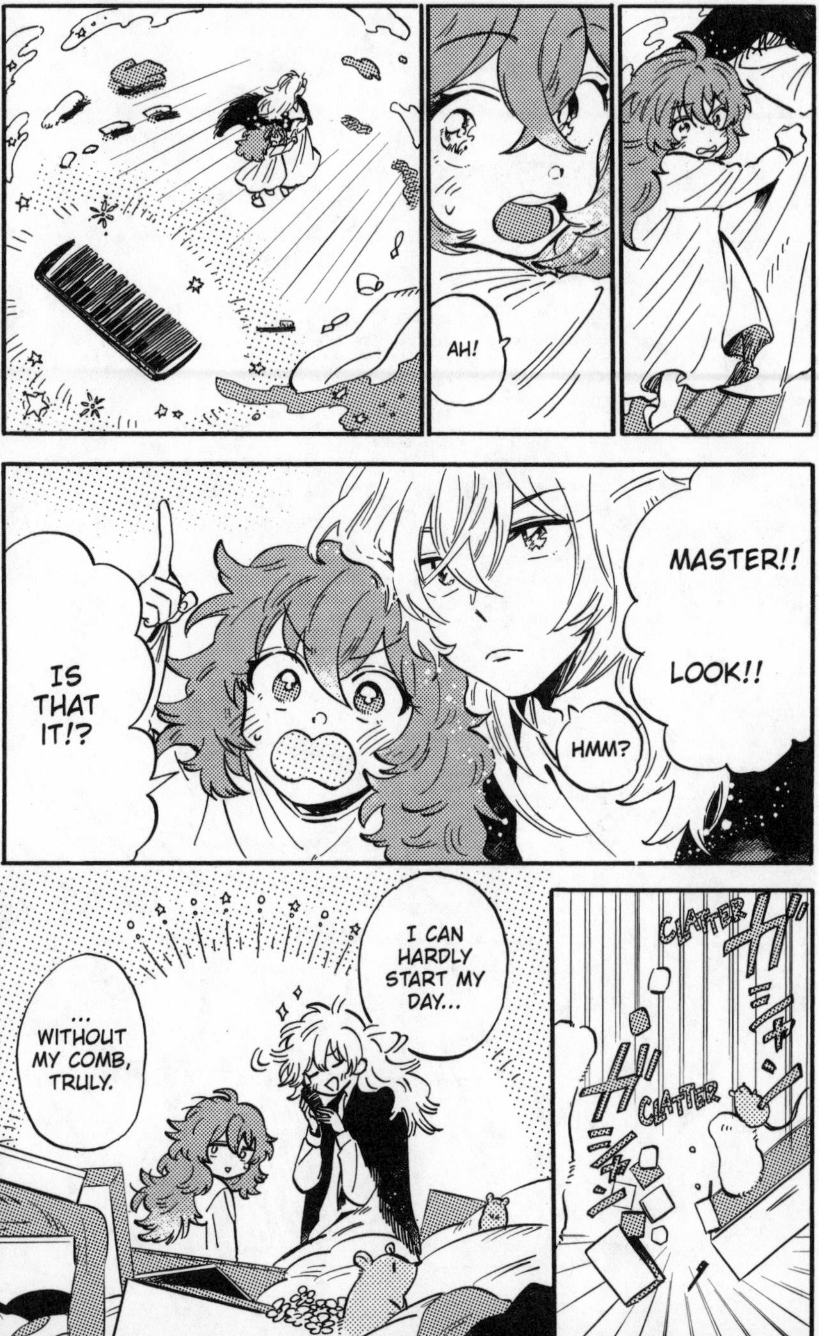
AH!
MASTER!! LOOK!!
HMM?
IS THAT IT!?
CLATTER
CLATTER
I CAN HARDLY START MY DAY...
...WITHOUT MY COMB, TRULY.

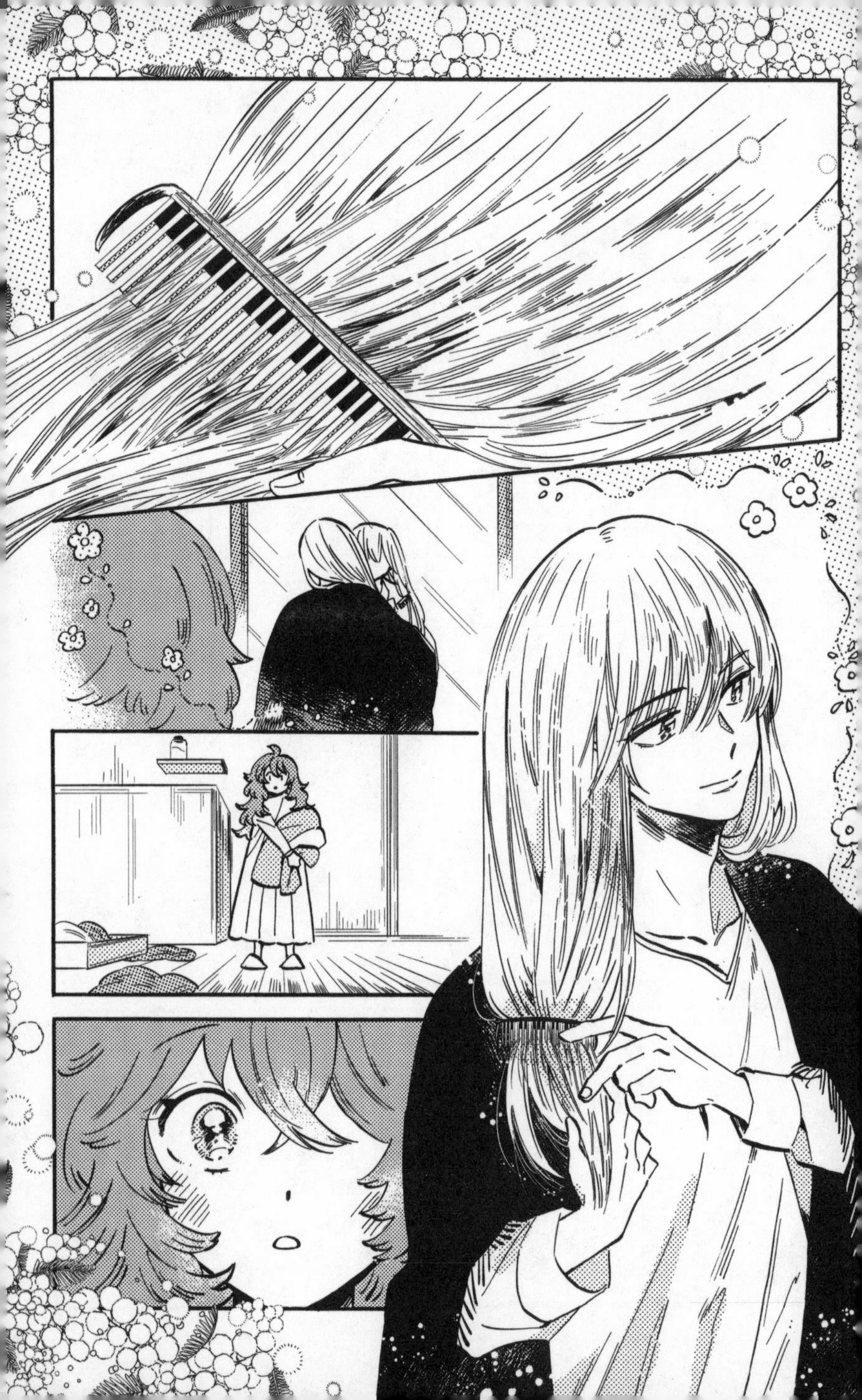

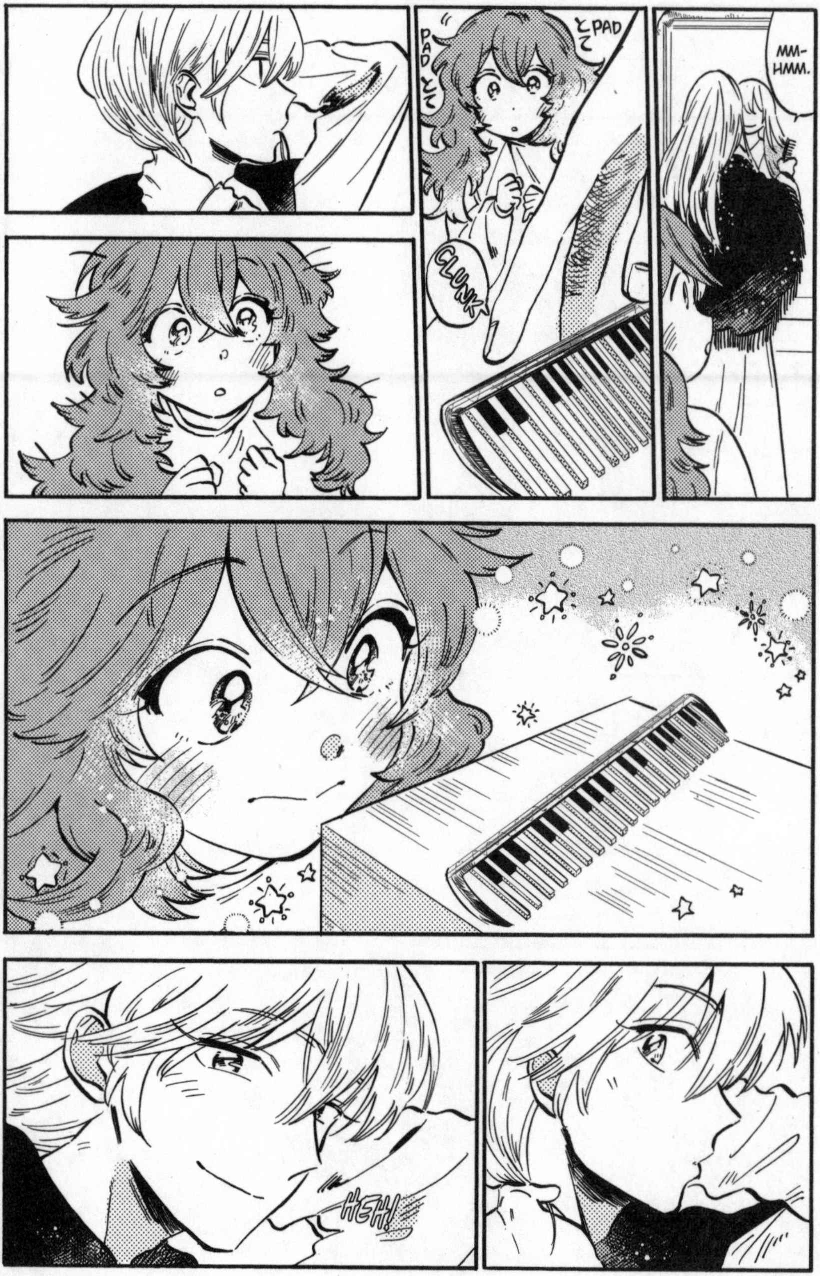
MM-HMM.
とて PAD
PAD とて
CLUNK
HEH!

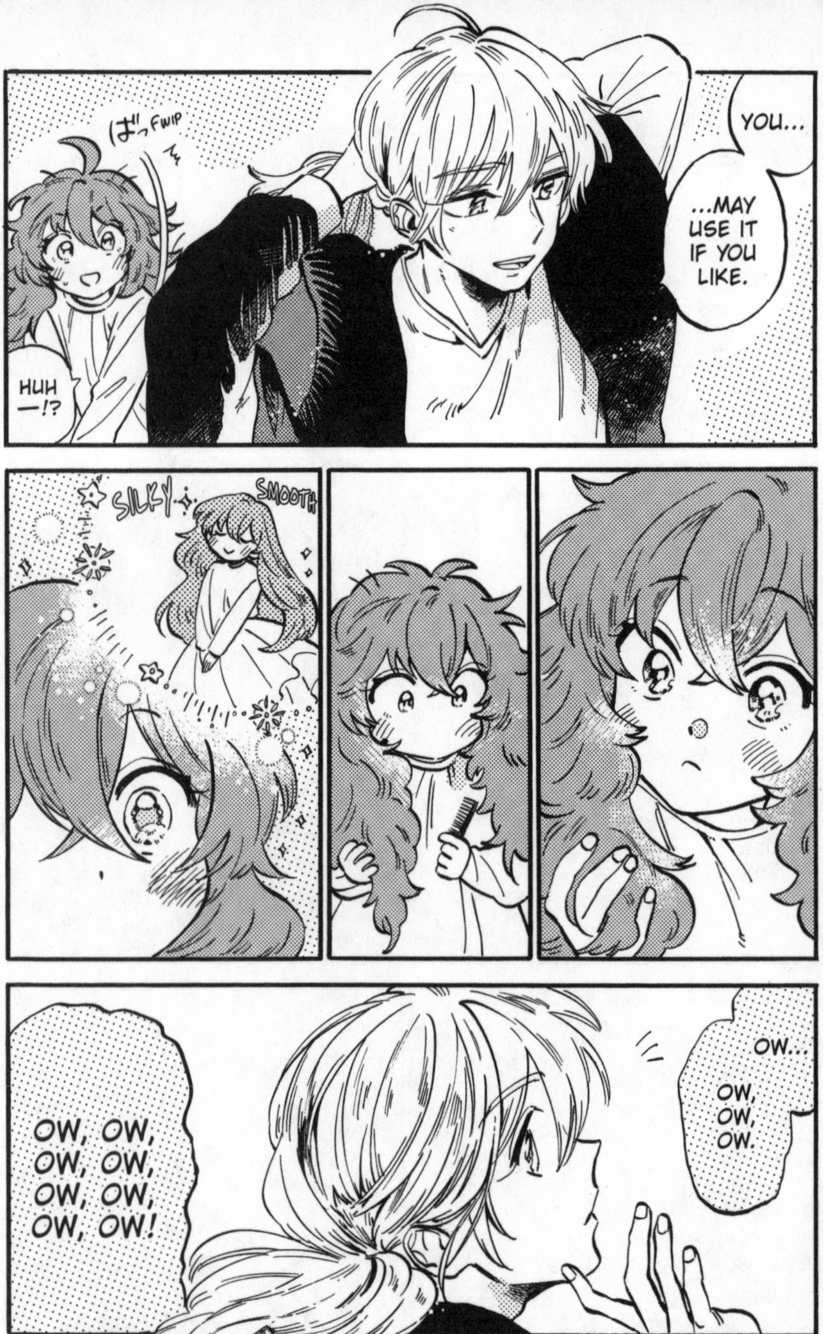
YOU...
...MAY USE IT IF YOU LIKE.
ぱっ FWIP
HUH—!?
SMOOTH
SILKY
OW...
OW, OW, OW.
OW, OW, OW, OW, OW, OW, OW, OW!

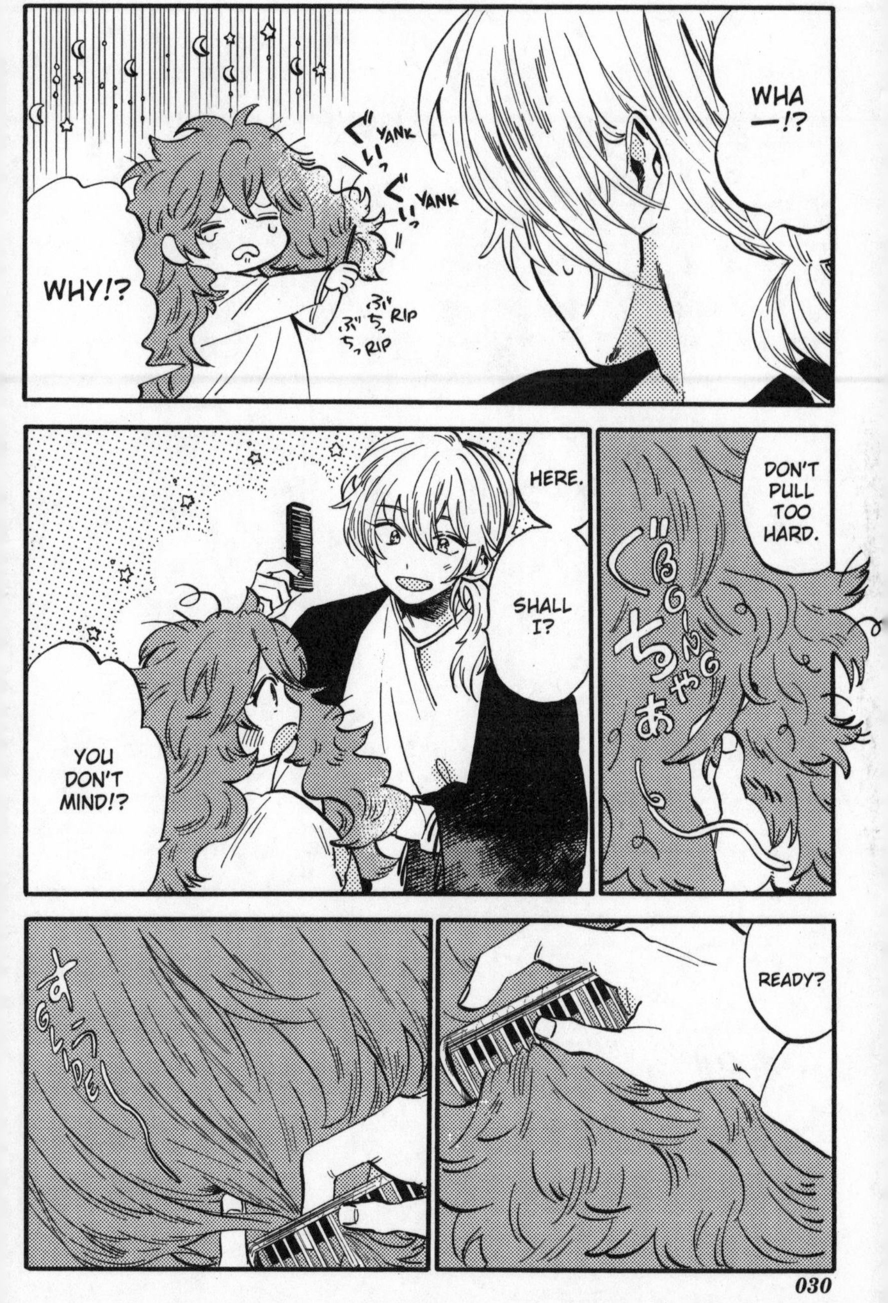
WHA—!?
YANK
YANK
WHY!?
RIP
RIP
DON'T PULL TOO HARD.
HERE.
SHALL I?
YOU DON'T MIND!?
READY?
GLIDE

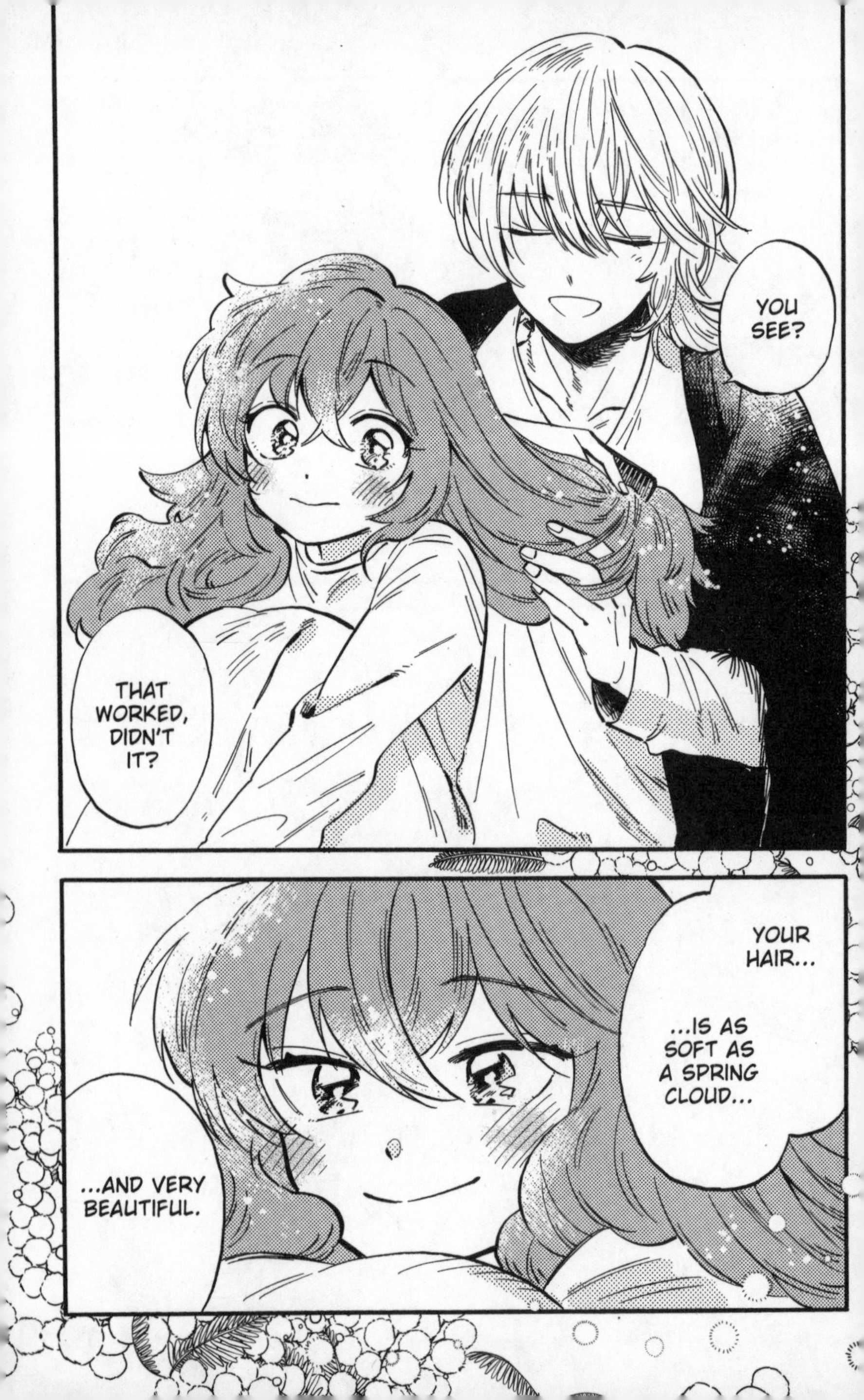
YOU SEE?
THAT WORKED, DIDN'T IT?
YOUR HAIR...
...IS AS SOFT AS A SPRING CLOUD...
...AND VERY BEAUTIFUL.

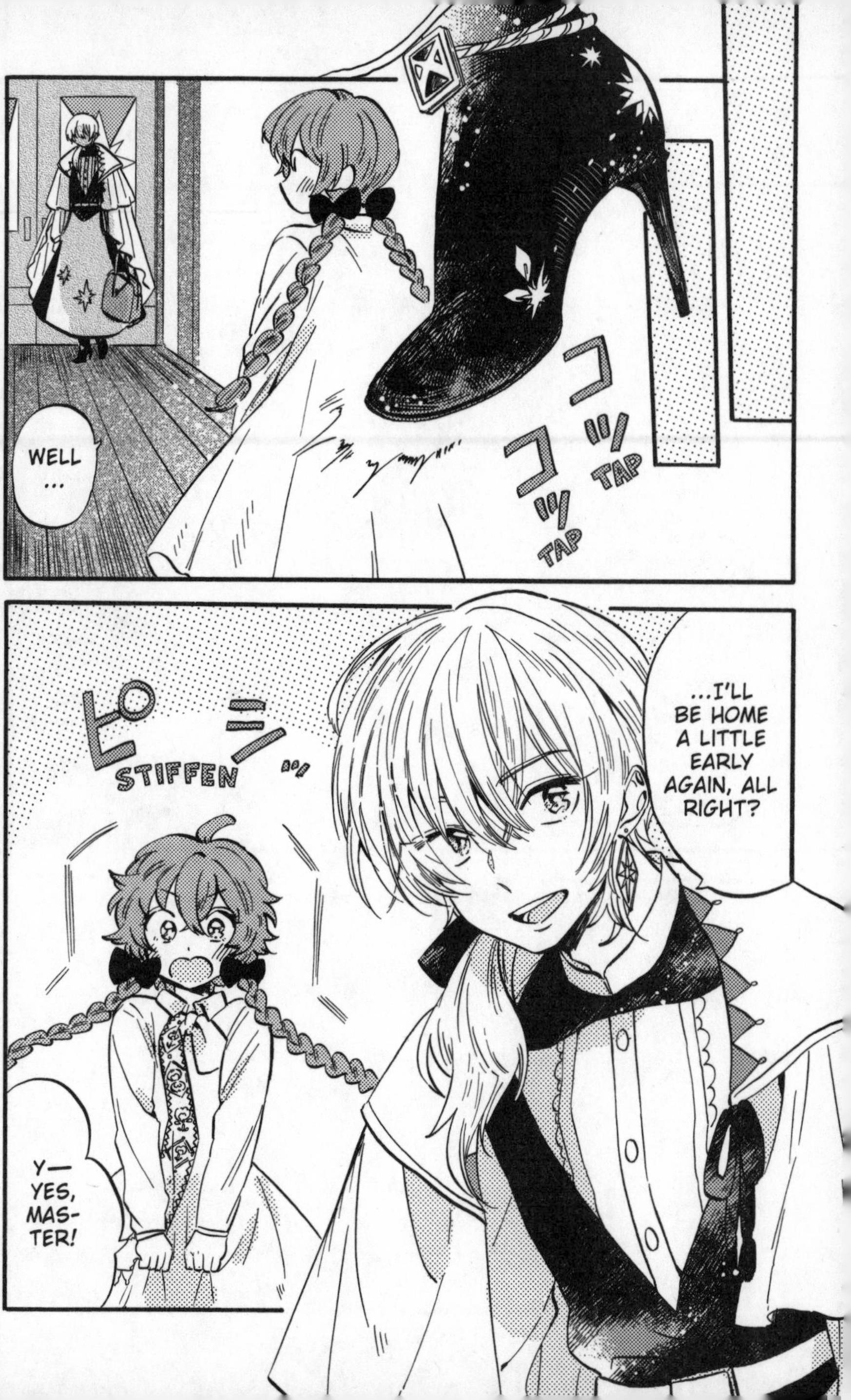
TAP
TAP
WELL ...
...I'LL BE HOME A LITTLE EARLY AGAIN, ALL RIGHT?
STIFFEN
Y— YES, MASTER!

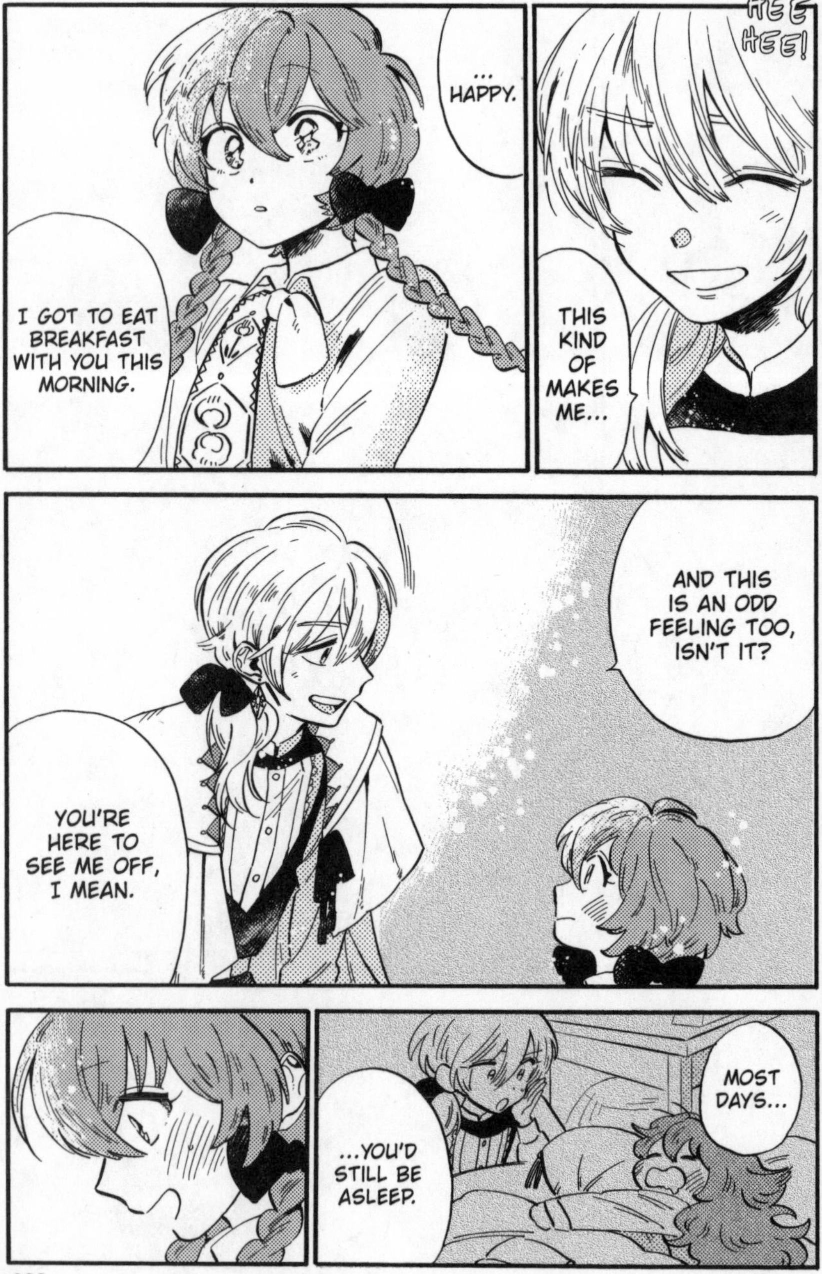
HEE HEE!
THIS KIND OF MAKES ME...
...HAPPY.
I GOT TO EAT BREAKFAST WITH YOU THIS MORNING.
AND THIS IS AN ODD FEELING TOO, ISN'T IT?
YOU'RE HERE TO SEE ME OFF, I MEAN.
MOST DAYS...
...YOU'D STILL BE ASLEEP.

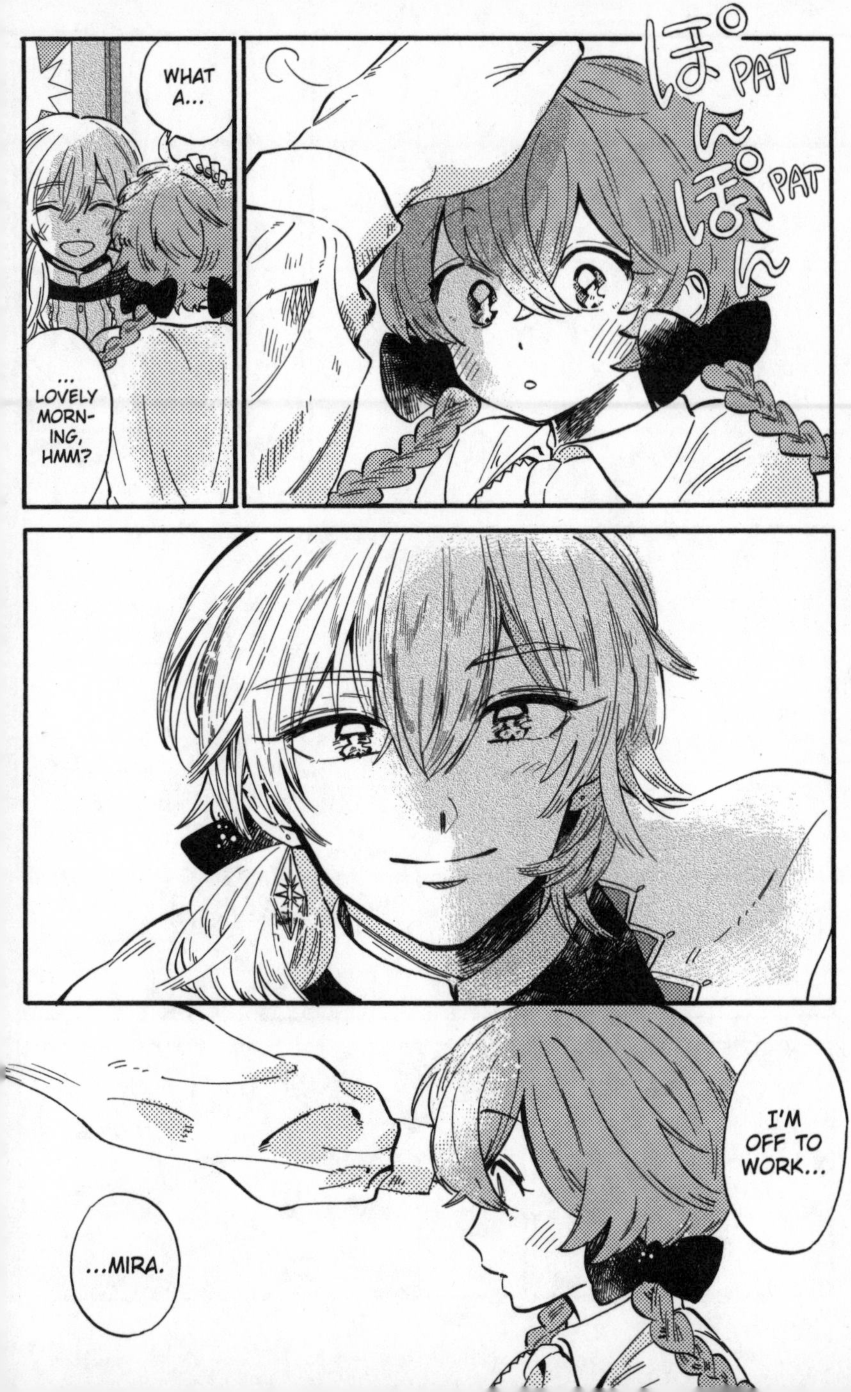
ぽんぽん
PAT PAT
WHAT A...
...LOVELY MORNING, HMM?
I'M OFF TO WORK...
...MIRA.

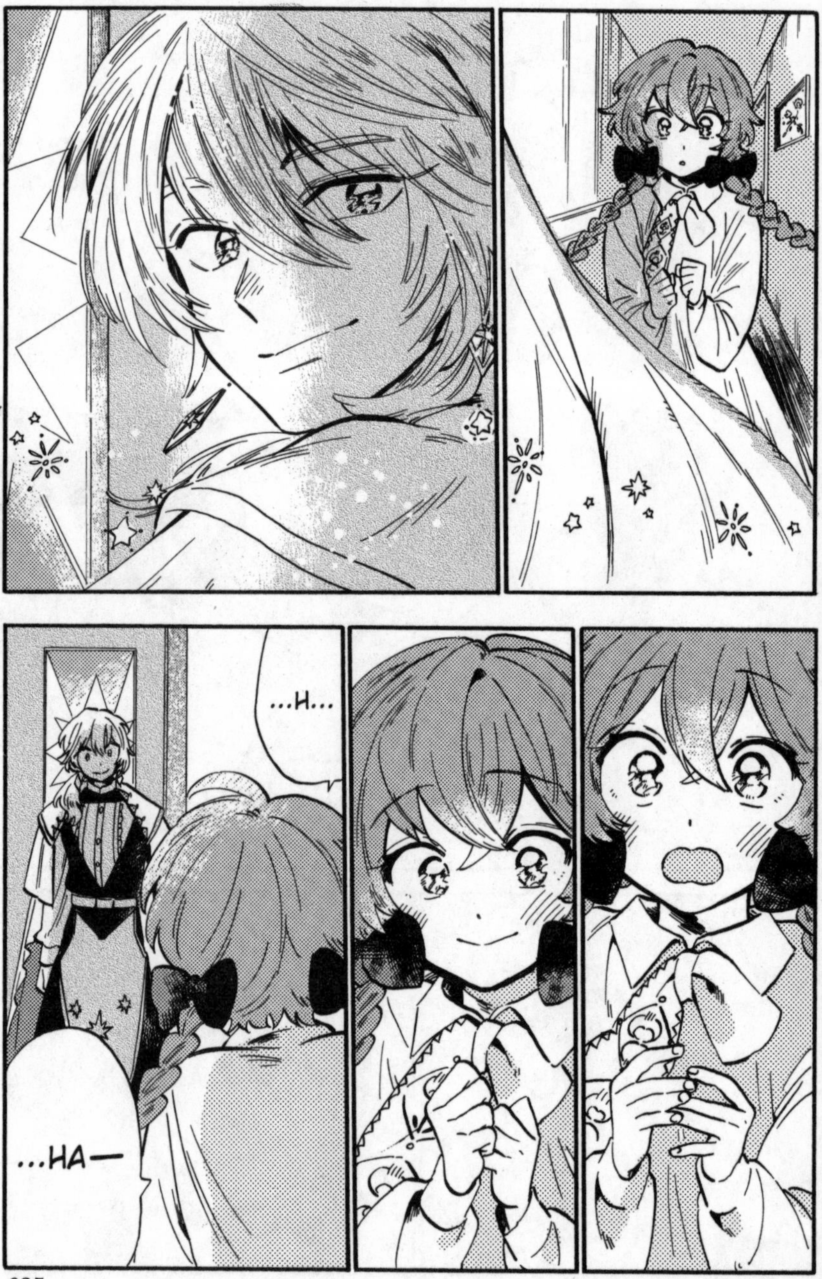
...H...
...HA—

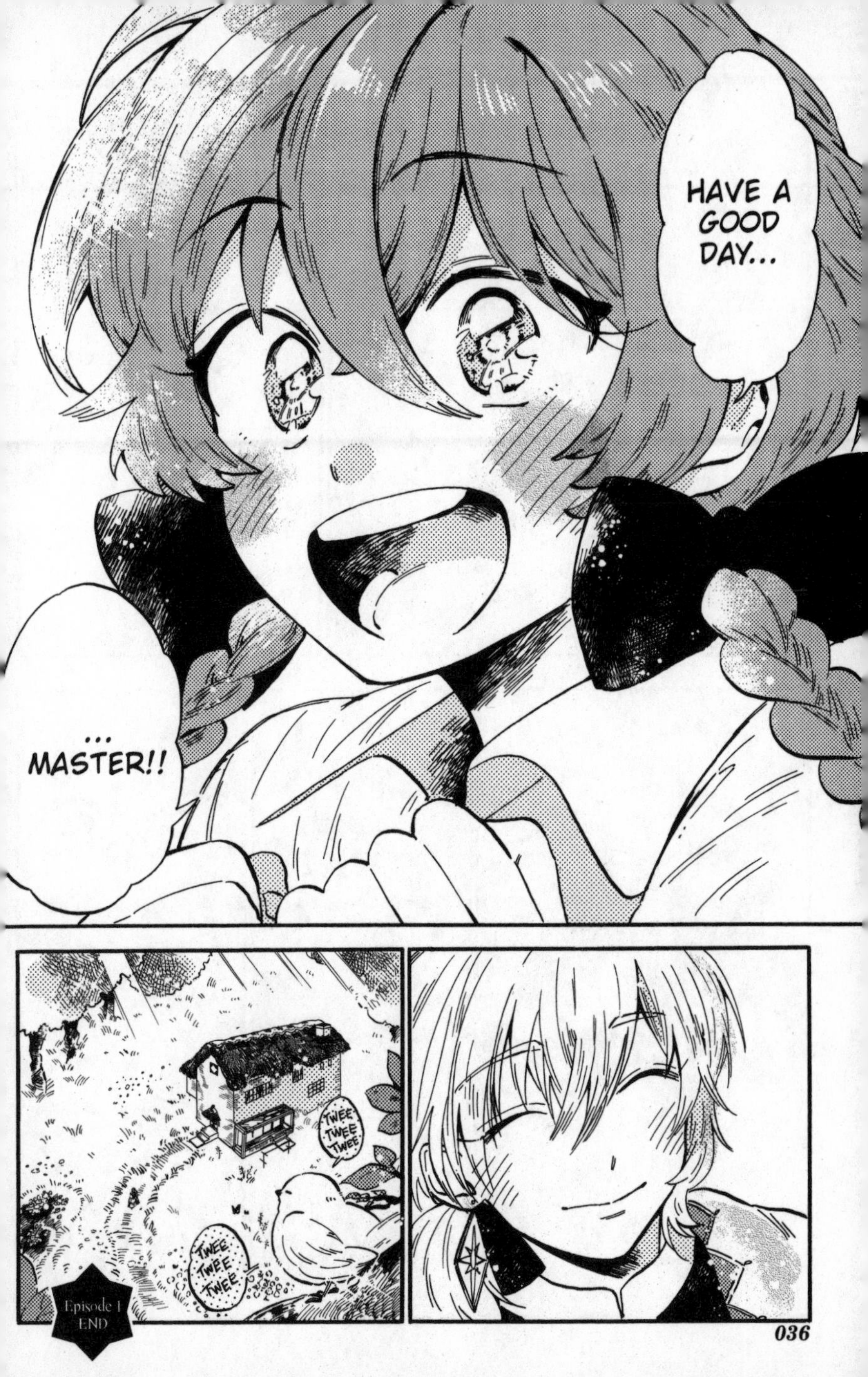
HAVE A GOOD DAY...
... MASTER!!
TWEE TWEE TWEE
TWEE TWEE TWEE
Episode 1 END

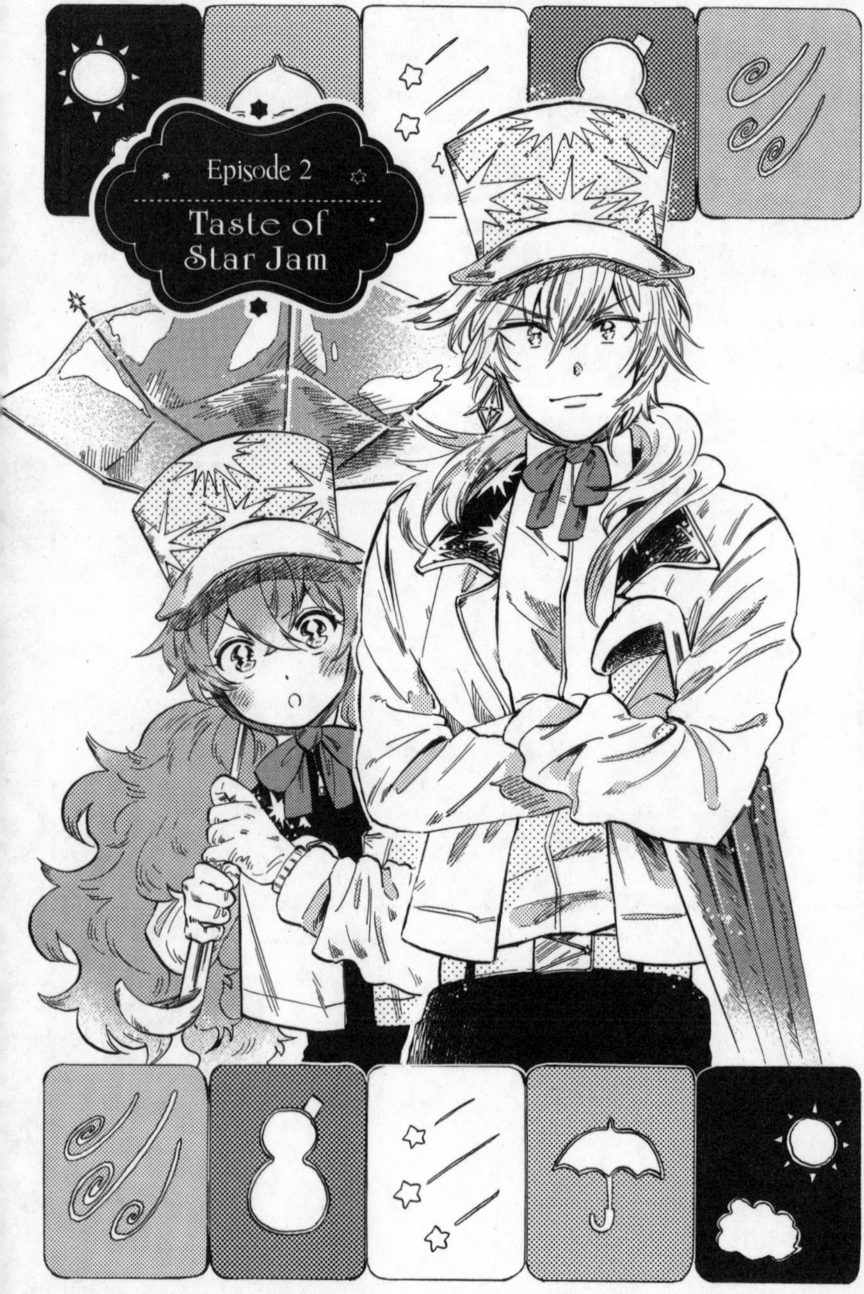
Episode 2
Taste of Star Jam

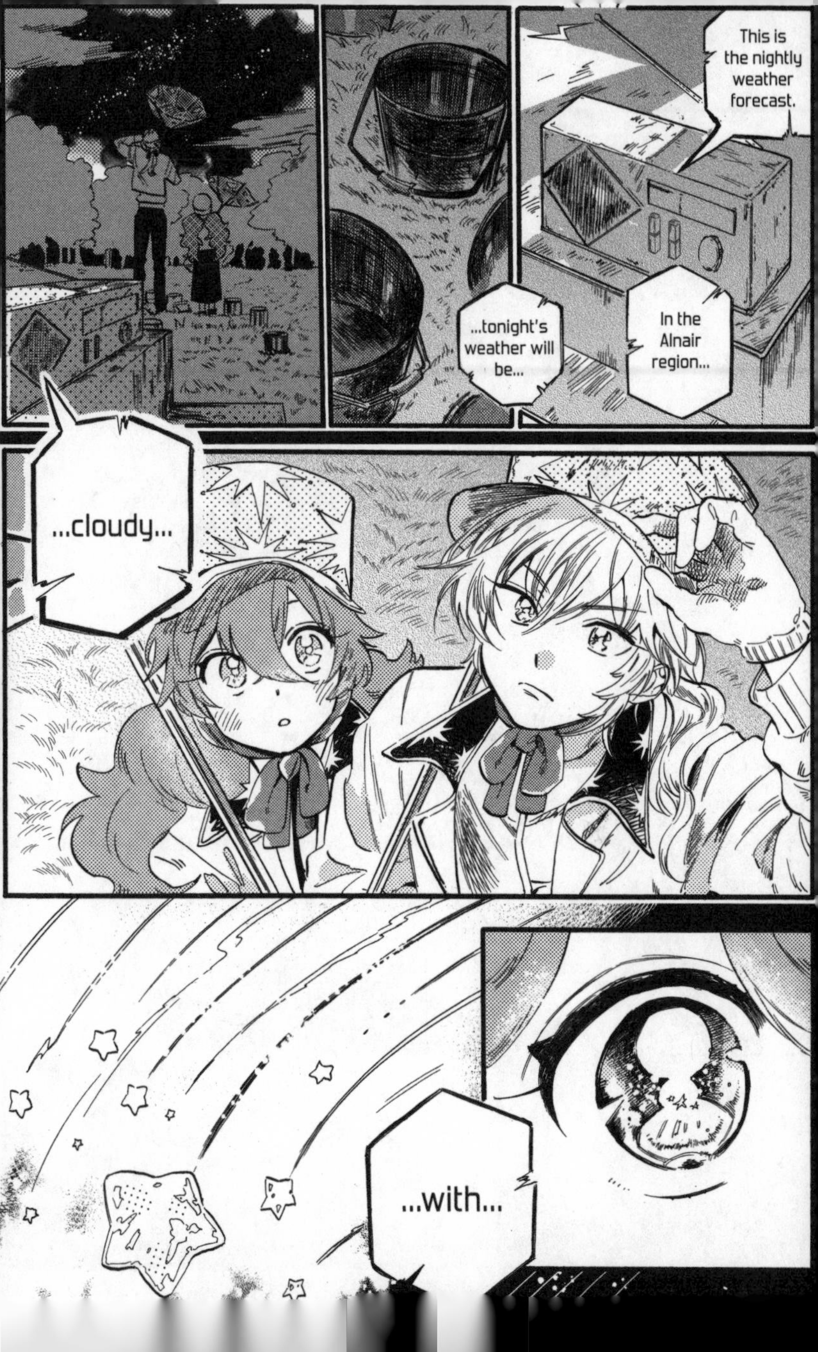
This is the nightly weather forecast.
In the Alnair region...
...tonight's weather will be...
...cloudy...
...with...

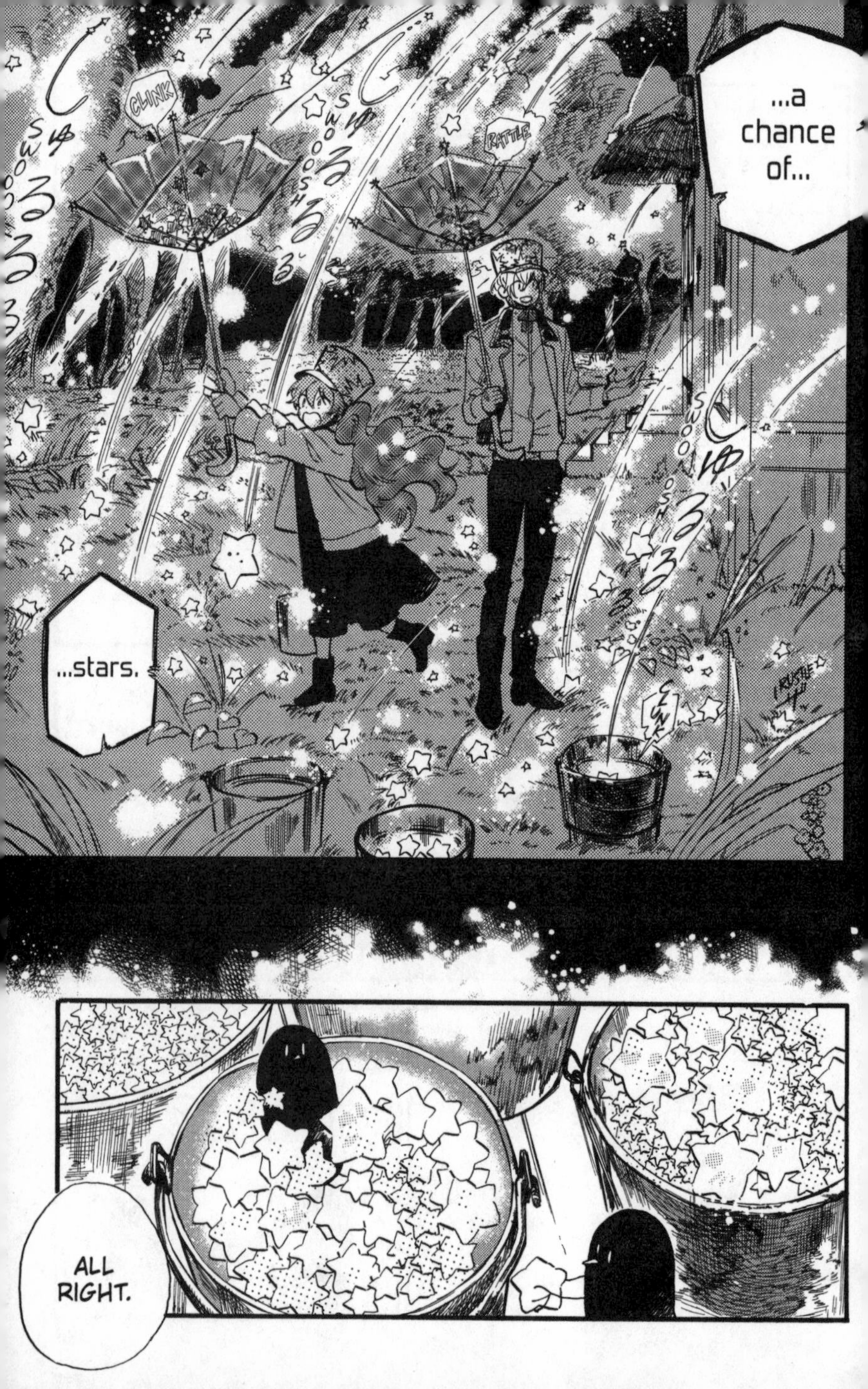
...a chance of...
RATTLE
SWOOOSH
CLINK
...stars.
SWOOOSH
RUSTLE
CLINK
ALL RIGHT.

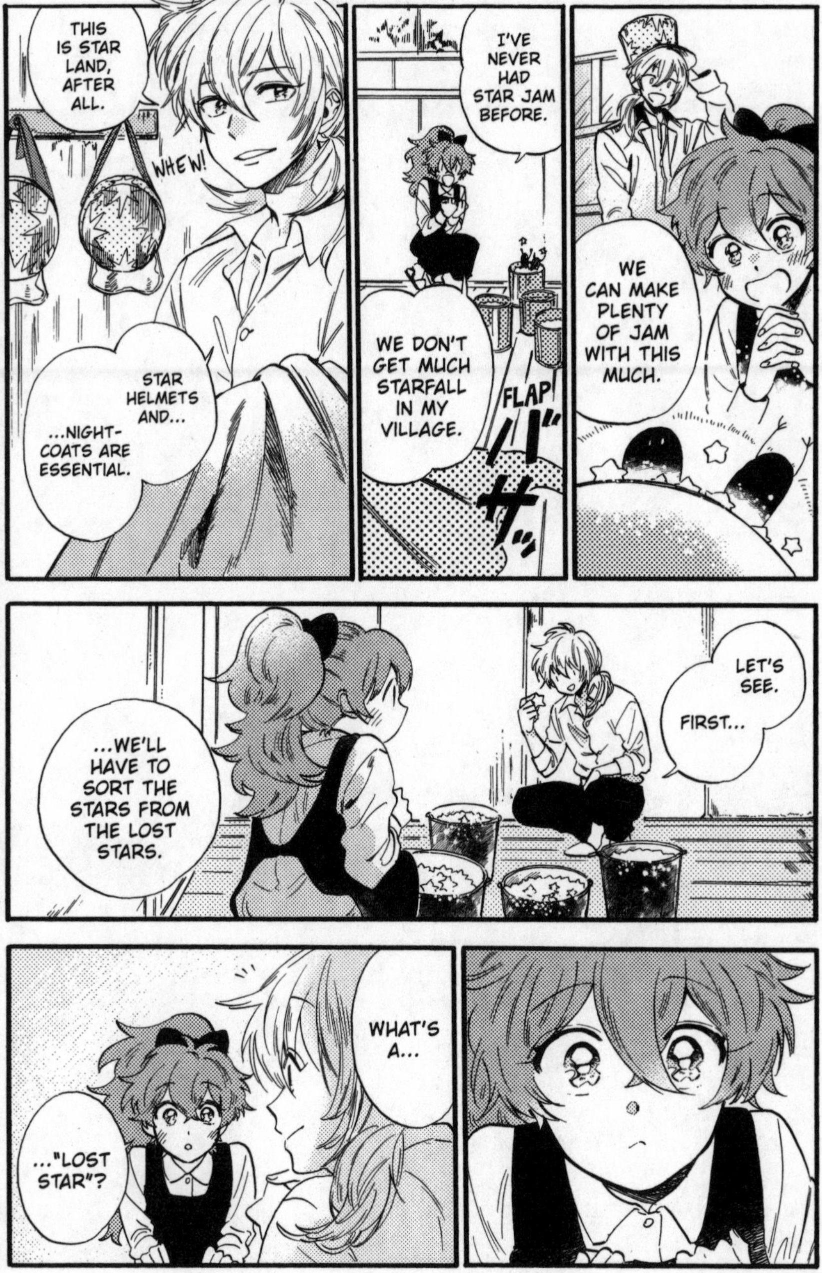
WE CAN MAKE PLENTY OF JAM WITH THIS MUCH.
I'VE NEVER HAD STAR JAM BEFORE.
WE DON'T GET MUCH STARFALL IN MY VILLAGE.
FLAP
THIS IS STAR LAND, AFTER ALL.
WHEW!
STAR HELMETS AND...
...NIGHT-COATS ARE ESSENTIAL.
LET'S SEE.
FIRST...
...WE'LL HAVE TO SORT THE STARS FROM THE LOST STARS.
WHAT'S A...
..."LOST STAR"?

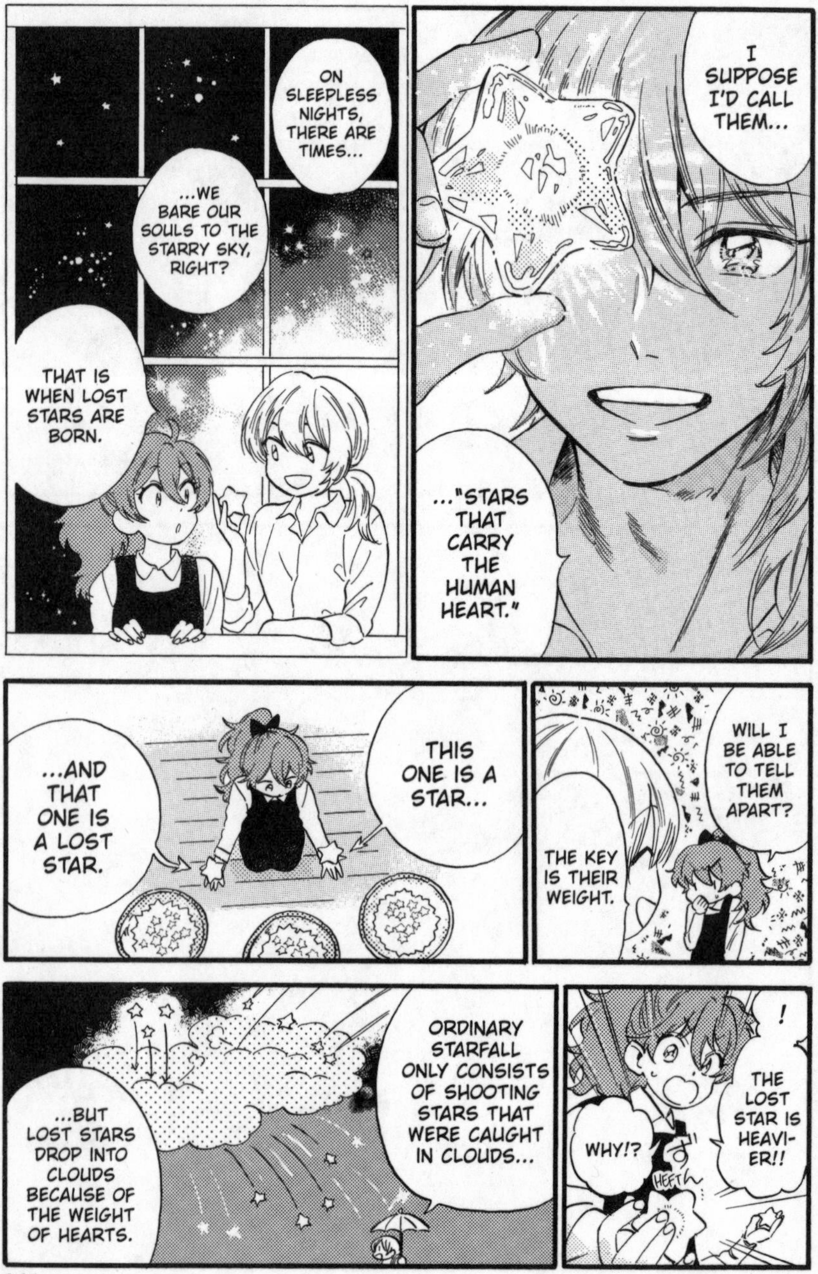
I SUPPOSE I'D CALL THEM...
..."STARS THAT CARRY THE HUMAN HEART."
ON SLEEPLESS NIGHTS, THERE ARE TIMES...
...WE BARE OUR SOULS TO THE STARRY SKY, RIGHT?
THAT IS WHEN LOST STARS ARE BORN.
WILL I BE ABLE TO TELL THEM APART?
THE KEY IS THEIR WEIGHT.
THIS ONE IS A STAR...
...AND THAT ONE IS A LOST STAR.
!
THE LOST STAR IS HEAVI-ER!!
WHY!?
HEFT
ORDINARY STARFALL ONLY CONSISTS OF SHOOTING STARS THAT WERE CAUGHT IN CLOUDS...
...BUT LOST STARS DROP INTO CLOUDS BECAUSE OF THE WEIGHT OF HEARTS.

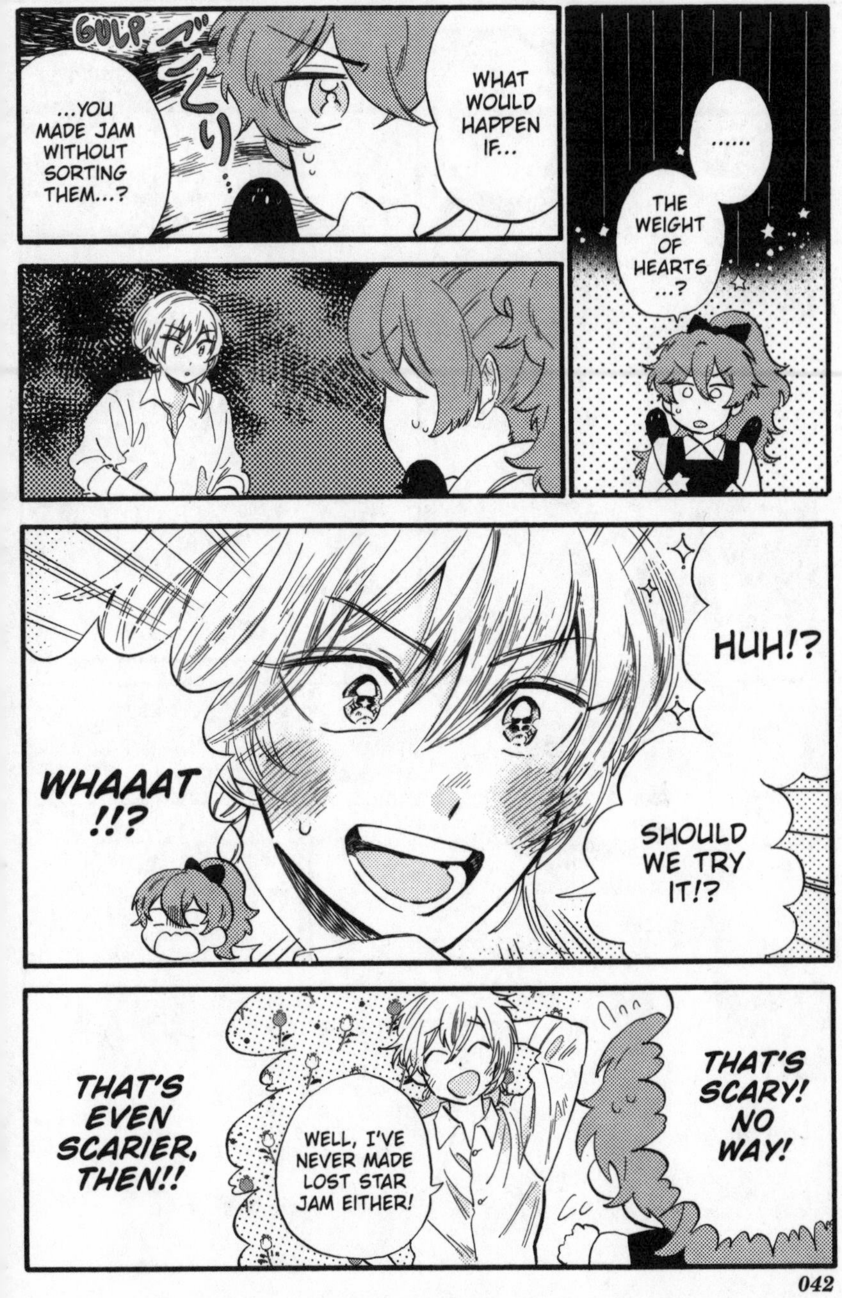
......
THE WEIGHT OF HEARTS ...?
WHAT WOULD HAPPEN IF...
GULP
...YOU MADE JAM WITHOUT SORTING THEM...?
HUH!?
SHOULD WE TRY IT!?
WHAAAT !!?
THAT'S SCARY! NO WAY!
WELL, I'VE NEVER MADE LOST STAR JAM EITHER!
THAT'S EVEN SCARIER, THEN!!

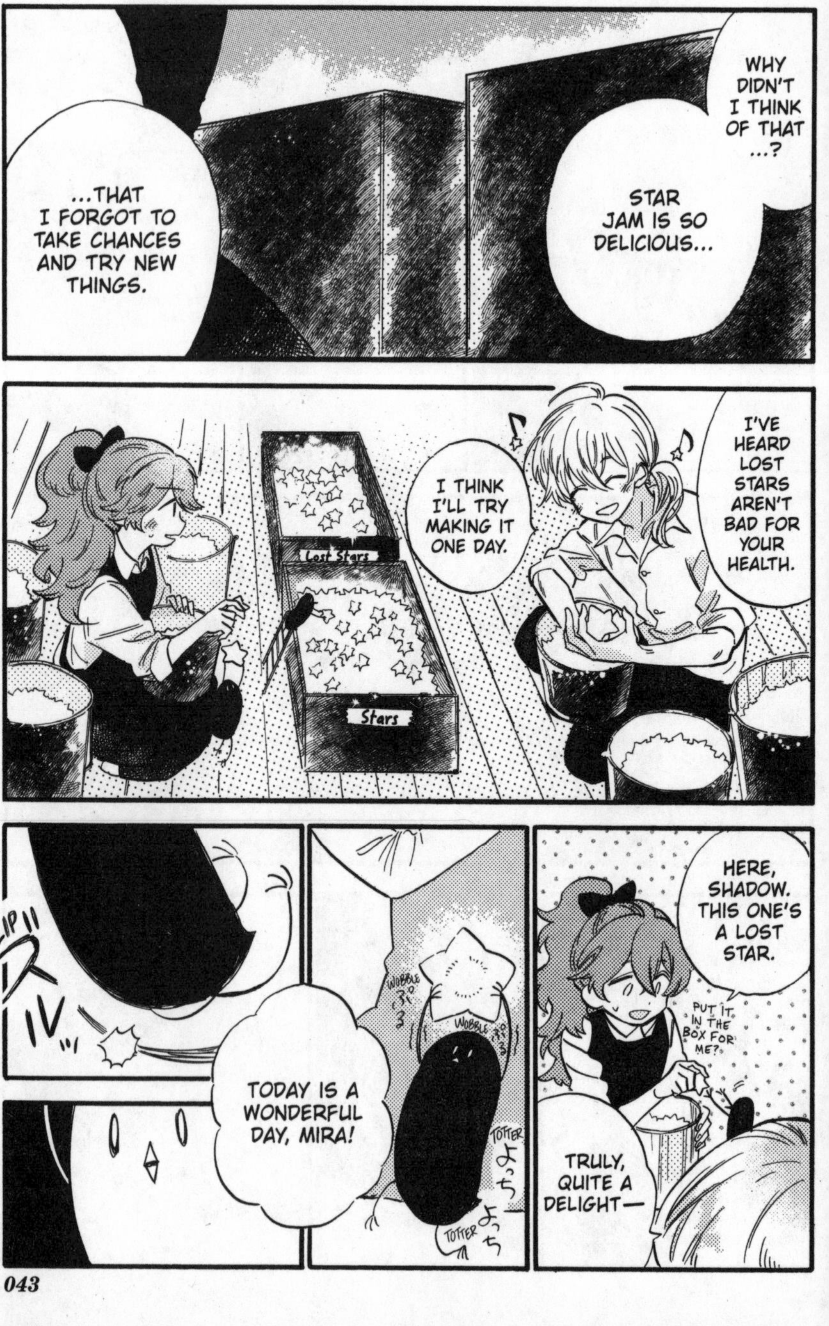
WHY DIDN'T I THINK OF THAT ...?
STAR JAM IS SO DELICIOUS...
...THAT I FORGOT TO TAKE CHANCES AND TRY NEW THINGS.
I'VE HEARD LOST STARS AREN'T BAD FOR YOUR HEALTH.
I THINK I'LL TRY MAKING IT ONE DAY.
Lost Stars
Stars
HERE, SHADOW. THIS ONE'S A LOST STAR.
PUT IT IN THE BOX FOR ME?
TRULY, QUITE A DELIGHT—
WOBBLE
WOBBLE
TODAY IS A WONDERFUL DAY, MIRA!
TOTTER
TOTTER
SLIP

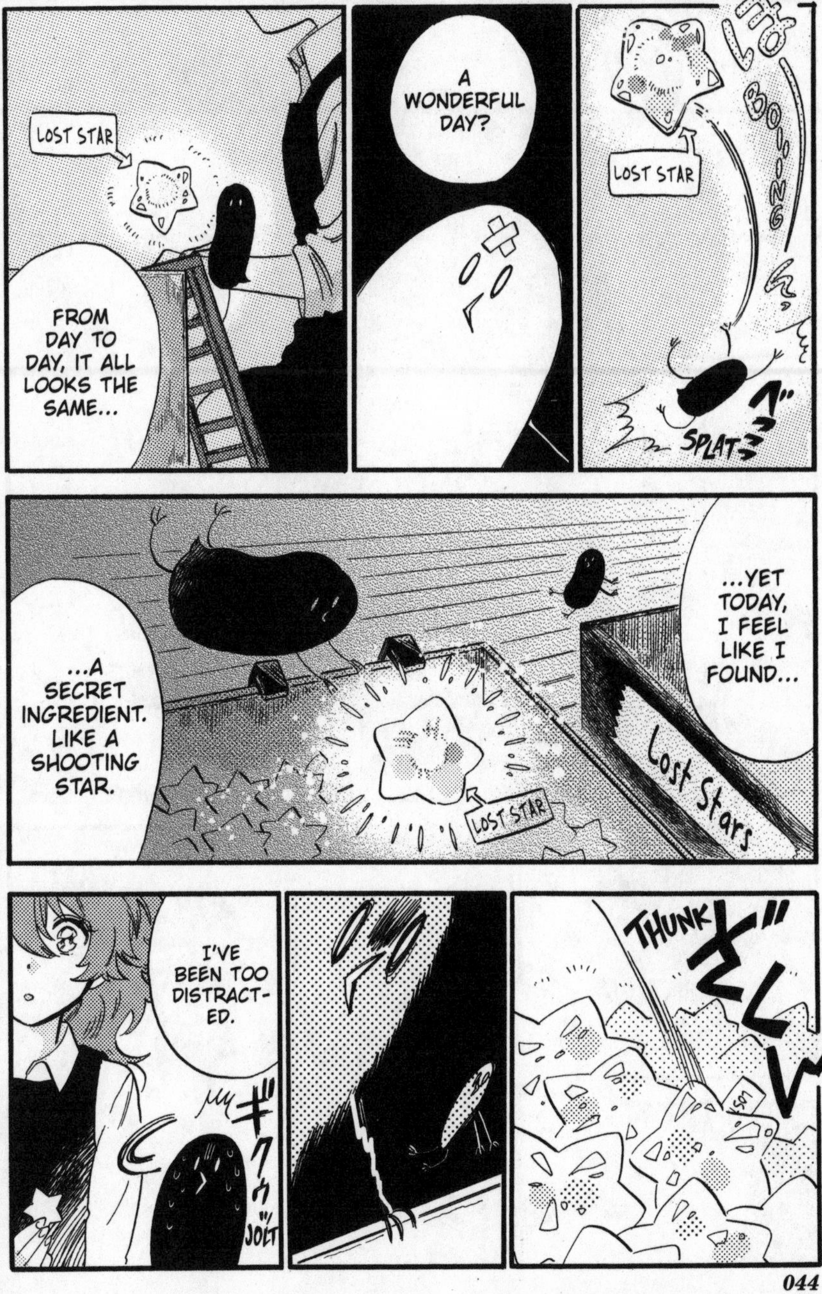
LOST STAR
BOING
SPLAT
A WONDERFUL DAY?
LOST STAR
FROM DAY TO DAY, IT ALL LOOKS THE SAME...
...YET TODAY, I FEEL LIKE I FOUND...
Lost Stars
LOST STAR
...A SECRET INGREDIENT. LIKE A SHOOTING STAR.
THUNK
I'VE BEEN TOO DISTRACT-ED.
JOLT

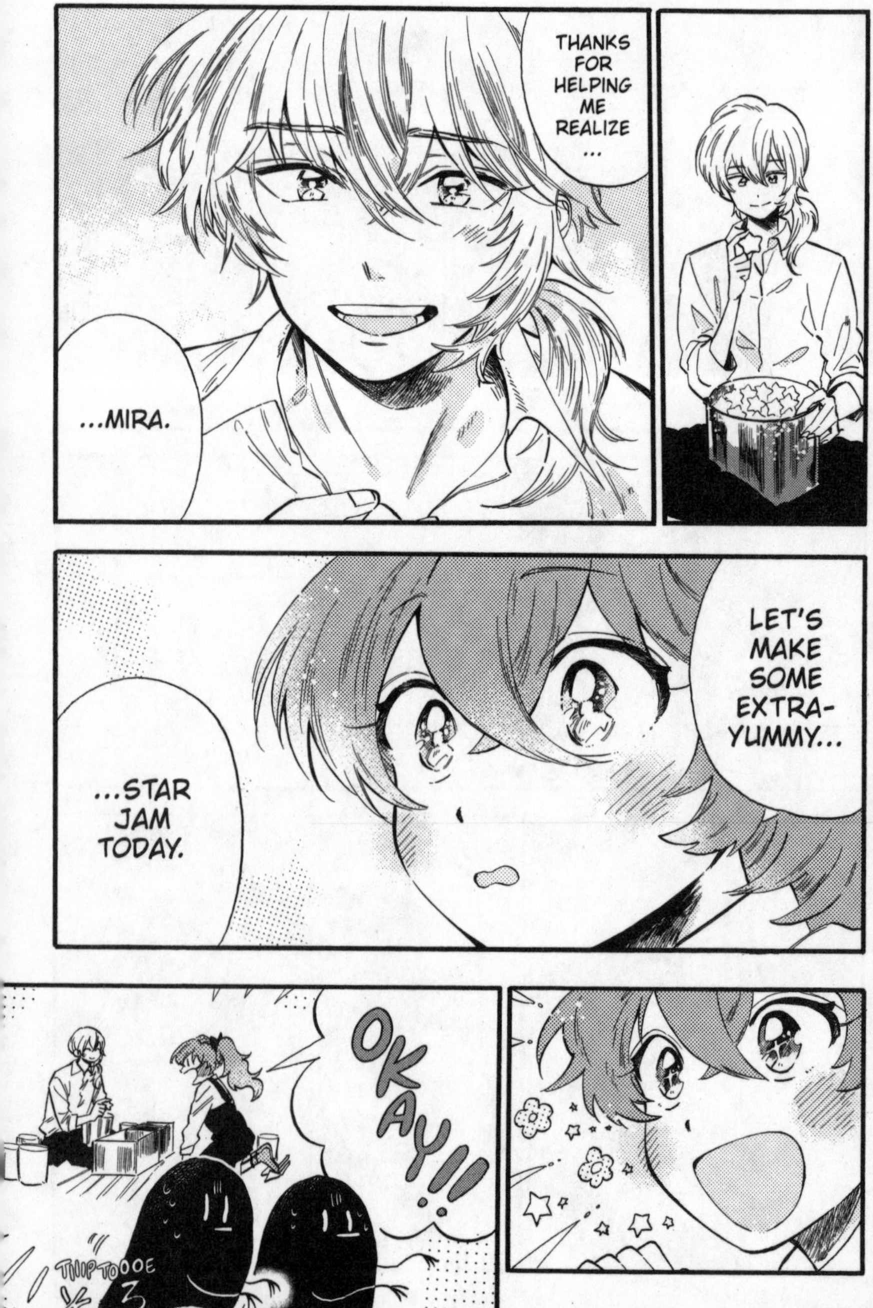
THANKS FOR HELPING ME REALIZE...
...MIRA.
LET'S MAKE SOME EXTRA-YUMMY...
...STAR JAM TODAY.
OKAY!!!
TIIIPTOOOE

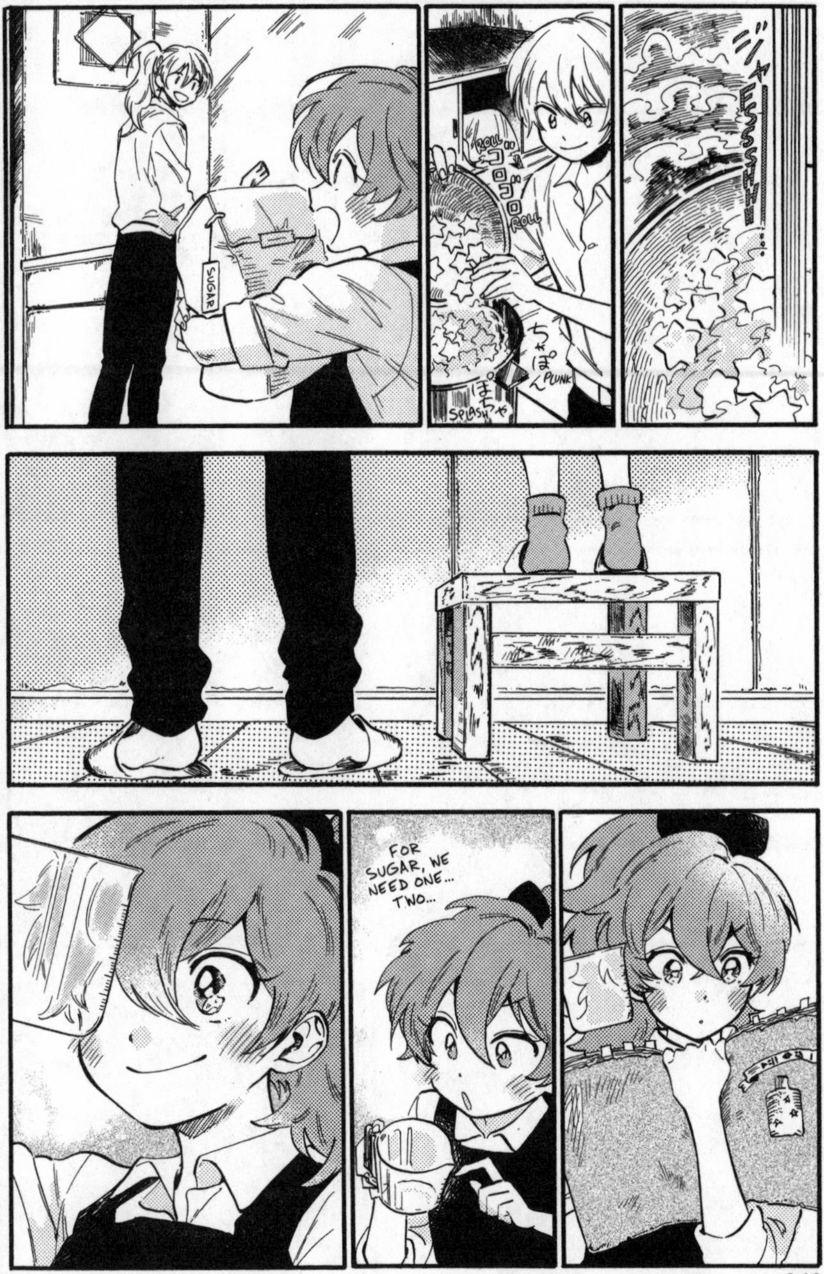
ジャー
ESSSHHH!!...
ROLL
ゴロゴロ
ROLL
ちゃぽん
PLUNK
ぽちゃ
SPLASH
SUGAR
FOR SUGAR, WE NEED ONE... TWO...

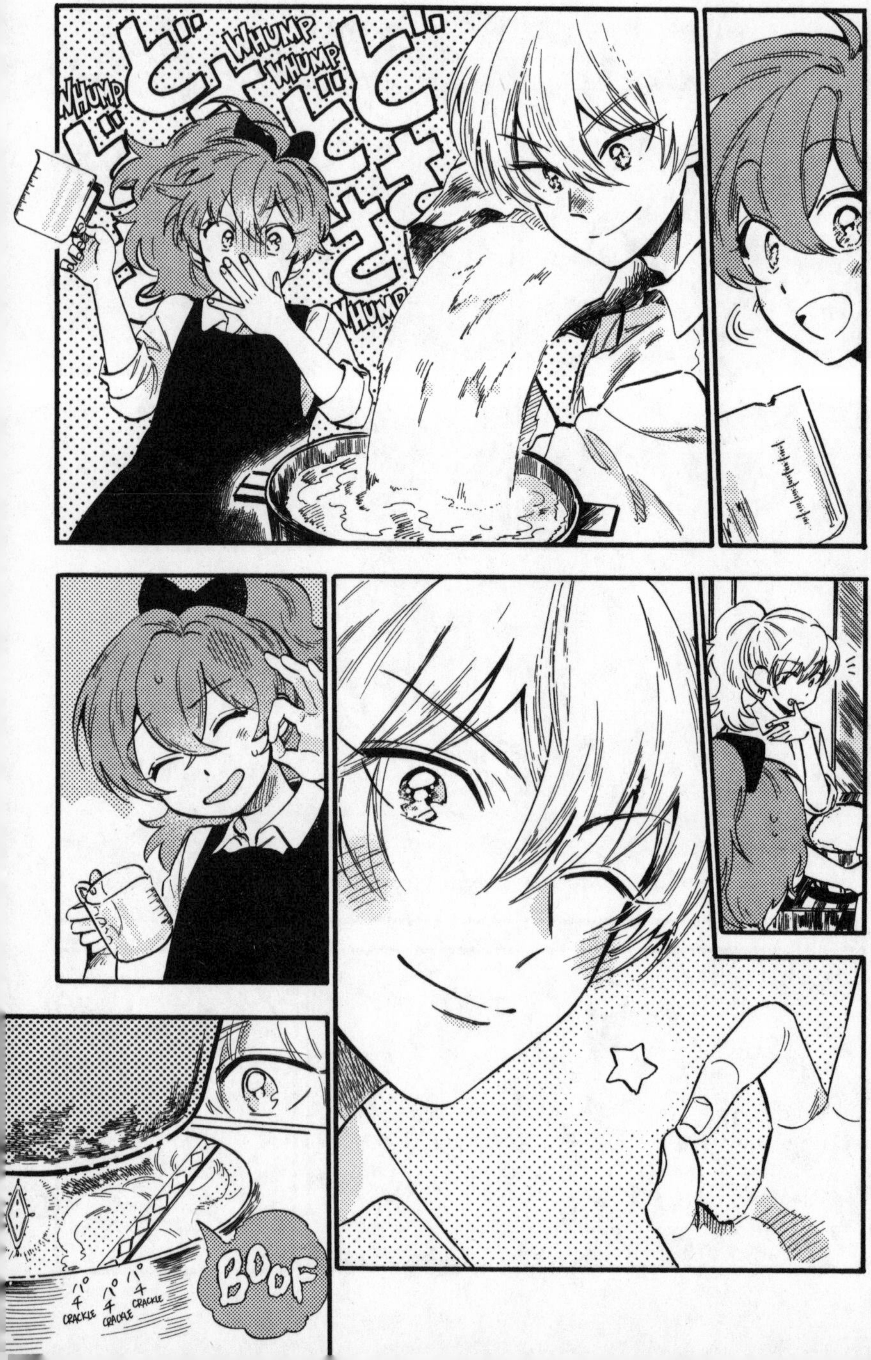
WHUMP
WHUMP
WHUMP
WHUMP
BOOF
パチ
CRACKLE
パチ
CRACKLE
パチ
CRACKLE

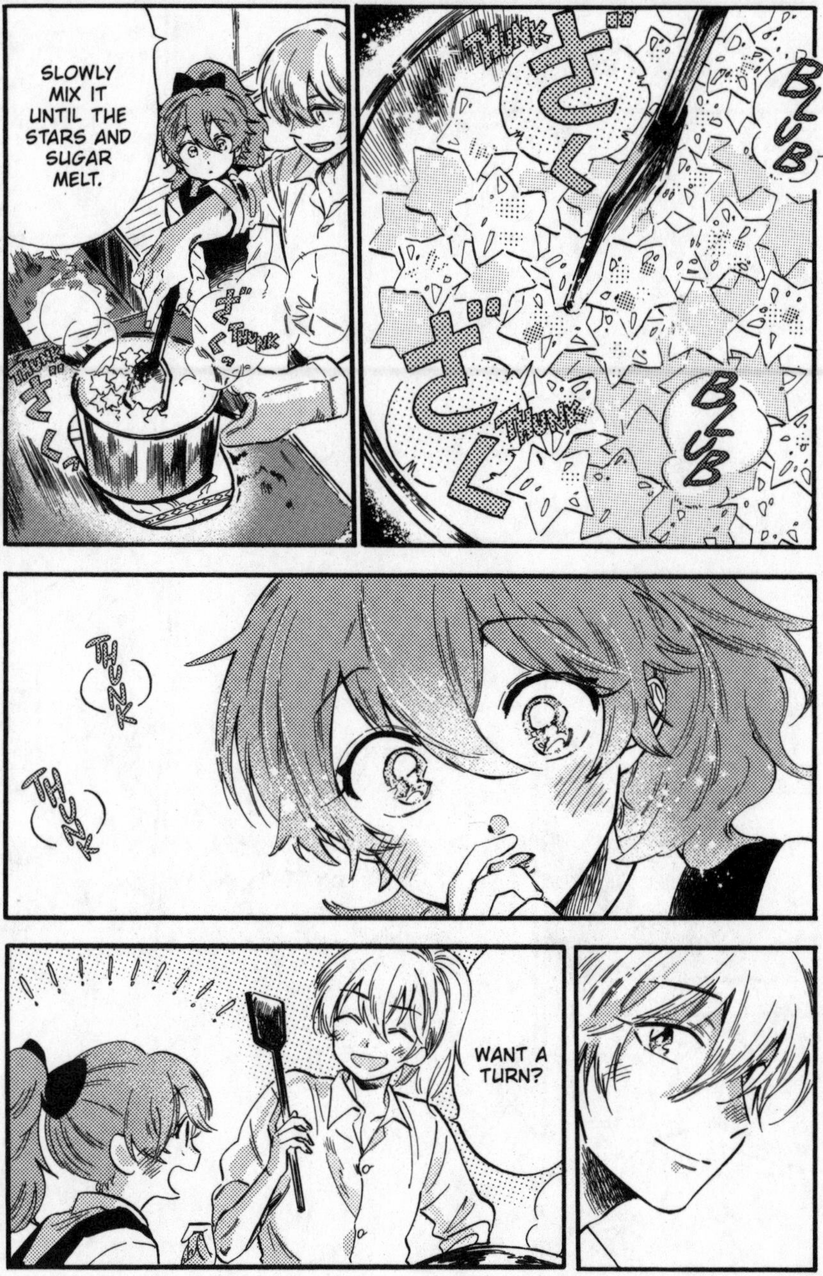
THUNK
ざく
BLUB
THUNK
ざく
BLUB
SLOWLY MIX IT UNTIL THE STARS AND SUGAR MELT.
THUNK
ざく
THUNK
ざく
THUNK
THUNK
WANT A TURN?
!!!!!!!!!

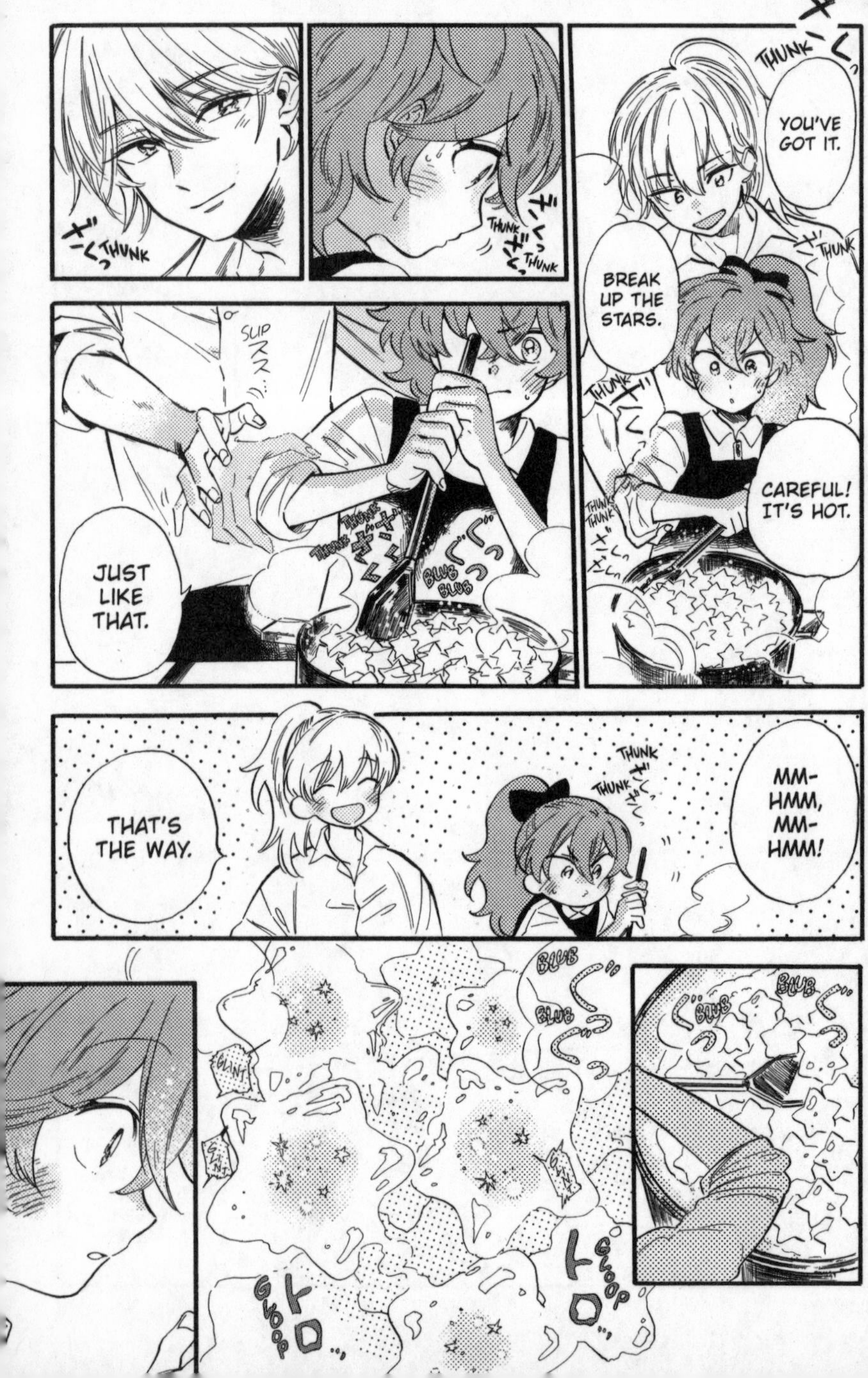
THUNK
YOU'VE GOT IT.
THUNK
BREAK UP THE STARS.
THUNK
THUNK THUNK
CAREFUL! IT'S HOT.
THUNK
THUNK
THUNK
SLIP
THUNK THUNK
BLUB BLUB
JUST LIKE THAT.
MM-HMM, MM-HMM!
THUNK
THUNK
THAT'S THE WAY.
BLUB
BLUB
BLUB
BLUB
GLINT
GLINT
GLINT
GLOOP
GLOOP

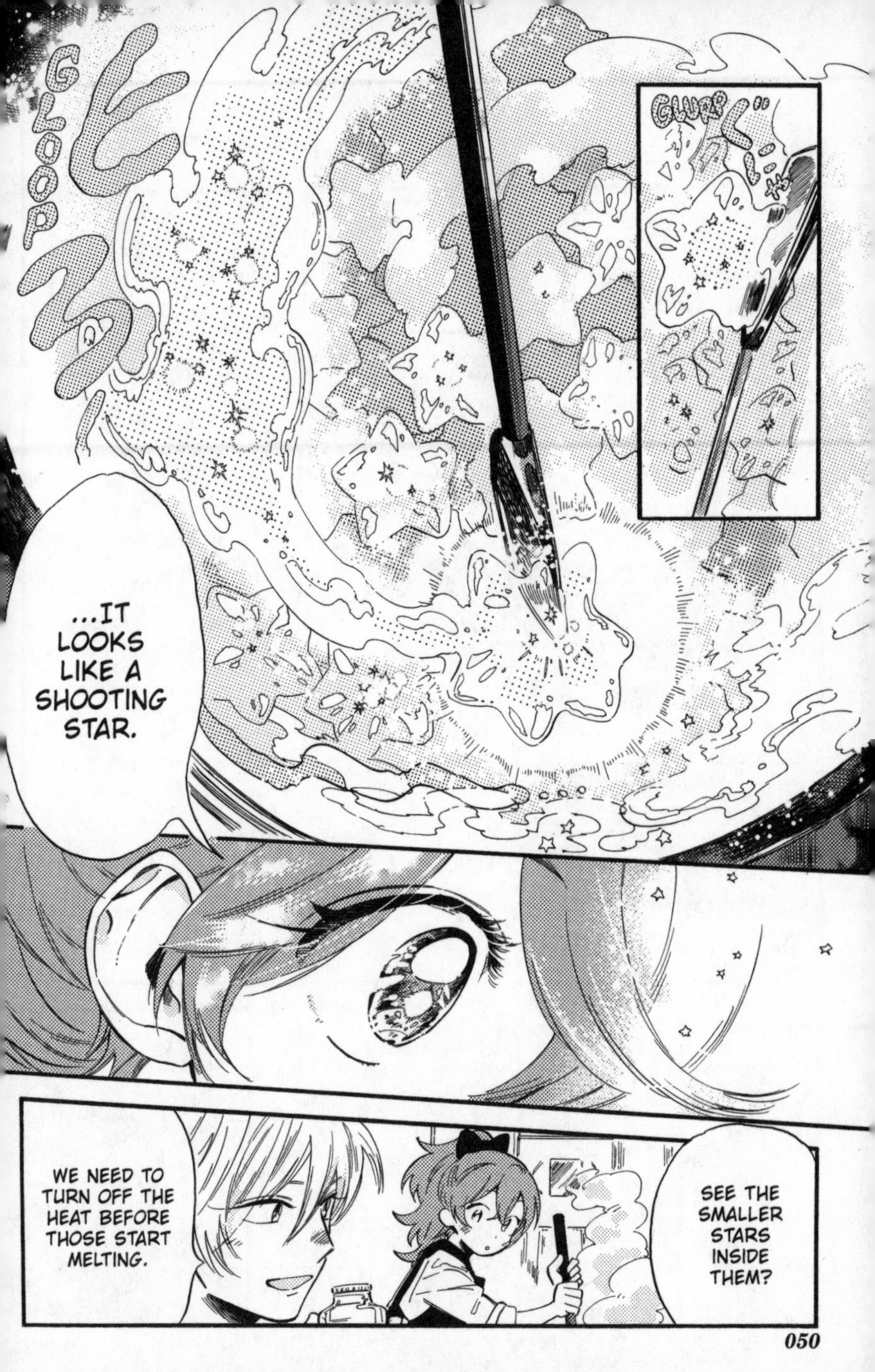
GLURP
GLOOP
...IT LOOKS LIKE A SHOOTING STAR.
SEE THE SMALLER STARS INSIDE THEM?
WE NEED TO TURN OFF THE HEAT BEFORE THOSE START MELTING.

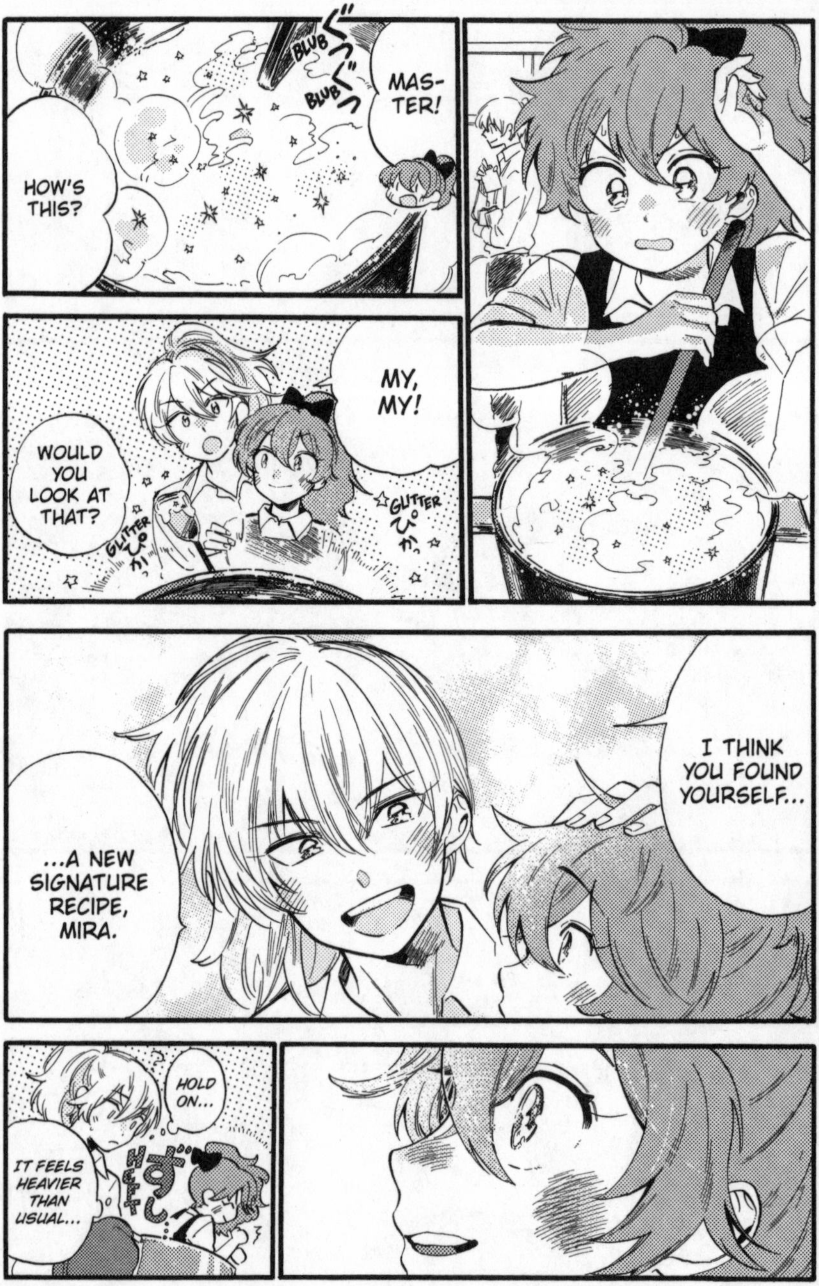
MAS-TER!
BLUB ぐつ BLUB ぐつ
HOW'S THIS?
MY, MY!
GLITTER ぴかっ
WOULD YOU LOOK AT THAT?
GLITTER ぴかっ
I THINK YOU FOUND YOURSELF...
...A NEW SIGNATURE RECIPE, MIRA.
HOLD ON...
HEFT ずしっ
IT FEELS HEAVIER THAN USUAL...

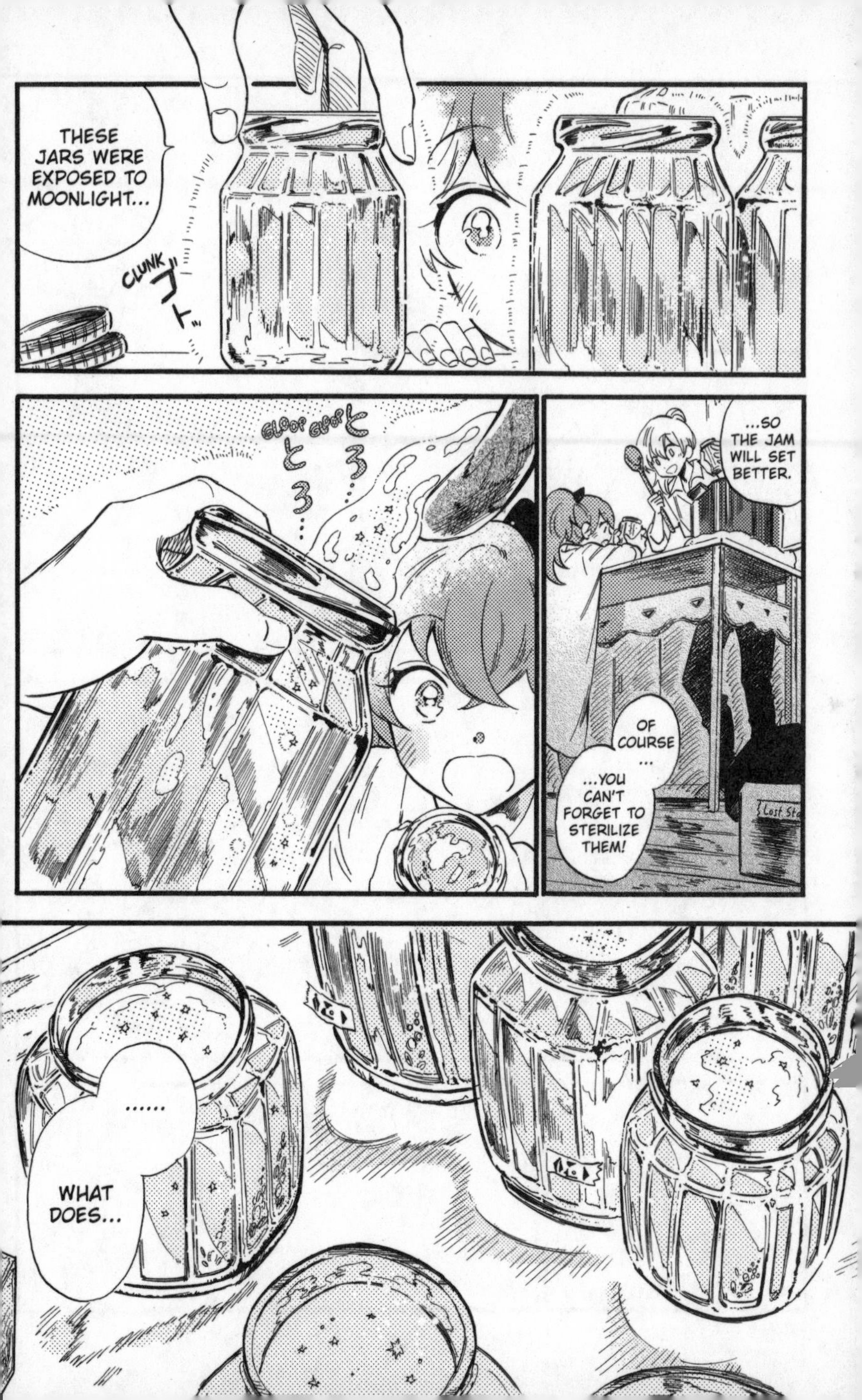
THESE JARS WERE EXPOSED TO MOONLIGHT...
CLUNK ゴトッ
...SO THE JAM WILL SET BETTER.
OF COURSE...
...YOU CAN'T FORGET TO STERILIZE THEM!
GLOOP GLOOP とろとろ...
......
WHAT DOES...

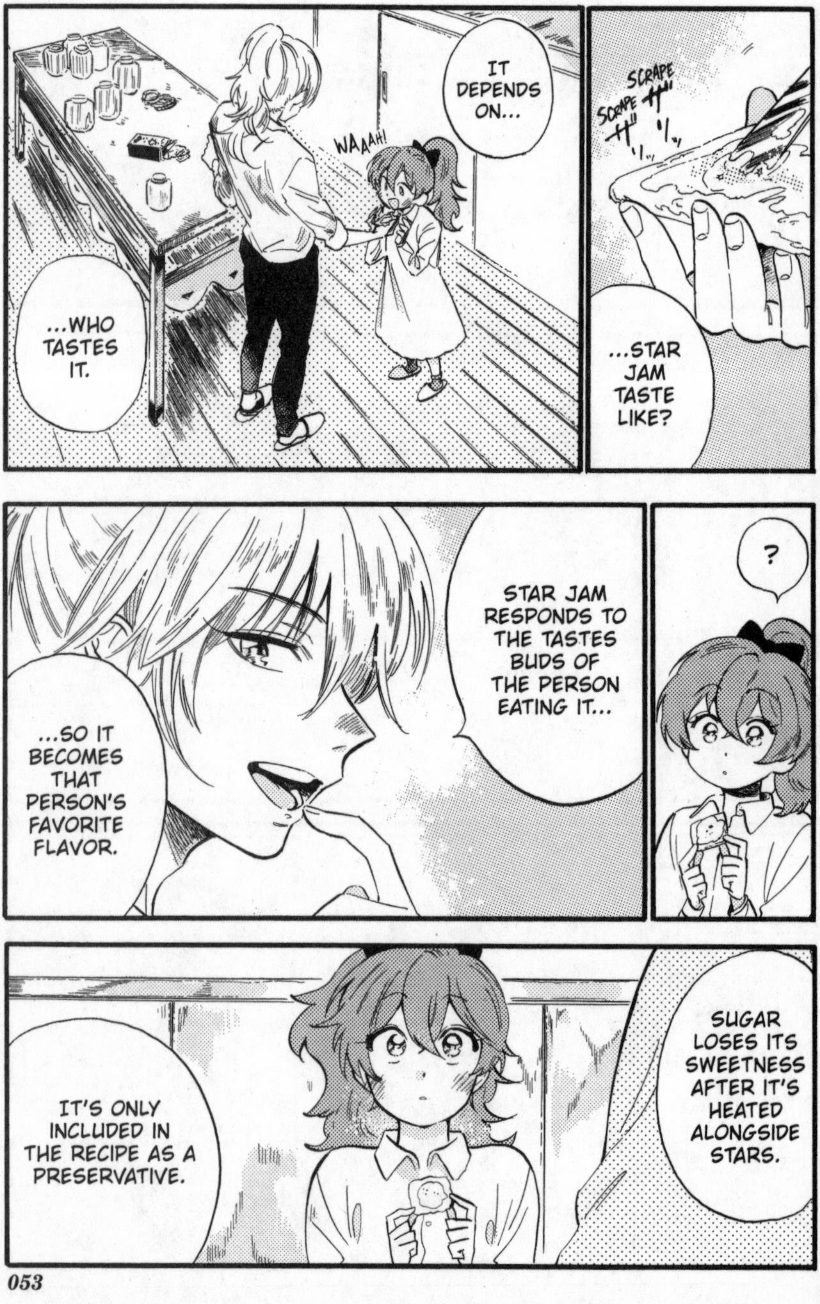
SCRAPE
SCRAPE
...STAR JAM TASTE LIKE?
IT DEPENDS ON...
WAAAH!
...WHO TASTES IT.
?
STAR JAM RESPONDS TO THE TASTES BUDS OF THE PERSON EATING IT...
...SO IT BECOMES THAT PERSON'S FAVORITE FLAVOR.
SUGAR LOSES ITS SWEETNESS AFTER IT'S HEATED ALONGSIDE STARS.
IT'S ONLY INCLUDED IN THE RECIPE AS A PRESERVATIVE.

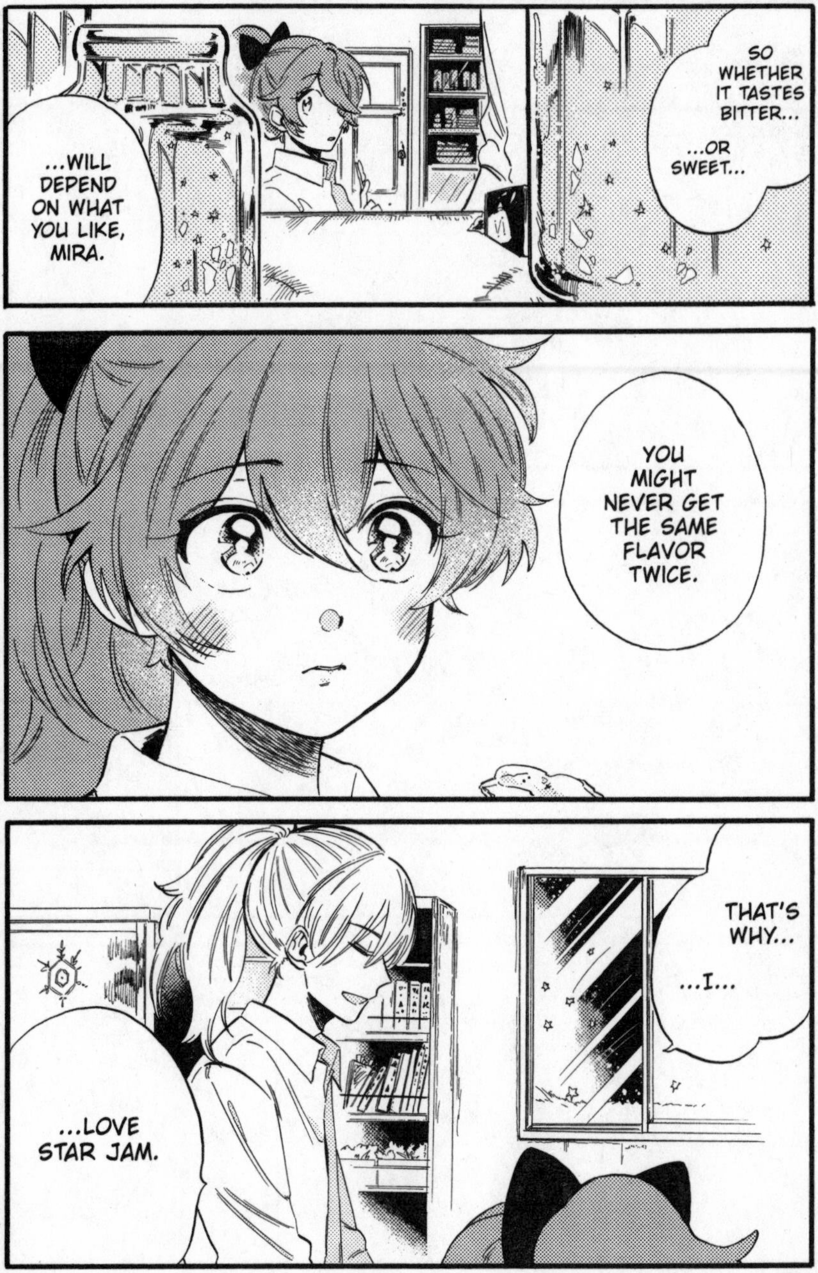
SO WHETHER IT TASTES BITTER... ...OR SWEET...
...WILL DEPEND ON WHAT YOU LIKE, MIRA.
YOU MIGHT NEVER GET THE SAME FLAVOR TWICE.
THAT'S WHY... ...I...
...LOVE STAR JAM.

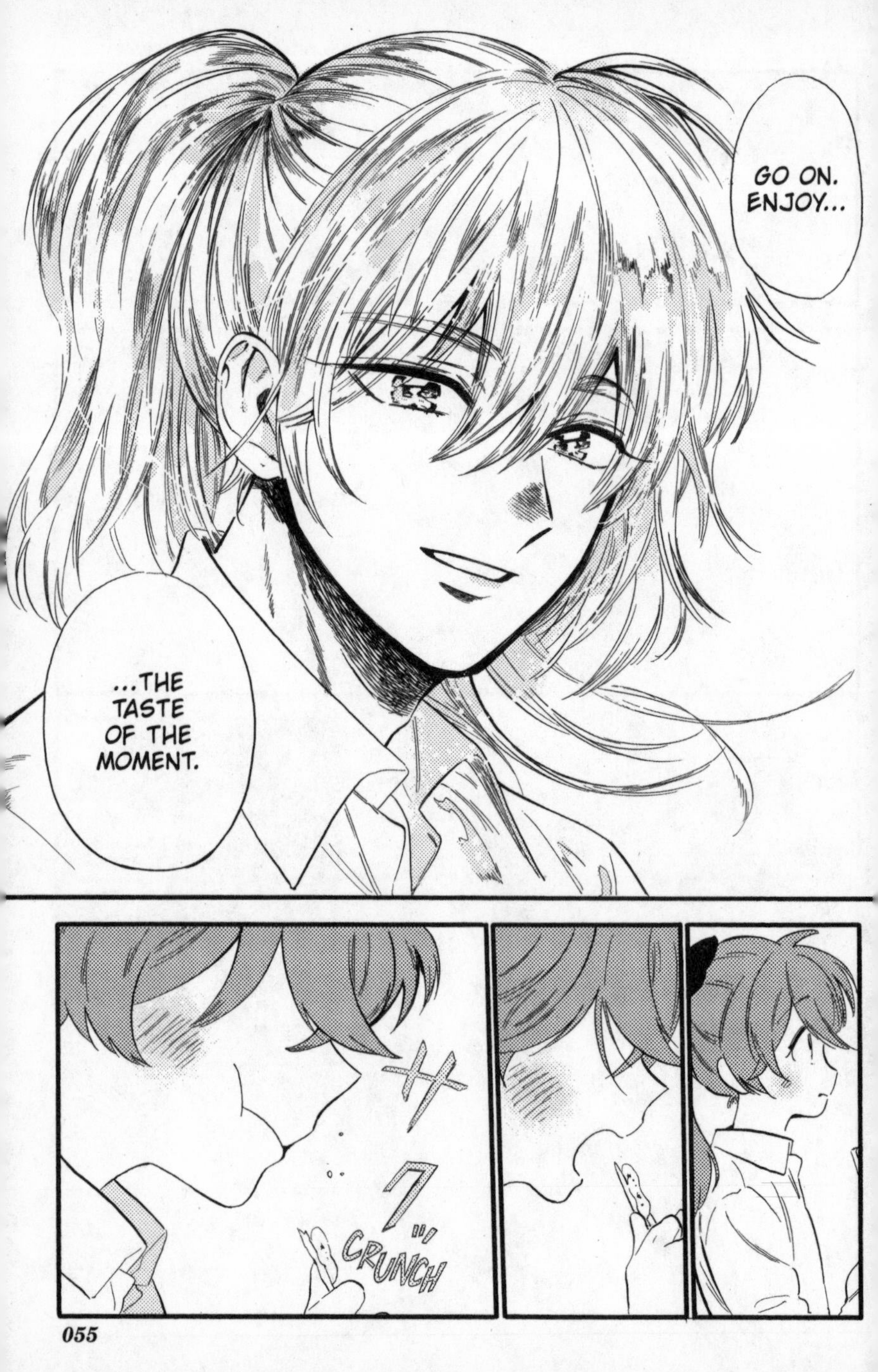
GO ON. ENJOY...
...THE TASTE OF THE MOMENT.
CRUNCH

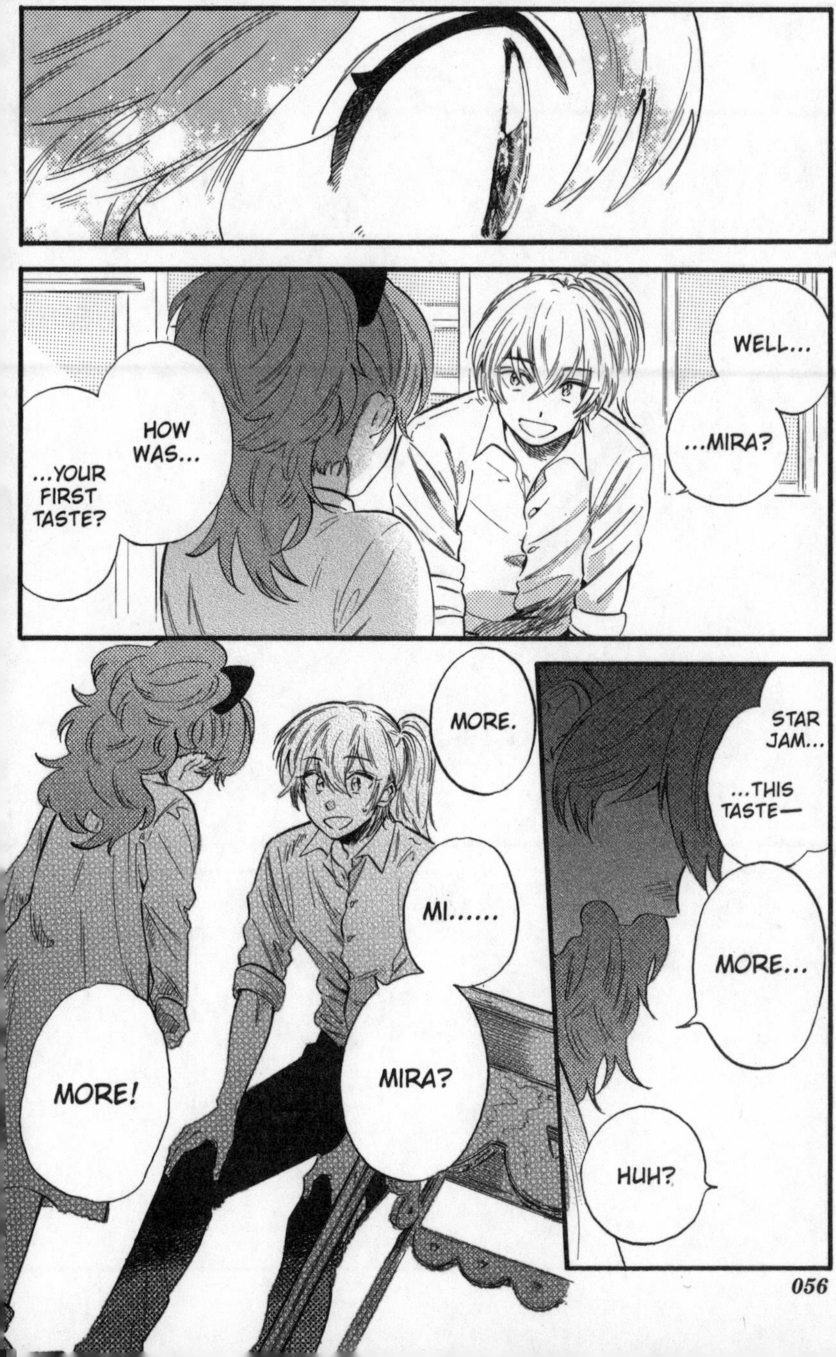
WELL...
...MIRA?
HOW WAS...
...YOUR FIRST TASTE?
STAR JAM...
...THIS TASTE—
MORE...
HUH?
MORE.
MI......
MIRA?
MORE!

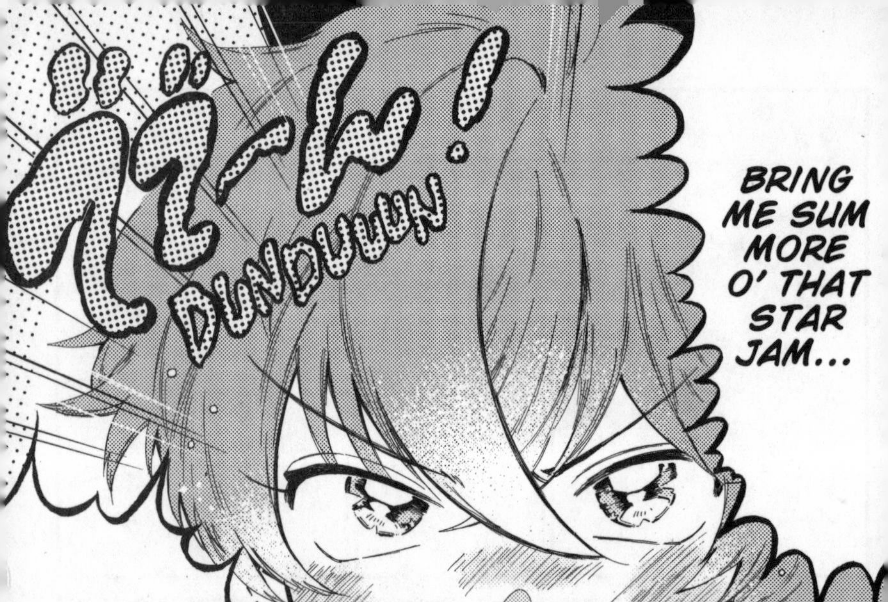
DUNDUUUN
BRING ME SUM MORE O' THAT STAR JAM...
...MASTAH!!

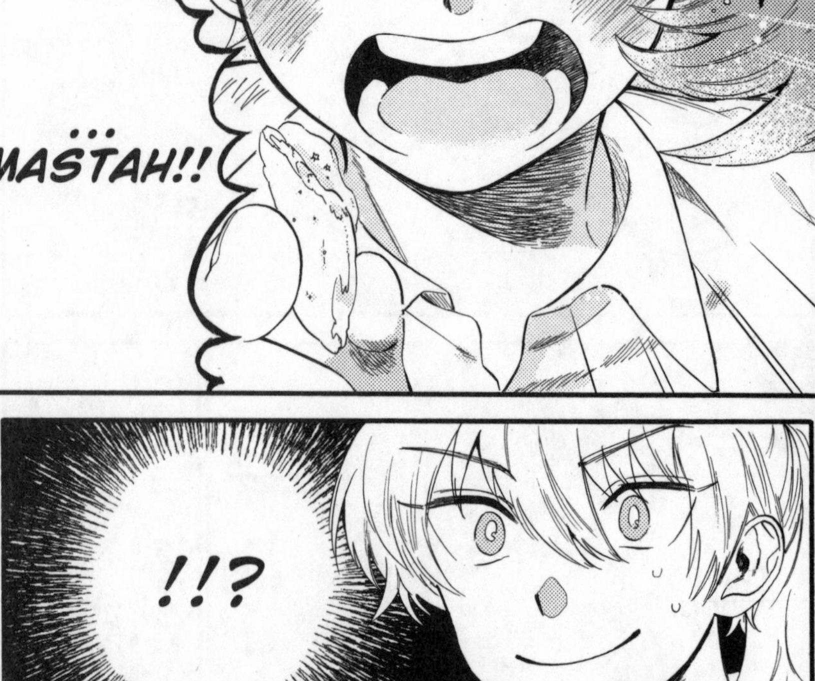
!!?

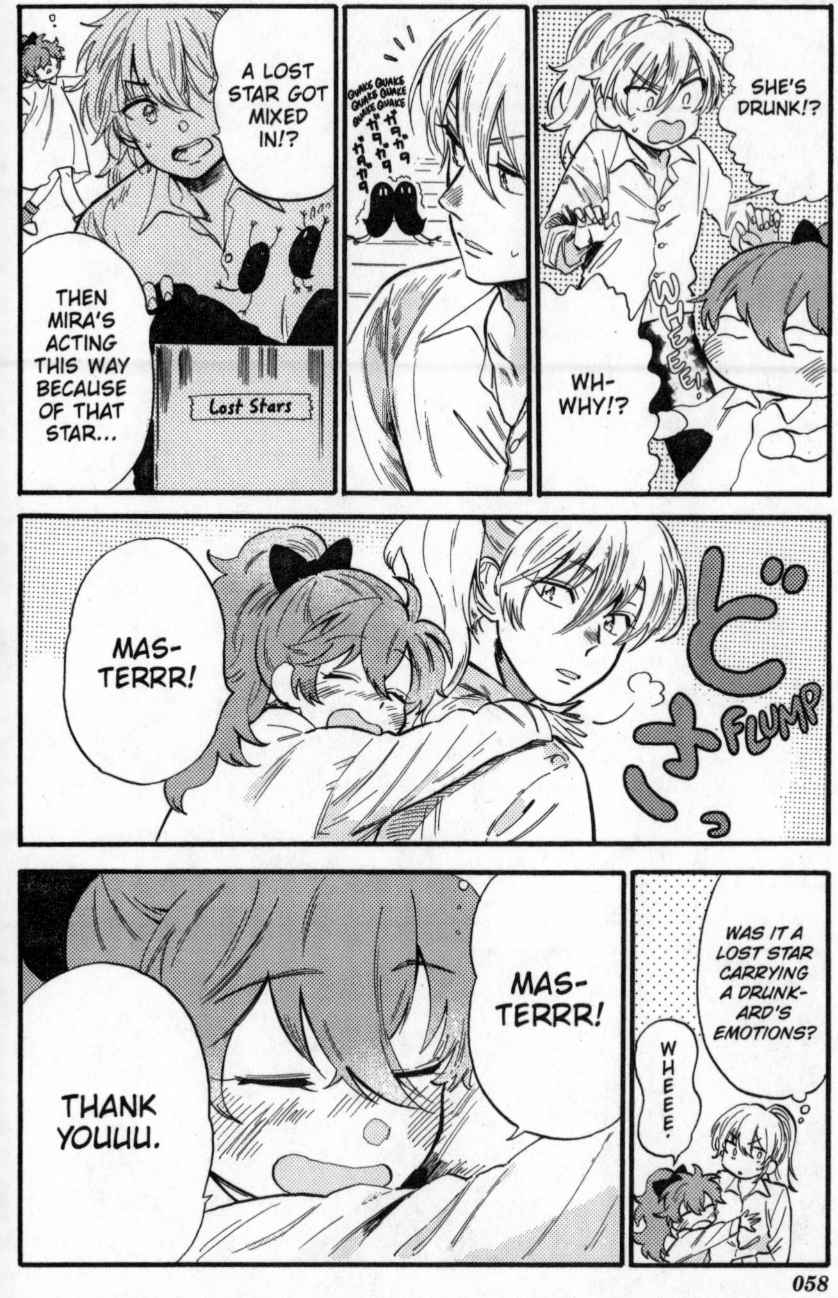
SHE'S DRUNK!?
WHEEE!
WH- WHY!?
QUAKE QUAKE QUAKE QUAKE QUAKE QUAKE
A LOST STAR GOT MIXED IN!?
THEN MIRA'S ACTING THIS WAY BECAUSE OF THAT STAR...
Lost Stars
どさっ
FLUMP
MAS-TERRR!
WAS IT A LOST STAR CARRYING A DRUNK-ARD'S EMOTIONS?
WHEEE.
MAS-TERRR!
THANK YOUUU.

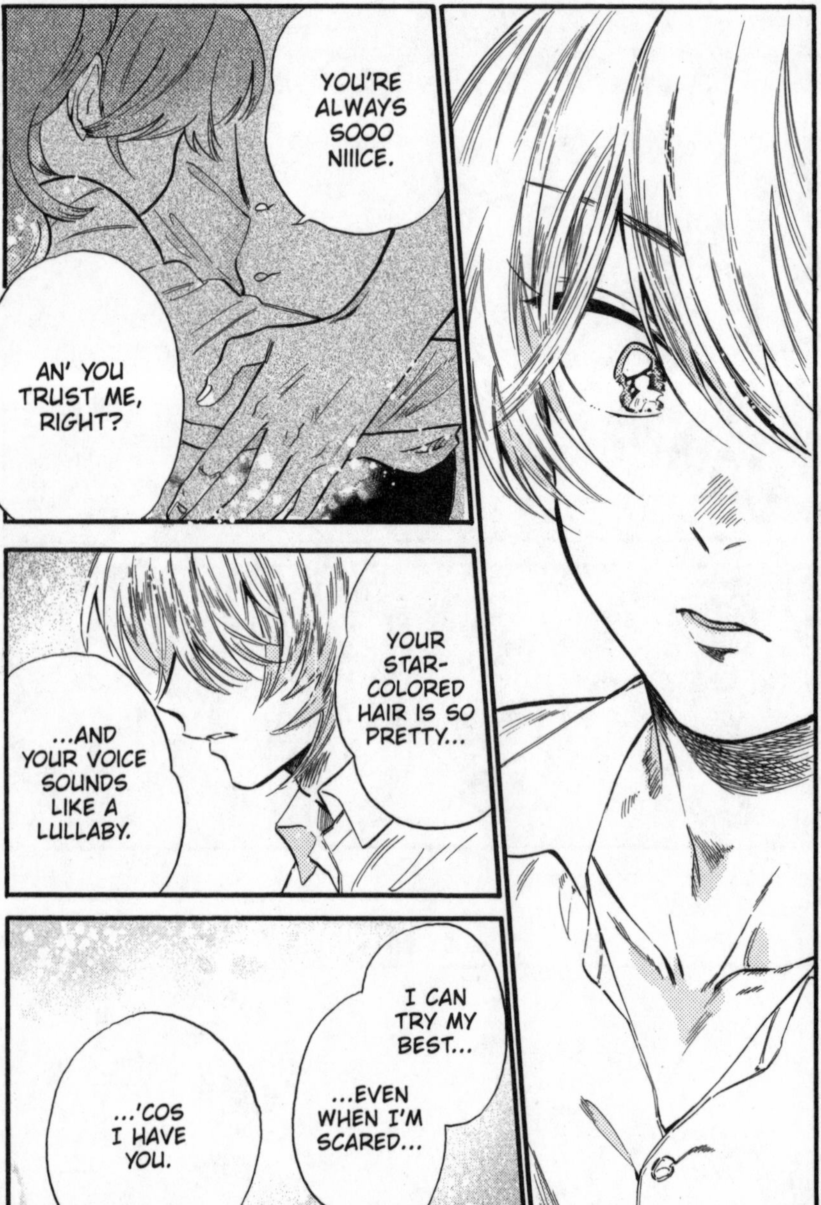
YOU'RE ALWAYS SOOO NIIICE.
AN' YOU TRUST ME, RIGHT?
YOUR STAR-COLORED HAIR IS SO PRETTY...
...AND YOUR VOICE SOUNDS LIKE A LULLABY.
I CAN TRY MY BEST...
...EVEN WHEN I'M SCARED...
...'COS I HAVE YOU.

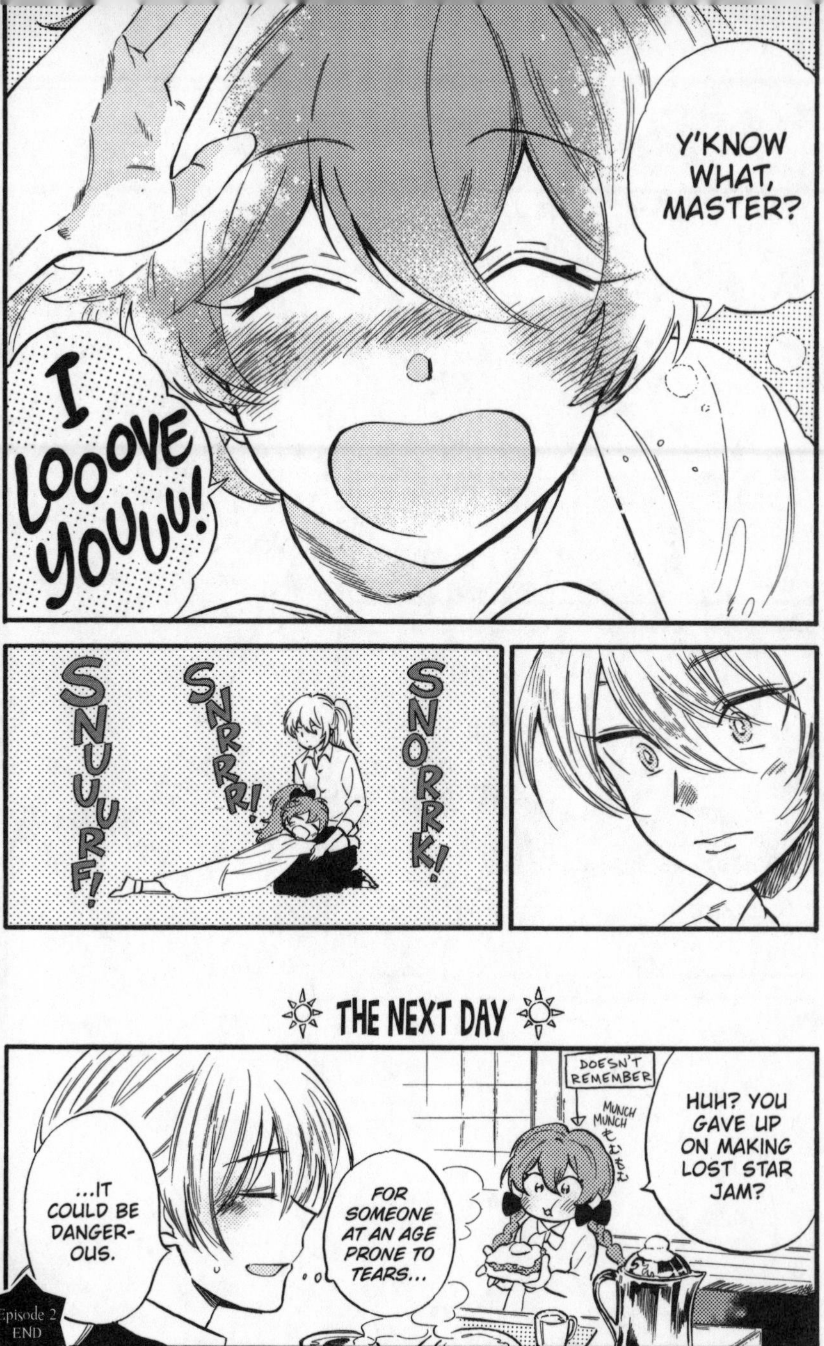
Y'KNOW WHAT, MASTER?
I LOOOVE YOUUU!
SNORRK!
SNRRR!
SNUUURF!
THE NEXT DAY
HUH? YOU GAVE UP ON MAKING LOST STAR JAM?
DOESN'T REMEMBER
MUNCH MUNCH
もむもむ
FOR SOMEONE AT AN AGE PRONE TO TEARS...
...IT COULD BE DANGER-OUS.
Episode 2 END

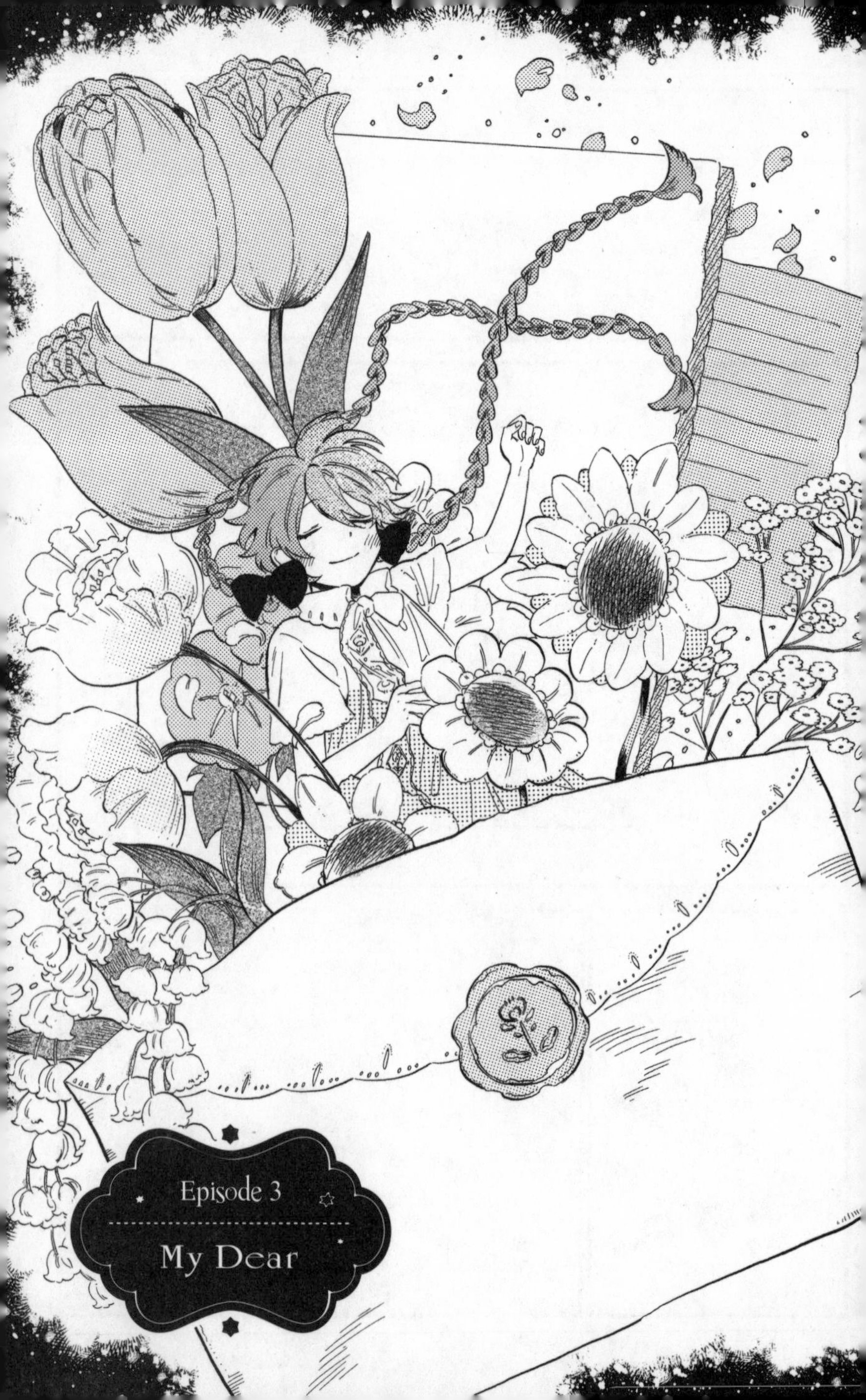
Episode 3
My Dear

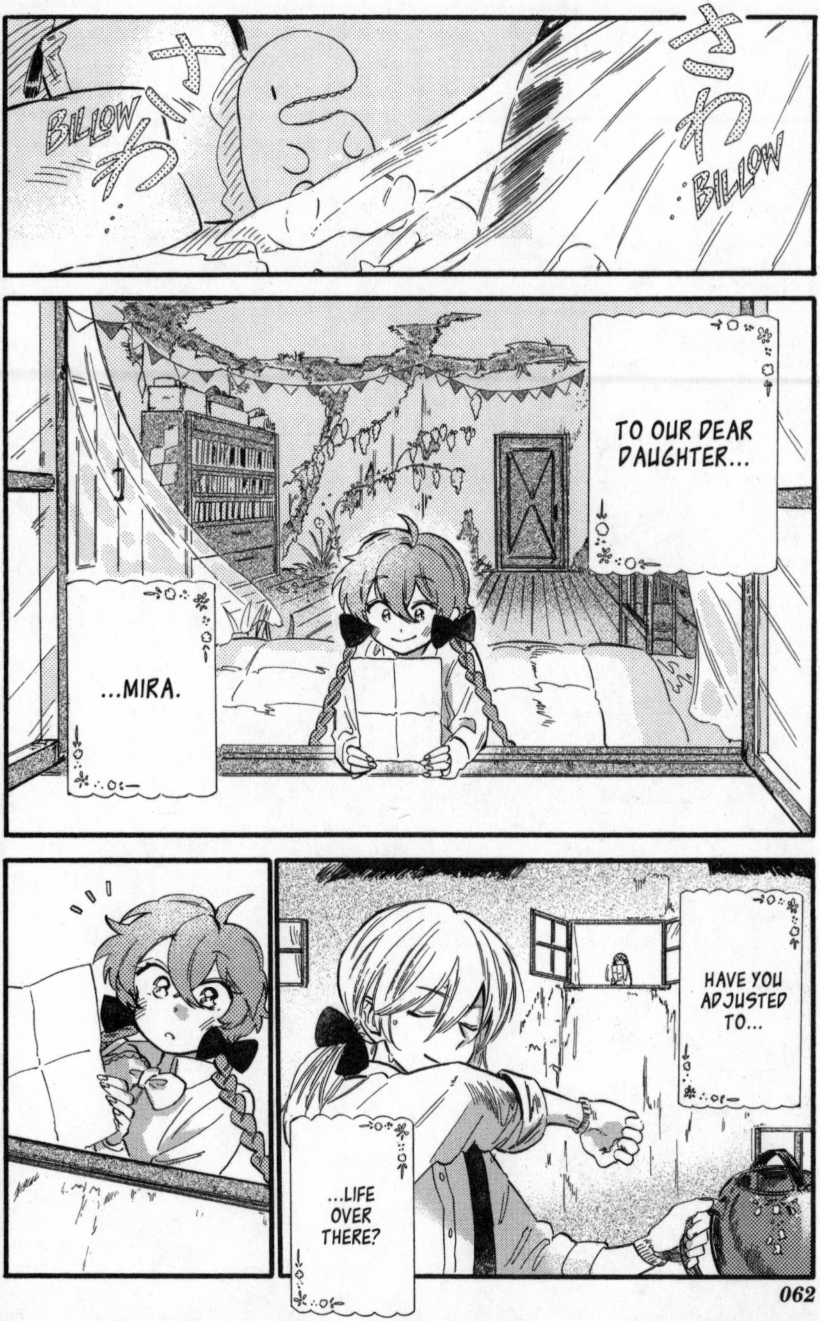
さわ
BILLOW
さわ
BILLOW
TO OUR DEAR DAUGHTER...
...MIRA.
HAVE YOU ADJUSTED TO...
...LIFE OVER THERE?

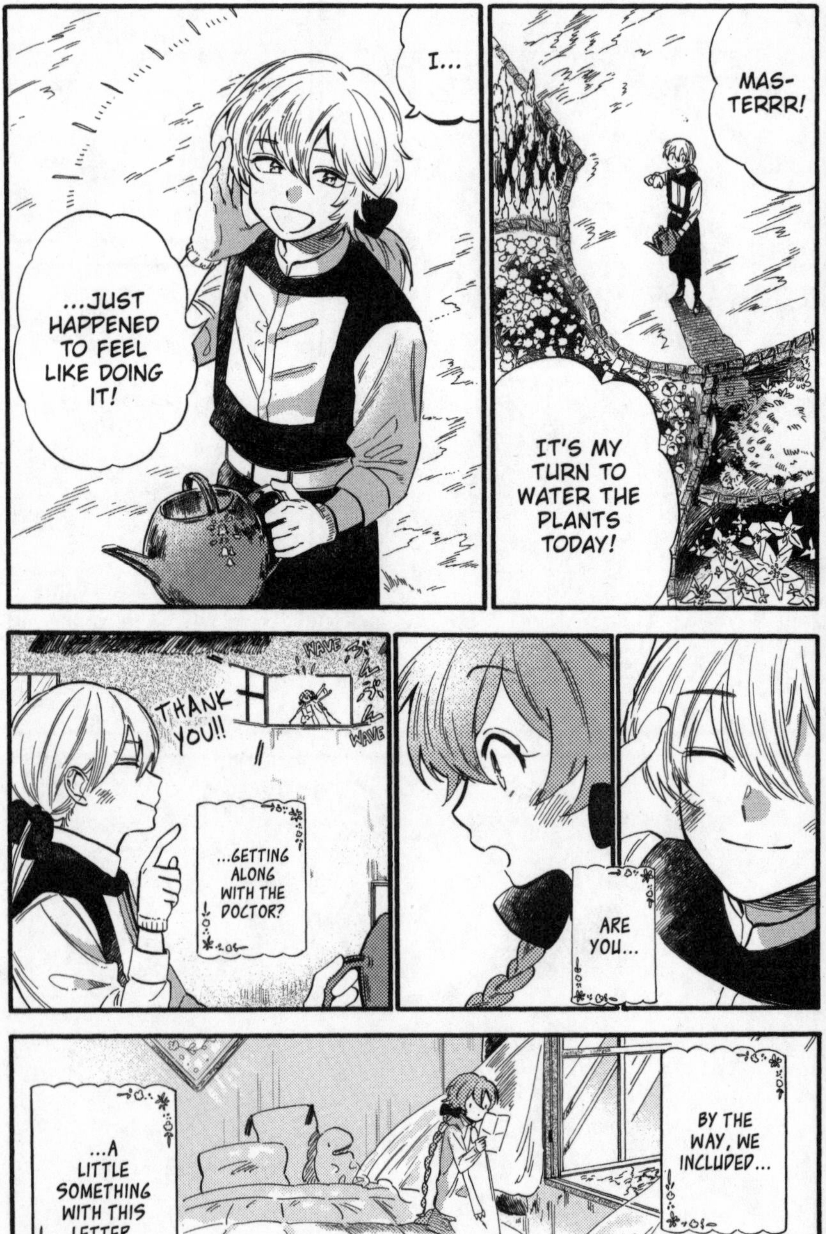
MAS-TERRR!
IT'S MY TURN TO WATER THE PLANTS TODAY!
I...
...JUST HAPPENED TO FEEL LIKE DOING IT!
ARE YOU...
WAVE
WAVE
THANK YOU!!
...GETTING ALONG WITH THE DOCTOR?
BY THE WAY, WE INCLUDED...
...A LITTLE SOMETHING WITH THIS LETTER.

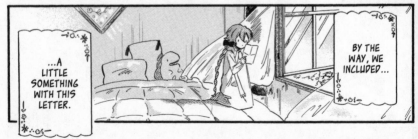

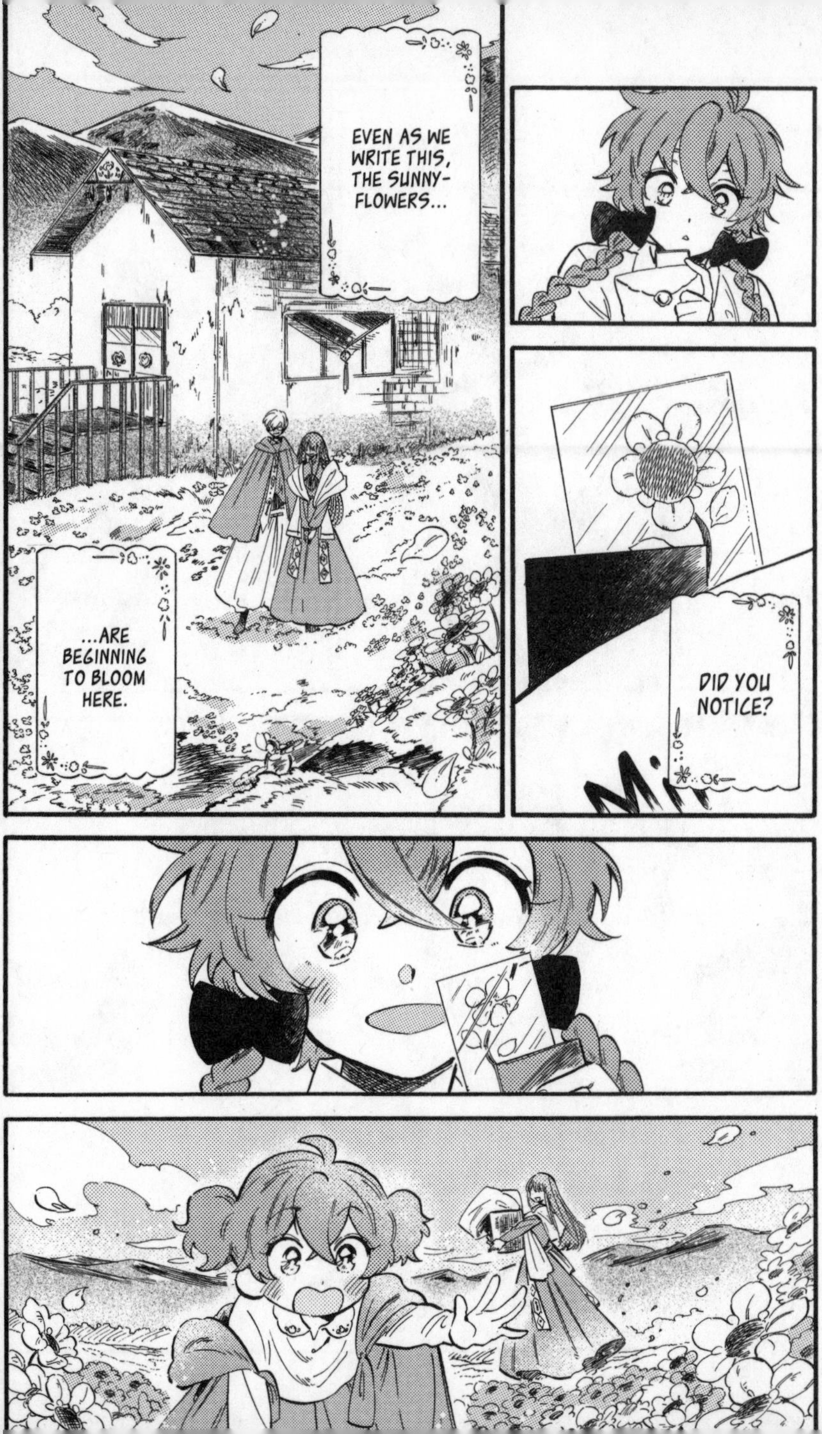
DID YOU NOTICE?
EVEN AS WE WRITE THIS, THE SUNNY-FLOWERS...
...ARE BEGINNING TO BLOOM HERE.

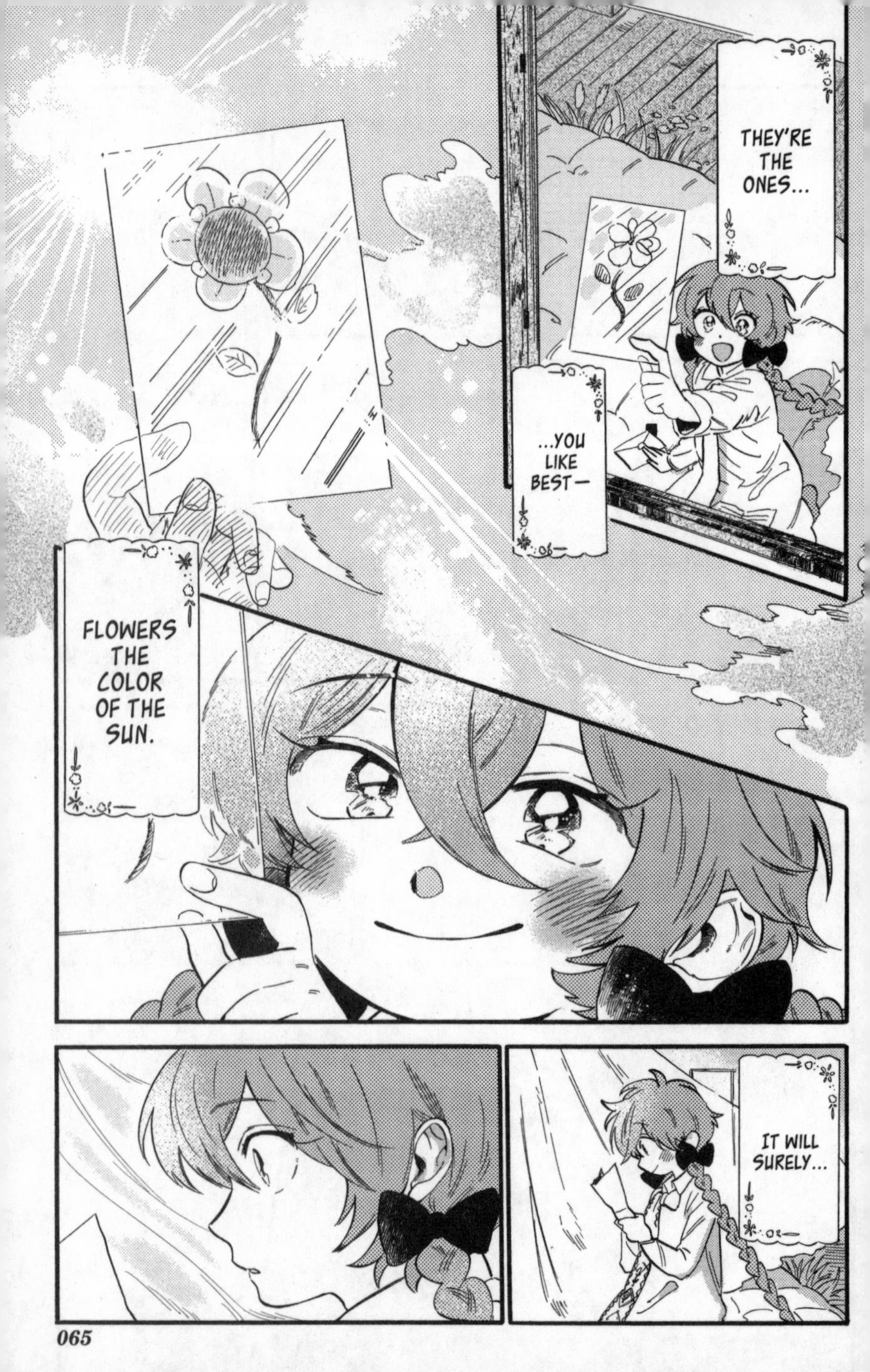
THEY'RE THE ONES...
...YOU LIKE BEST—
FLOWERS THE COLOR OF THE SUN.
IT WILL SURELY...

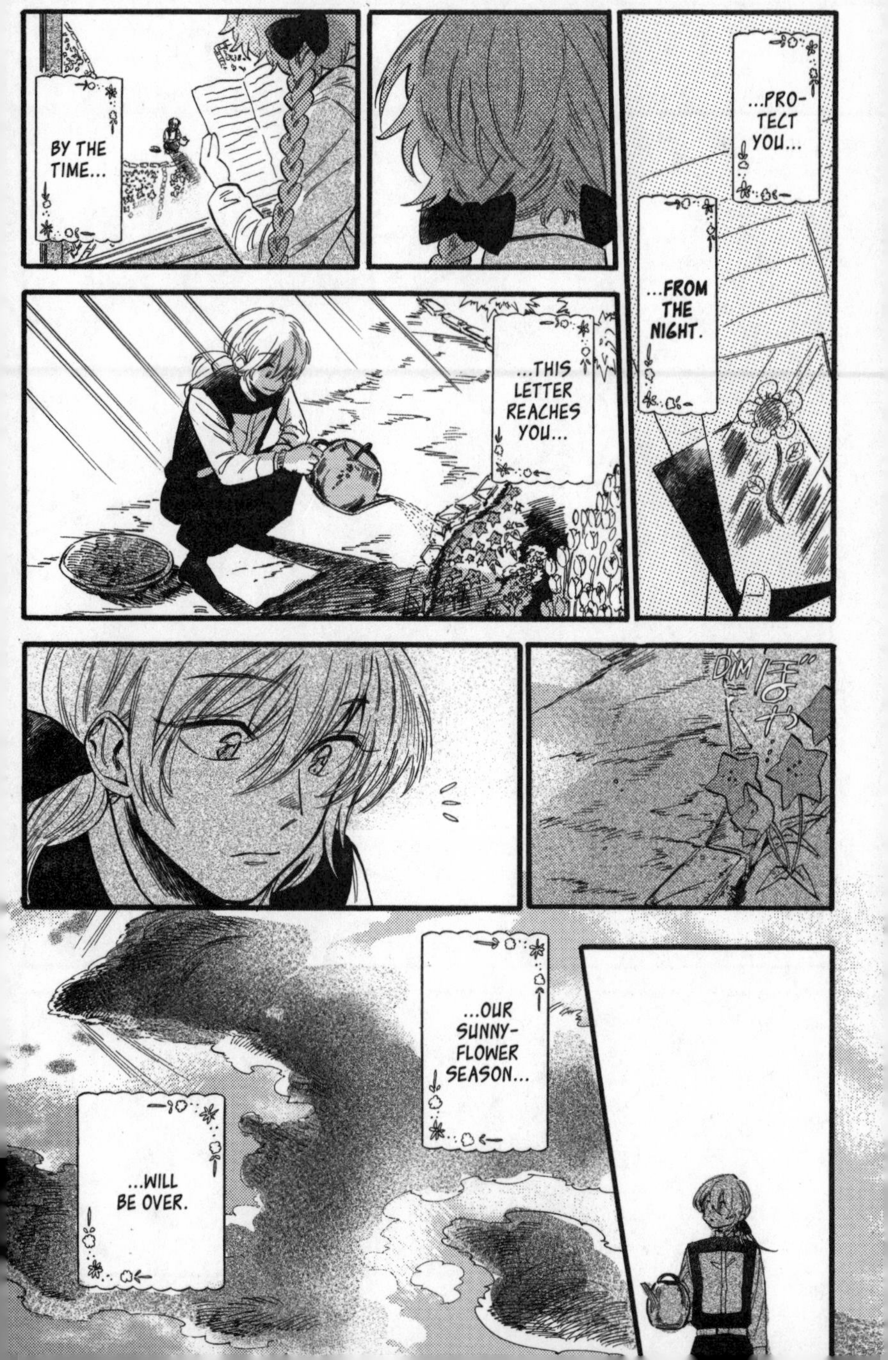
...PRO-TECT YOU...
...FROM THE NIGHT.
BY THE TIME...
...THIS LETTER REACHES YOU...
DIM
ぼや
...OUR SUNNY-FLOWER SEASON...
...WILL BE OVER.

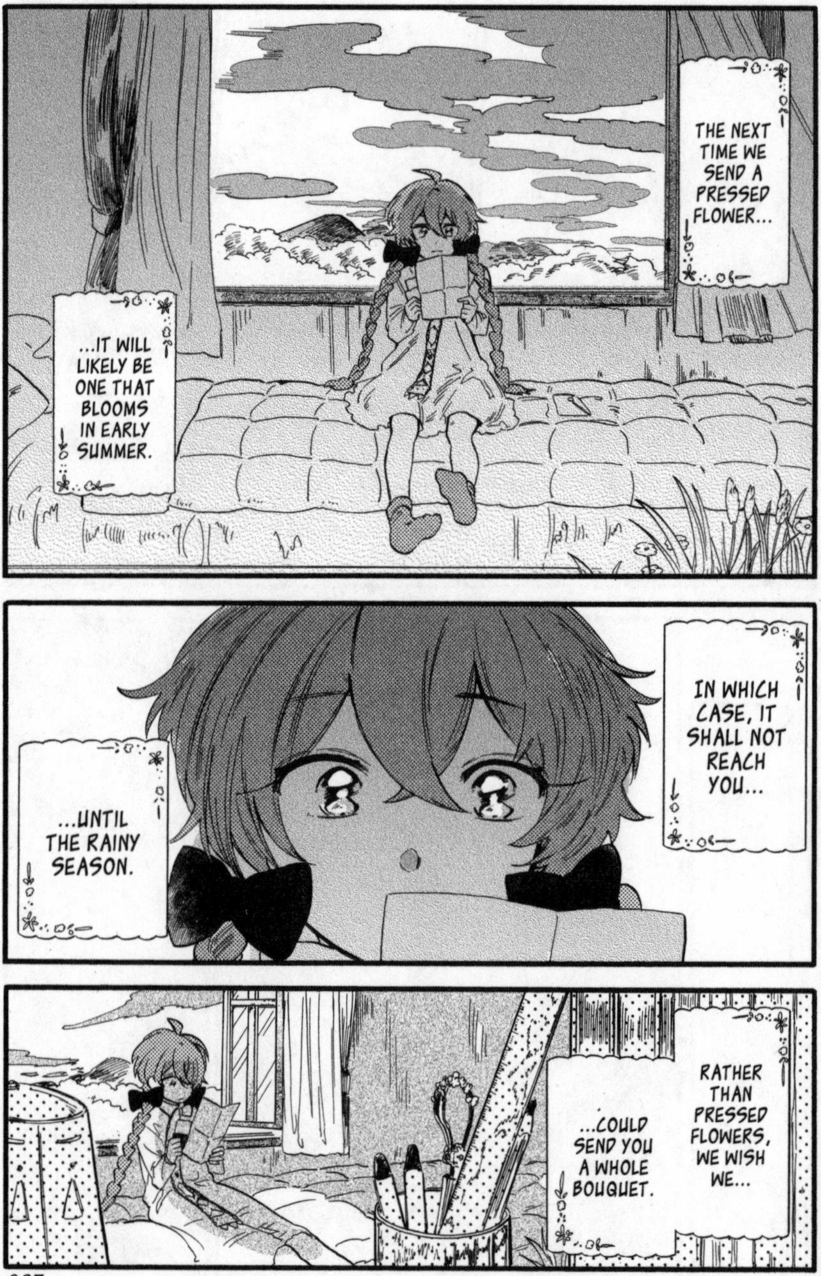
THE NEXT TIME WE SEND A PRESSED FLOWER...
...IT WILL LIKELY BE ONE THAT BLOOMS IN EARLY SUMMER.
IN WHICH CASE, IT SHALL NOT REACH YOU...
...UNTIL THE RAINY SEASON.
RATHER THAN PRESSED FLOWERS, WE WISH WE...
...COULD SEND YOU A WHOLE BOUQUET.

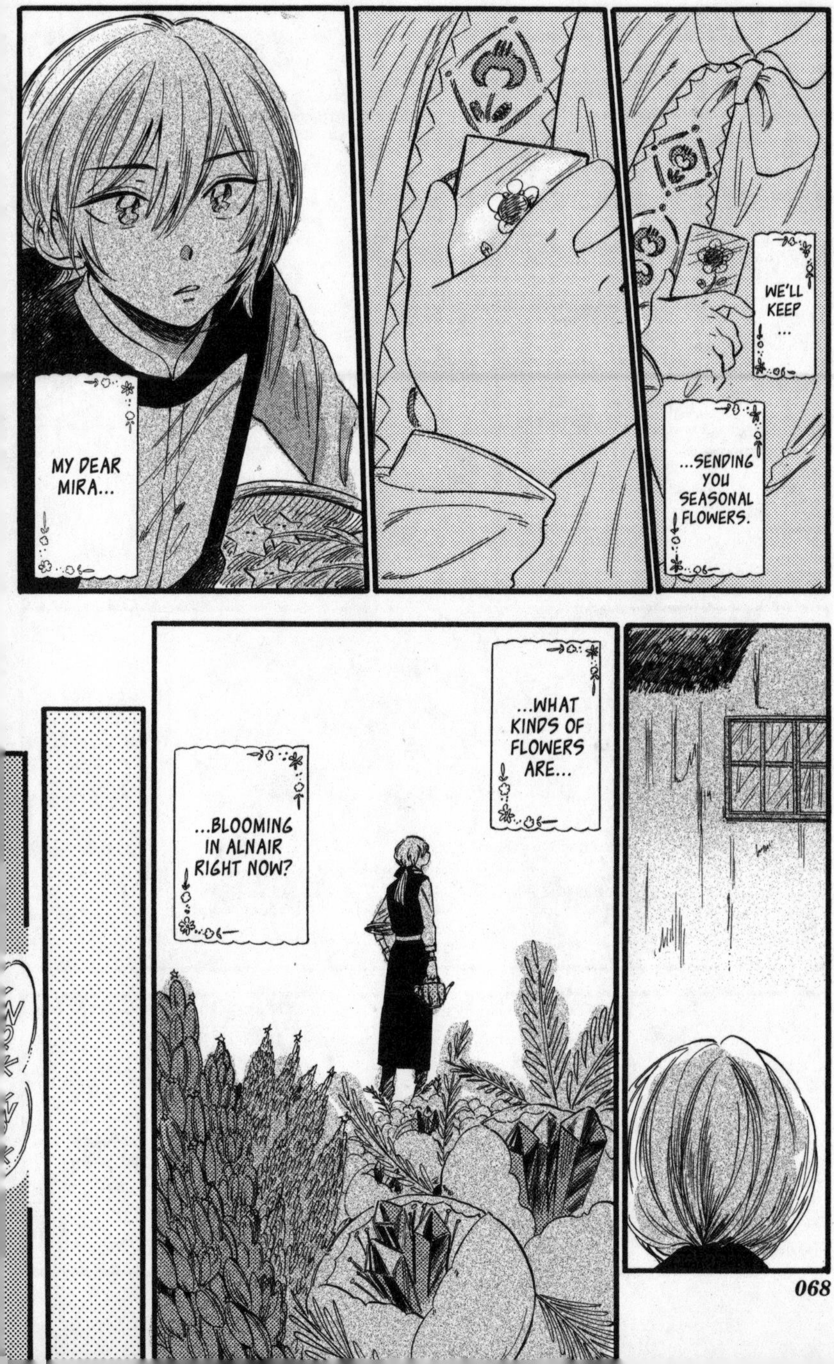
WE'LL KEEP ...
...SENDING YOU SEASONAL FLOWERS.
MY DEAR MIRA...
...WHAT KINDS OF FLOWERS ARE...
...BLOOMING IN ALNAIR RIGHT NOW?

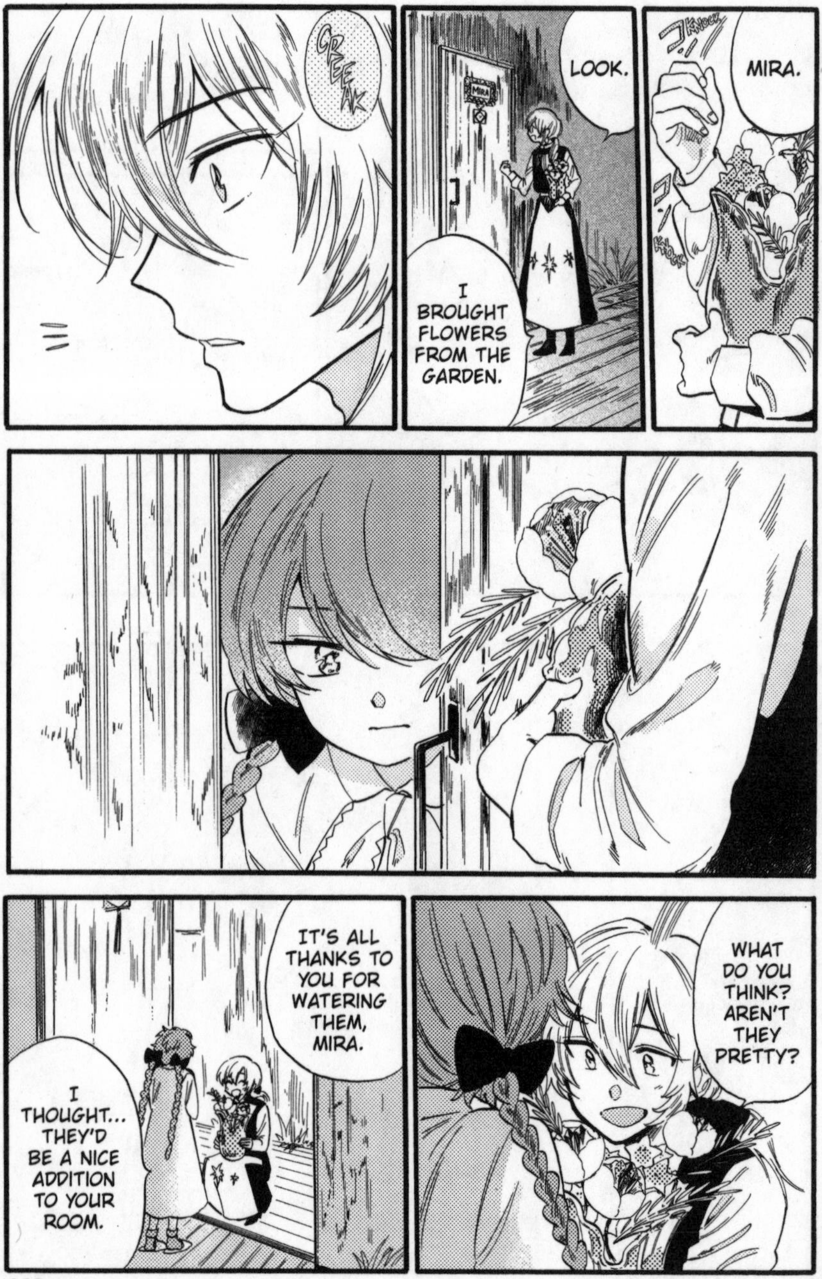
KNOCK
MIRA.
KNOCK
LOOK.
MIRA
I BROUGHT FLOWERS FROM THE GARDEN.
CREEAK
WHAT DO YOU THINK? AREN'T THEY PRETTY?
IT'S ALL THANKS TO YOU FOR WATERING THEM, MIRA.
I THOUGHT... THEY'D BE A NICE ADDITION TO YOUR ROOM.

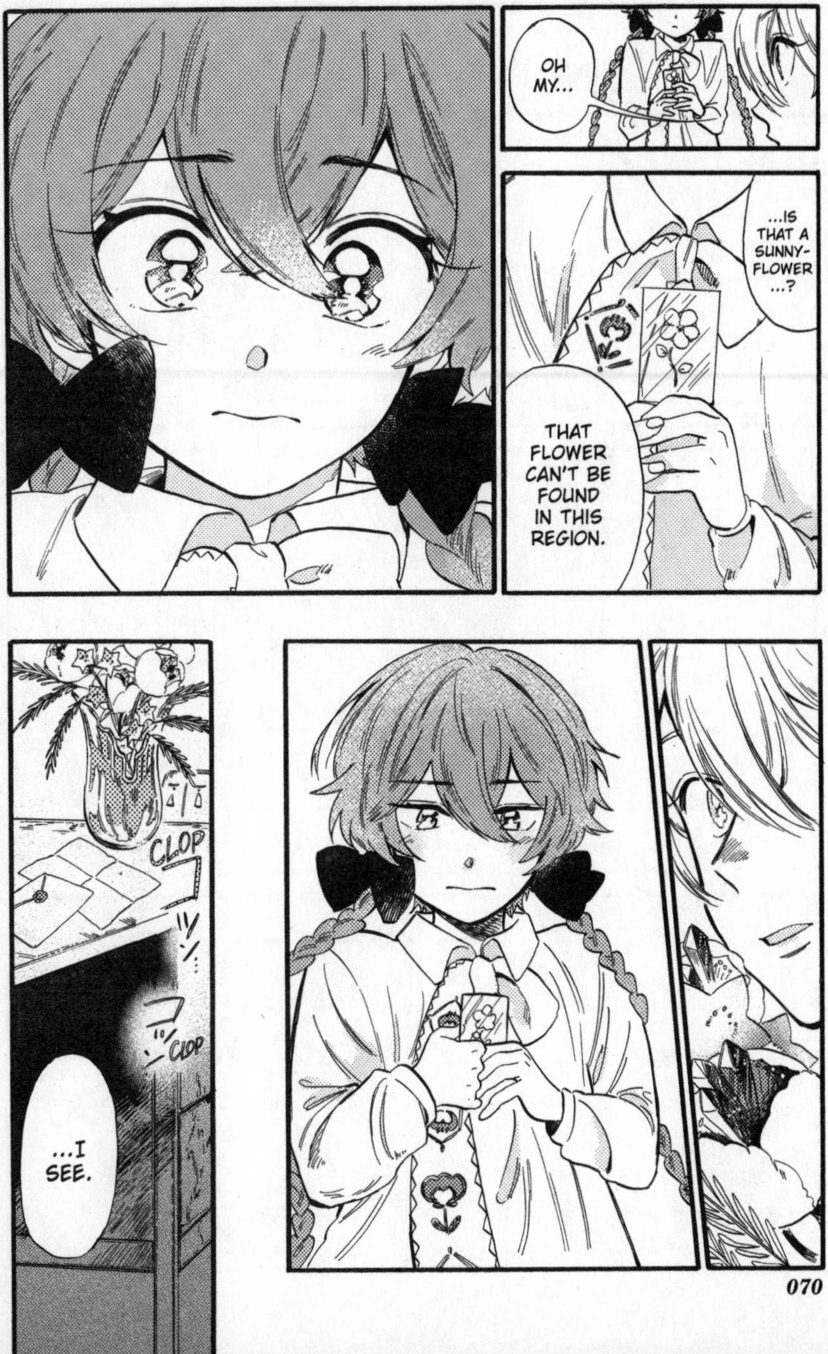
OH MY...
...IS THAT A SUNNY-FLOWER ...?
THAT FLOWER CAN'T BE FOUND IN THIS REGION.
CLOP
CLOP
...I SEE.

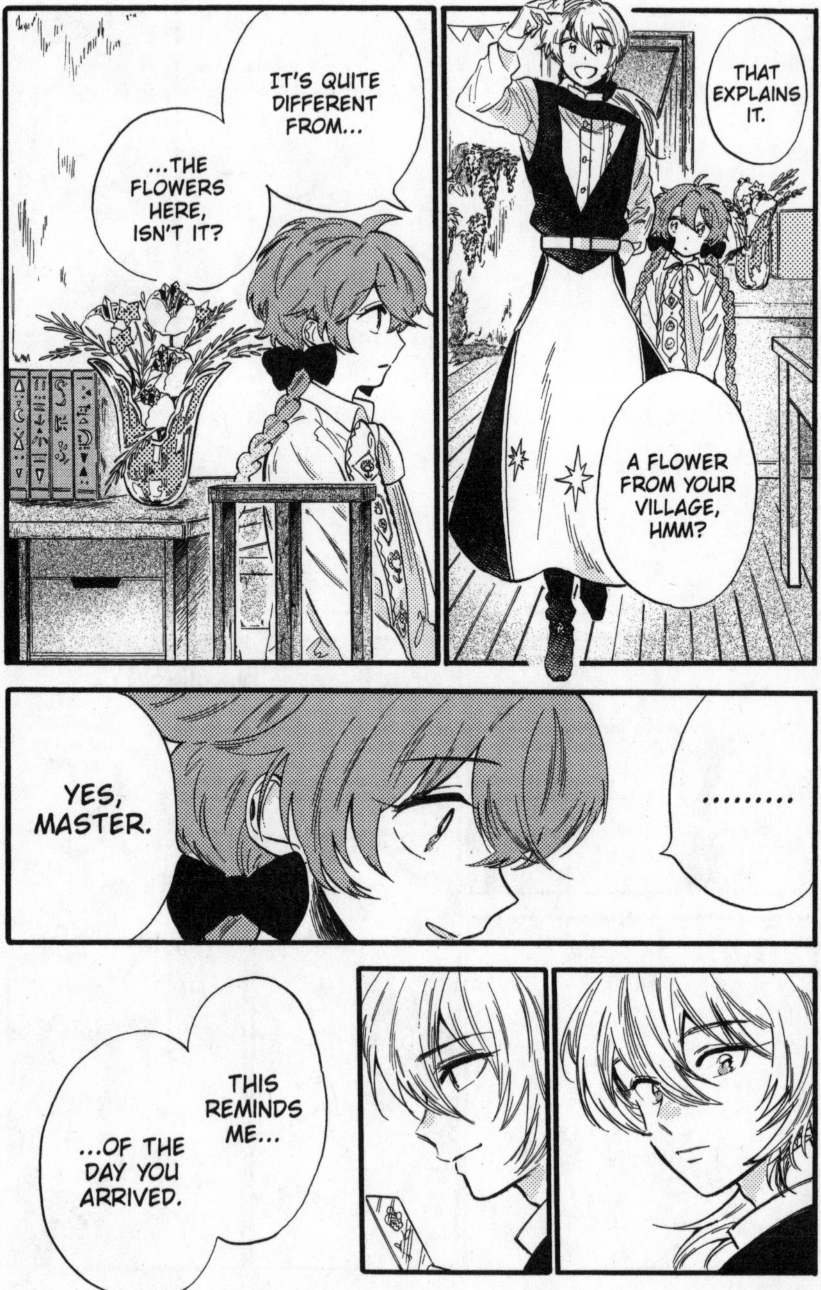
THAT EXPLAINS IT.
A FLOWER FROM YOUR VILLAGE, HMM?
IT'S QUITE DIFFERENT FROM...
...THE FLOWERS HERE, ISN'T IT?
....
YES, MASTER.
THIS REMINDS ME...
...OF THE DAY YOU ARRIVED.

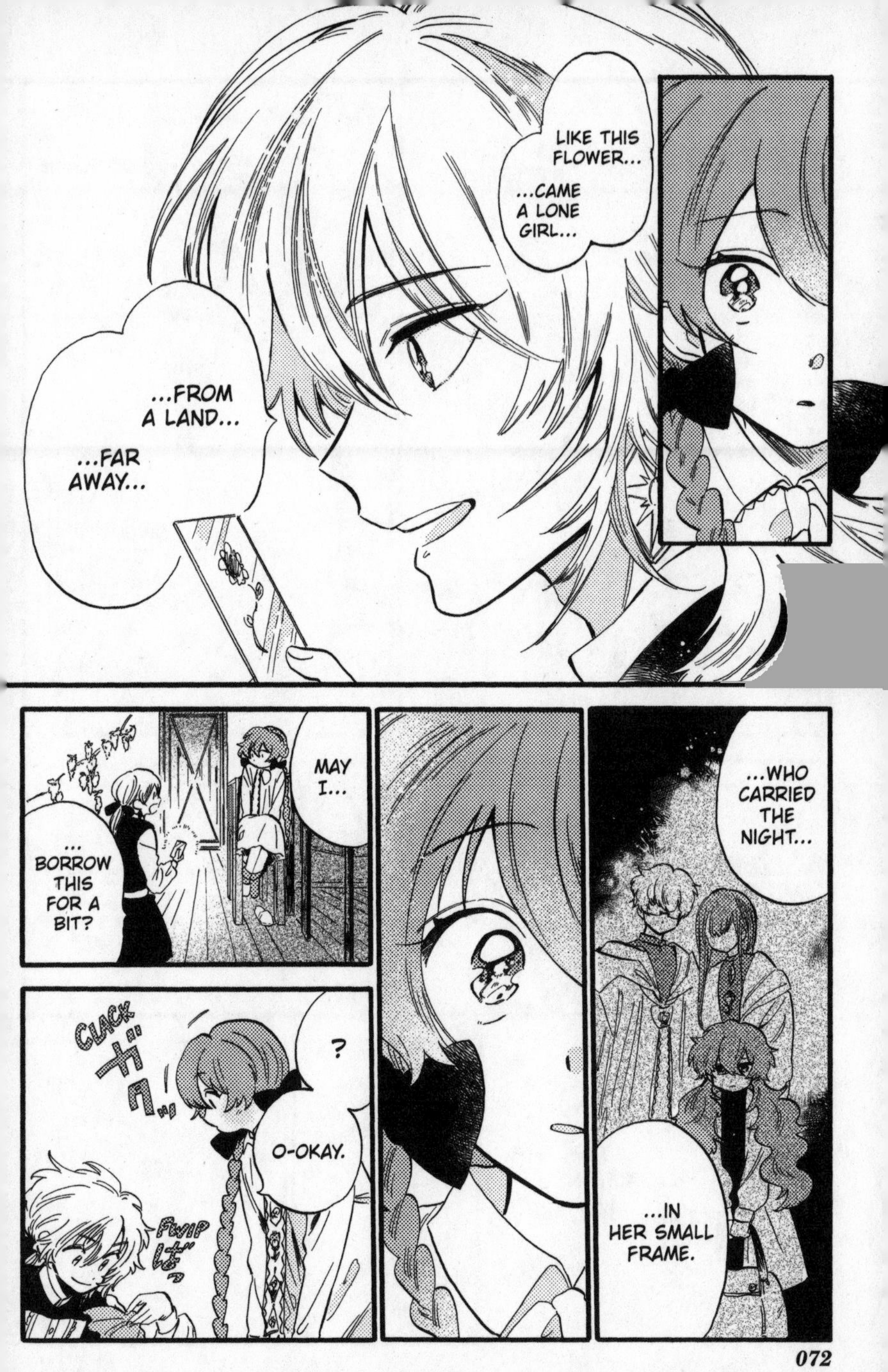
LIKE THIS FLOWER...
...CAME A LONE GIRL...
...FROM A LAND...
...FAR AWAY...
...WHO CARRIED THE NIGHT...
...IN HER SMALL FRAME.
MAY I...
...BORROW THIS FOR A BIT?
?
O-OKAY.
CLACK
FWIP

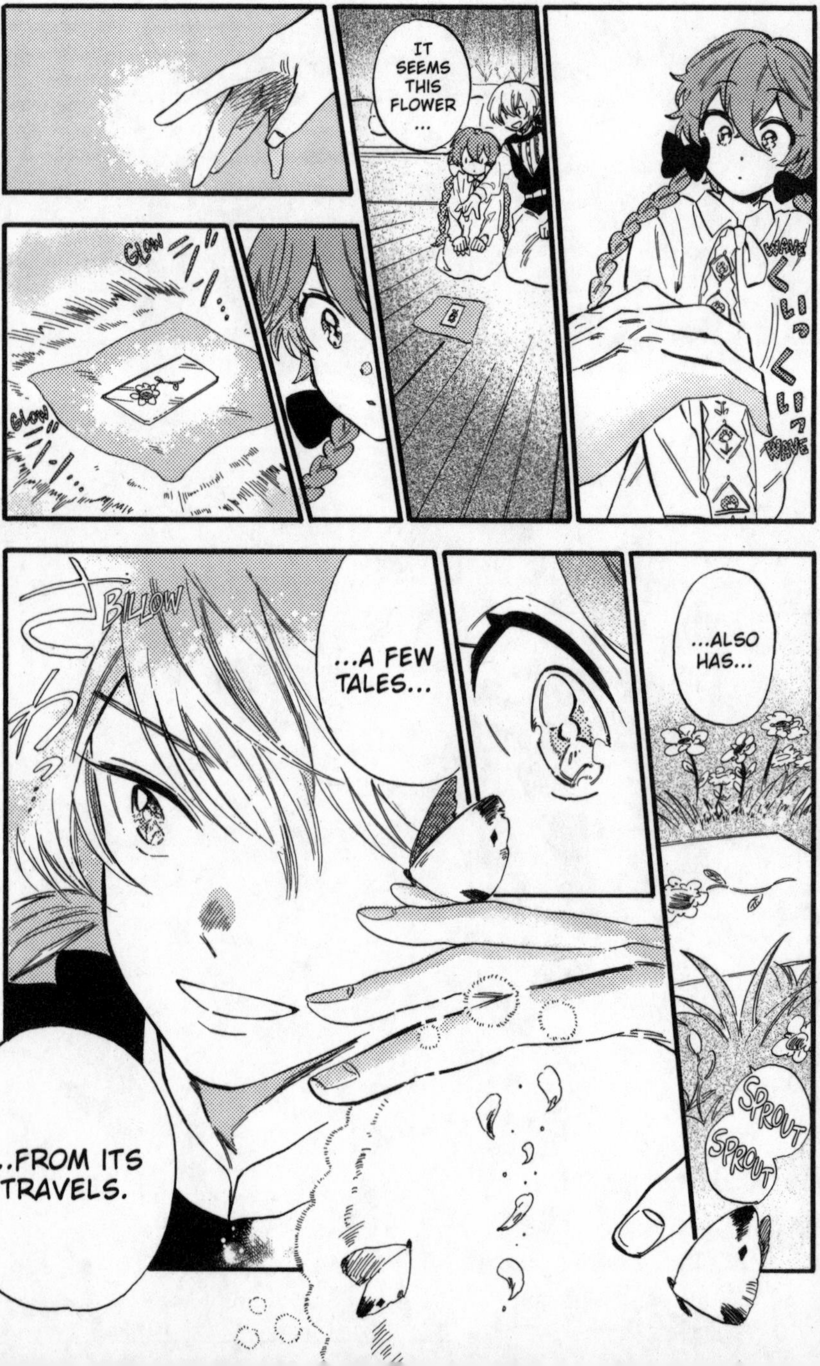
WAVE
くいっ
くいっ
WAVE
IT SEEMS THIS FLOWER ...
GLOW
GLOW
...ALSO HAS...
SPROUT
SPROUT
...A FEW TALES...
BILLOW
...FROM ITS TRAVELS.

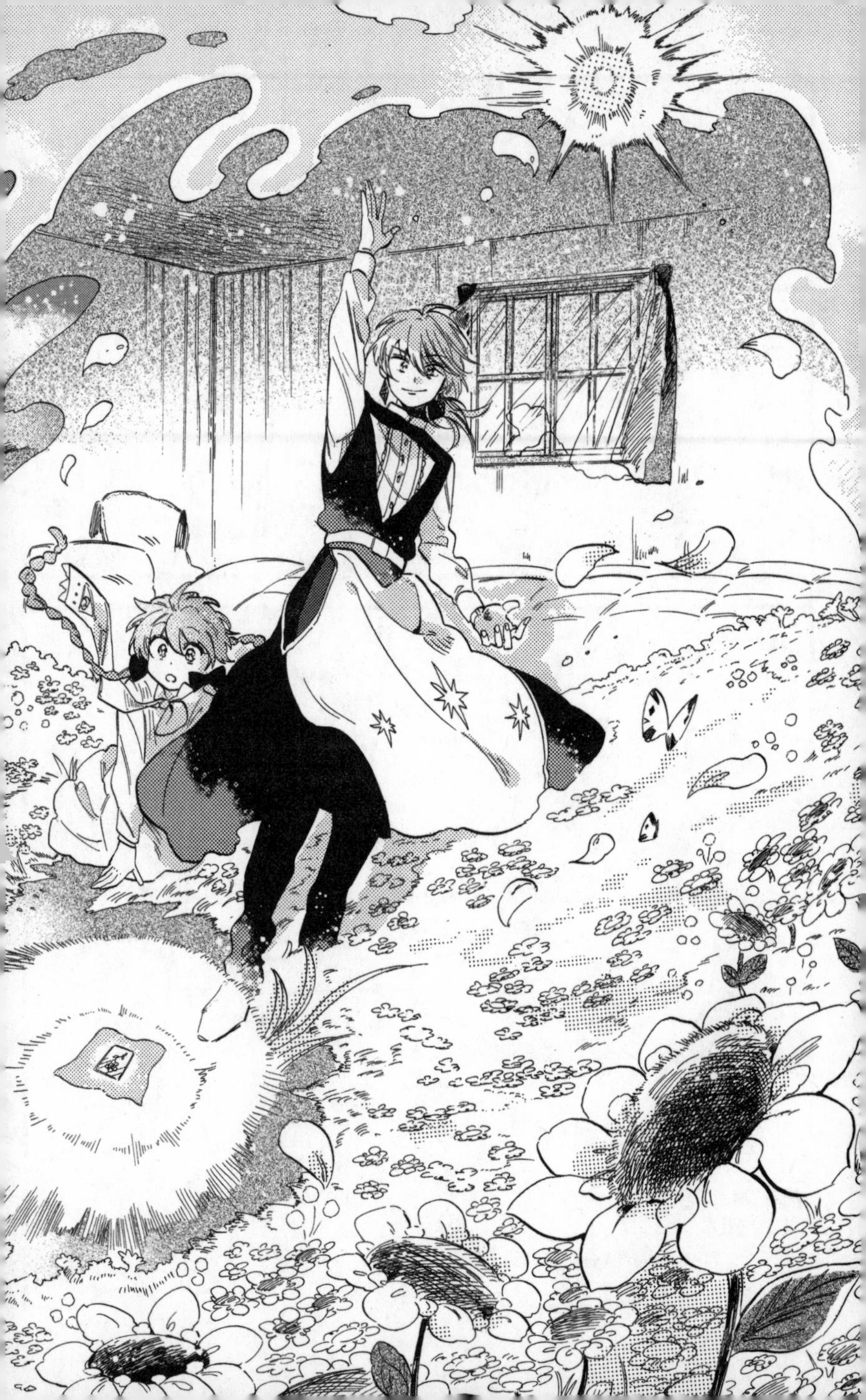

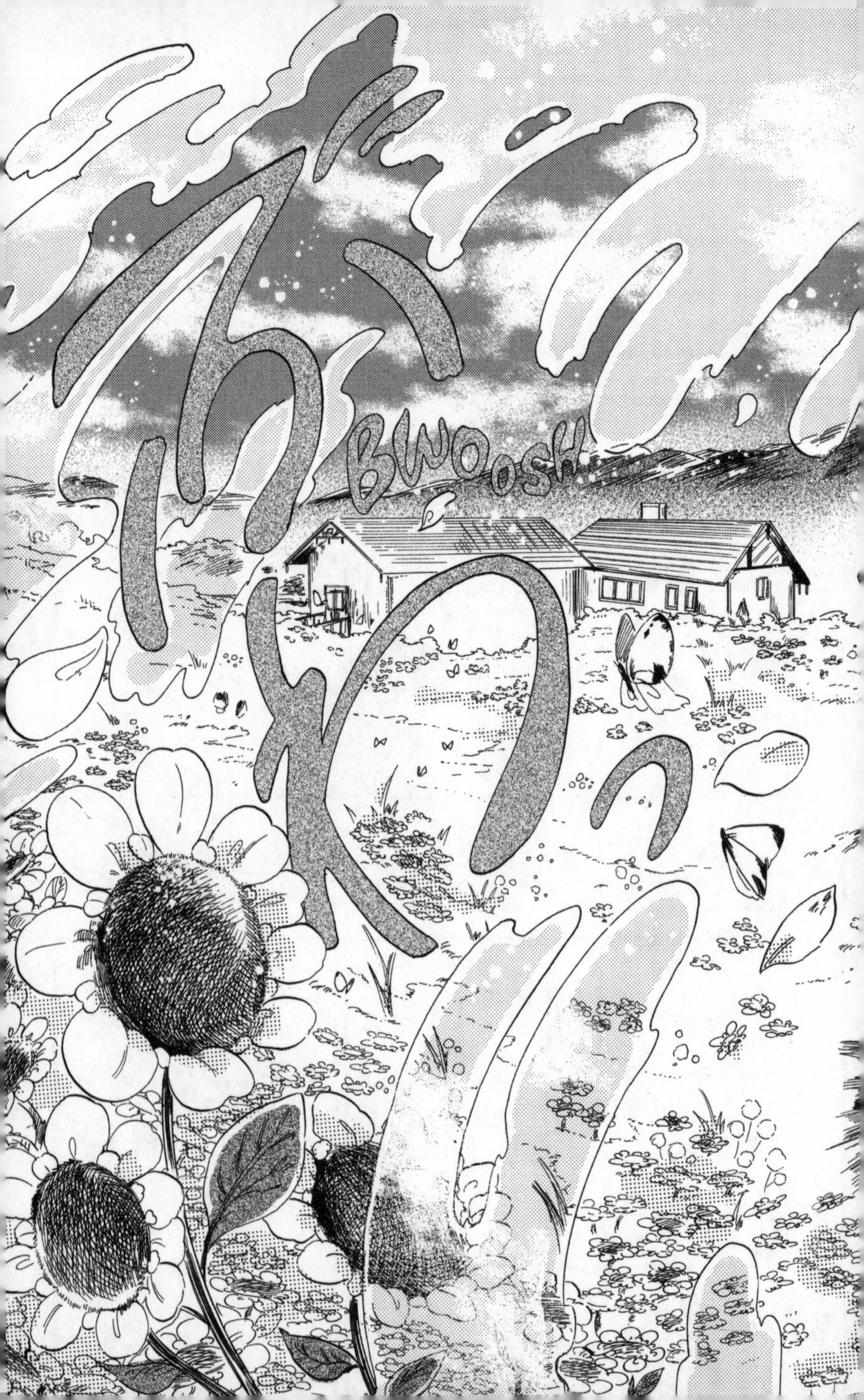
BWOOSH

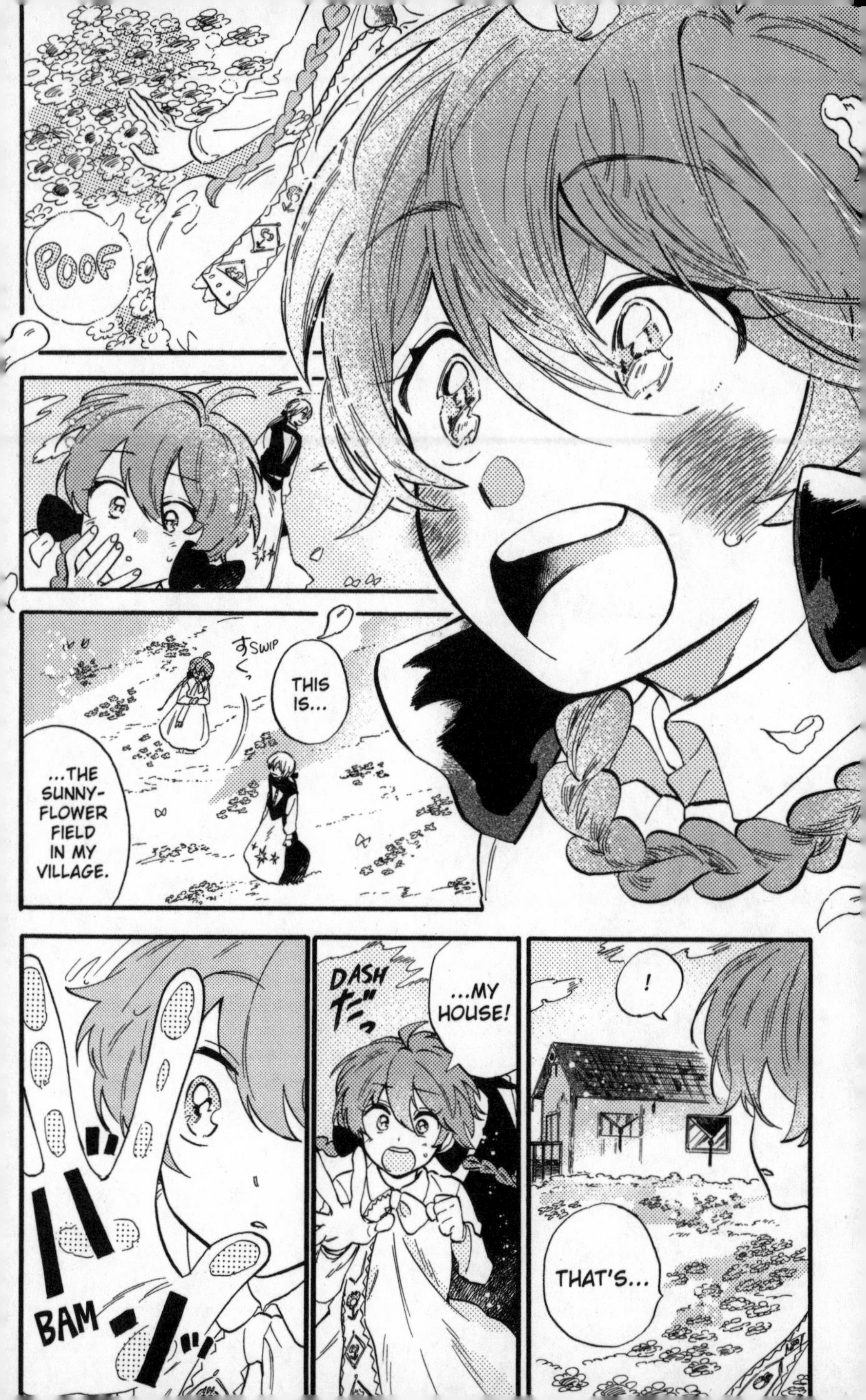
POOF
SWIP
THIS IS...
...THE SUNNY-FLOWER FIELD IN MY VILLAGE.
!
THAT'S...
DASH
...MY HOUSE!
BAM

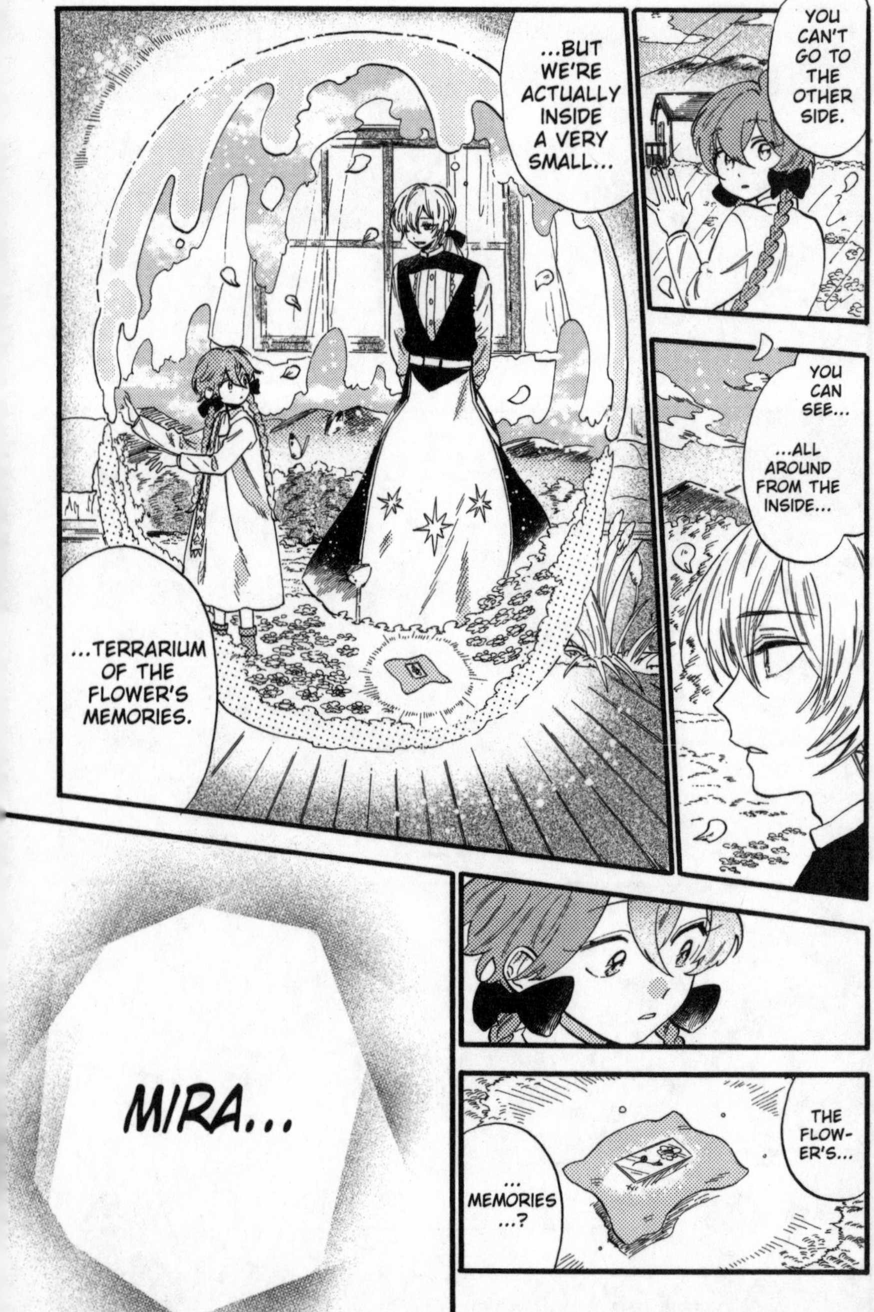
YOU CAN'T GO TO THE OTHER SIDE.
YOU CAN SEE...
...ALL AROUND FROM THE INSIDE...
...BUT WE'RE ACTUALLY INSIDE A VERY SMALL...
...TERRARIUM OF THE FLOWER'S MEMORIES.
THE FLOWER'S...
...MEMORIES...?
MIRA...

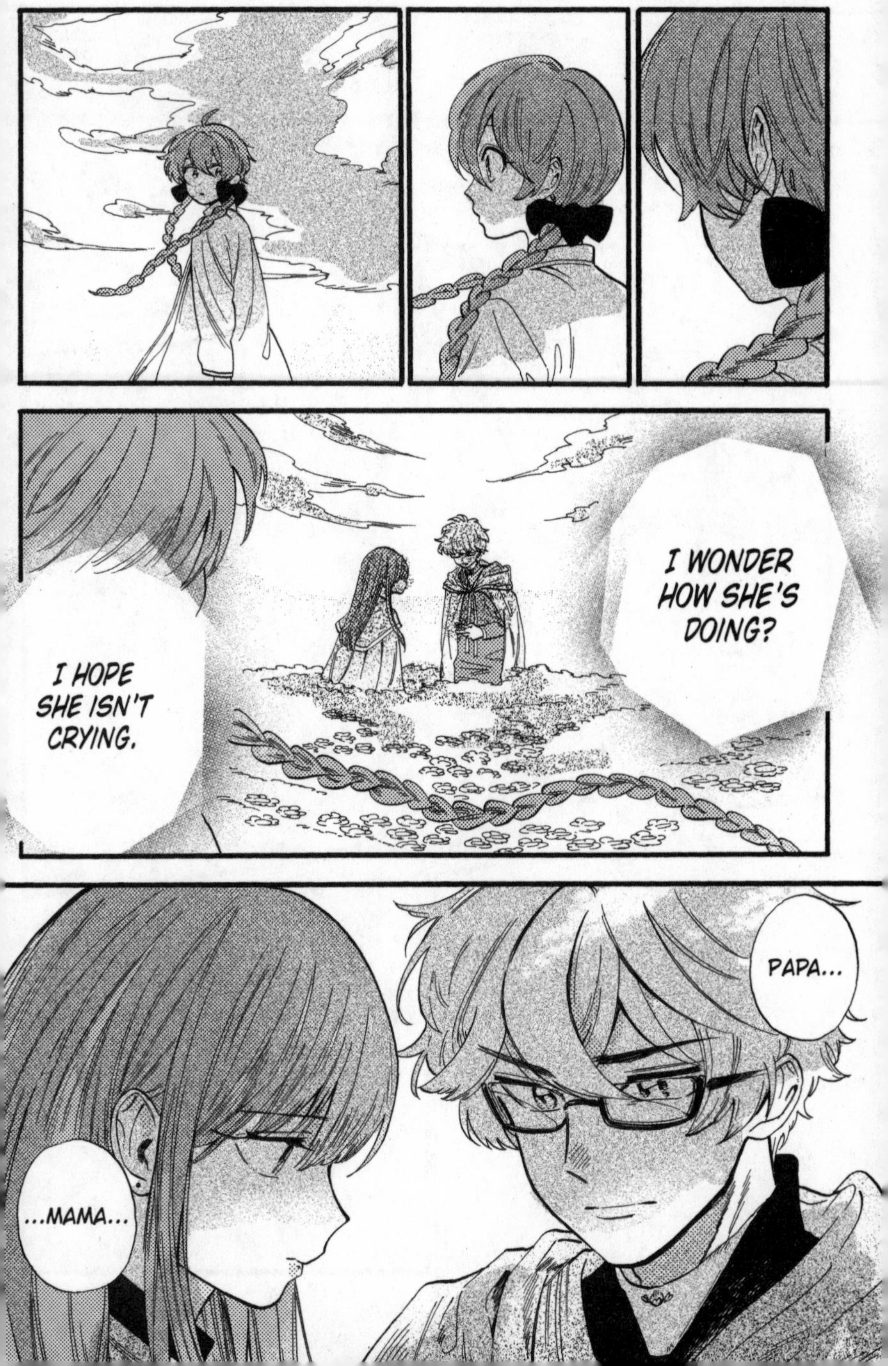
I WONDER HOW SHE'S DOING?
I HOPE SHE ISN'T CRYING.
PAPA...
...MAMA...

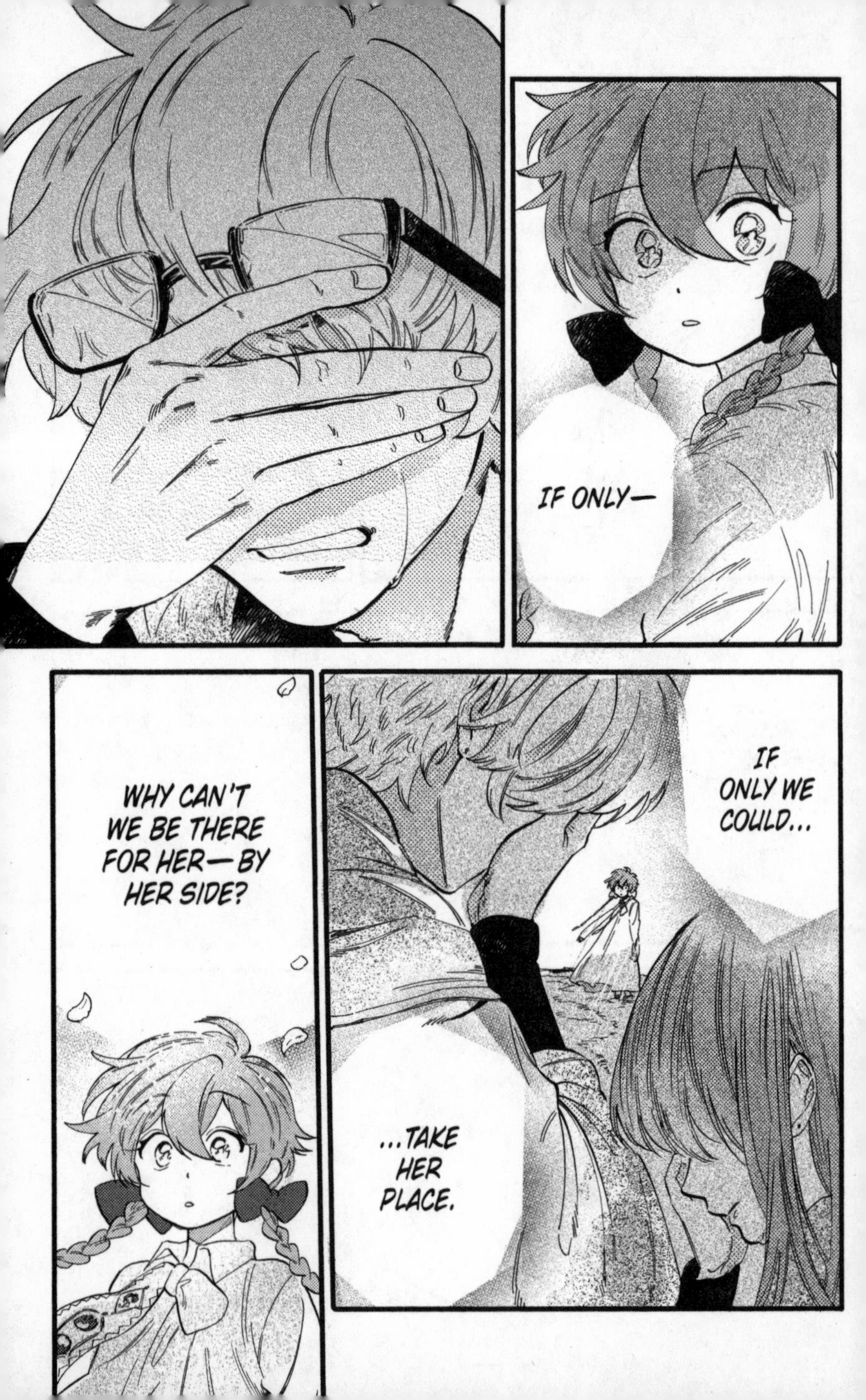
IF ONLY—
IF ONLY WE COULD...
...TAKE HER PLACE.
WHY CAN'T WE BE THERE FOR HER—BY HER SIDE?

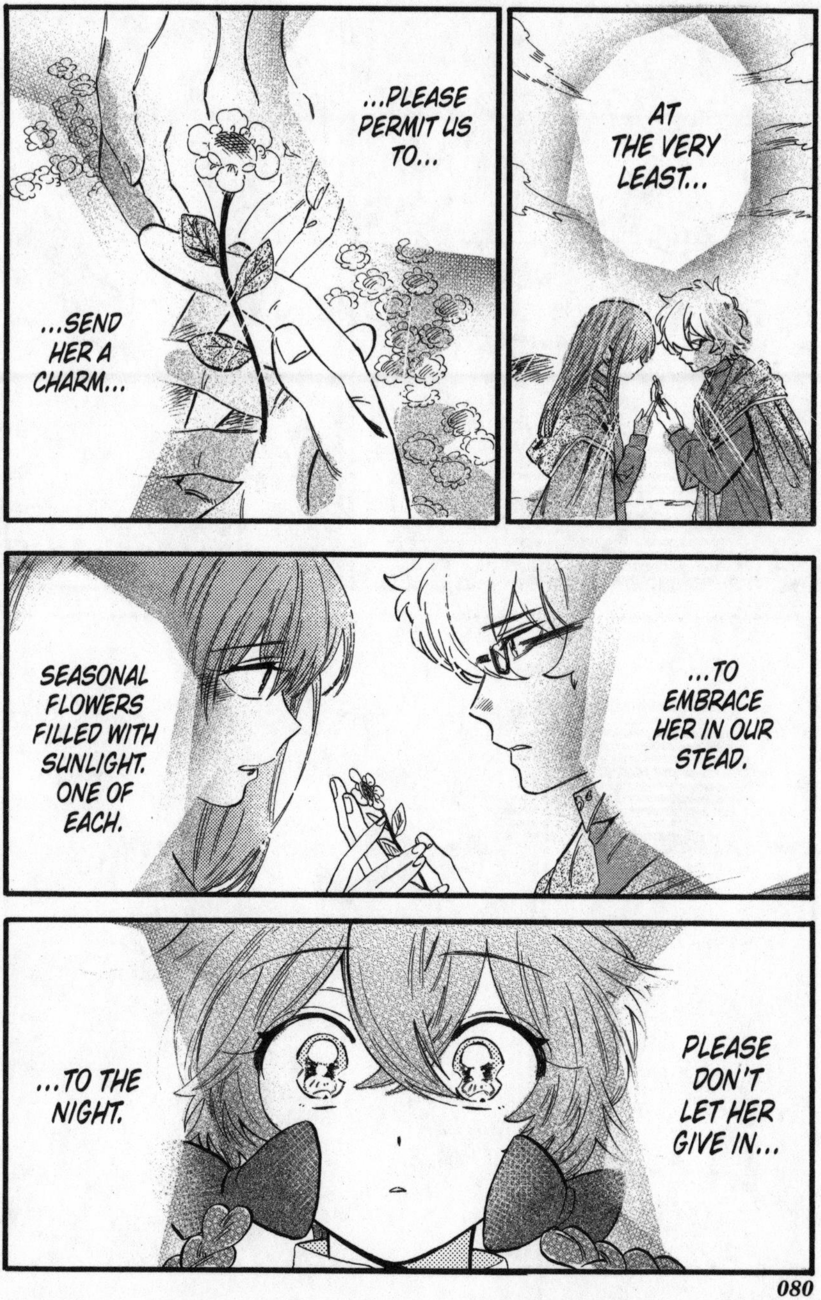
AT THE VERY LEAST...
...PLEASE PERMIT US TO...
...SEND HER A CHARM...
...TO EMBRACE HER IN OUR STEAD.
SEASONAL FLOWERS FILLED WITH SUNLIGHT. ONE OF EACH.
PLEASE DON'T LET HER GIVE IN...
...TO THE NIGHT.

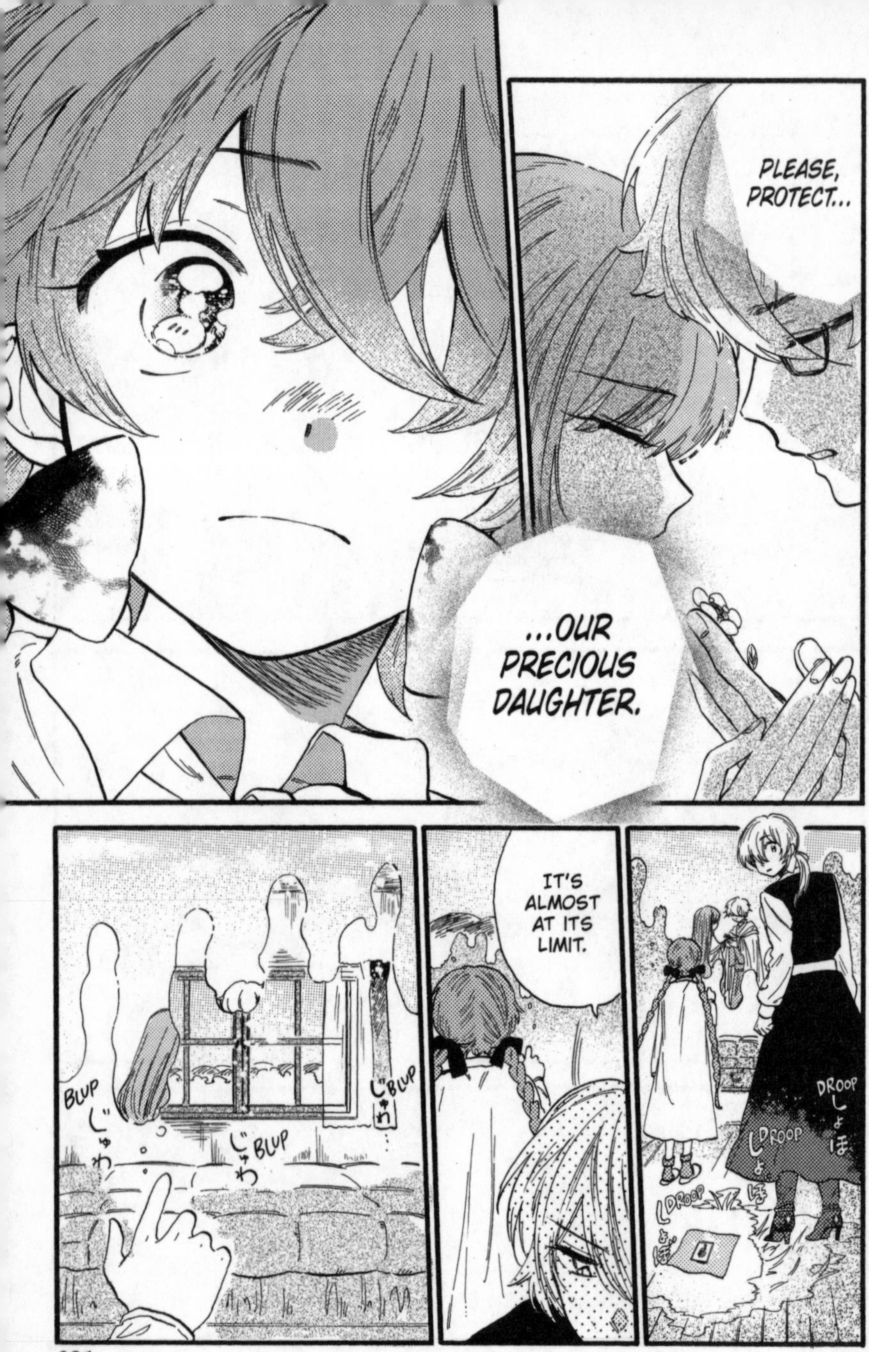
PLEASE, PROTECT...
...OUR PRECIOUS DAUGHTER.
DROOP しょぼ
DROOP しょぼ
DROOP しょぼ
IT'S ALMOST AT ITS LIMIT.
BLUP じゅわ
BLUP じゅわ
BLUP じゅわ

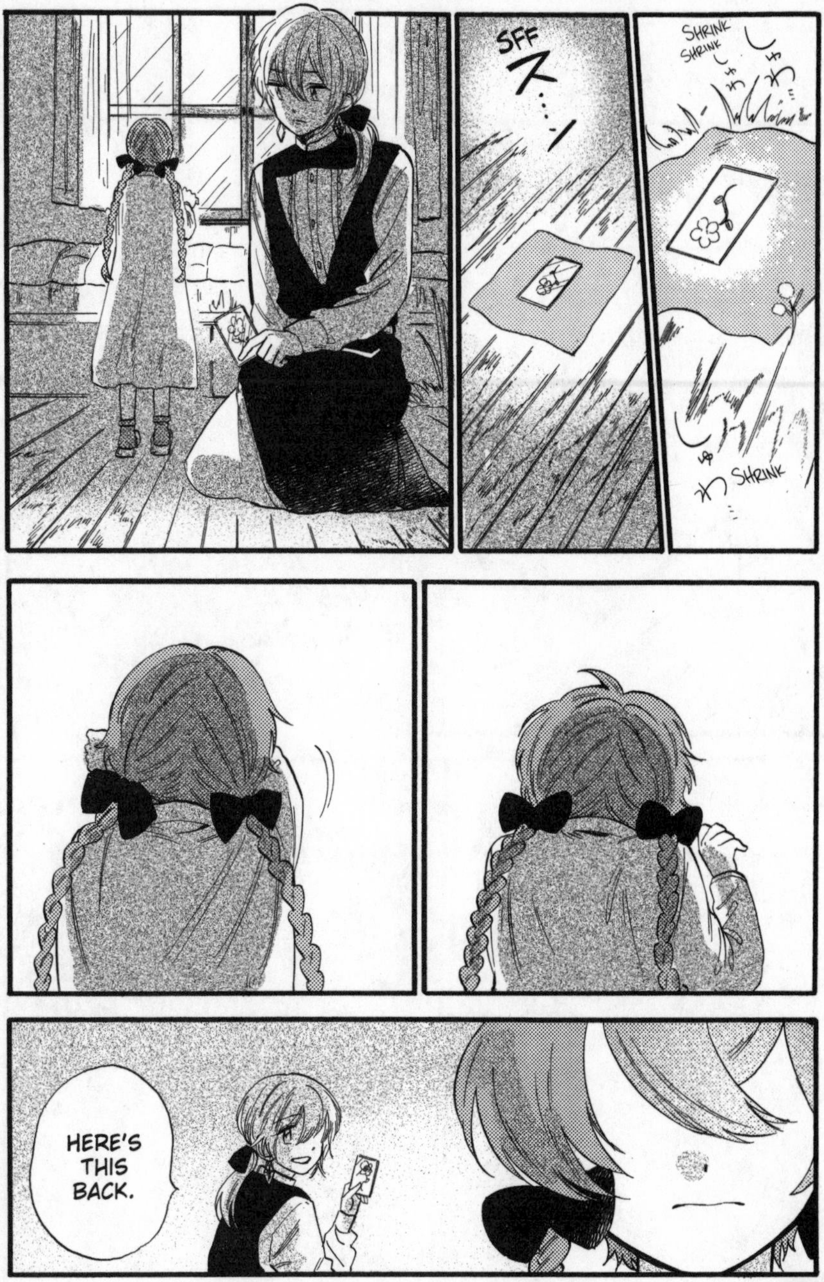
SHRINK SHRINK
SFF
ス…ー
SHRINK
HERE'S THIS BACK.

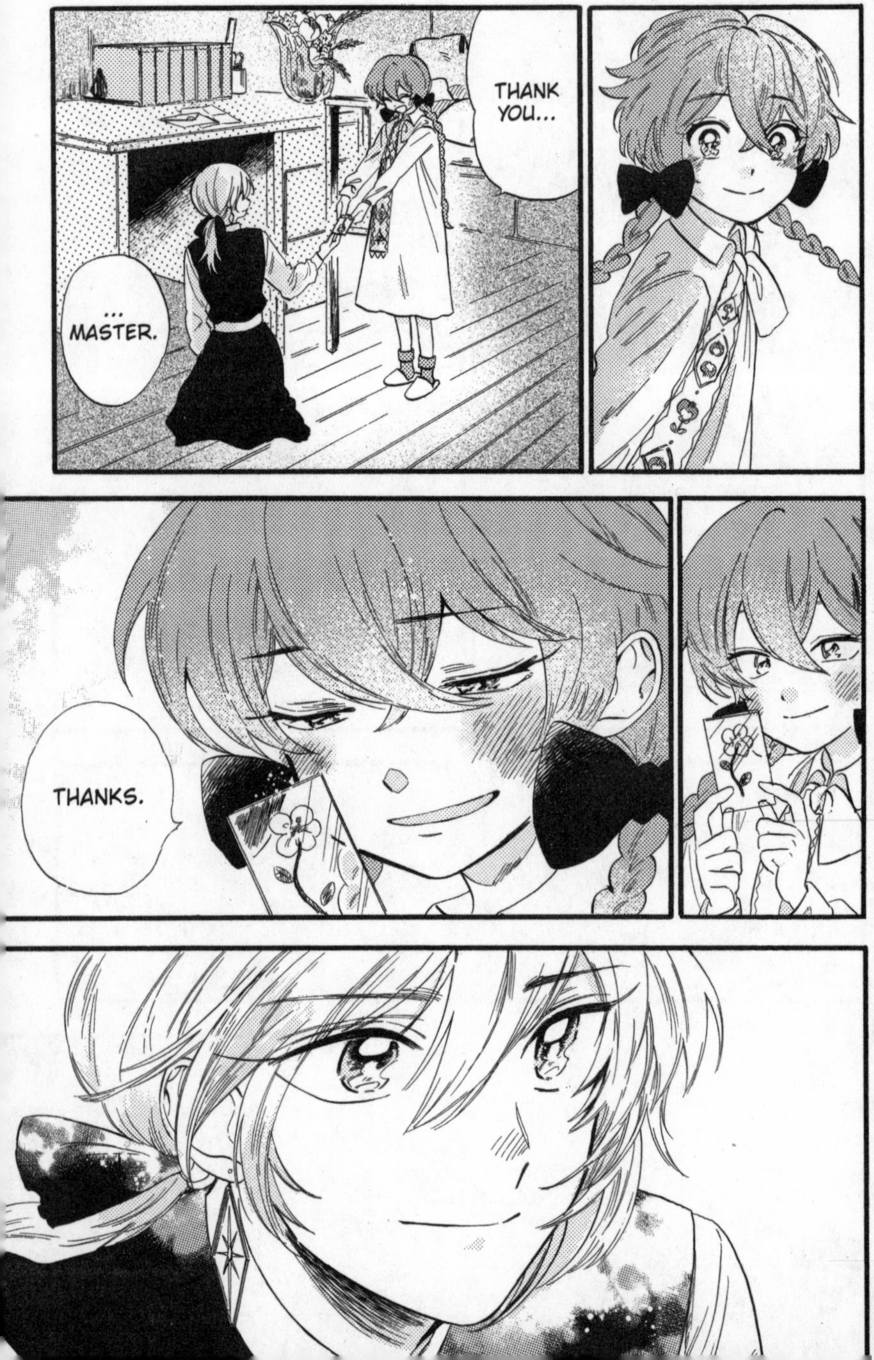
THANK YOU...
... MASTER.
THANKS.

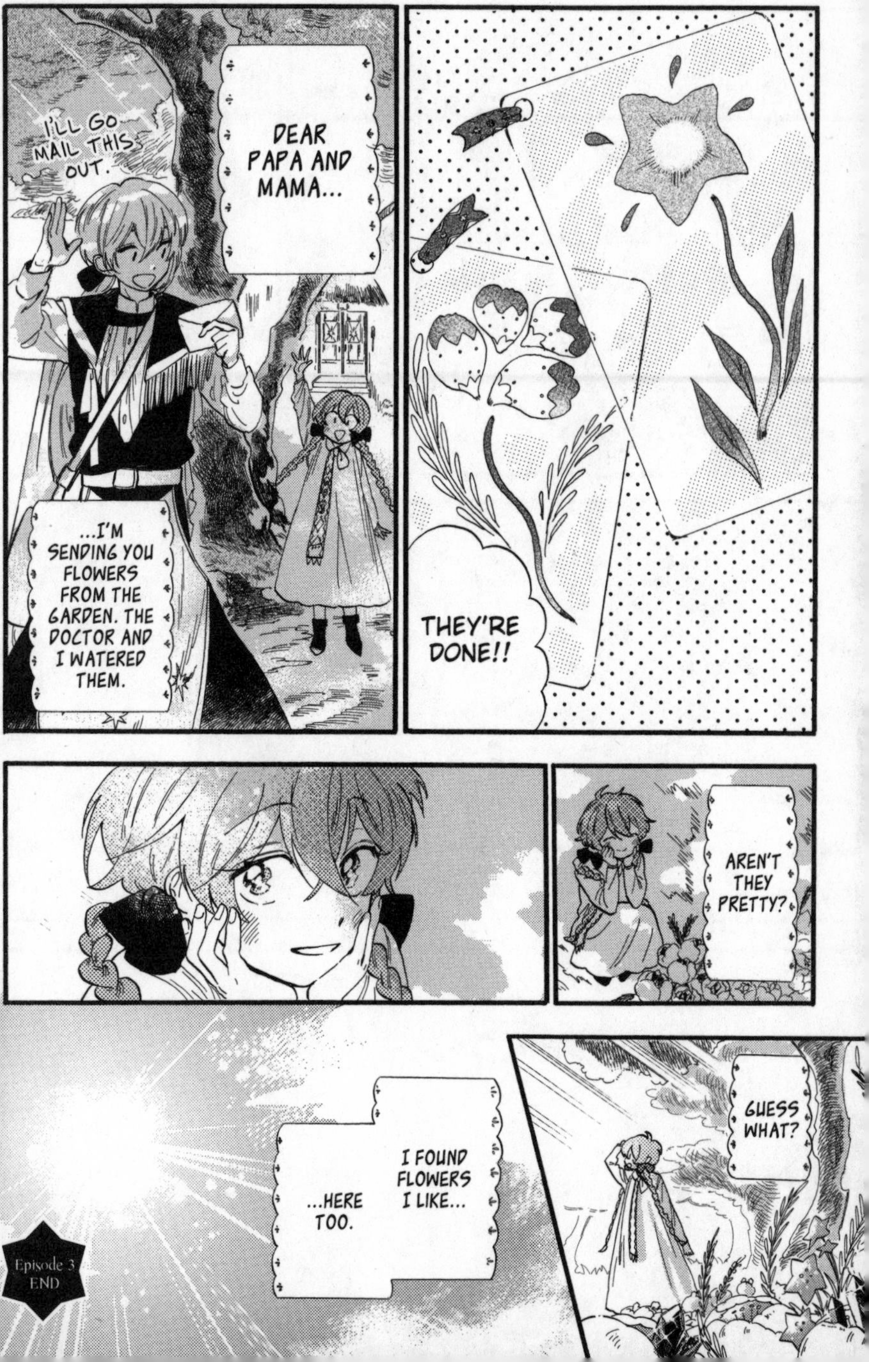
THEY'RE DONE!!
DEAR PAPA AND MAMA...
I'LL GO MAIL THIS OUT.
...I'M SENDING YOU FLOWERS FROM THE GARDEN. THE DOCTOR AND I WATERED THEM.
AREN'T THEY PRETTY?
GUESS WHAT?
I FOUND FLOWERS I LIKE...
...HERE TOO.
Episode 3 END

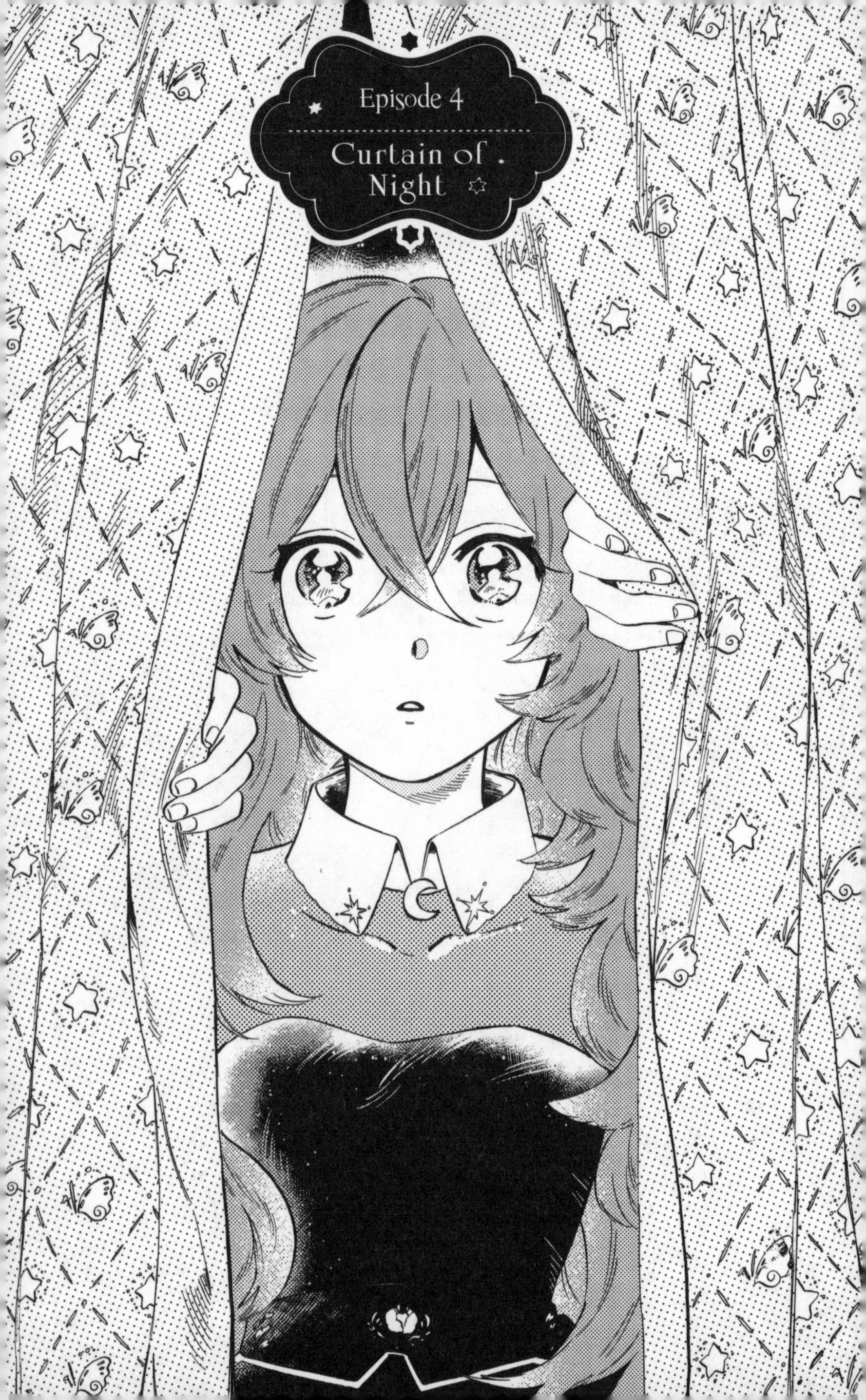
Episode 4
Curtain of Night

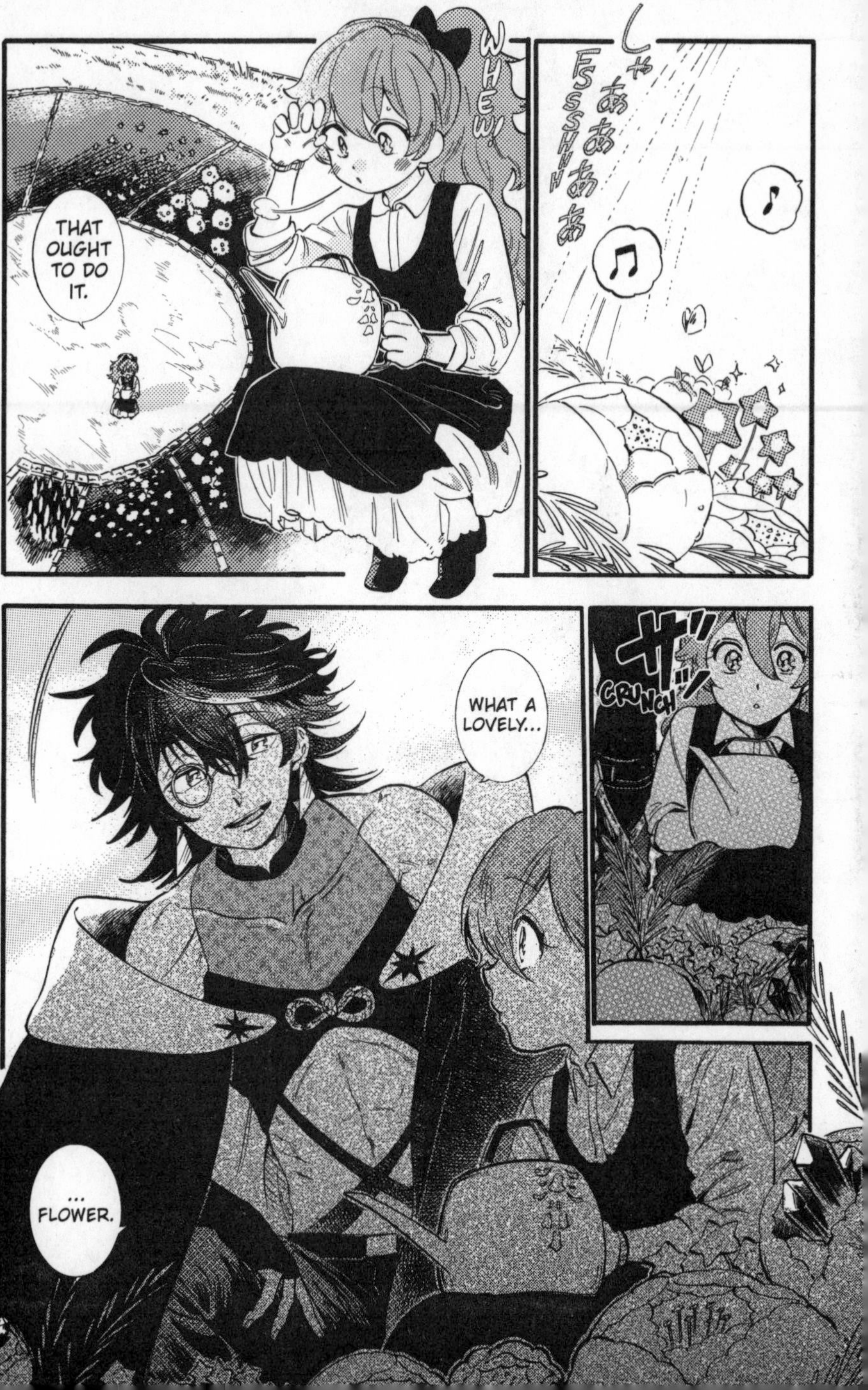

しゃああああ
FSSHHH
♫
♪
WHEW
THAT OUGHT TO DO IT.
ザッ
CRUNCH
WHAT A LOVELY...
...FLOWER.

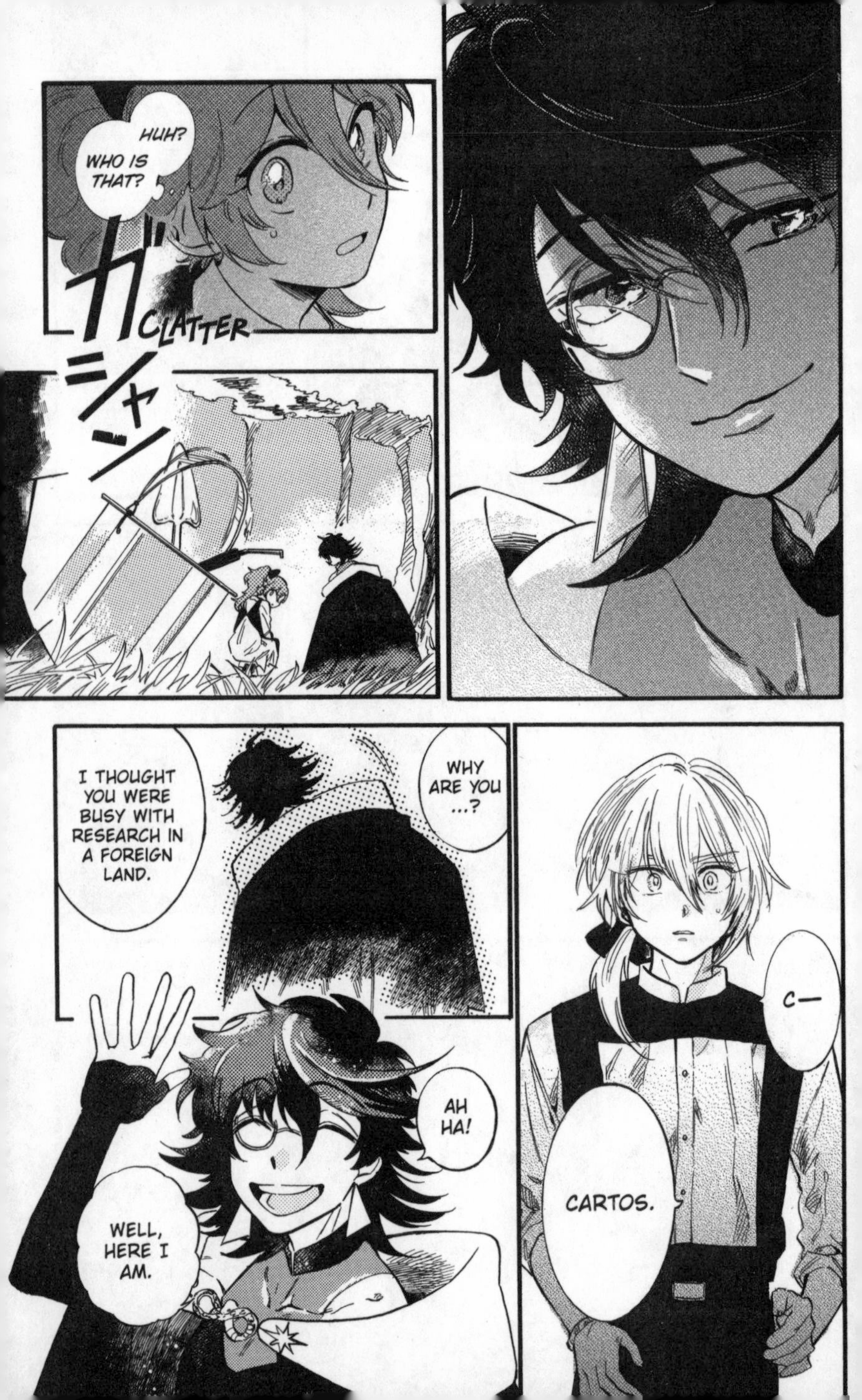
HUH? WHO IS THAT?
ガ CLATTER
シャン
WHY ARE YOU ...?
I THOUGHT YOU WERE BUSY WITH RESEARCH IN A FOREIGN LAND.
AH HA!
WELL, HERE I AM.
C—
CARTOS.

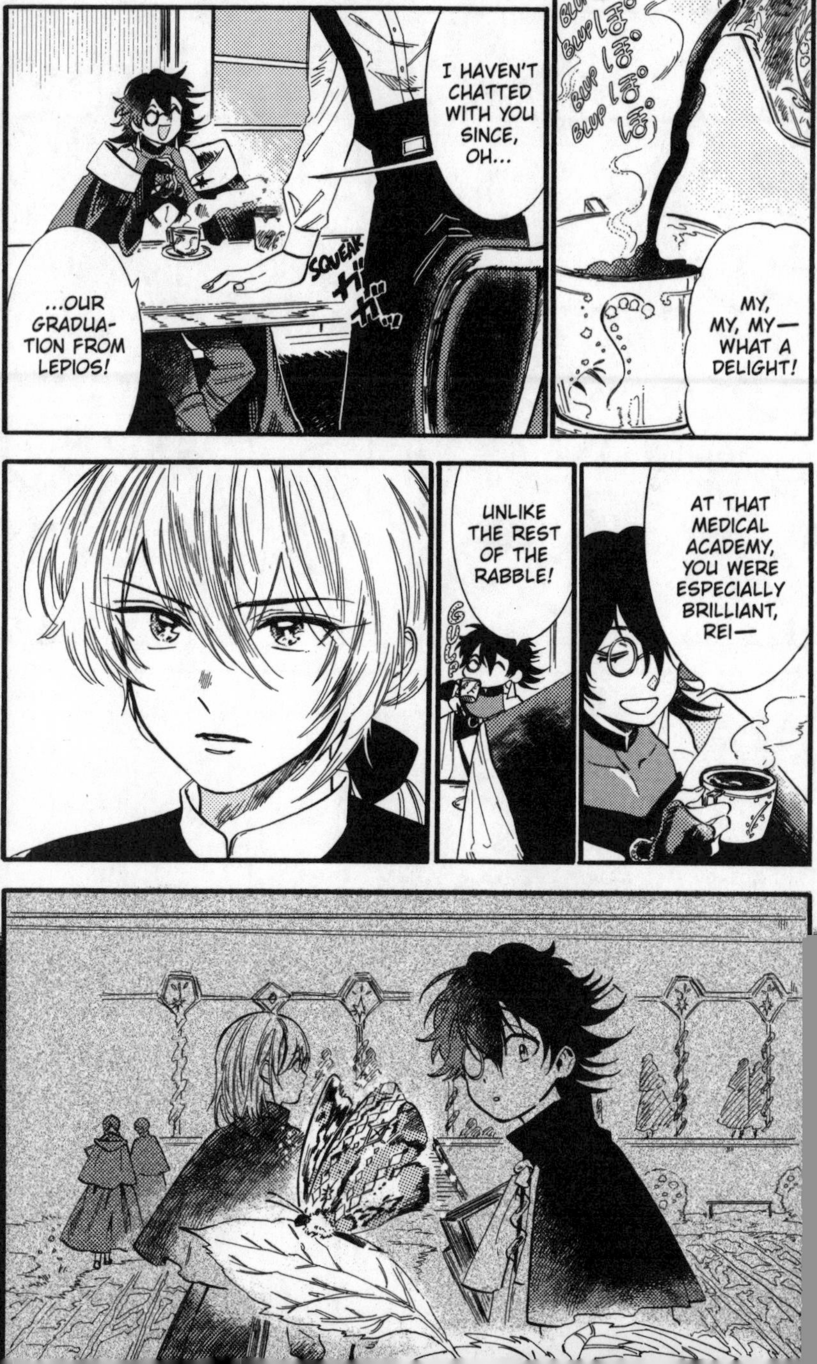
BLUP BLUP BLUP BLUP
MY, MY, MY—WHAT A DELIGHT!
I HAVEN'T CHATTED WITH YOU SINCE, OH...
SQUEAK
...OUR GRADUATION FROM LEPIOS!
AT THAT MEDICAL ACADEMY, YOU WERE ESPECIALLY BRILLIANT, REI—
UNLIKE THE REST OF THE RABBLE!

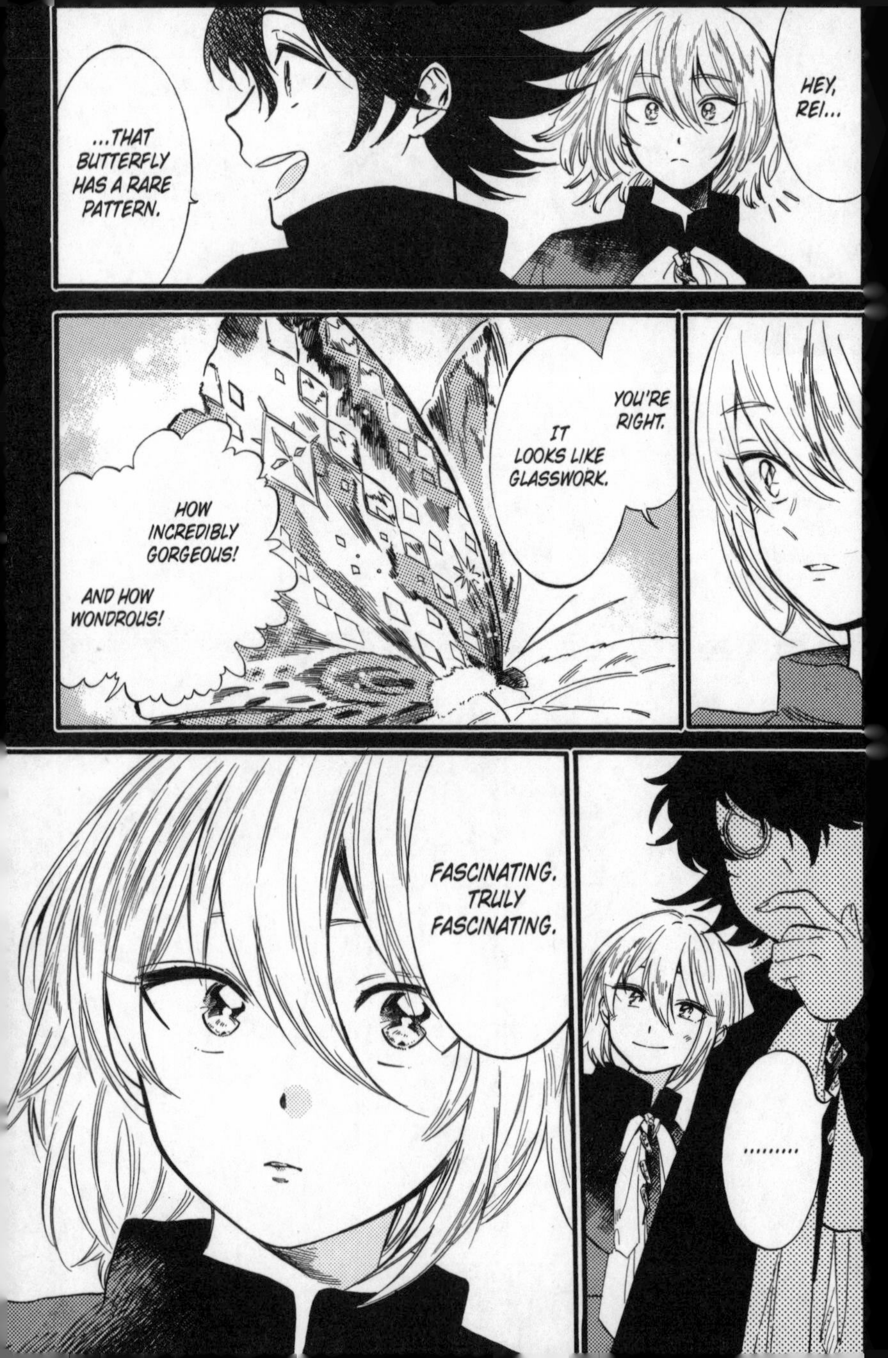
HEY, REI...
...THAT BUTTERFLY HAS A RARE PATTERN.
YOU'RE RIGHT.
IT LOOKS LIKE GLASSWORK.
HOW INCREDIBLY GORGEOUS!
AND HOW WONDROUS!
....
FASCINATING. TRULY FASCINATING.

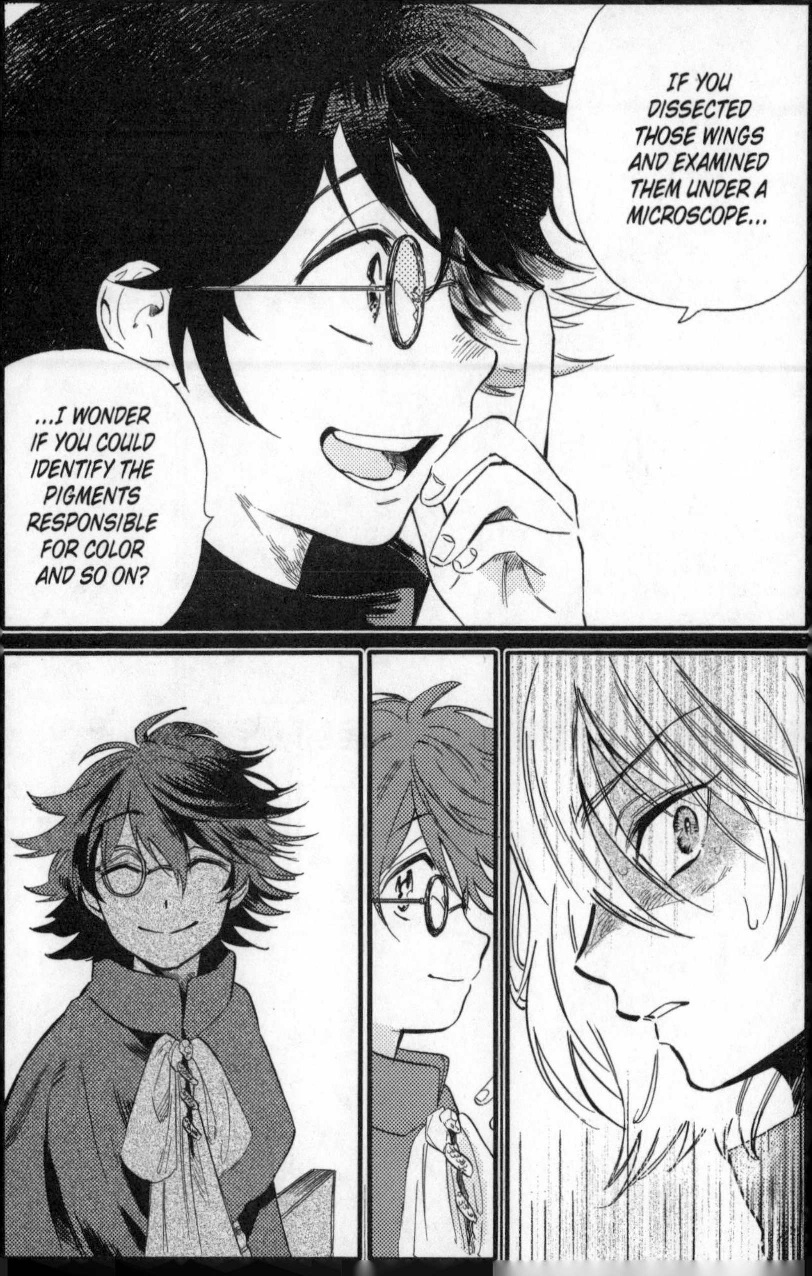
IF YOU DISSECTED THOSE WINGS AND EXAMINED THEM UNDER A MICROSCOPE...
...I WONDER IF YOU COULD IDENTIFY THE PIGMENTS RESPONSIBLE FOR COLOR AND SO ON?

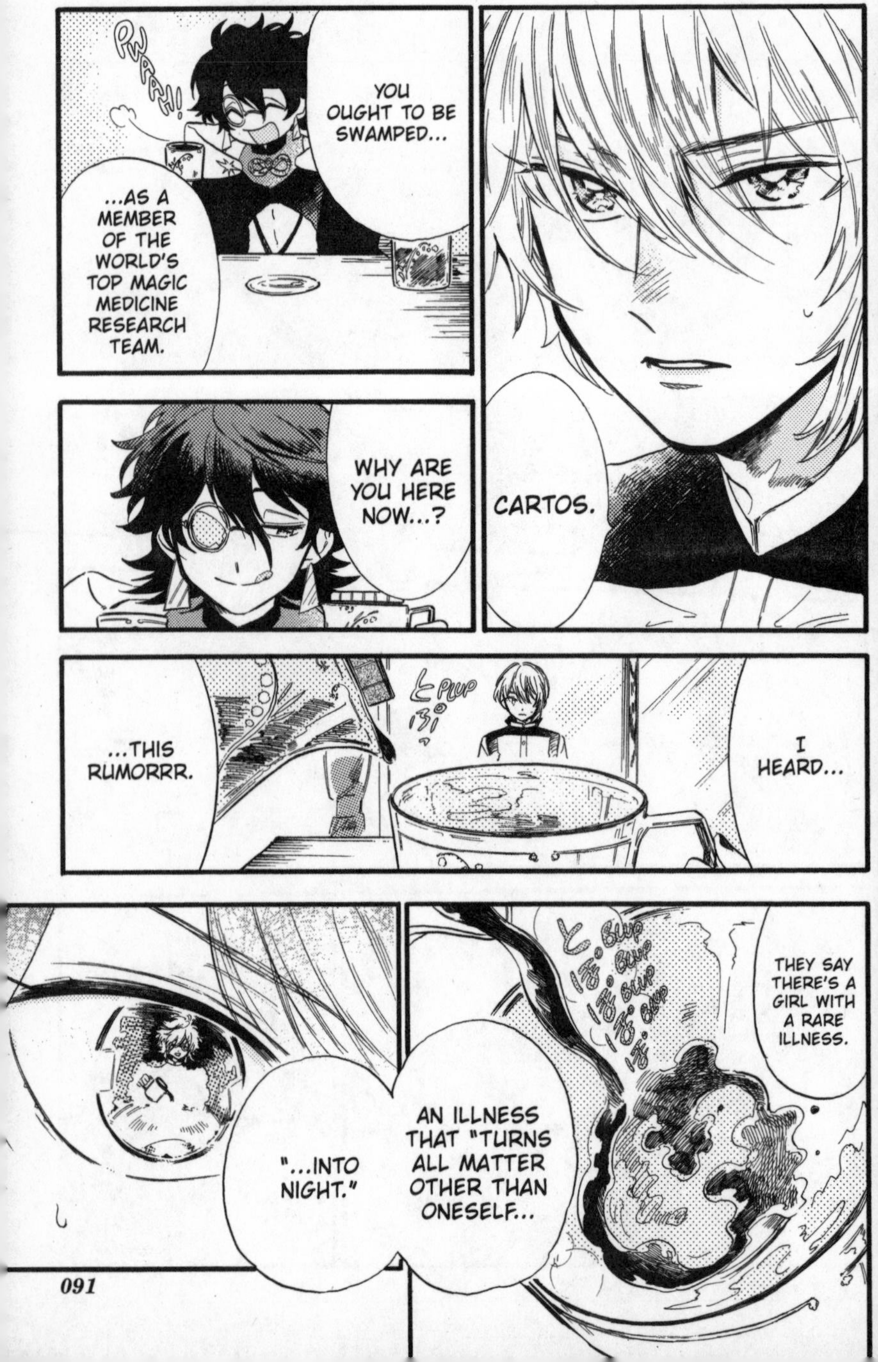
CARTOS.
YOU OUGHT TO BE SWAMPED...
...AS A MEMBER OF THE WORLD'S TOP MAGIC MEDICINE RESEARCH TEAM.
PWAAH!
WHY ARE YOU HERE NOW...?
I HEARD...
PLUP
...THIS RUMORRR.
THEY SAY THERE'S A GIRL WITH A RARE ILLNESS.
BLUP BLUP BLUP BLUP
AN ILLNESS THAT "TURNS ALL MATTER OTHER THAN ONESELF...
"...INTO NIGHT."

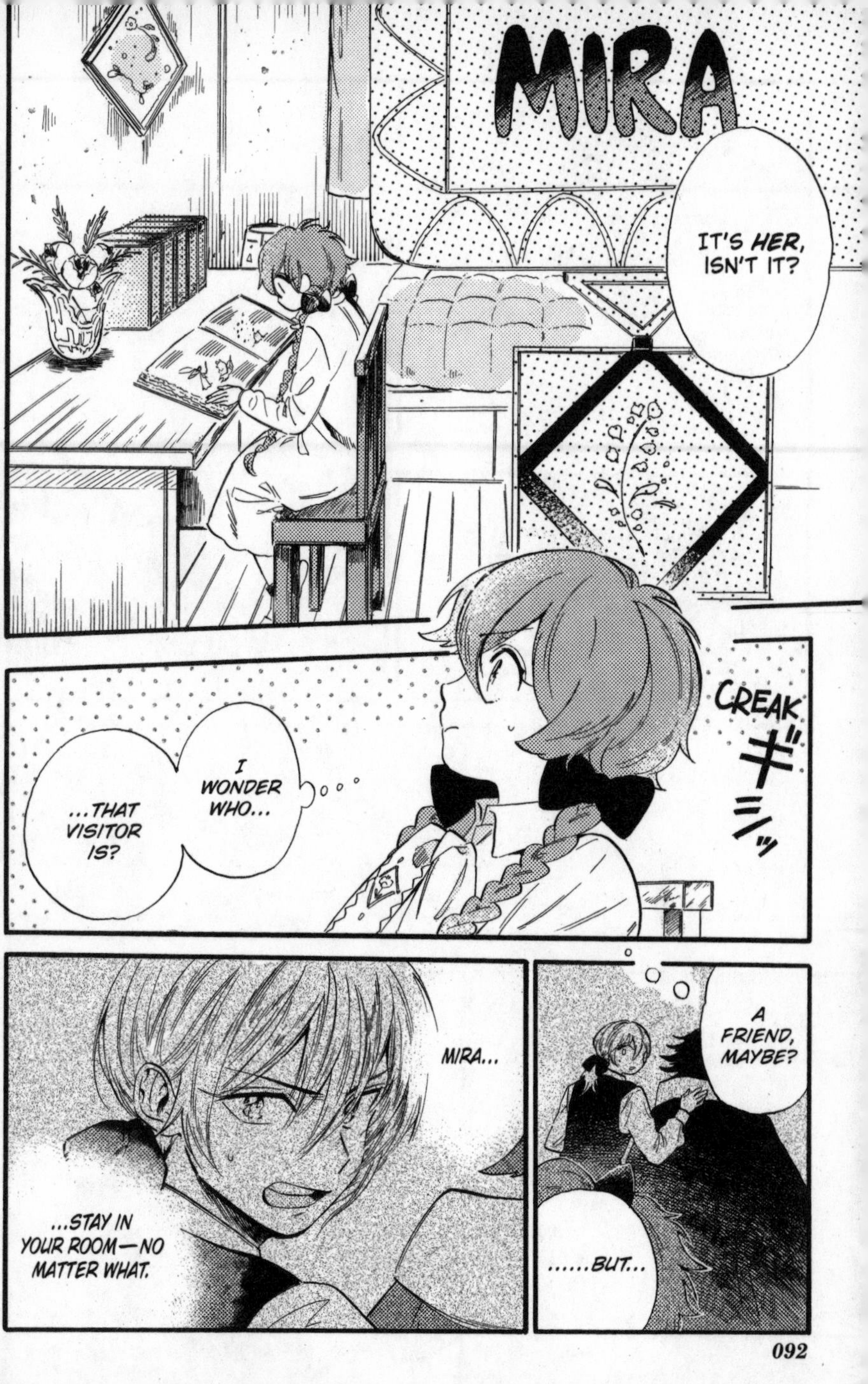
MIRA
IT'S *HER*, ISN'T IT?
CREAK
ギシッ
I WONDER WHO...
...THAT VISITOR IS?
A FRIEND, MAYBE?
......BUT...
MIRA...
...STAY IN YOUR ROOM—NO MATTER WHAT.

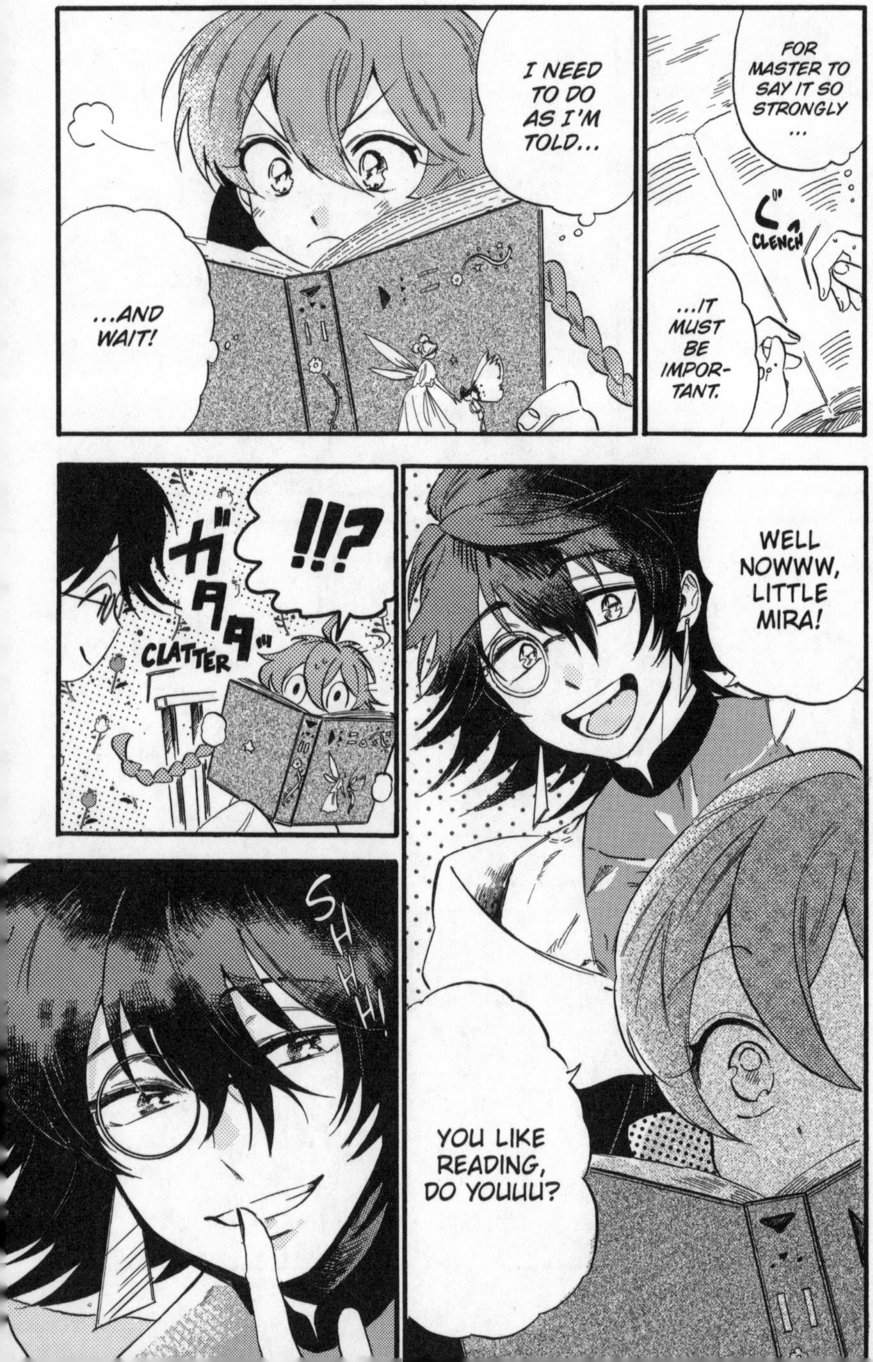
FOR MASTER TO SAY IT SO STRONGLY...
CLENCH
...IT MUST BE IMPORTANT.
I NEED TO DO AS I'M TOLD...
...AND WAIT!
WELL NOWWW, LITTLE MIRA!
YOU LIKE READING, DO YOUUU?
!!?
ガタタ
CLATTER
SHHHH!

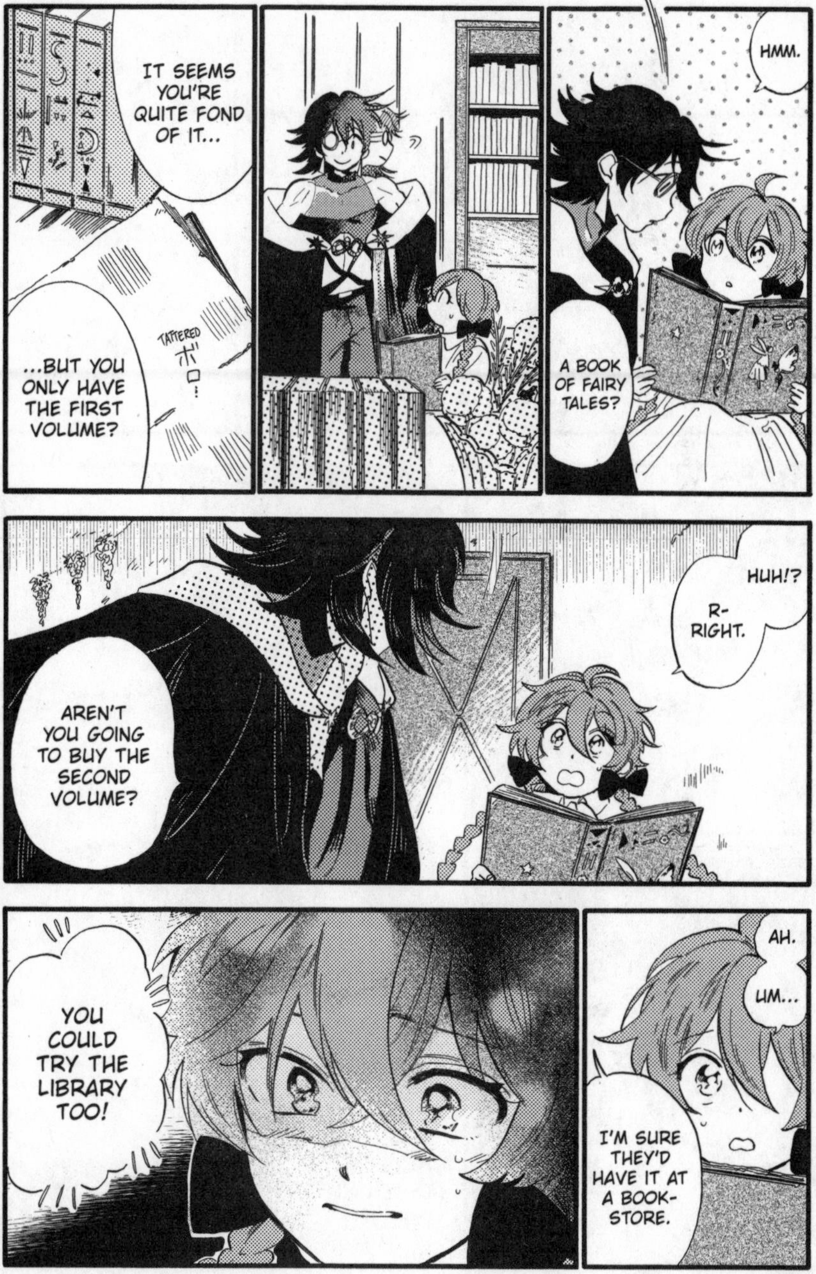
HMM.
A BOOK OF FAIRY TALES?
IT SEEMS YOU'RE QUITE FOND OF IT...
TATTERED ボロ…
...BUT YOU ONLY HAVE THE FIRST VOLUME?
HUH!?
R-RIGHT.
AREN'T YOU GOING TO BUY THE SECOND VOLUME?
AH.
UM...
I'M SURE THEY'D HAVE IT AT A BOOK-STORE.
YOU COULD TRY THE LIBRARY TOO!

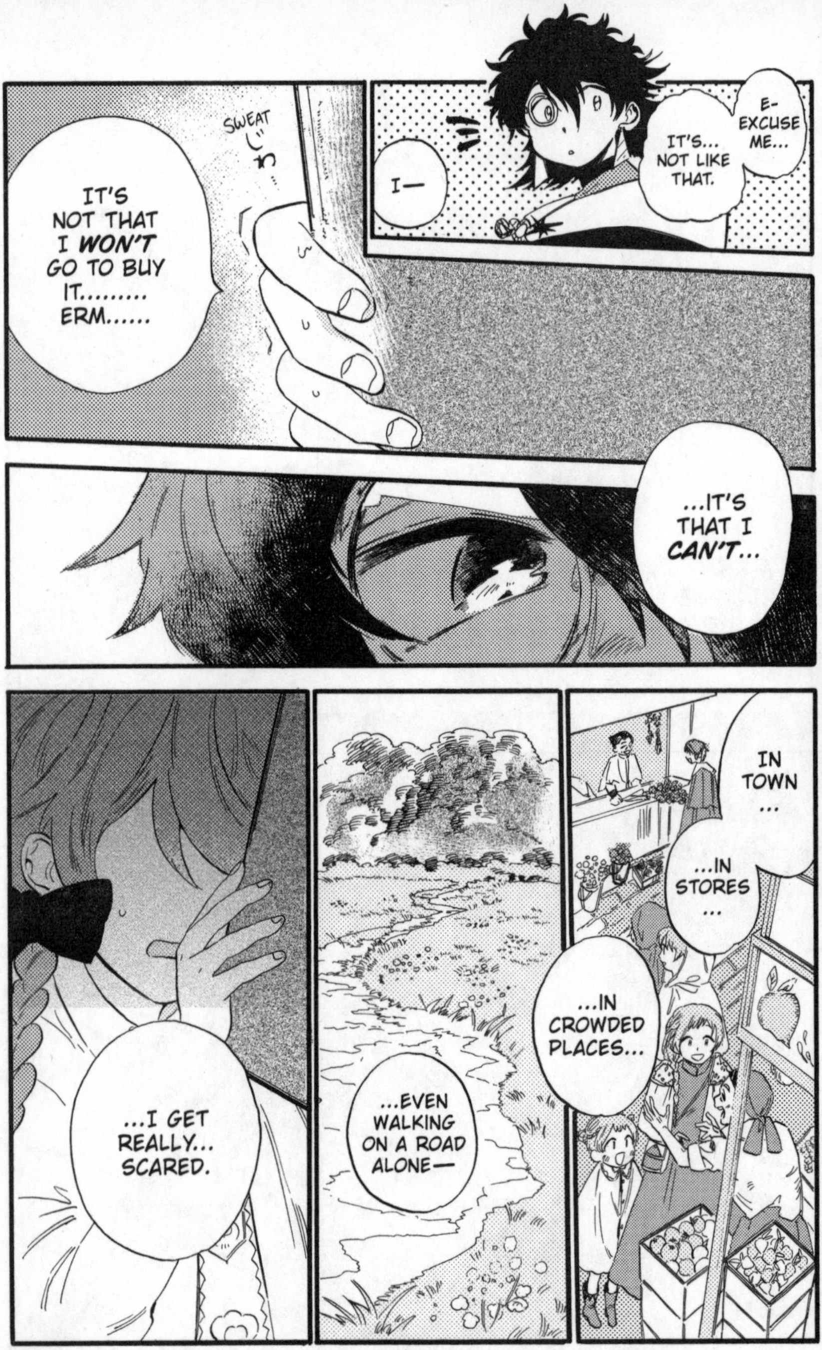
E-EXCUSE ME...
IT'S... NOT LIKE THAT.
I—
SWEAT
じわ…
IT'S NOT THAT I WON'T GO TO BUY IT......... ERM......
...IT'S THAT I CAN'T...
IN TOWN...
...IN STORES...
...IN CROWDED PLACES...
...EVEN WALKING ON A ROAD ALONE—
...I GET REALLY... SCARED.

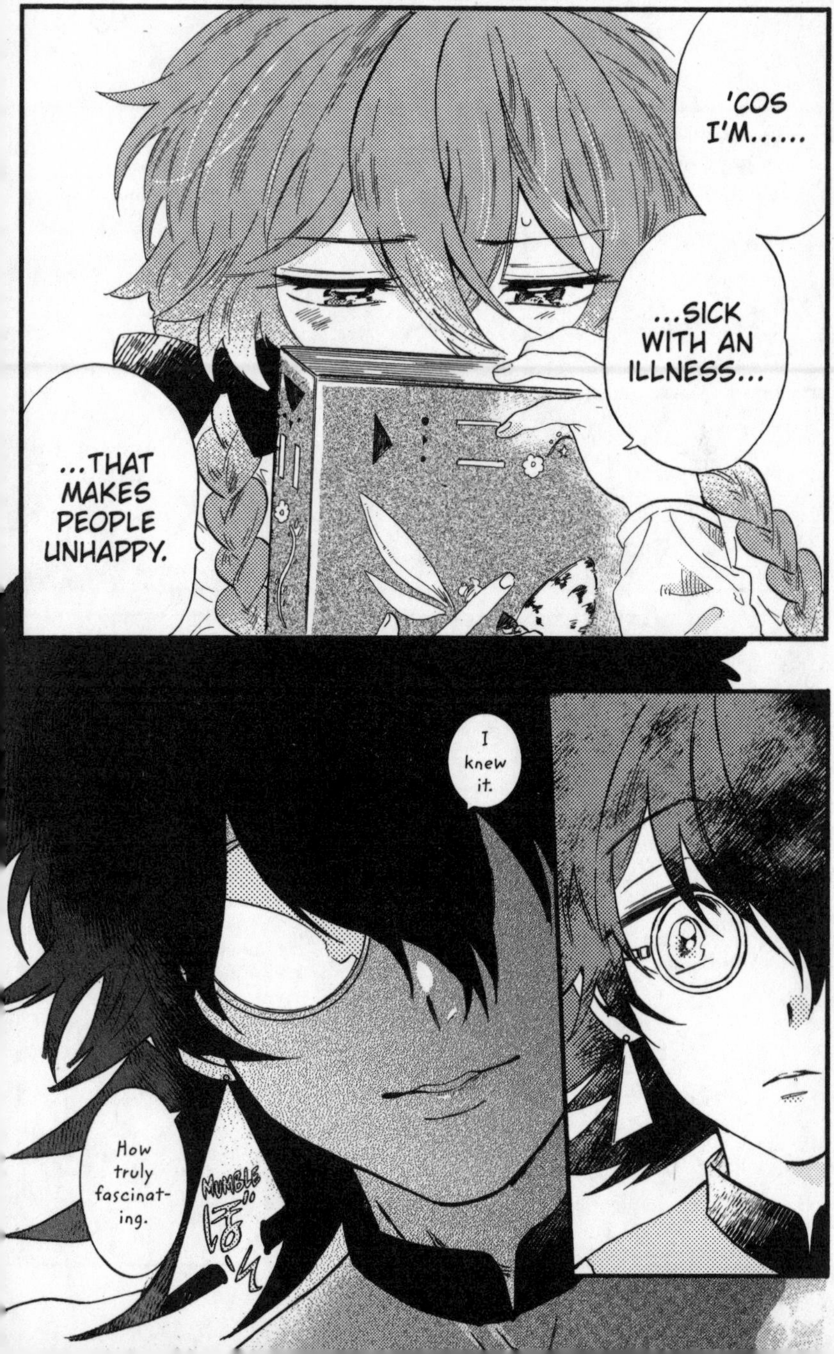
'COS I'M......
...SICK WITH AN ILLNESS...
...THAT MAKES PEOPLE UNHAPPY.
I knew it.
How truly fascinat-ing.
MUMBLE

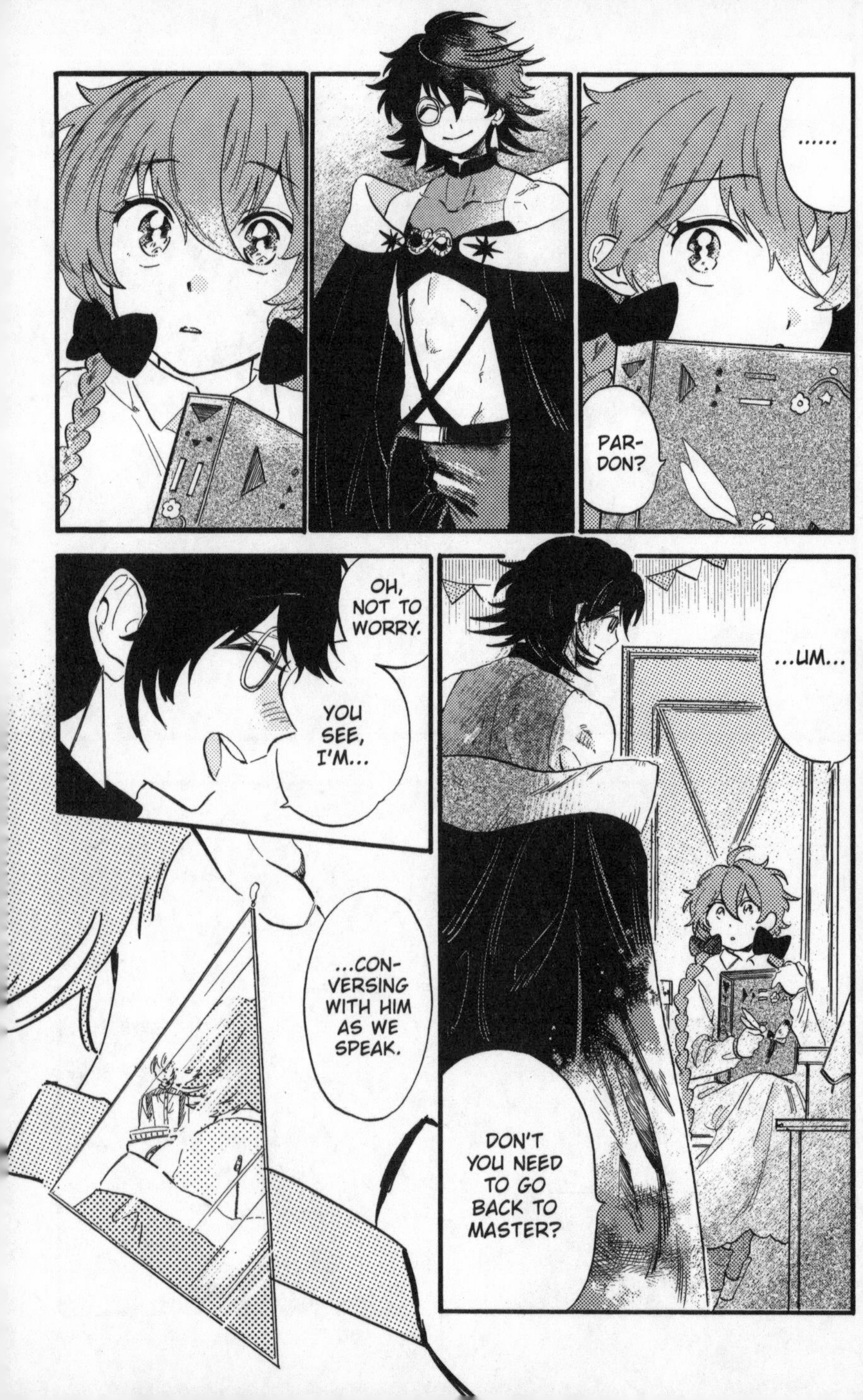
......
PAR-DON?
...UM...
DON'T YOU NEED TO GO BACK TO MASTER?
OH, NOT TO WORRY.
YOU SEE, I'M...
...CON-VERSING WITH HIM AS WE SPEAK.

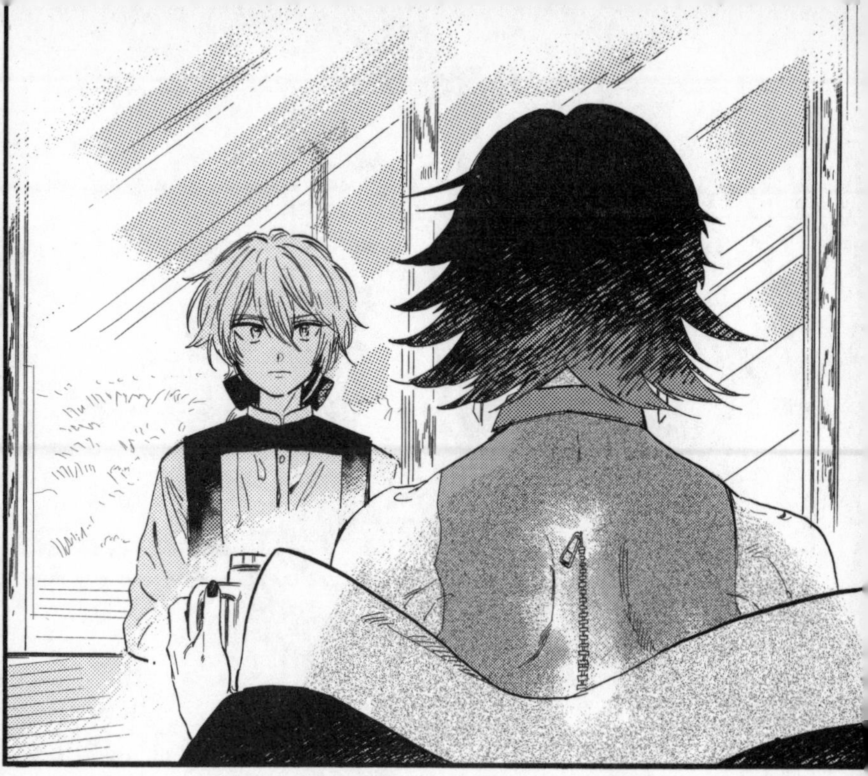

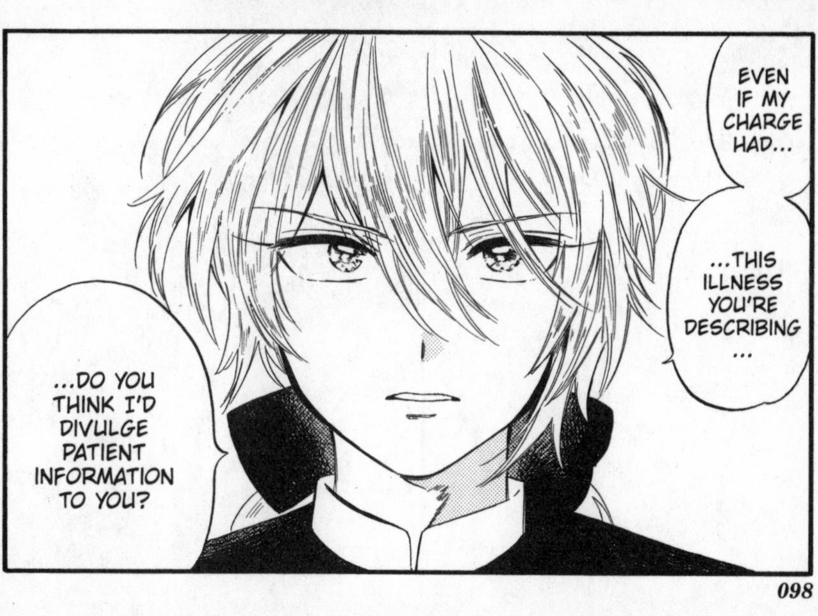
EVEN IF MY CHARGE HAD...
...THIS ILLNESS YOU'RE DESCRIBING ...
...DO YOU THINK I'D DIVULGE PATIENT INFORMATION TO YOU?

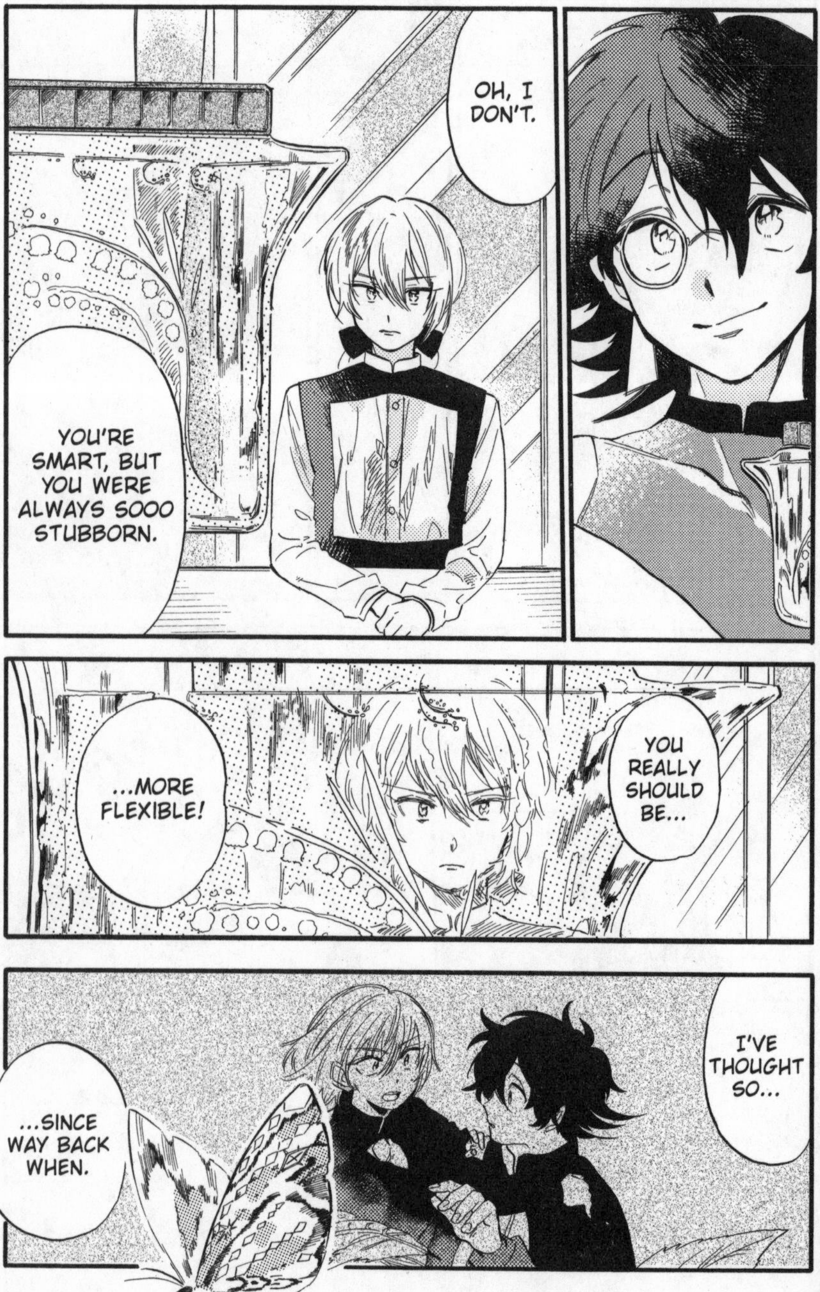
OH, I DON'T.
YOU'RE SMART, BUT YOU WERE ALWAYS SOOO STUBBORN.
YOU REALLY SHOULD BE...
...MORE FLEXIBLE!
I'VE THOUGHT SO...
...SINCE WAY BACK WHEN.

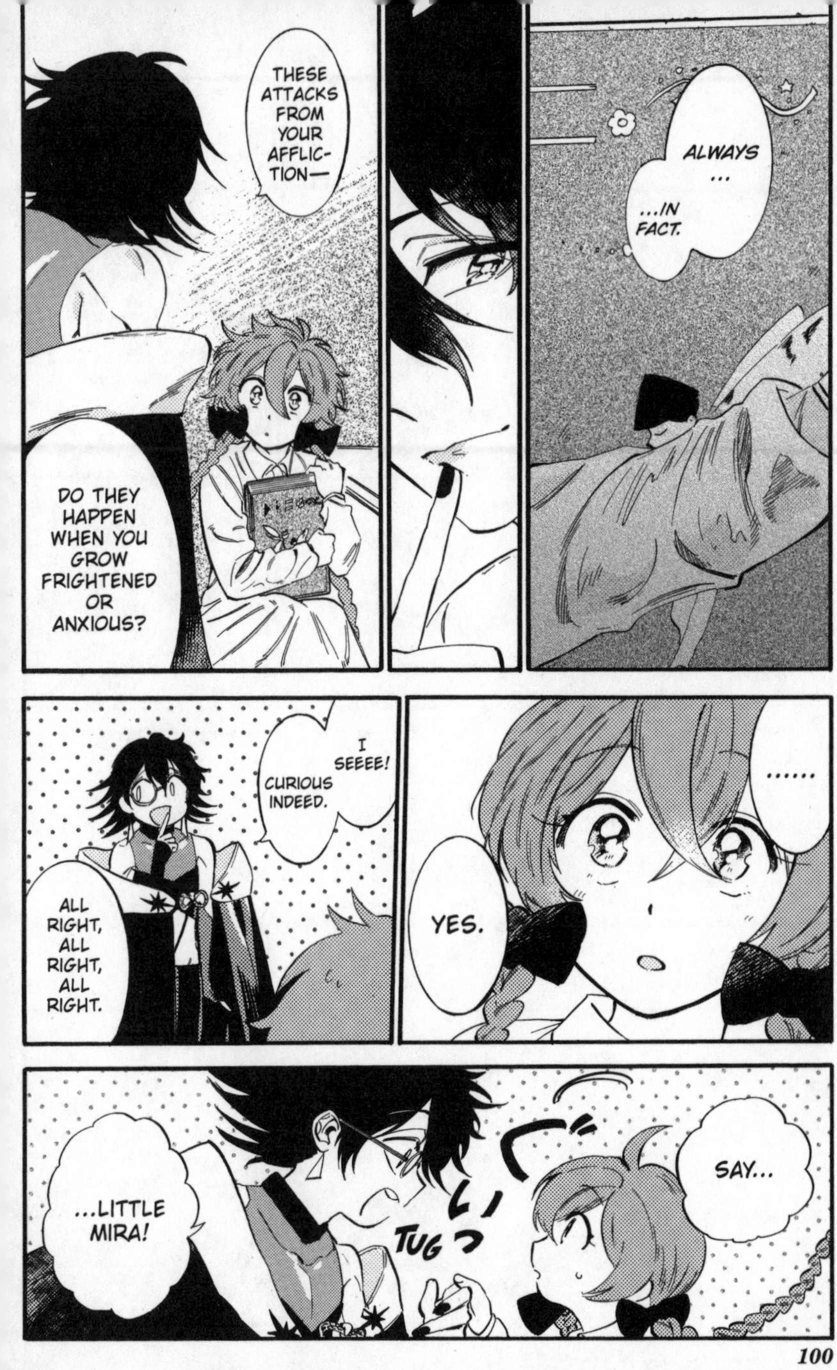
ALWAYS ... ...IN FACT.
THESE ATTACKS FROM YOUR AFFLICTION—
DO THEY HAPPEN WHEN YOU GROW FRIGHTENED OR ANXIOUS?
......
YES.
I SEEEE!
CURIOUS INDEED.
ALL RIGHT, ALL RIGHT, ALL RIGHT.
SAY...
TUG
...LITTLE MIRA!

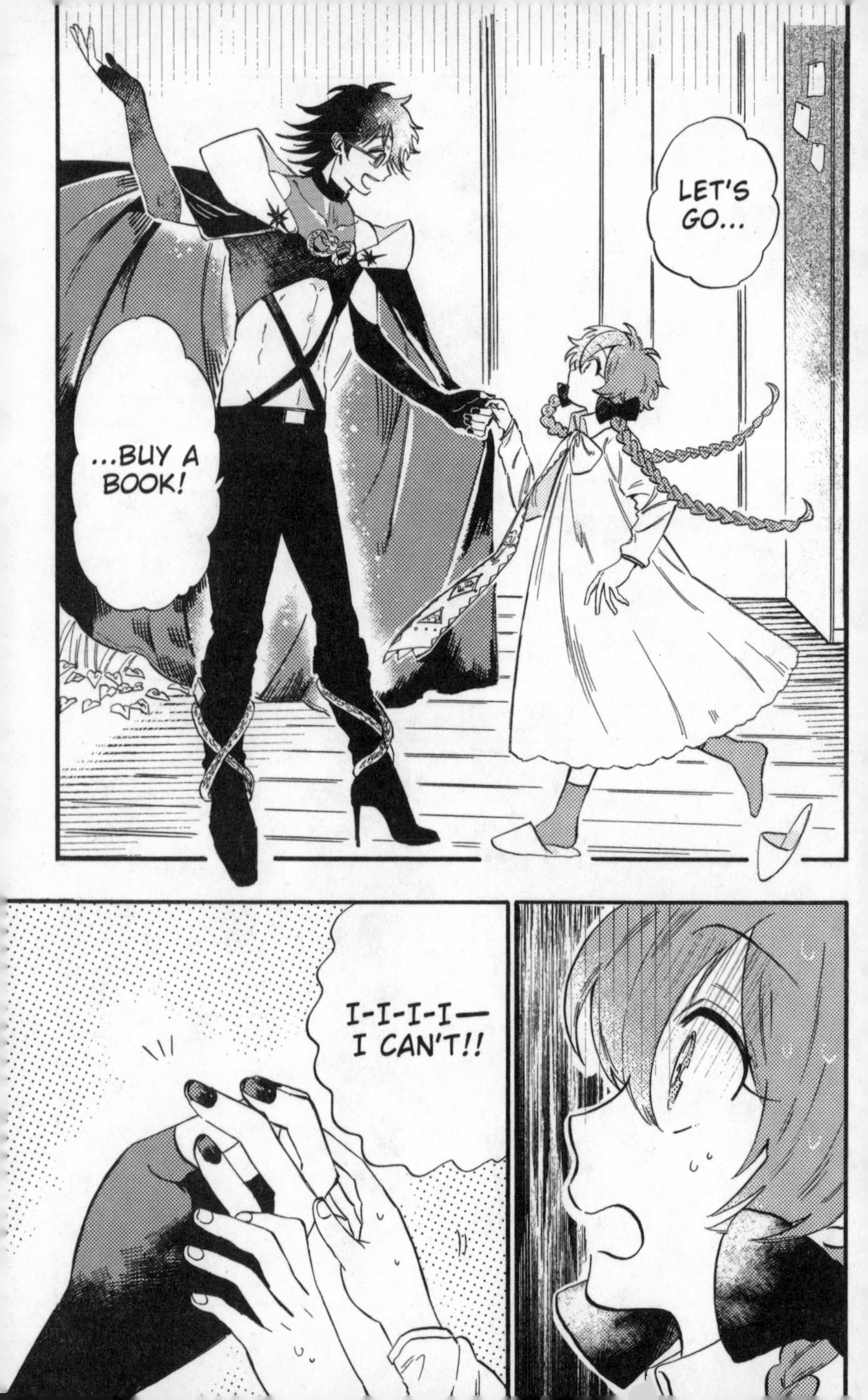
LET'S GO...
...BUY A BOOK!
I-I-I-I— I CAN'T!!

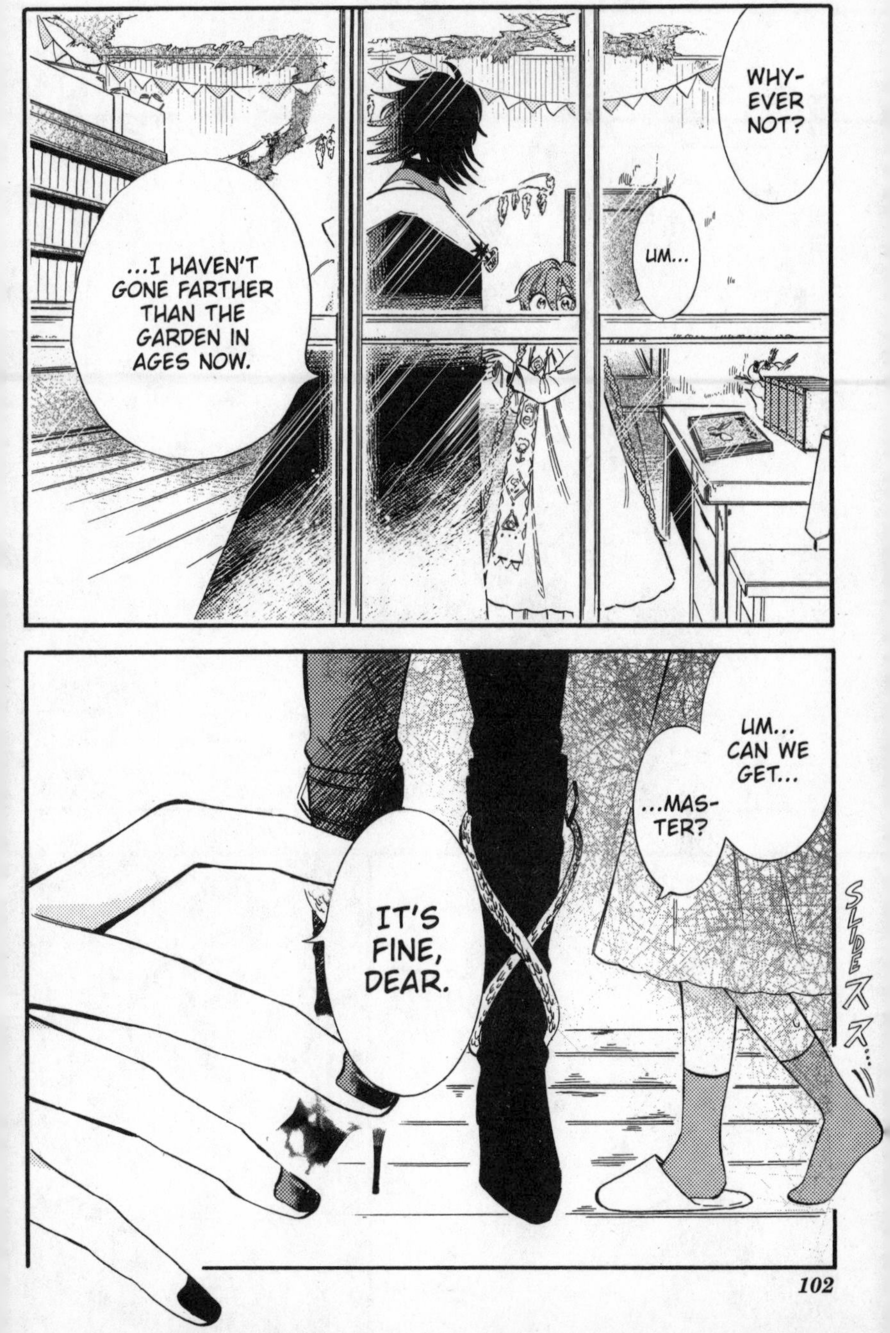
WHY-EVER NOT?
UM...
...I HAVEN'T GONE FARTHER THAN THE GARDEN IN AGES NOW.
UM... CAN WE GET...
...MAS-TER?
SLIDE スス...
IT'S FINE, DEAR.

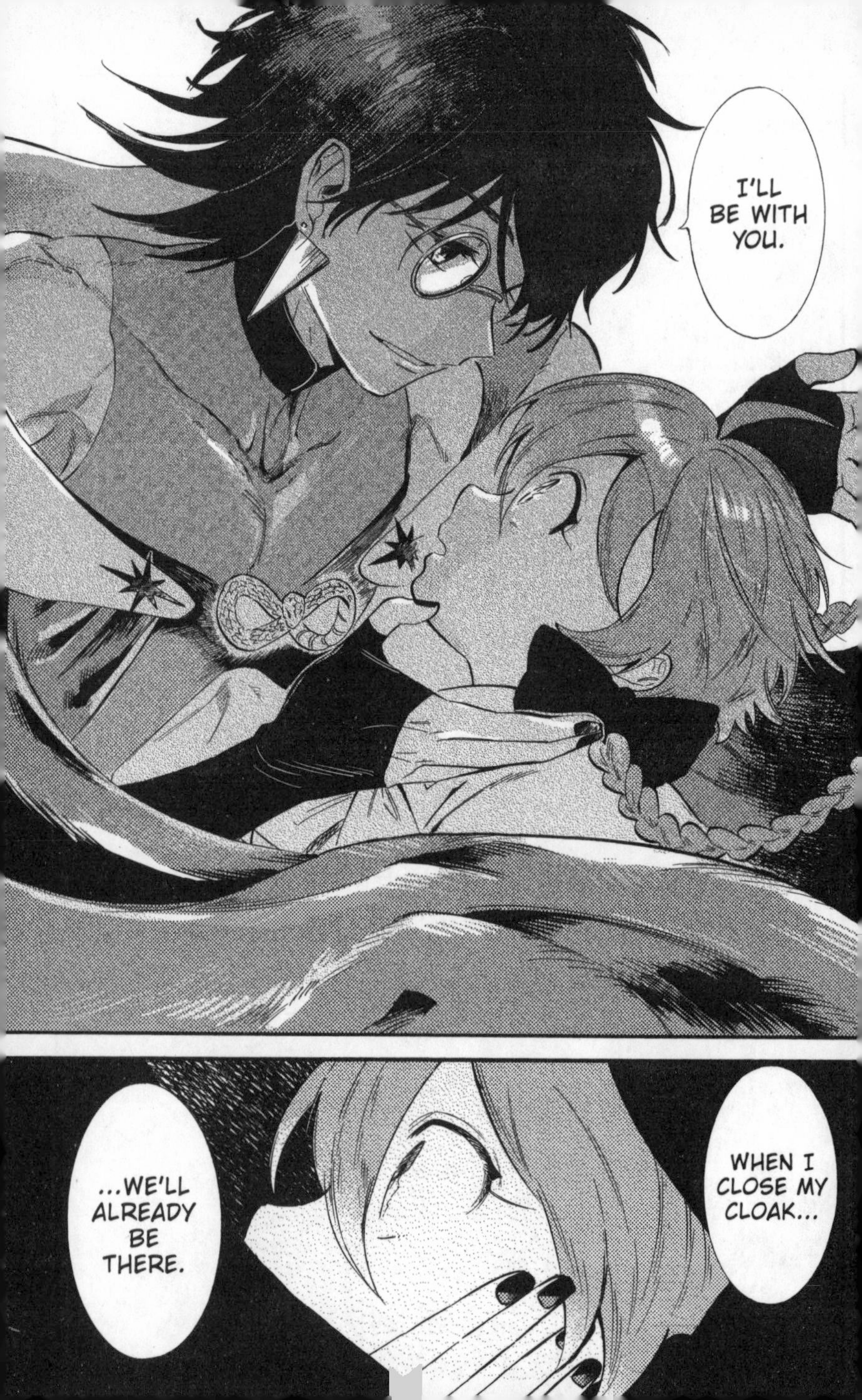
I'LL BE WITH YOU.
WHEN I CLOSE MY CLOAK...
...WE'LL ALREADY BE THERE.

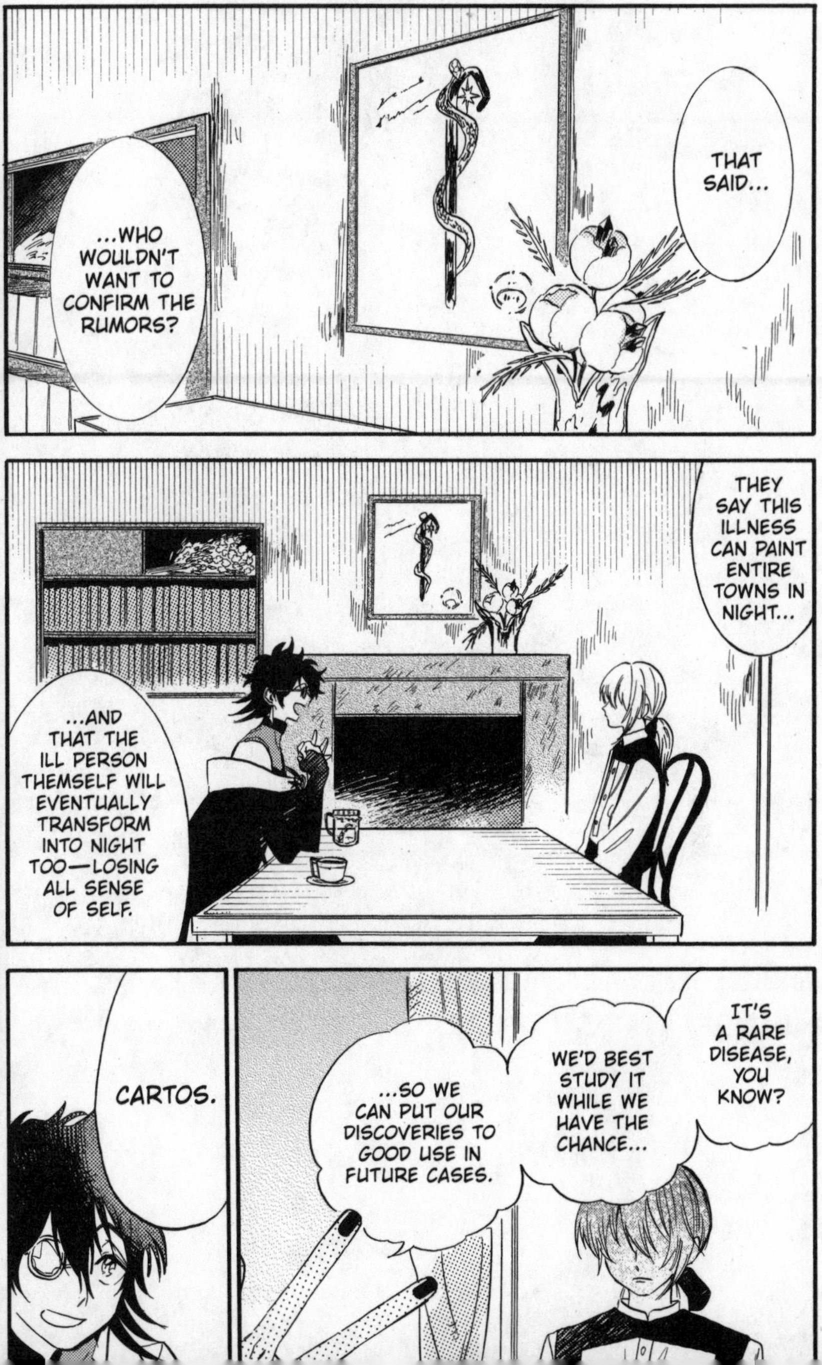
THAT SAID...
...WHO WOULDN'T WANT TO CONFIRM THE RUMORS?
THEY SAY THIS ILLNESS CAN PAINT ENTIRE TOWNS IN NIGHT...
...AND THAT THE ILL PERSON THEMSELF WILL EVENTUALLY TRANSFORM INTO NIGHT TOO—LOSING ALL SENSE OF SELF.
IT'S A RARE DISEASE, YOU KNOW?
WE'D BEST STUDY IT WHILE WE HAVE THE CHANCE...
...SO WE CAN PUT OUR DISCOVERIES TO GOOD USE IN FUTURE CASES.
CARTOS.

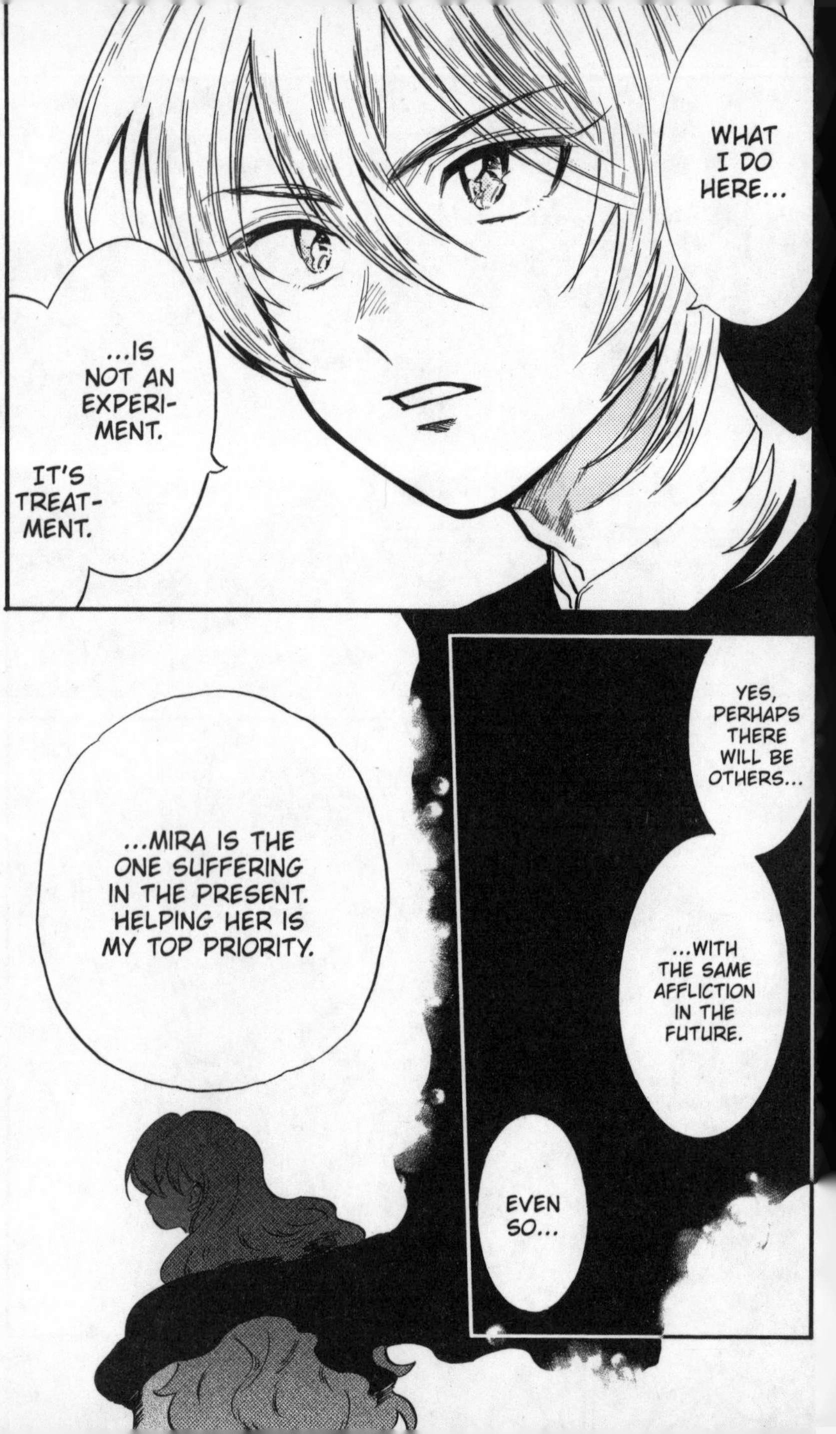
WHAT I DO HERE...
...IS NOT AN EXPERIMENT.
IT'S TREATMENT.
YES, PERHAPS THERE WILL BE OTHERS...
...WITH THE SAME AFFLICTION IN THE FUTURE.
EVEN SO...
...MIRA IS THE ONE SUFFERING IN THE PRESENT. HELPING HER IS MY TOP PRIORITY.

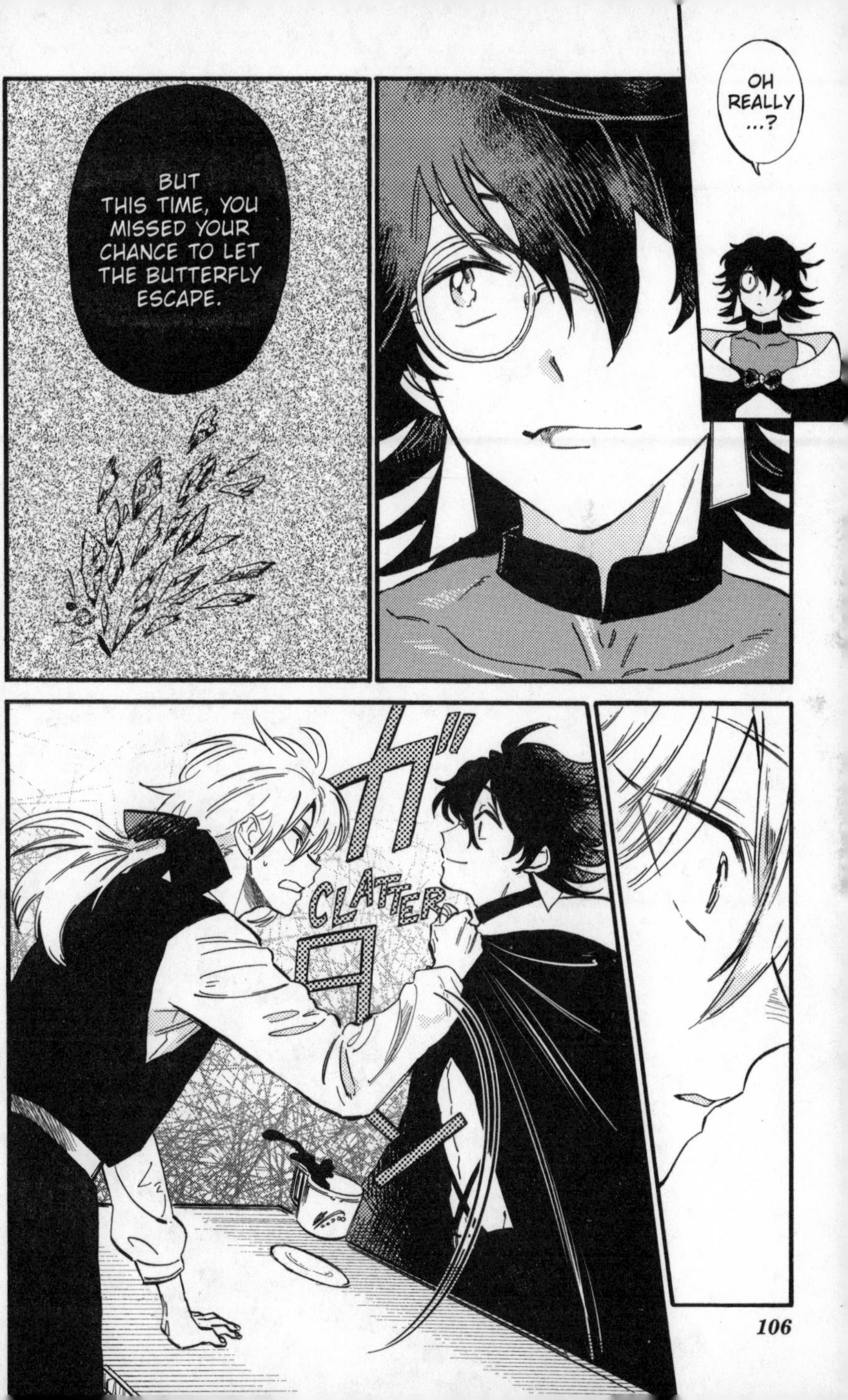
OH REALLY ...?
BUT THIS TIME, YOU MISSED YOUR CHANCE TO LET THE BUTTERFLY ESCAPE.
ガ
CLATTER

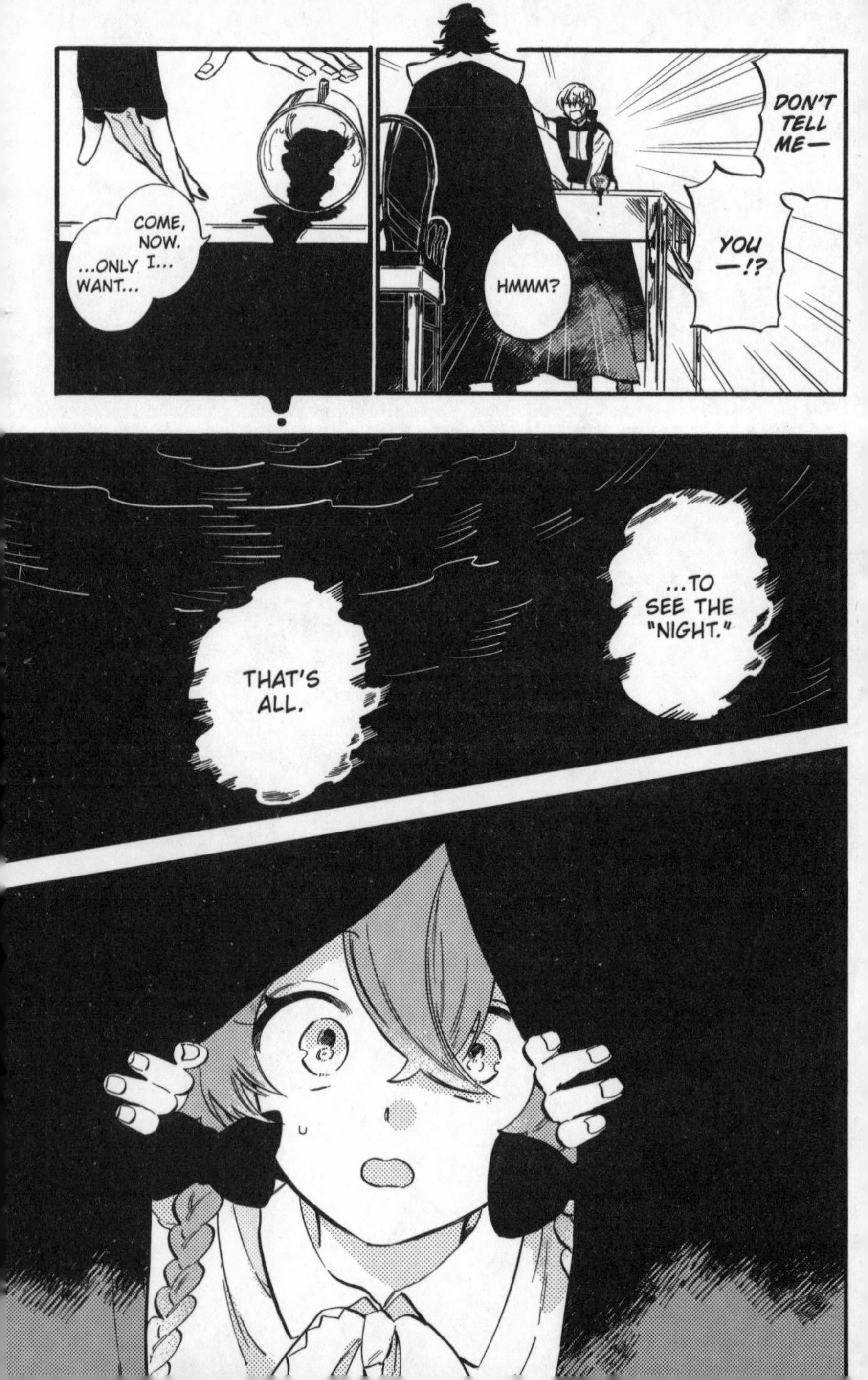
DON'T TELL ME—
YOU—!?
HMMM?
COME, NOW. ...ONLY I... WANT...
...TO SEE THE "NIGHT."
THAT'S ALL.

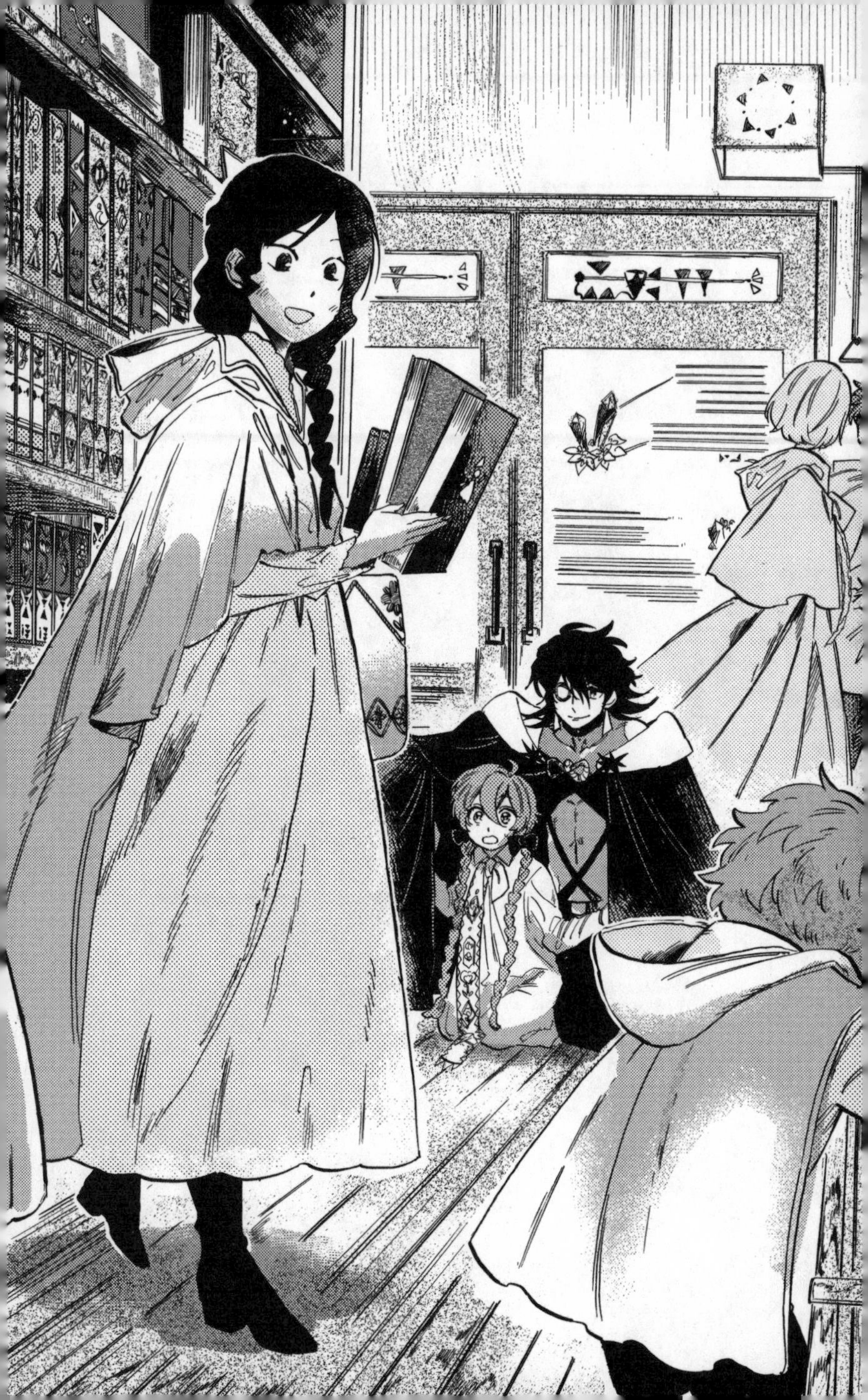

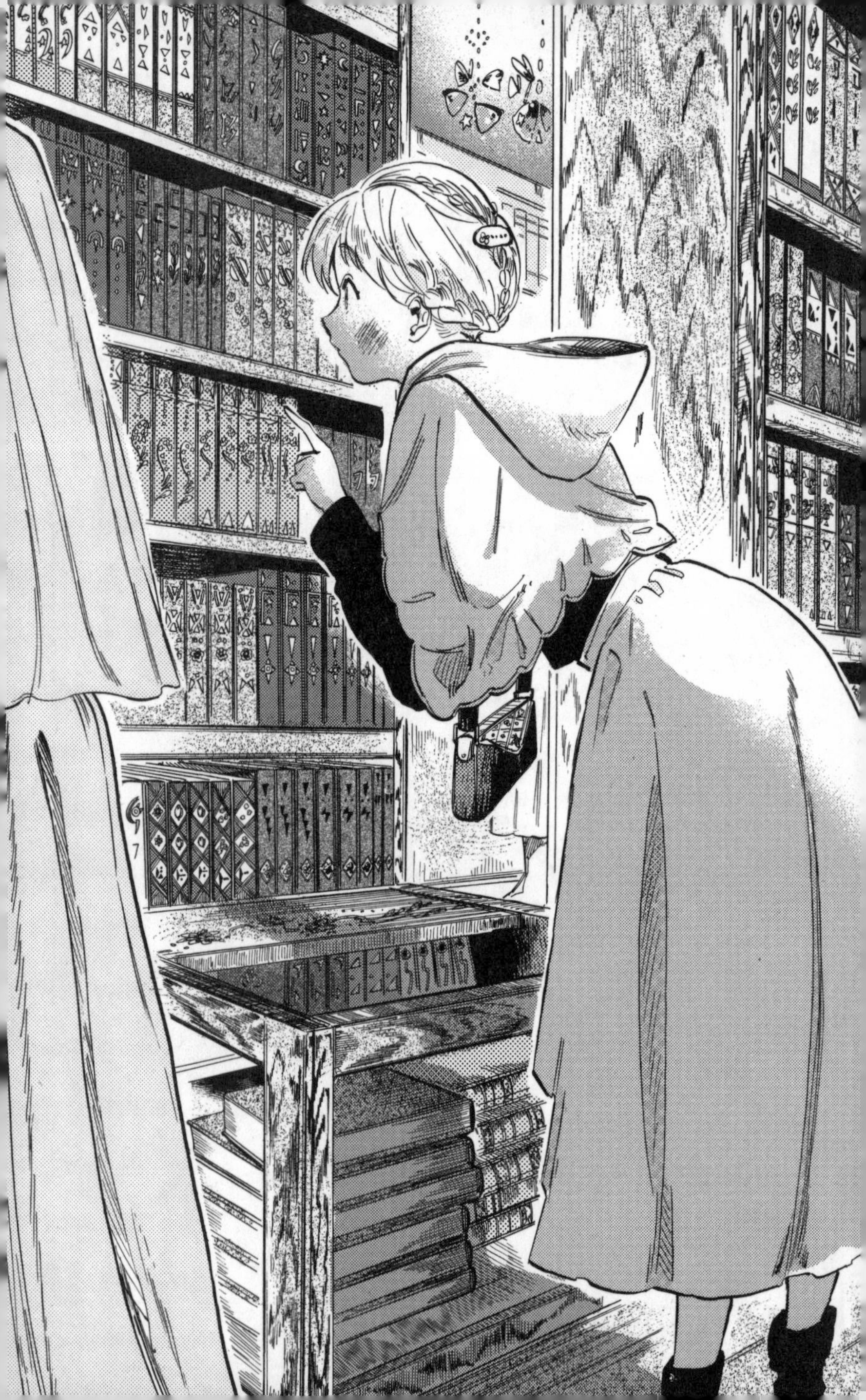

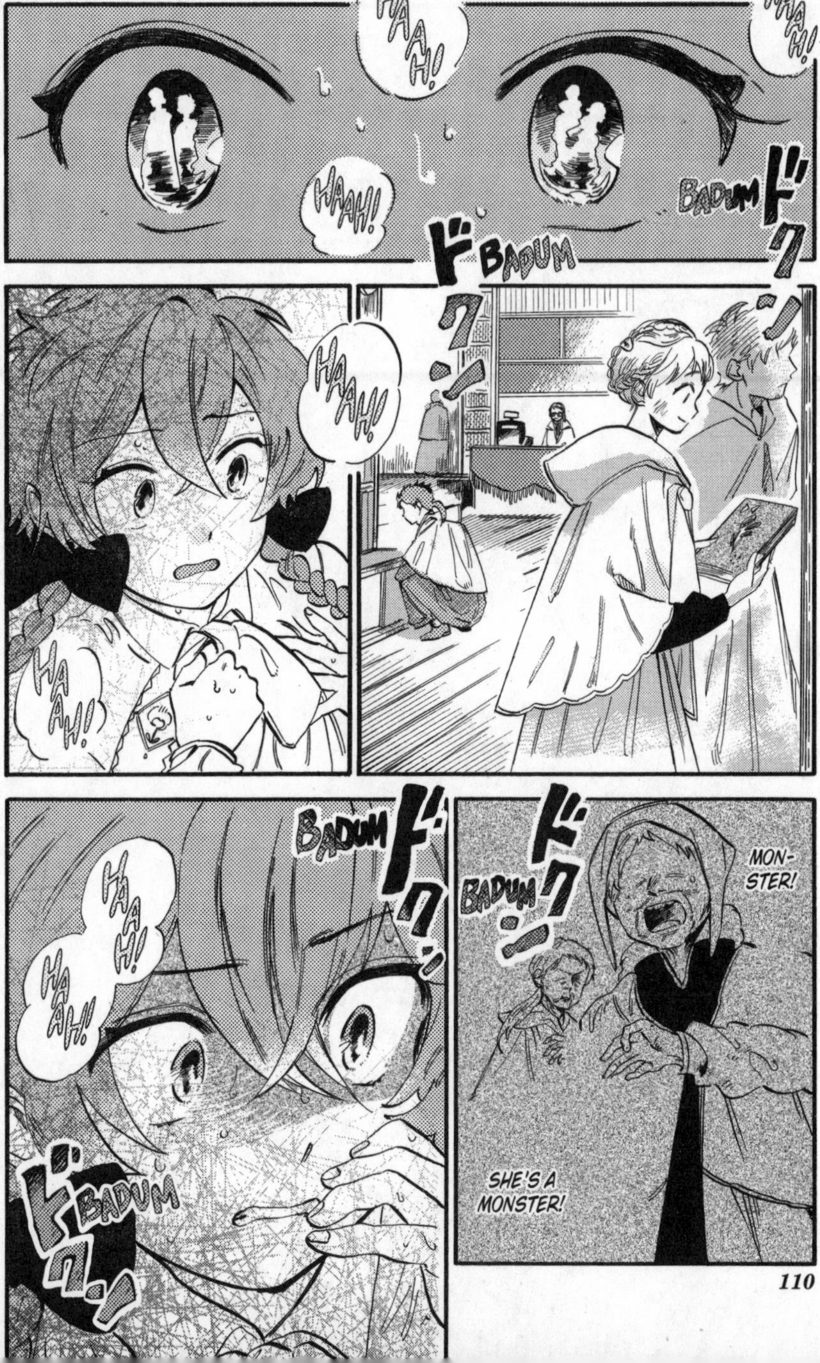
HAAAH!
HAAAH!
BADUM
ドクン
HAAAH!
BADUM
ドクン!
HAAAH!
HAAAH!
BADUM
ドクン
MON-
STER!
SHE'S A
MONSTER!
BADUM
ドクン
HAAAH!
HAAAH!
BADUM
ドクン!

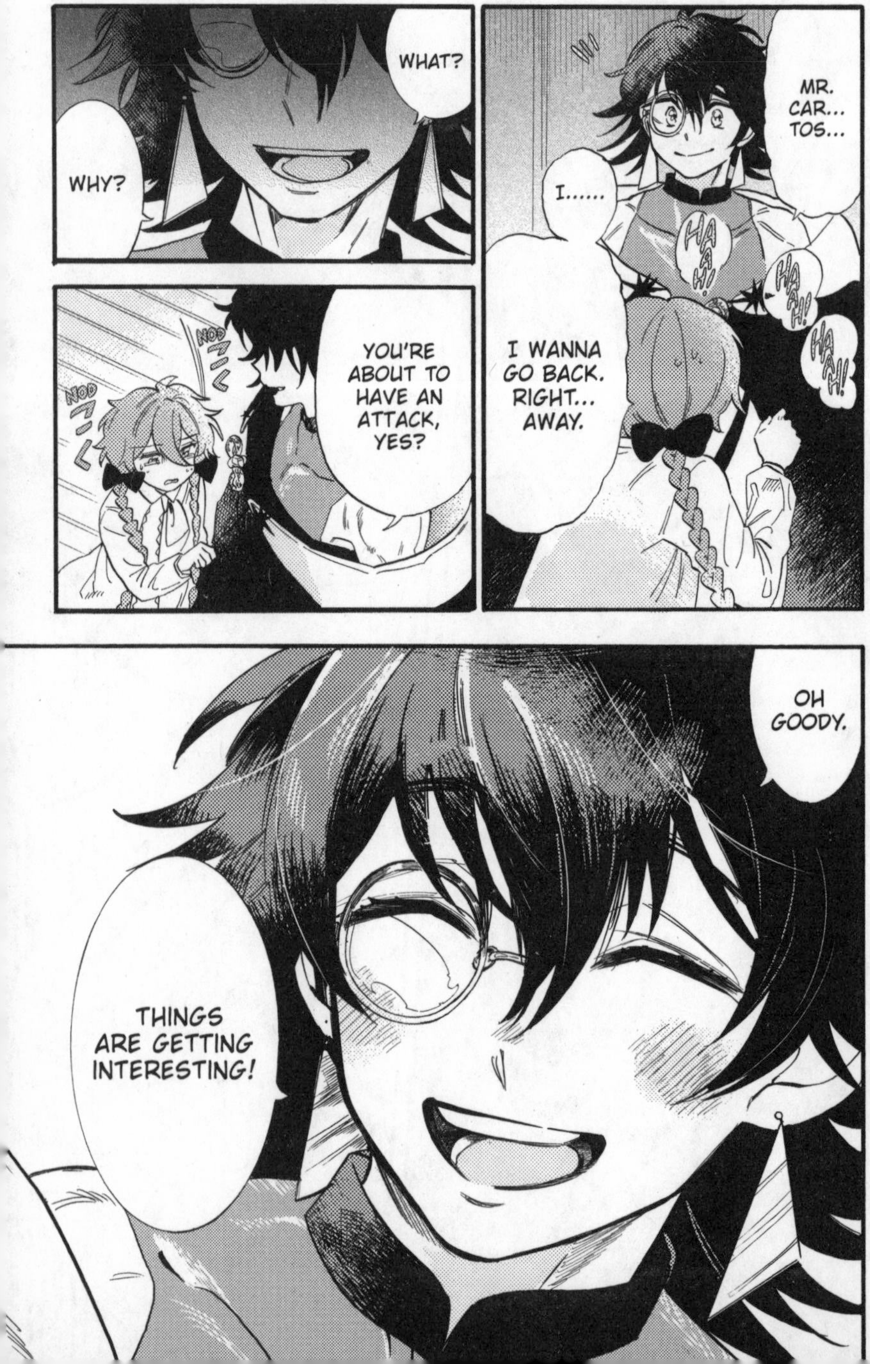
MR. CAR... TOS...
I......
HAAH!
HAAH!
HAAH!
I WANNA GO BACK. RIGHT... AWAY.
WHAT?
WHY?
YOU'RE ABOUT TO HAVE AN ATTACK, YES?
NOD
NOD
OH GOODY.
THINGS ARE GETTING INTERESTING!

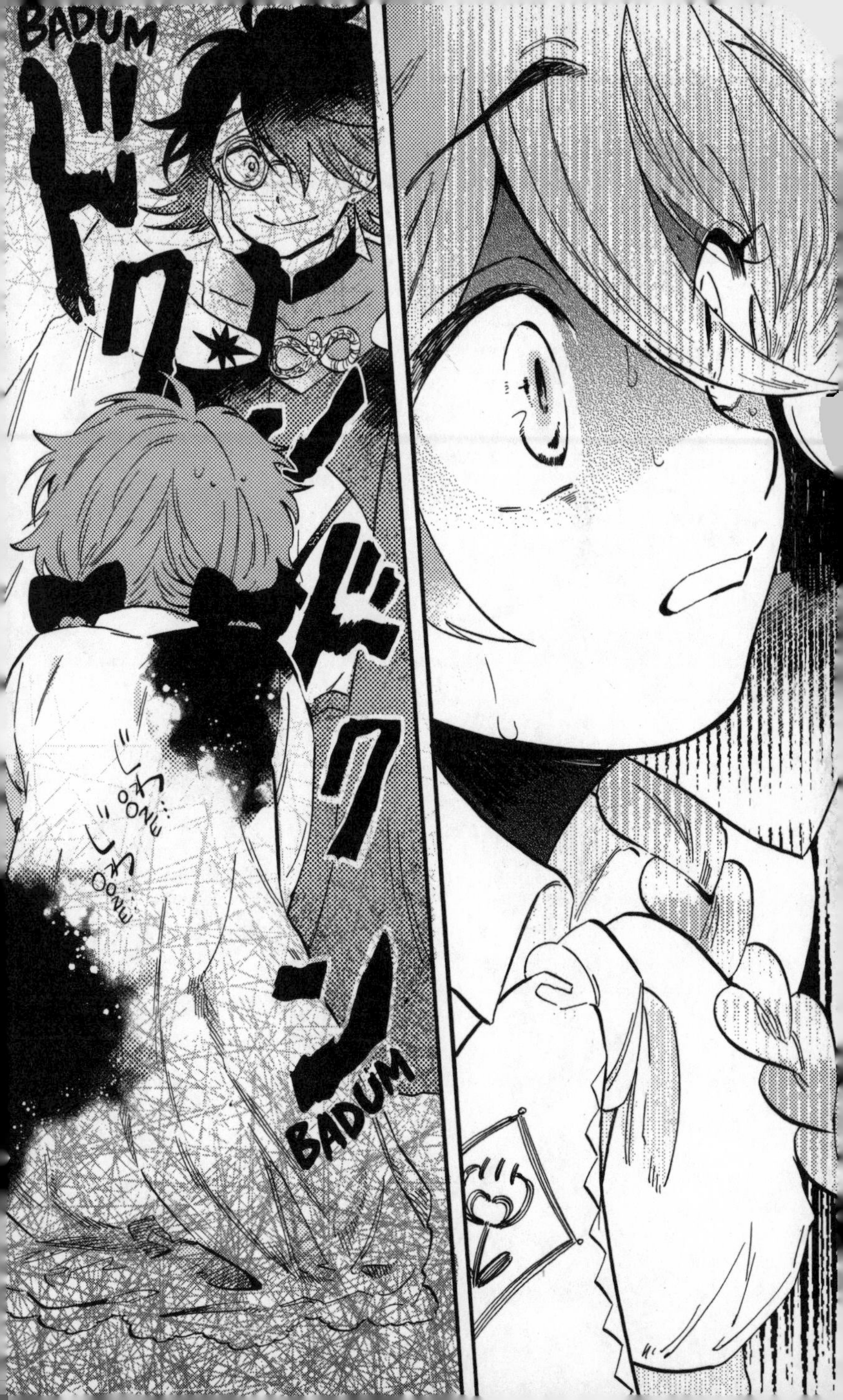
BADUM
BADUM
OONU
OONU

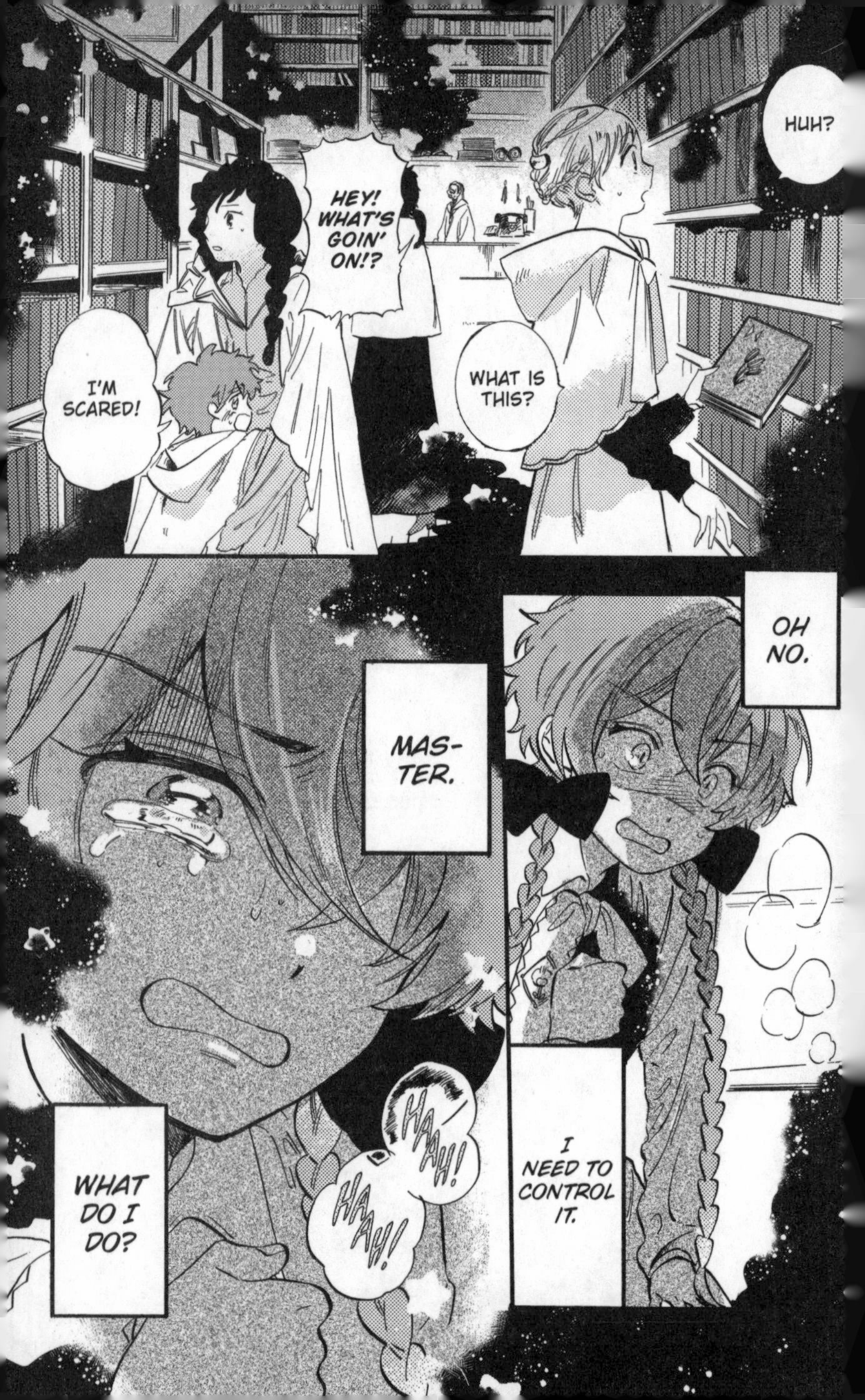
HUH?
HEY! WHAT'S GOIN' ON!?
WHAT IS THIS?
I'M SCARED!
OH NO.
I NEED TO CONTROL IT.
MAS-TER.
HAAH!
HAAH!
WHAT DO I DO?

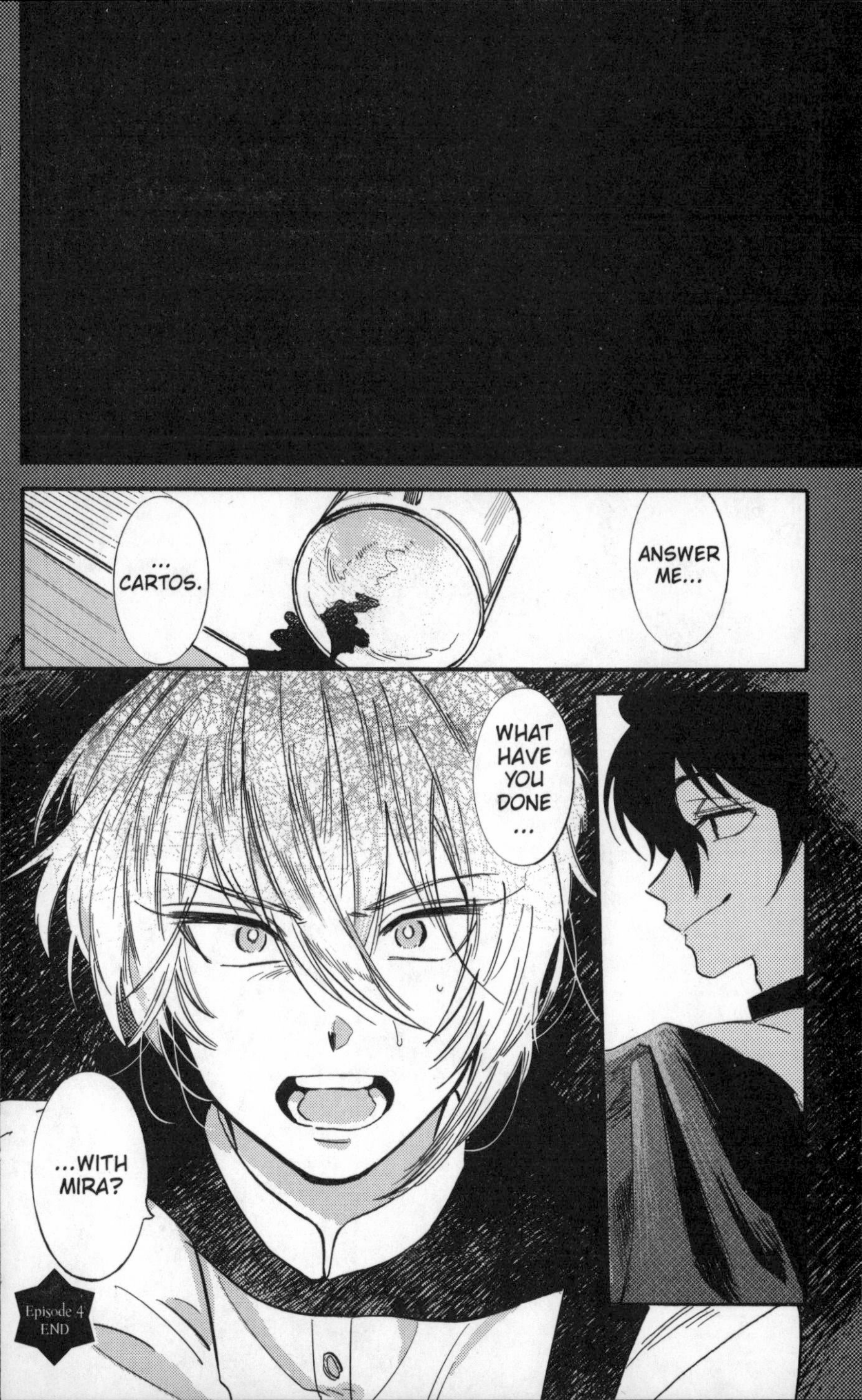
ANSWER ME...
...CARTOS.
WHAT HAVE YOU DONE...
...WITH MIRA?
Episode 4 END

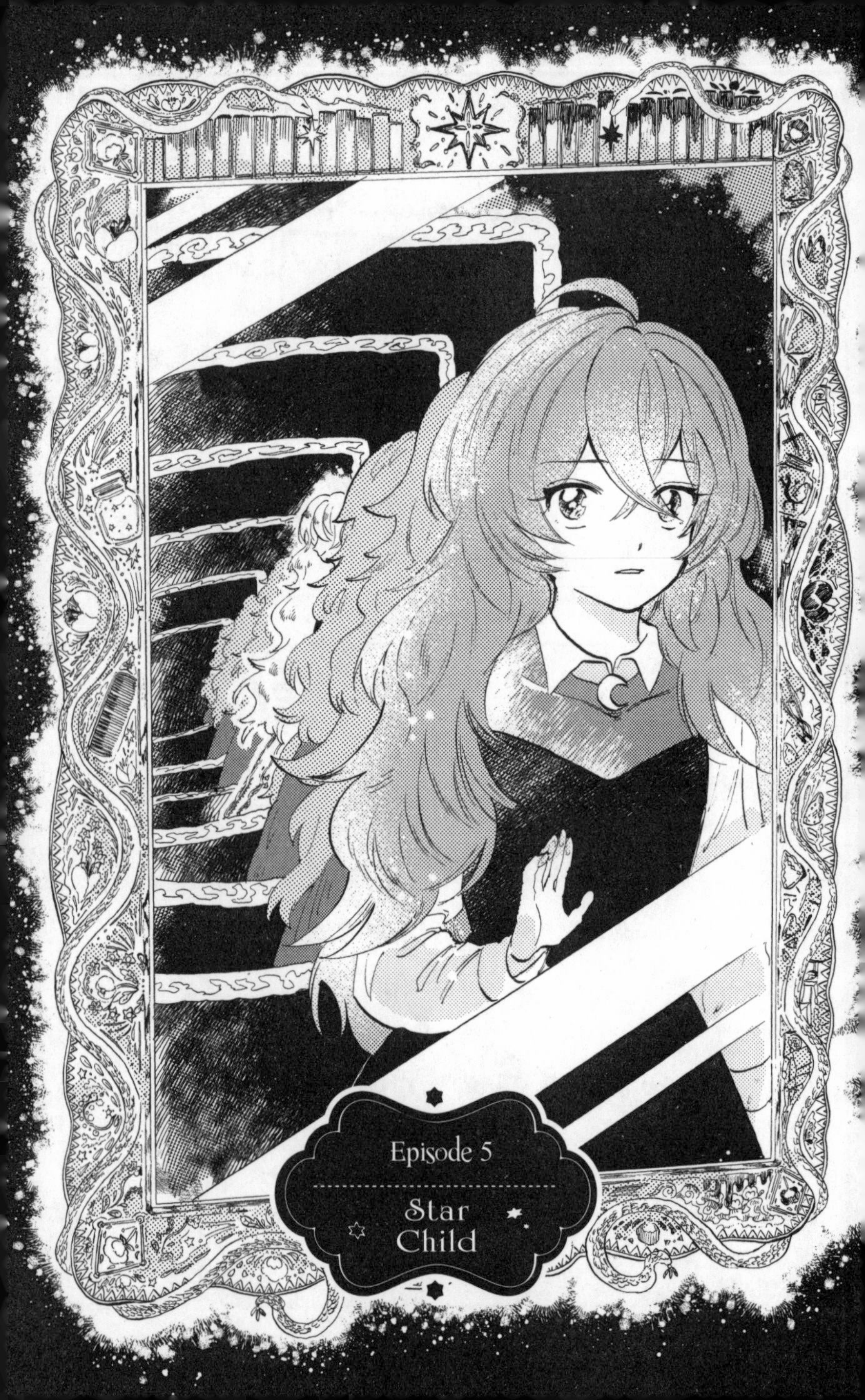
Episode 5
Star Child

...HAVE YOU TAKEN MIRA!?

WHERE...

CAR-TOS!

IT'S INCOMPATIBLE WITH...

...SUNLIGHT, CORRECT?

SO THIS "NIGHT"...

...ILLNESS—

116

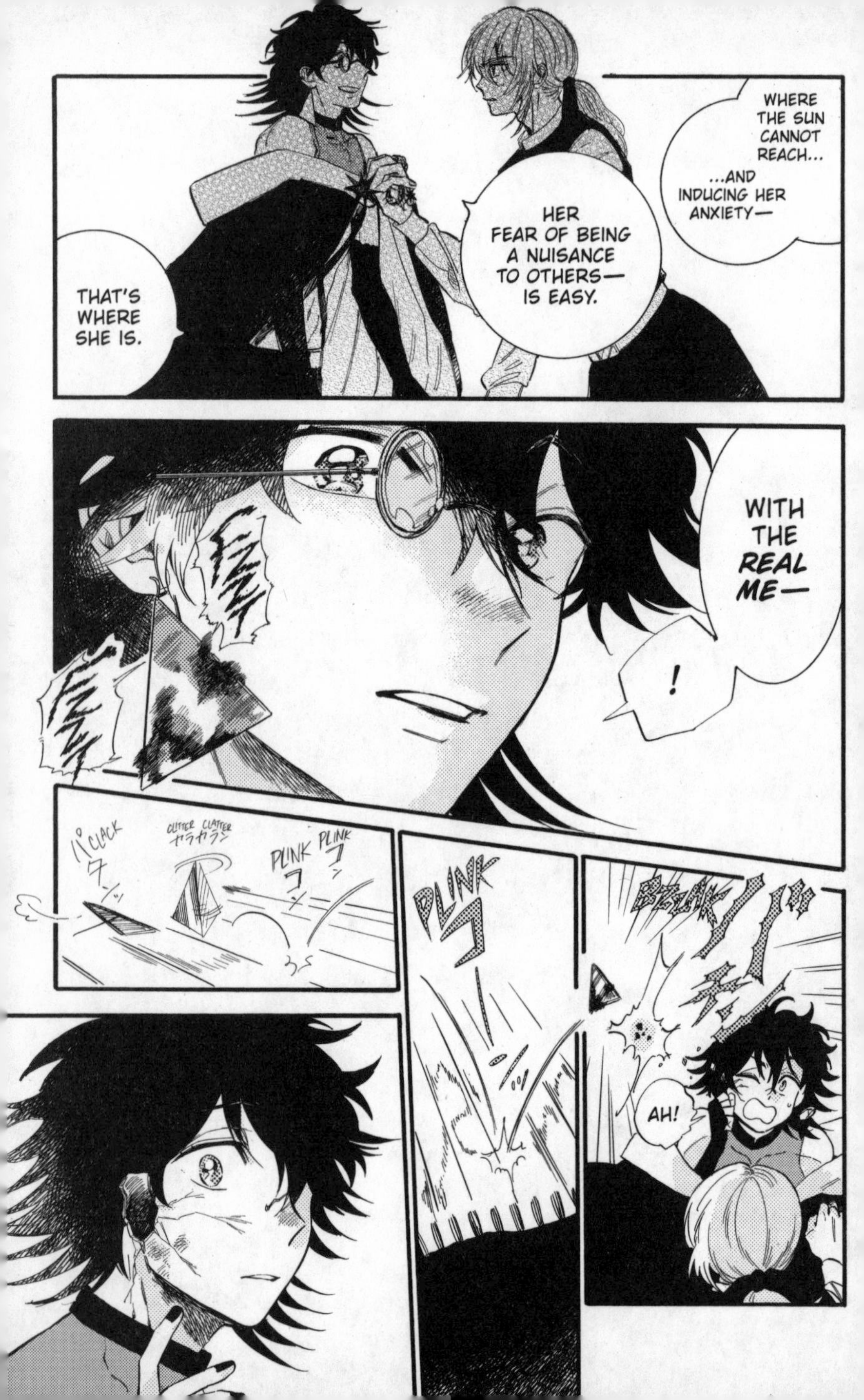
WHERE THE SUN CANNOT REACH...
...AND INDUCING HER ANXIETY—
HER FEAR OF BEING A NUISANCE TO OTHERS— IS EASY.
THAT'S WHERE SHE IS.
WITH THE REAL ME—
!
BZZAK
AH!
PLINK
CLACK
CLITTER CLATTER
ガラガラン
PLINK PLINK

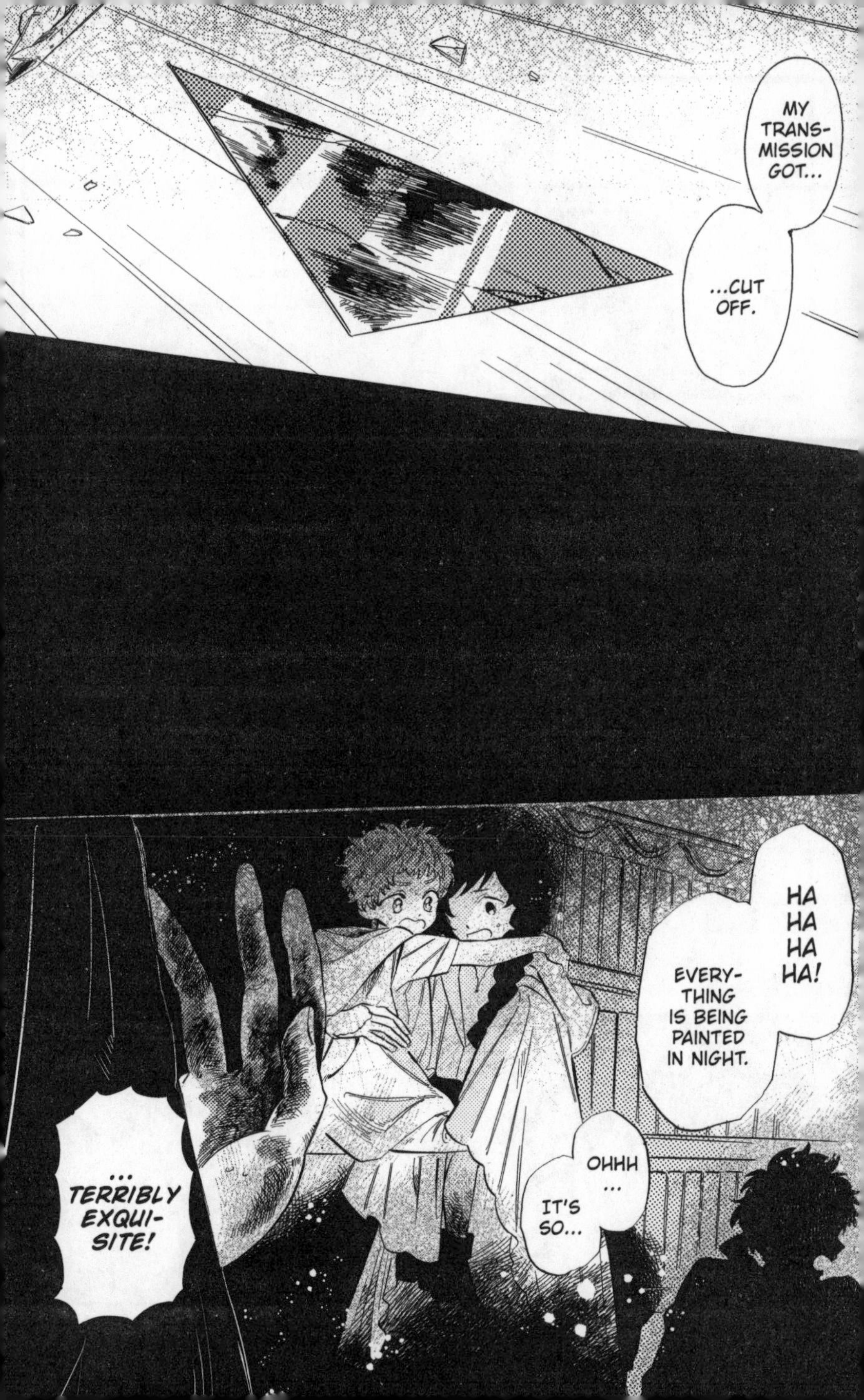
MY TRANS-MISSION GOT...
...CUT OFF.
HA HA HA HA!
EVERY-THING IS BEING PAINTED IN NIGHT.
OHHH... IT'S SO...
...TERRIBLY EXQUI-SITE!

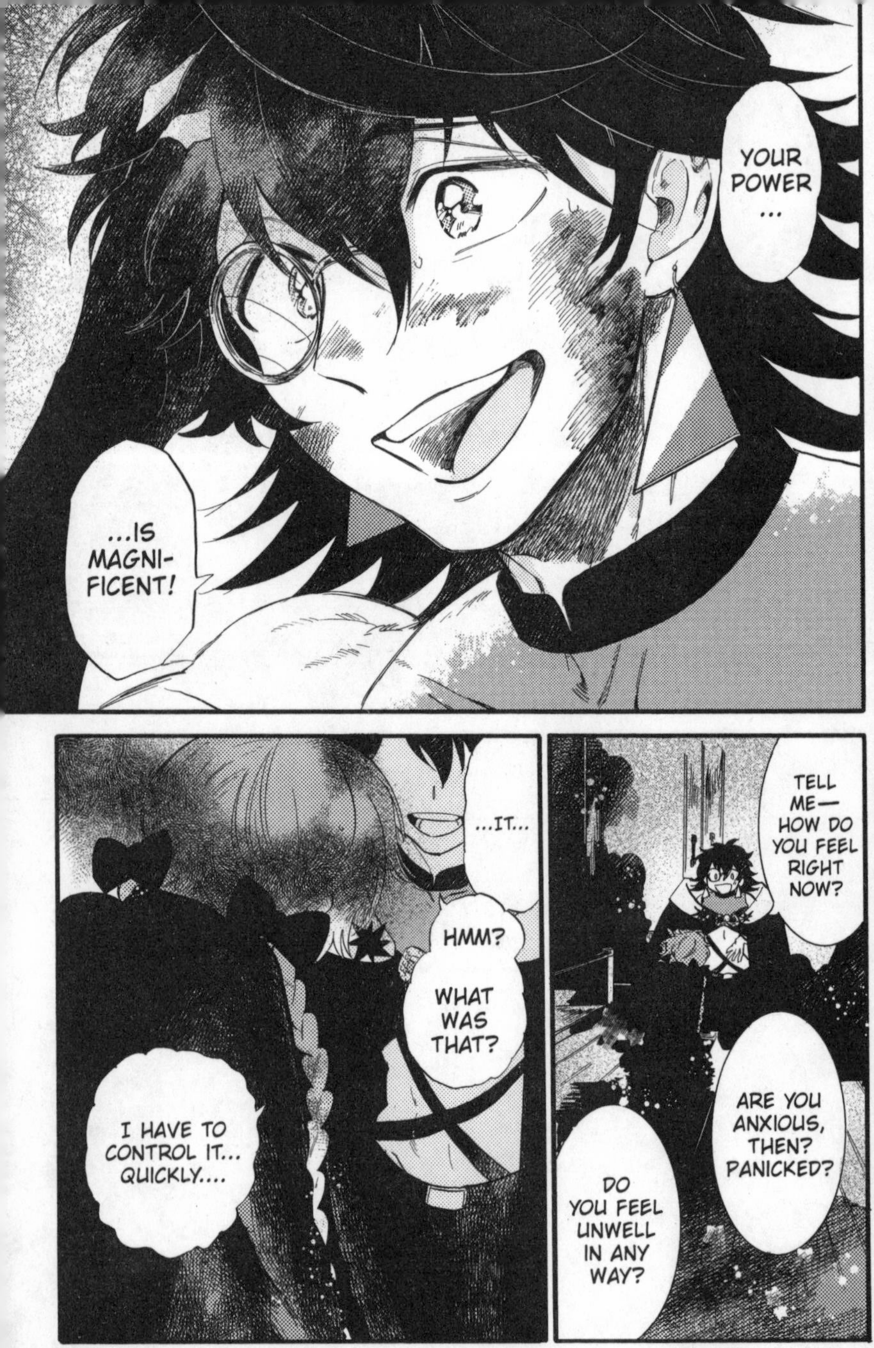
YOUR POWER ...
...IS MAGNIFICENT!
TELL ME— HOW DO YOU FEEL RIGHT NOW?
ARE YOU ANXIOUS, THEN? PANICKED?
DO YOU FEEL UNWELL IN ANY WAY?
...IT...
HMM?
WHAT WAS THAT?
I HAVE TO CONTROL IT... QUICKLY....

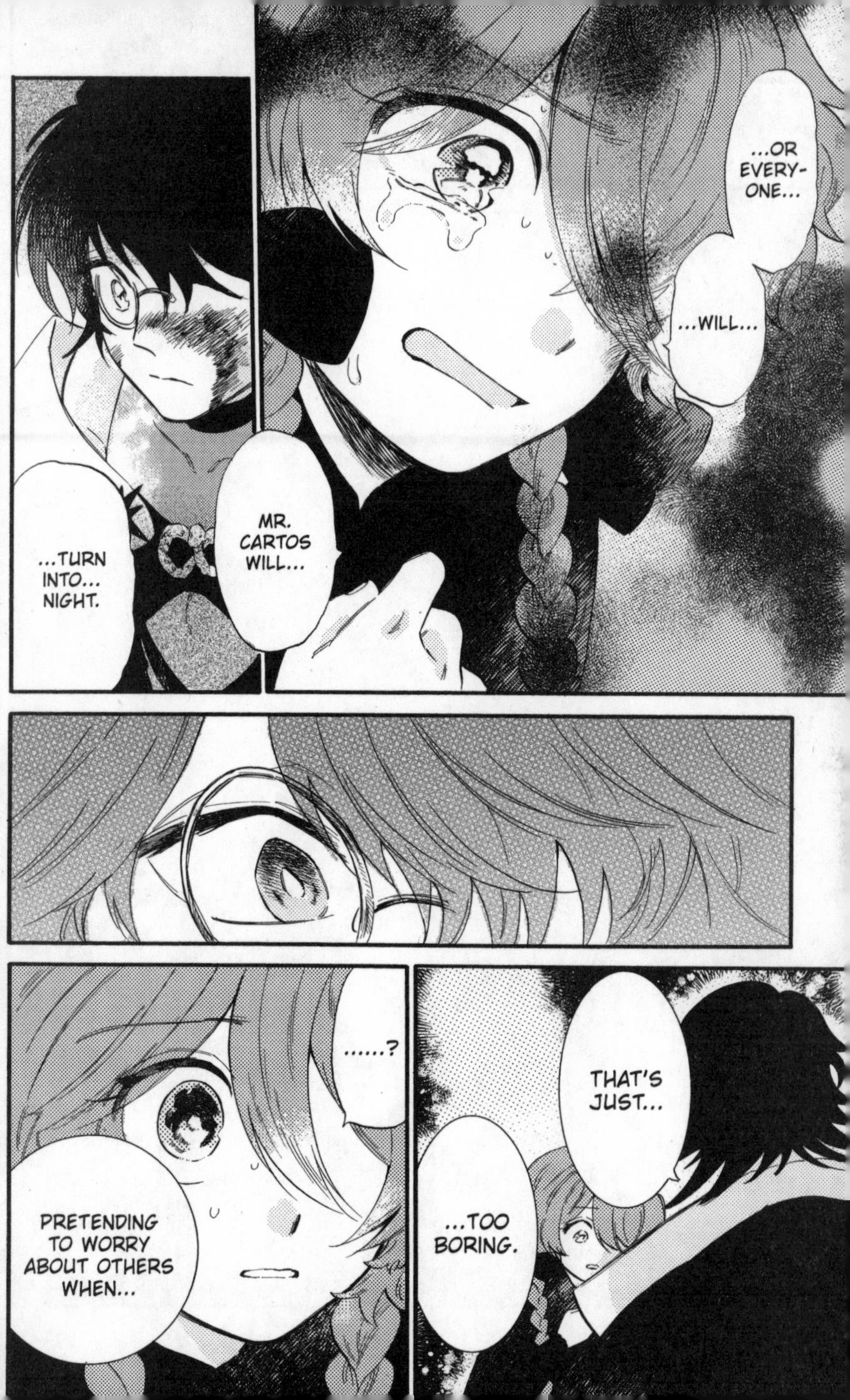
...OR EVERY-ONE...
...WILL...
MR. CARTOS WILL...
...TURN INTO... NIGHT.
THAT'S JUST...
...TOO BORING.
......?
PRETENDING TO WORRY ABOUT OTHERS WHEN...

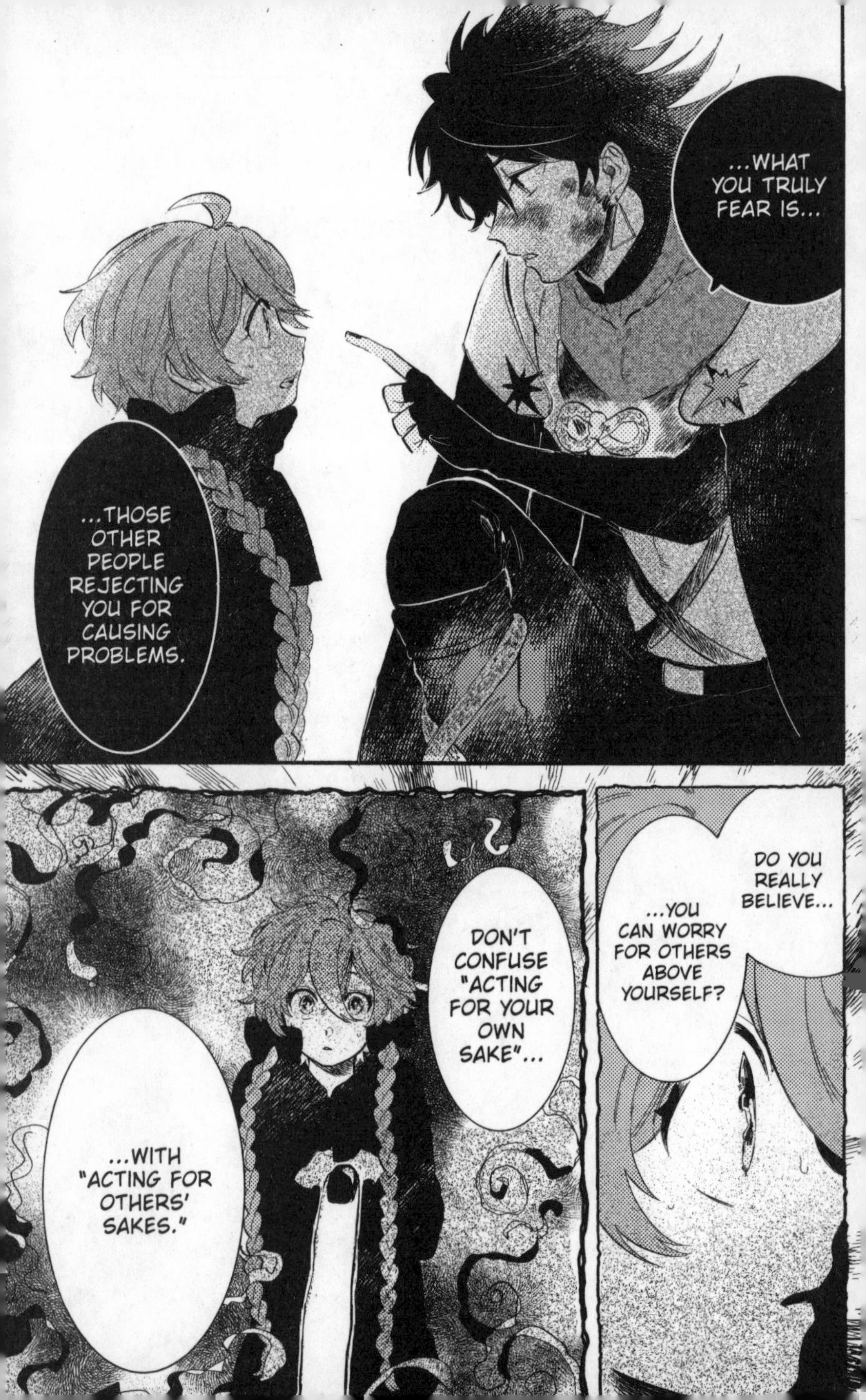
...WHAT YOU TRULY FEAR IS...
...THOSE OTHER PEOPLE REJECTING YOU FOR CAUSING PROBLEMS.
DO YOU REALLY BELIEVE...
...YOU CAN WORRY FOR OTHERS ABOVE YOURSELF?
DON'T CONFUSE "ACTING FOR YOUR OWN SAKE"...
...WITH "ACTING FOR OTHERS' SAKES."

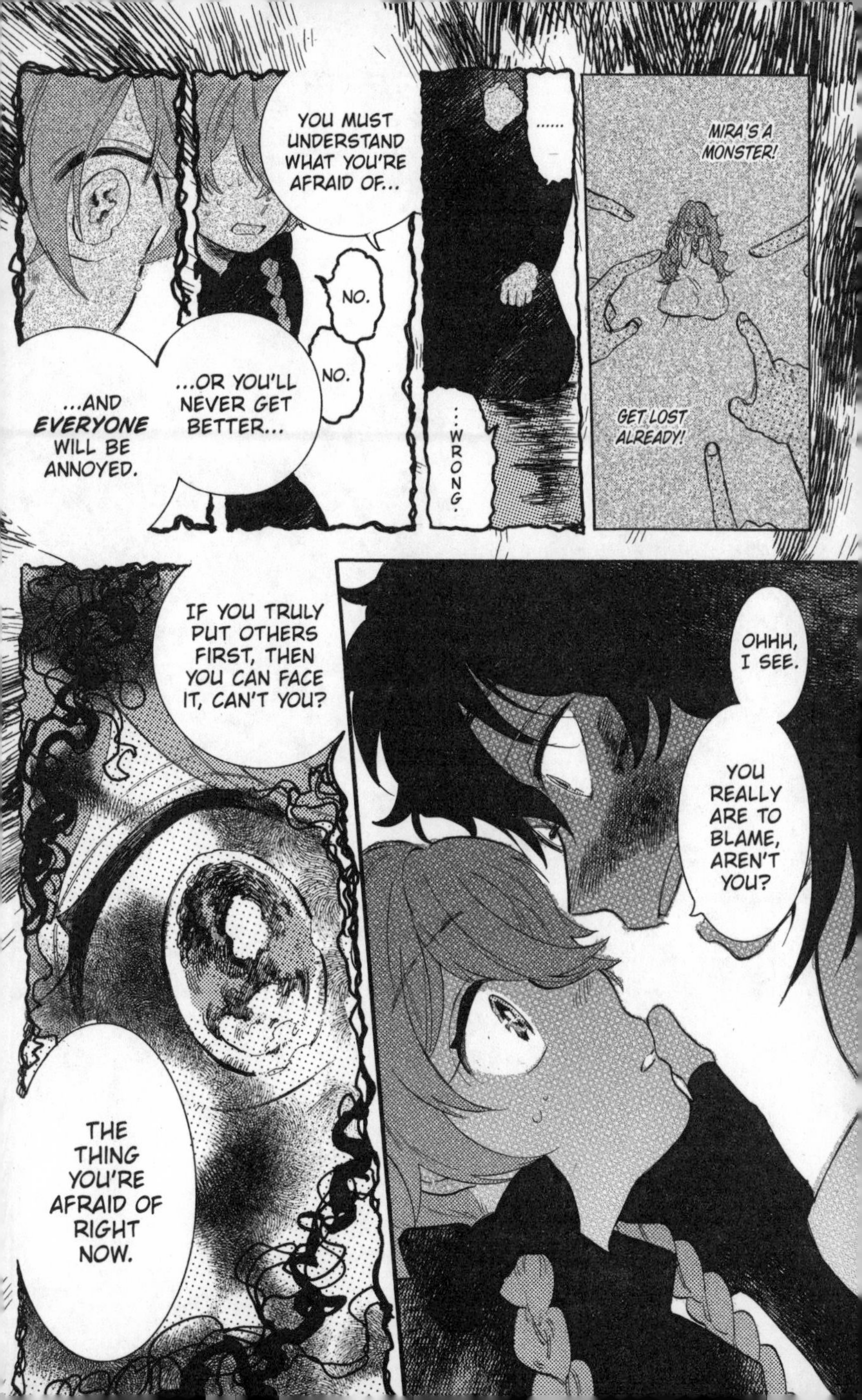
MIRA'S A MONSTER!
GET LOST ALREADY!
......
...WRONG.
YOU MUST UNDERSTAND WHAT YOU'RE AFRAID OF...
NO.
NO.
...OR YOU'LL NEVER GET BETTER...
...AND *EVERYONE* WILL BE ANNOYED.
OHHH, I SEE.
YOU REALLY ARE TO BLAME, AREN'T YOU?
IF YOU TRULY PUT OTHERS FIRST, THEN YOU CAN FACE IT, CAN'T YOU?
THE THING YOU'RE AFRAID OF RIGHT NOW.

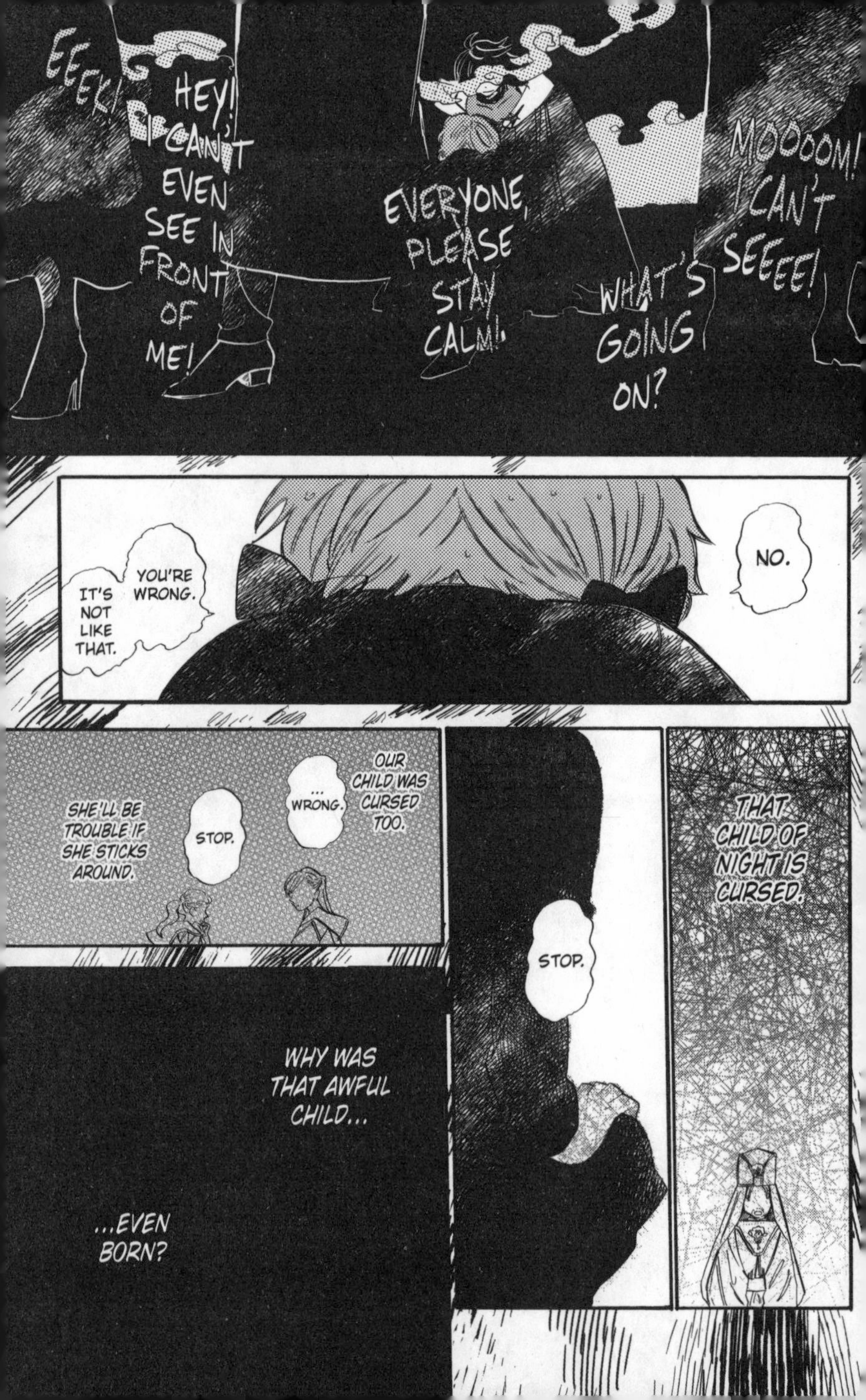
MOOOOM! I CAN'T SEEEEE!
WHAT'S GOING ON?
EVERYONE, PLEASE STAY CALM!
HEY! I CAN'T EVEN SEE IN FRONT OF ME!
EEEK!
NO.
YOU'RE WRONG. IT'S NOT LIKE THAT.
THAT CHILD OF NIGHT IS CURSED.
STOP.
OUR CHILD WAS CURSED TOO.
... WRONG.
STOP.
SHE'LL BE TROUBLE IF SHE STICKS AROUND.
WHY WAS THAT AWFUL CHILD...
...EVEN BORN?

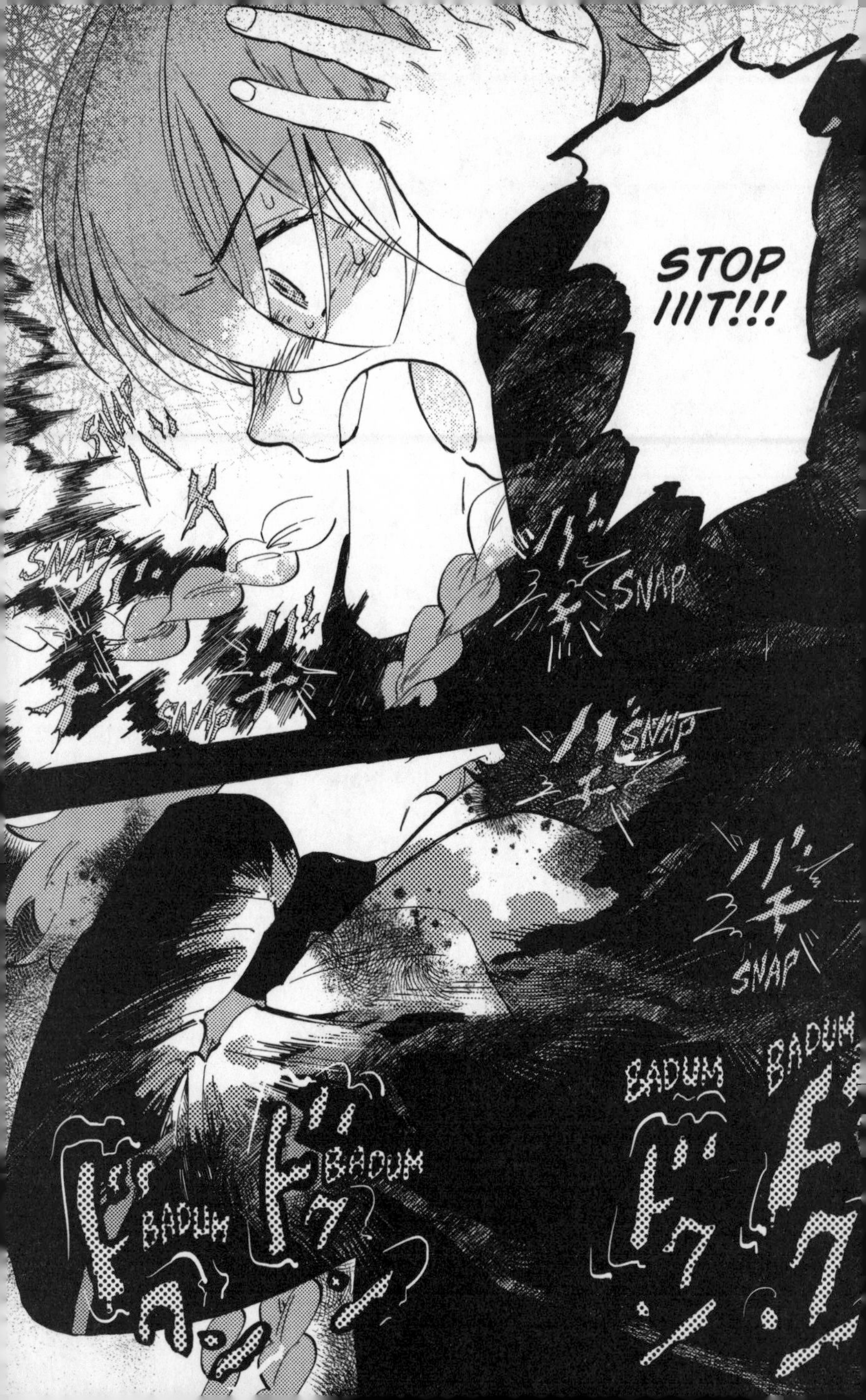
STOP IIIT!!!
SNAP
SNAP
SNAP
SNAP
SNAP
SNAP
BADUM
BADUM
BADUM
BADUM

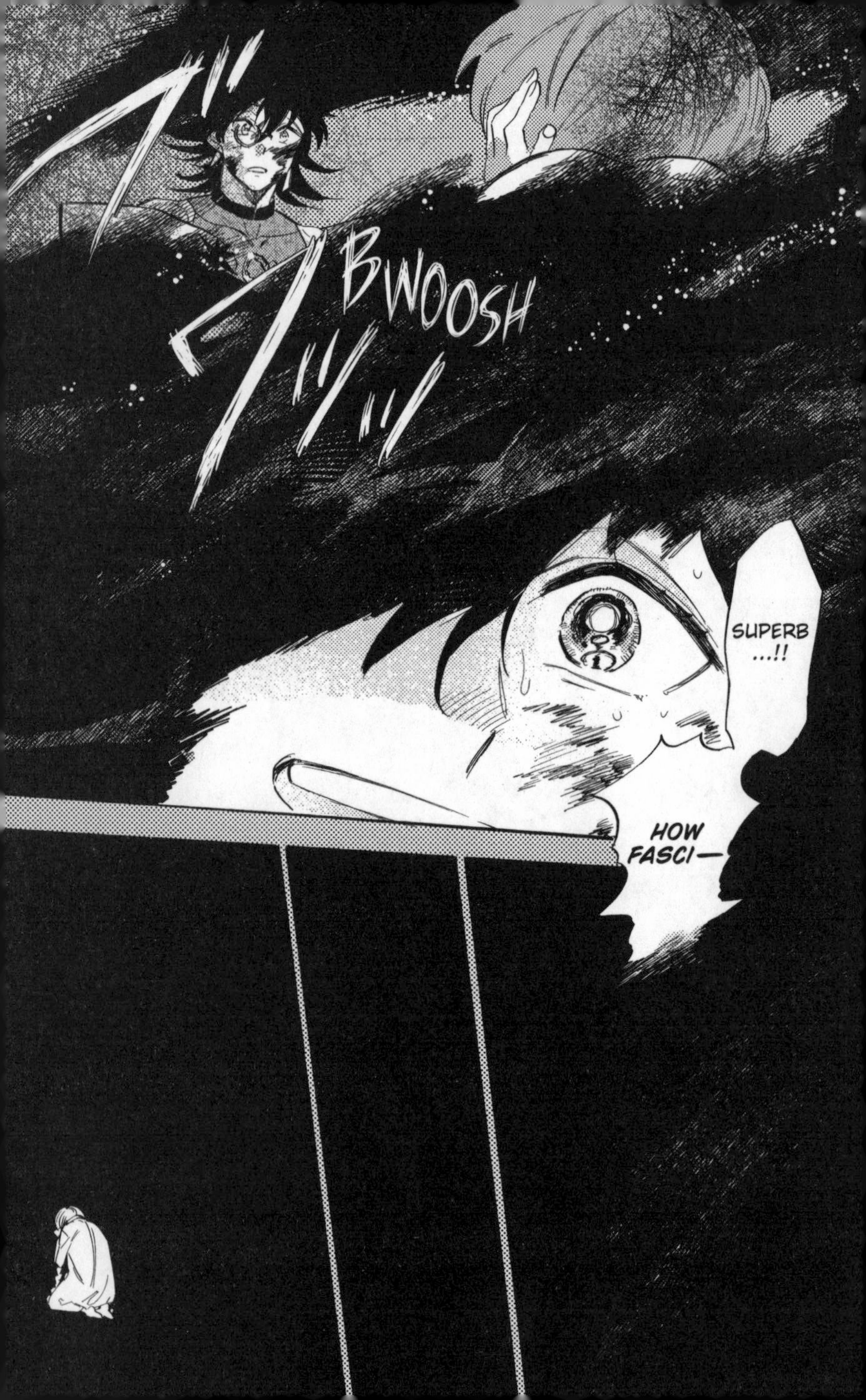
ブ
BWOOSH
ツッ
SUPERB ...!!
HOW FASCI—

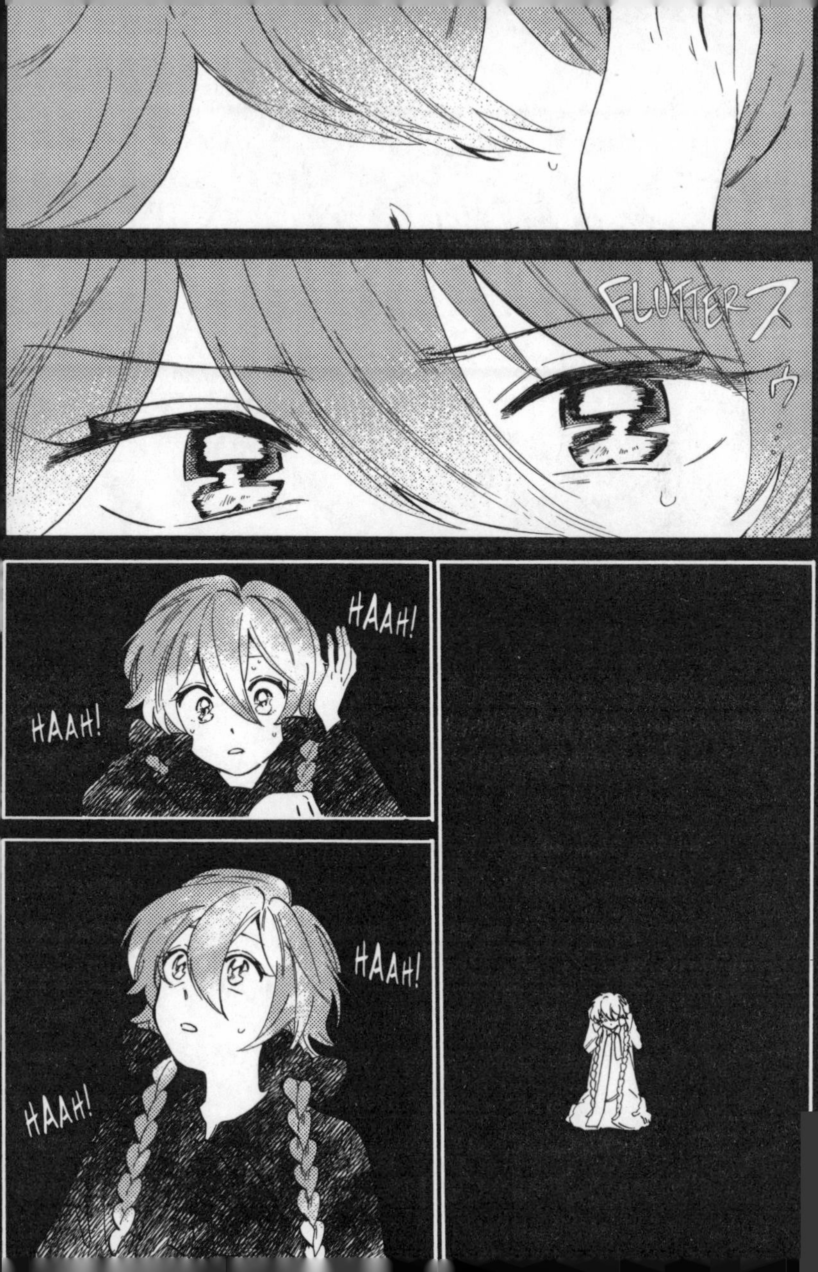
FLUTTER
スゥ…
HAAH!
HAAH!
HAAH!
HAAH!

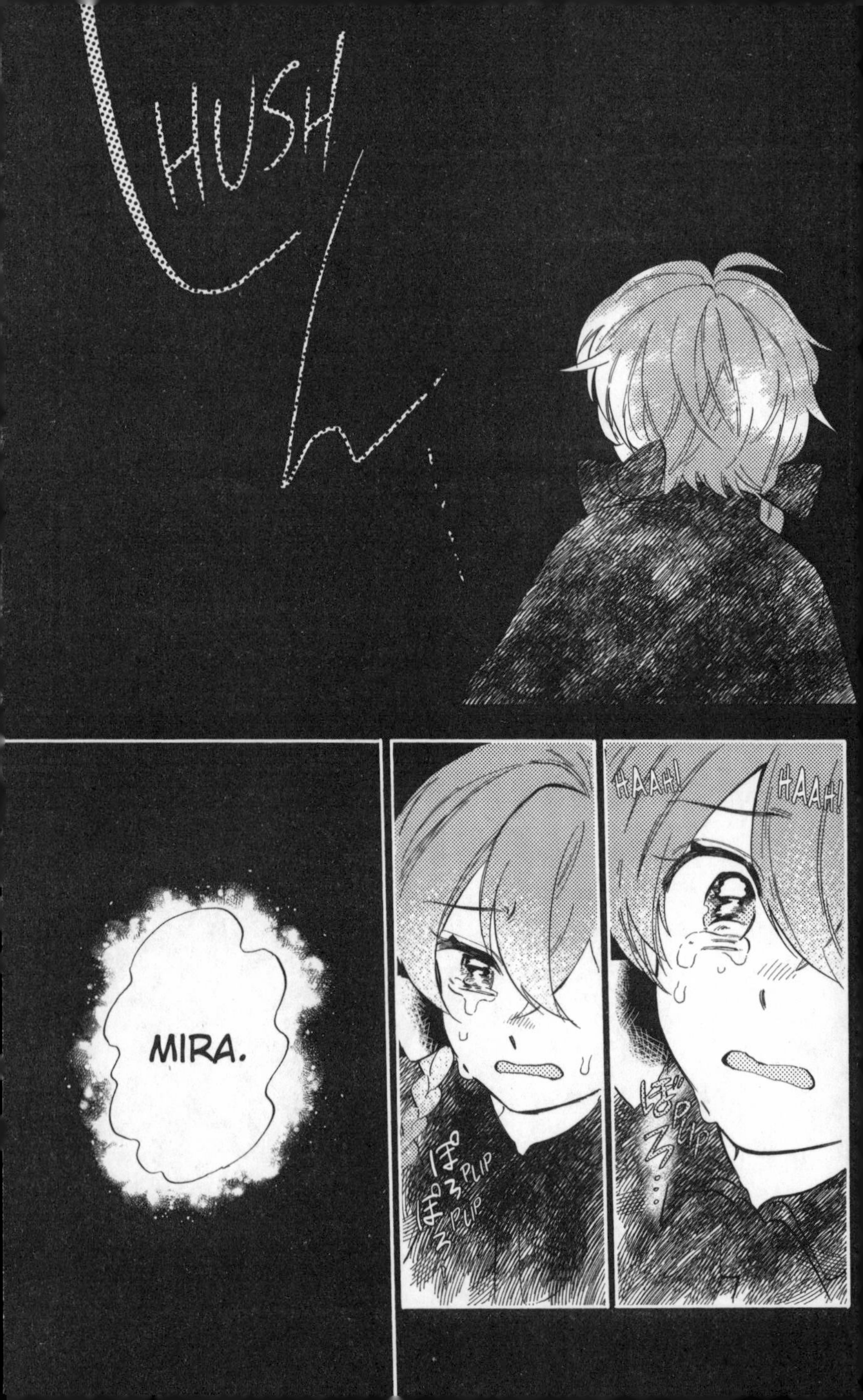
HUSH
HAAAH!
HAAAH!
ぽろ PLIP ろ...
ぽろ PLIP
ぽろ PLIP
MIRA.

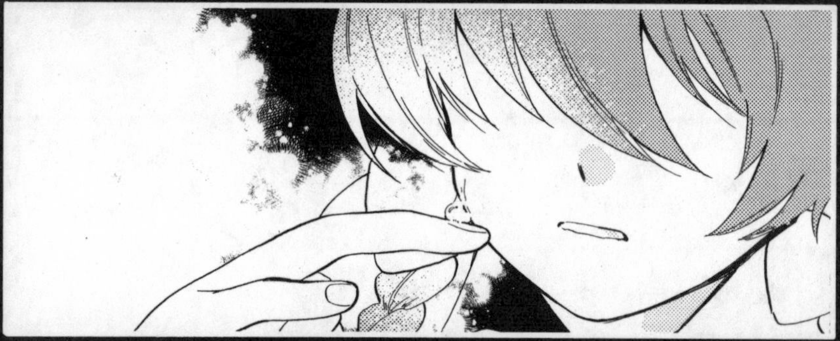
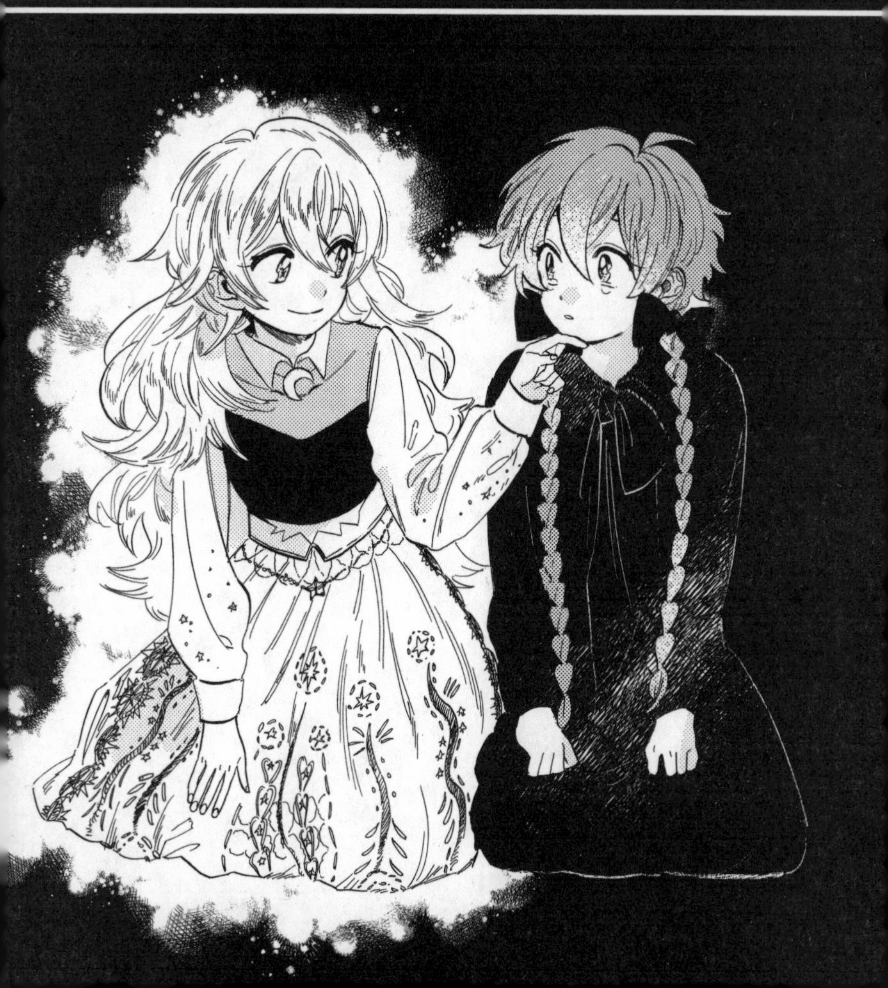

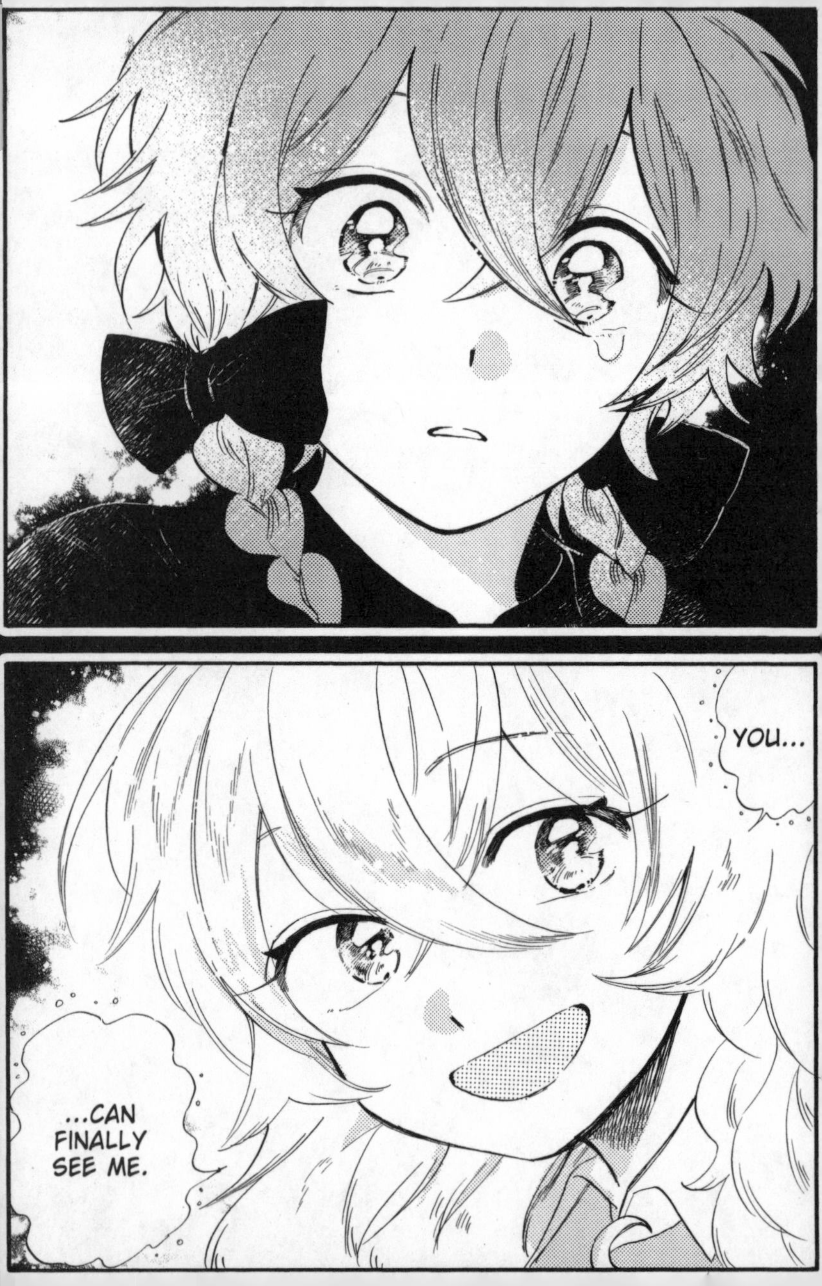
YOU...
...CAN FINALLY SEE ME.

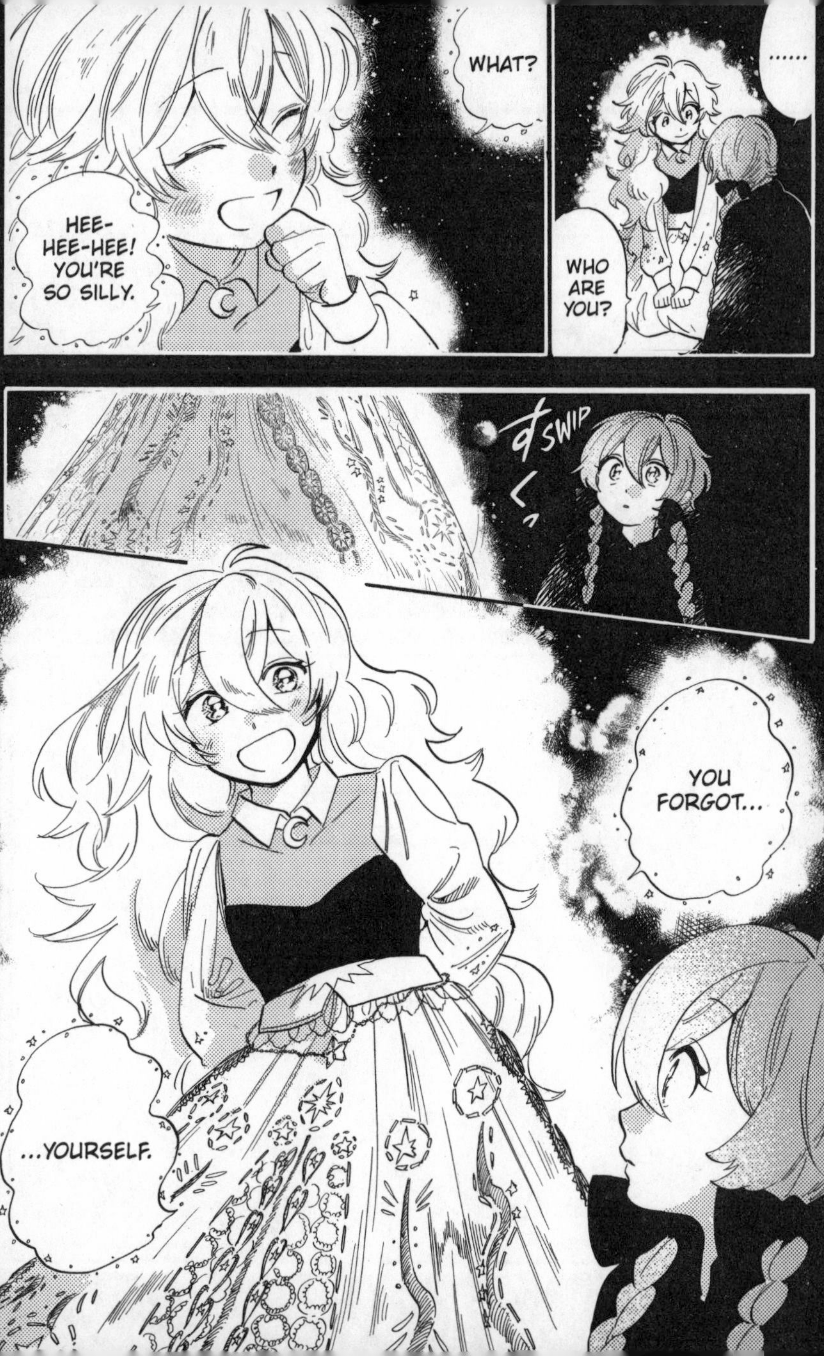
......
WHO ARE YOU?
WHAT?
HEE-HEE-HEE! YOU'RE SO SILLY.
SWIP
YOU FORGOT...
...YOURSELF.

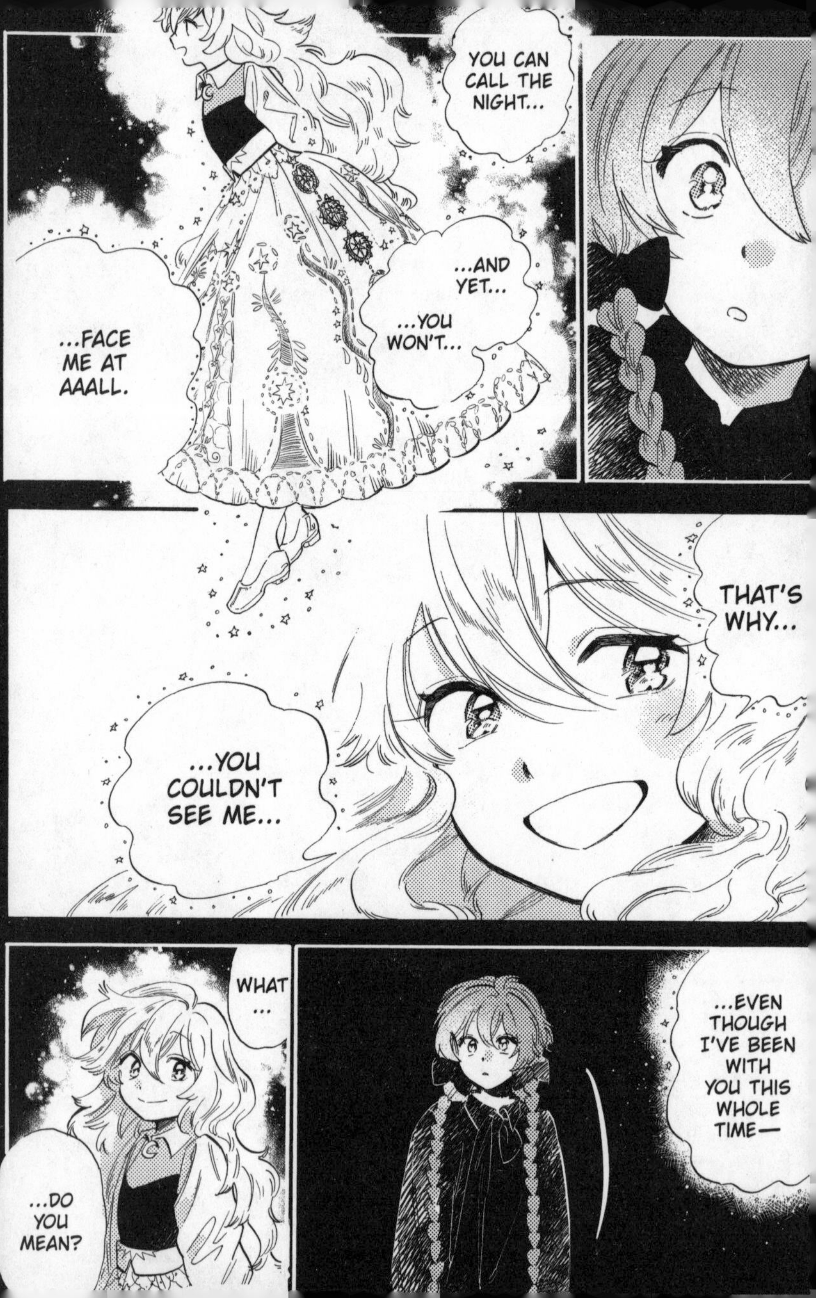
YOU CAN CALL THE NIGHT...
...AND YET...
...YOU WON'T...
...FACE ME AT AAALL.
THAT'S WHY...
...YOU COULDN'T SEE ME...
...EVEN THOUGH I'VE BEEN WITH YOU THIS WHOLE TIME—
WHAT ...
...DO YOU MEAN?

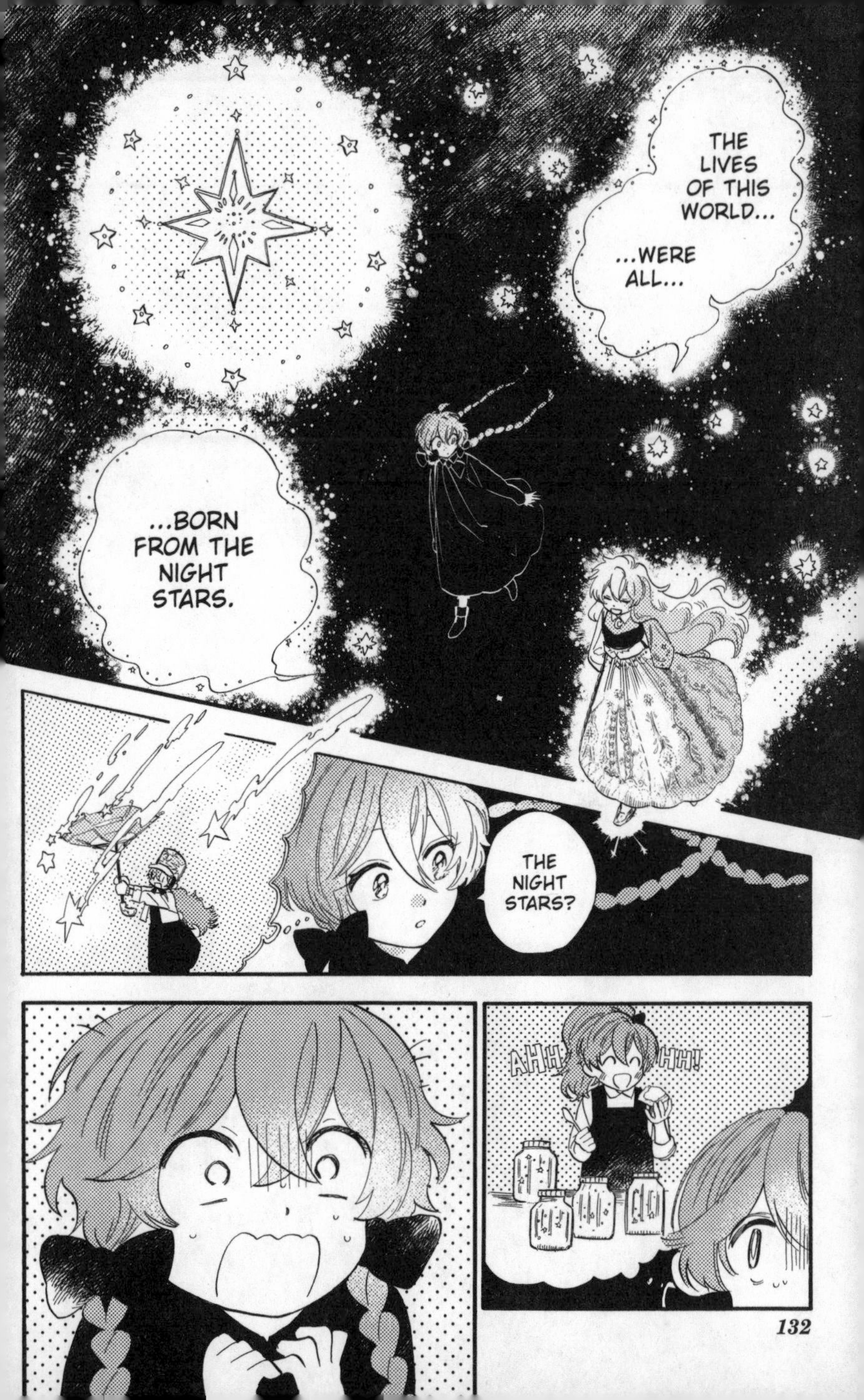
THE LIVES OF THIS WORLD...
...WERE ALL...
...BORN FROM THE NIGHT STARS.
THE NIGHT STARS?
AHH HH!

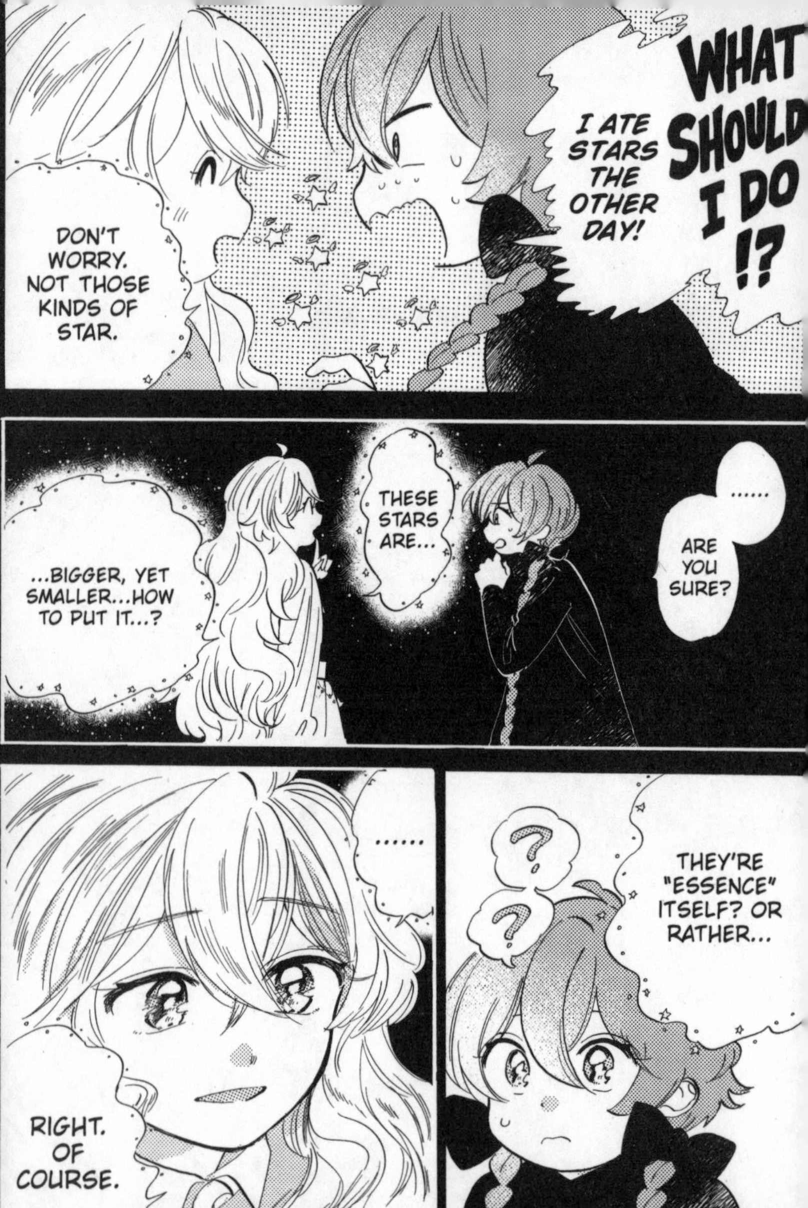
WHAT SHOULD I DO !?
I ATE STARS THE OTHER DAY!
DON'T WORRY. NOT THOSE KINDS OF STAR.
......
ARE YOU SURE?
THESE STARS ARE...
...BIGGER, YET SMALLER...HOW TO PUT IT...?
THEY'RE "ESSENCE" ITSELF? OR RATHER...
......
RIGHT. OF COURSE.

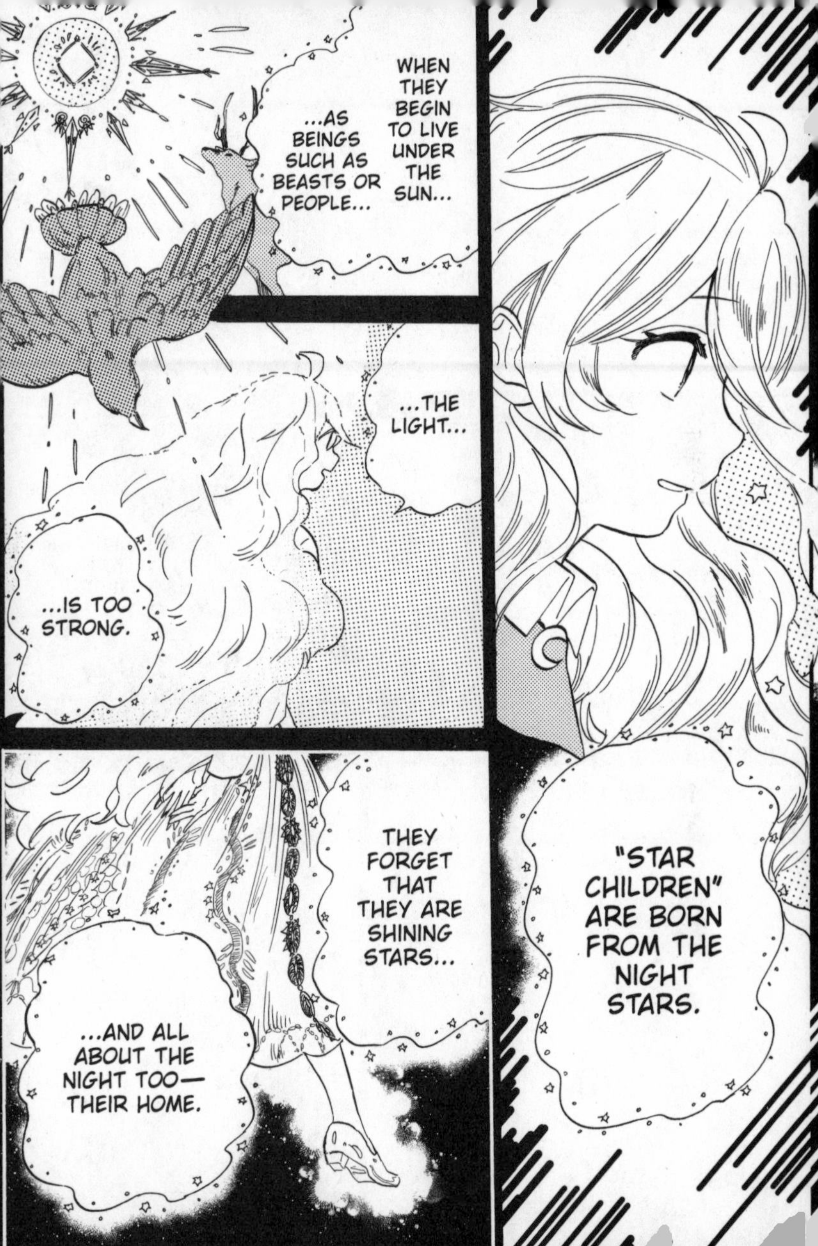
"STAR CHILDREN" ARE BORN FROM THE NIGHT STARS.
WHEN THEY BEGIN TO LIVE UNDER THE SUN...
...AS BEINGS SUCH AS BEASTS OR PEOPLE...
...THE LIGHT...
...IS TOO STRONG.
THEY FORGET THAT THEY ARE SHINING STARS...
...AND ALL ABOUT THE NIGHT TOO—THEIR HOME.

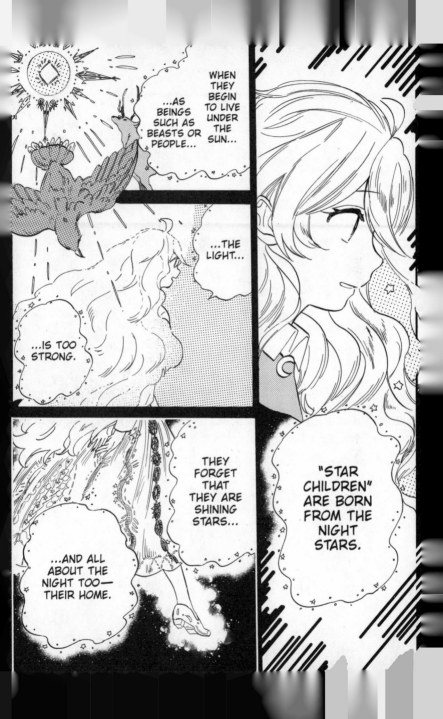

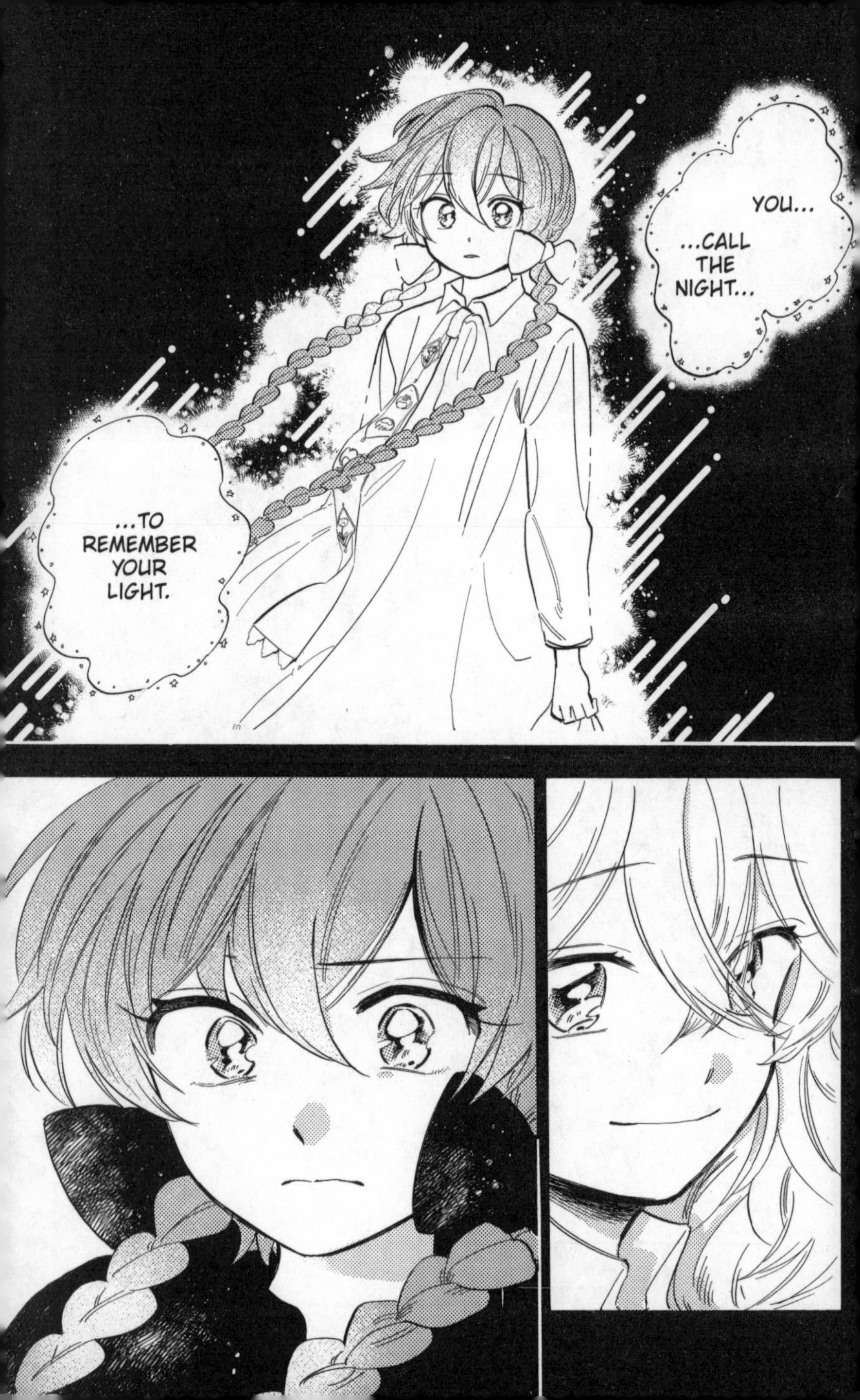
YOU...
...CALL THE NIGHT...
...TO REMEMBER YOUR LIGHT.

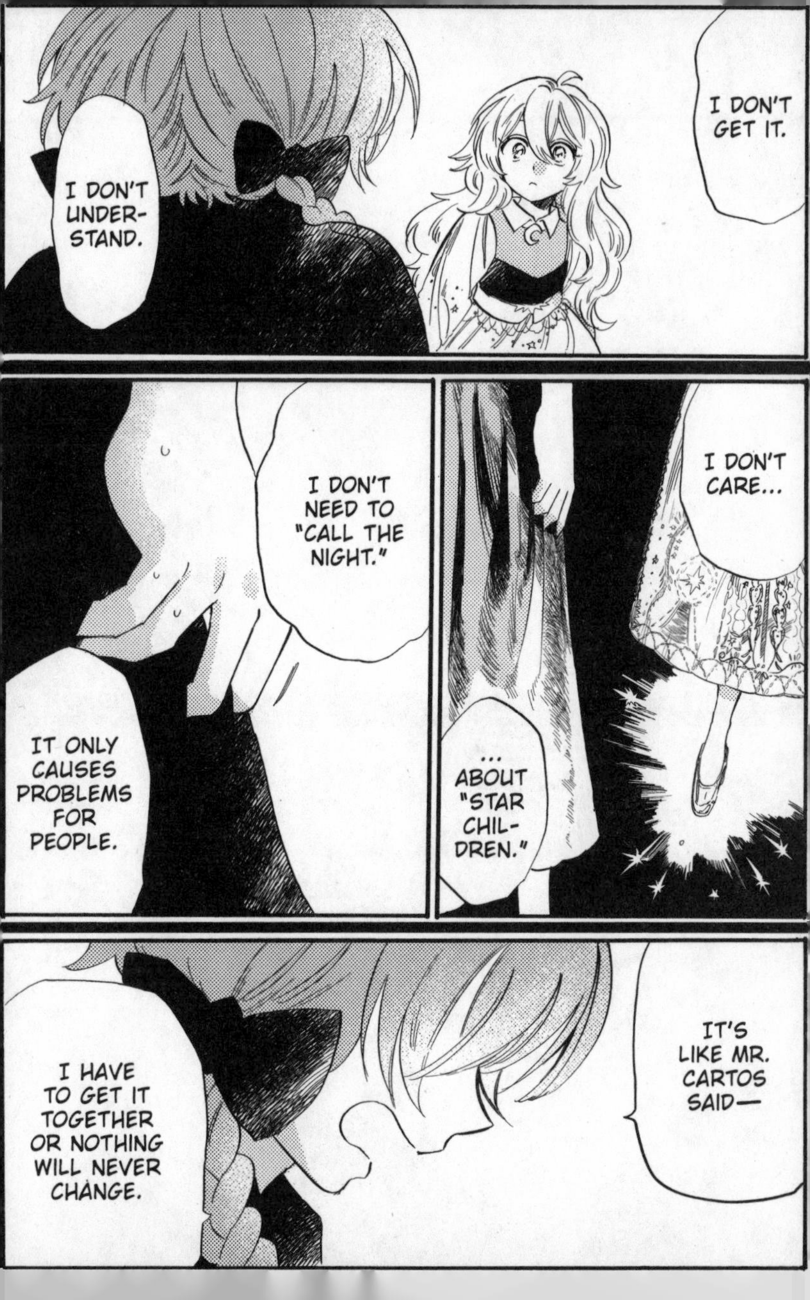
I DON'T GET IT.
I DON'T UNDER-STAND.
I DON'T CARE...
... ABOUT "STAR CHIL-DREN."
I DON'T NEED TO "CALL THE NIGHT."
IT ONLY CAUSES PROBLEMS FOR PEOPLE.
IT'S LIKE MR. CARTOS SAID—
I HAVE TO GET IT TOGETHER OR NOTHING WILL NEVER CHANGE.

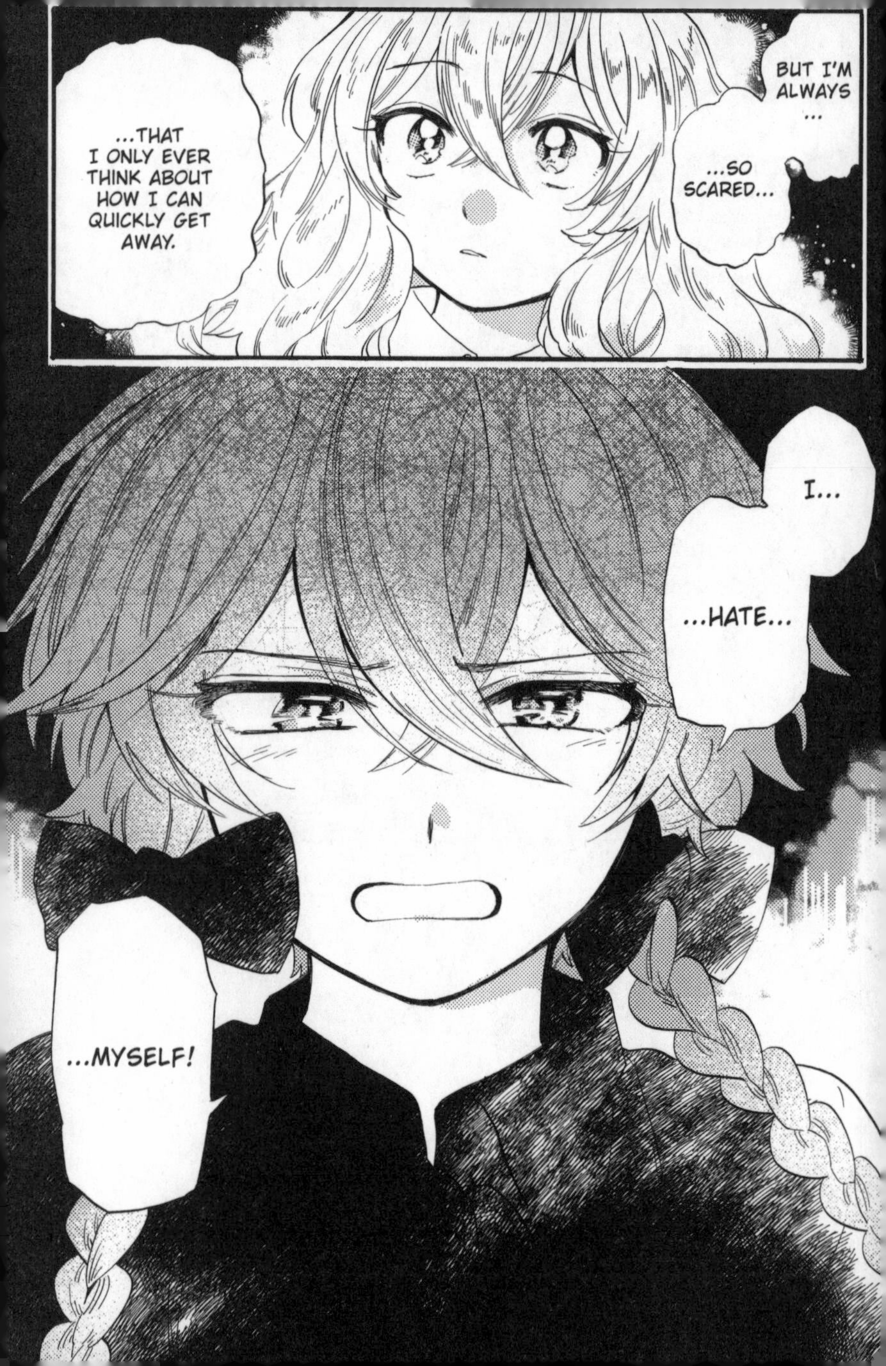
BUT I'M ALWAYS ...
...SO SCARED...
...THAT I ONLY EVER THINK ABOUT HOW I CAN QUICKLY GET AWAY.
I...
...HATE...
...MYSELF!

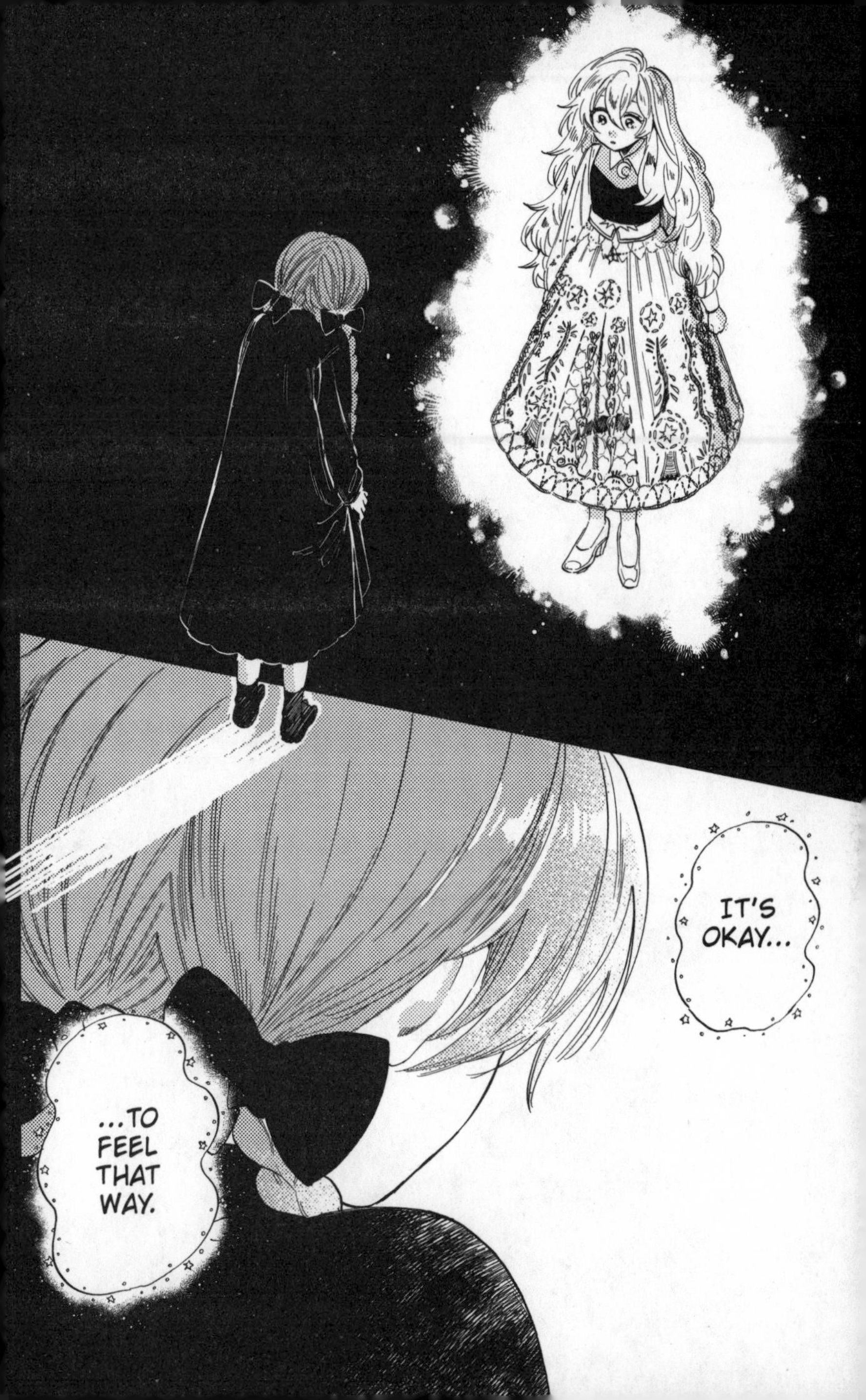
IT'S OKAY...
...TO FEEL THAT WAY.

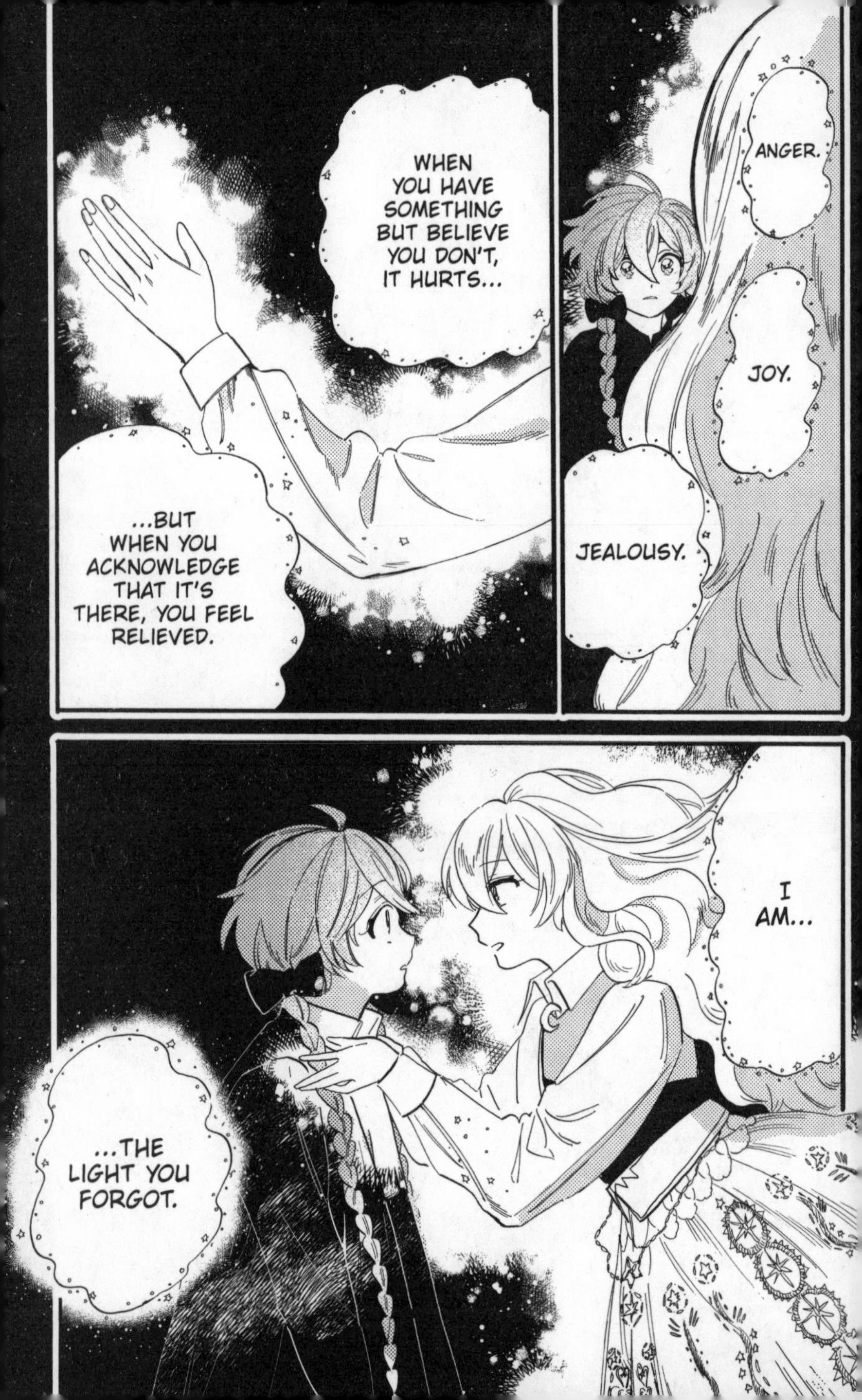
ANGER.
JOY.
JEALOUSY.
WHEN YOU HAVE SOMETHING BUT BELIEVE YOU DON'T, IT HURTS...
...BUT WHEN YOU ACKNOWLEDGE THAT IT'S THERE, YOU FEEL RELIEVED.
I AM...
...THE LIGHT YOU FORGOT.

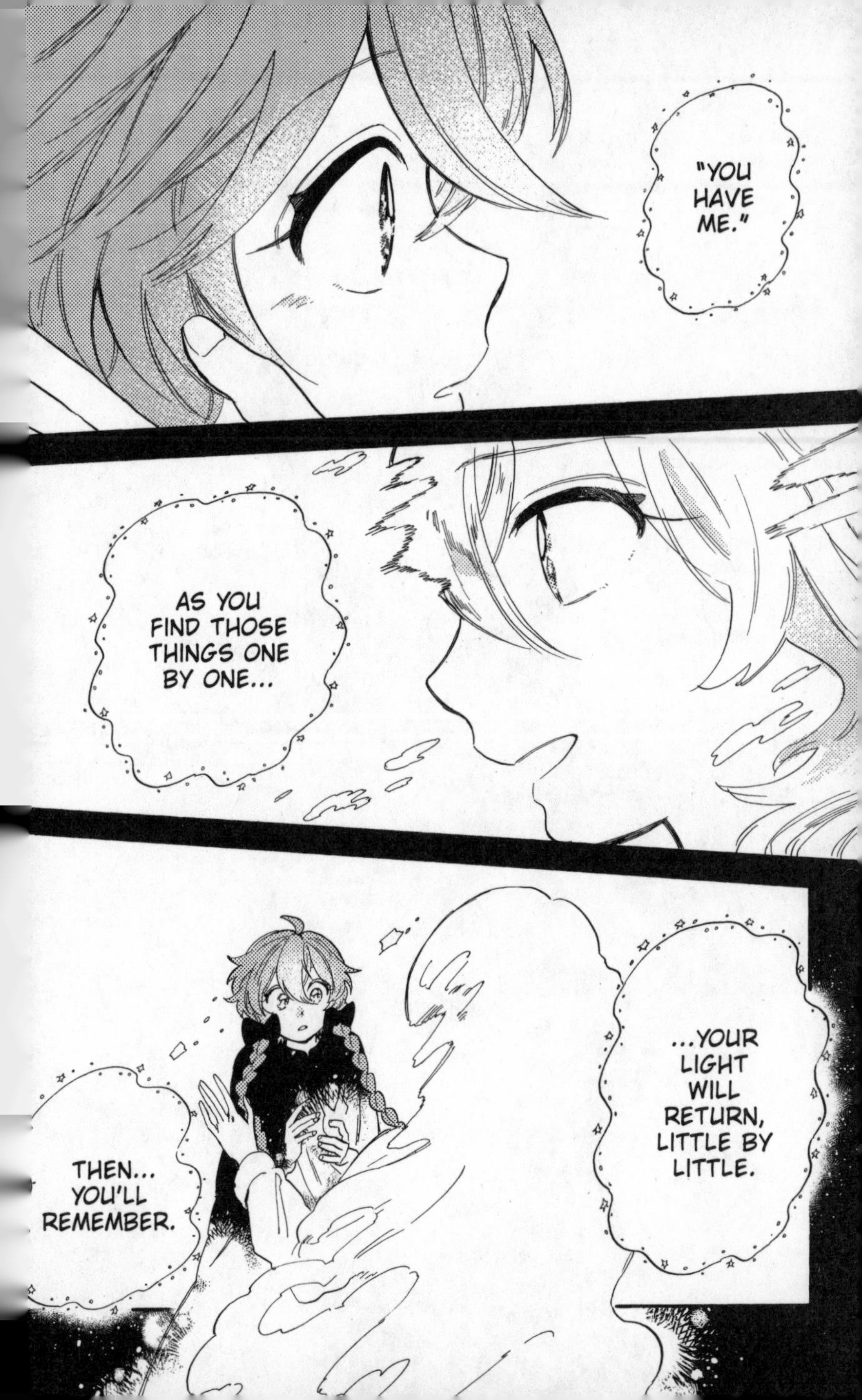
"YOU HAVE ME."
AS YOU FIND THOSE THINGS ONE BY ONE...
...YOUR LIGHT WILL RETURN, LITTLE BY LITTLE.
THEN... YOU'LL REMEMBER.

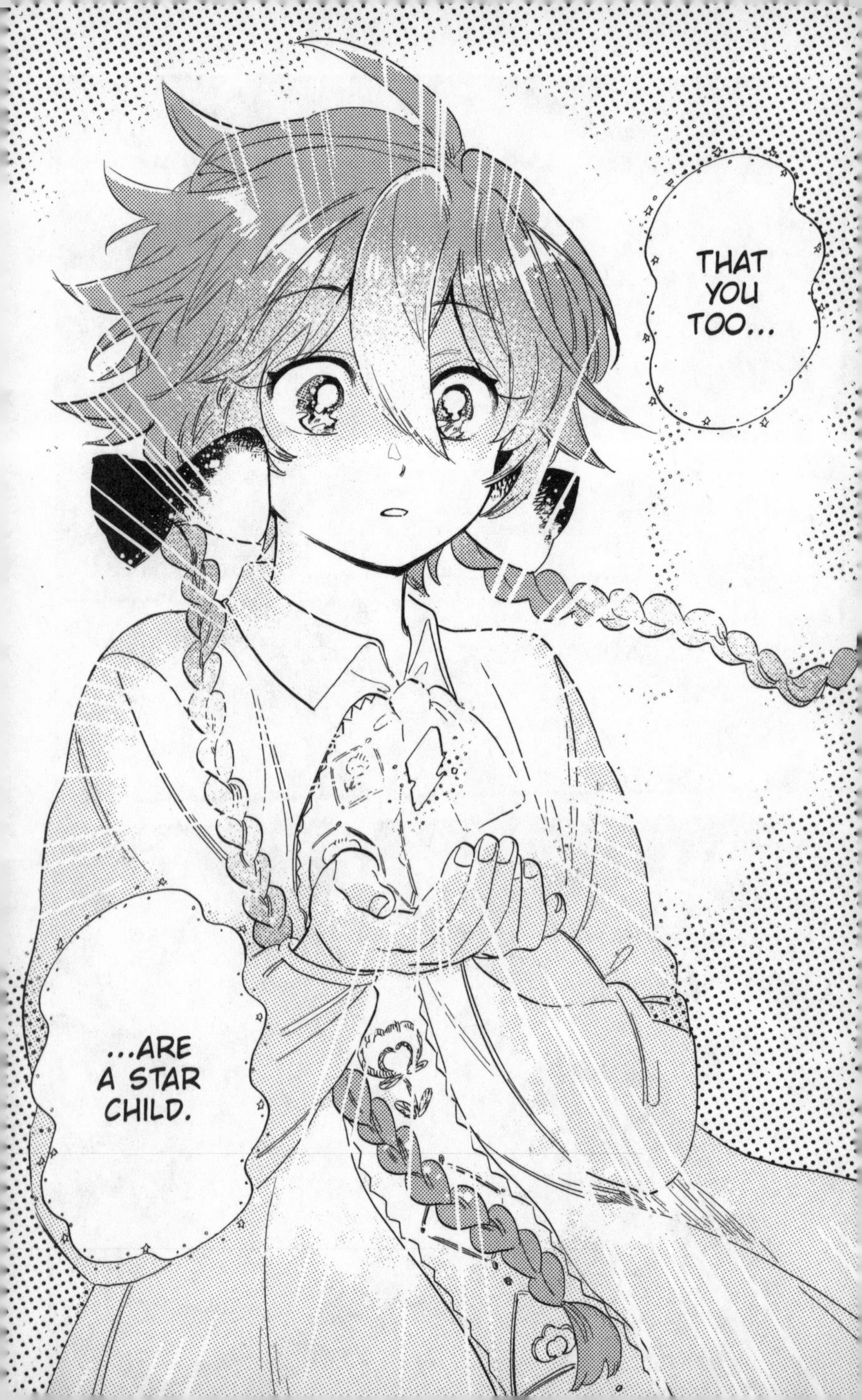
THAT YOU TOO...
...ARE A STAR CHILD.

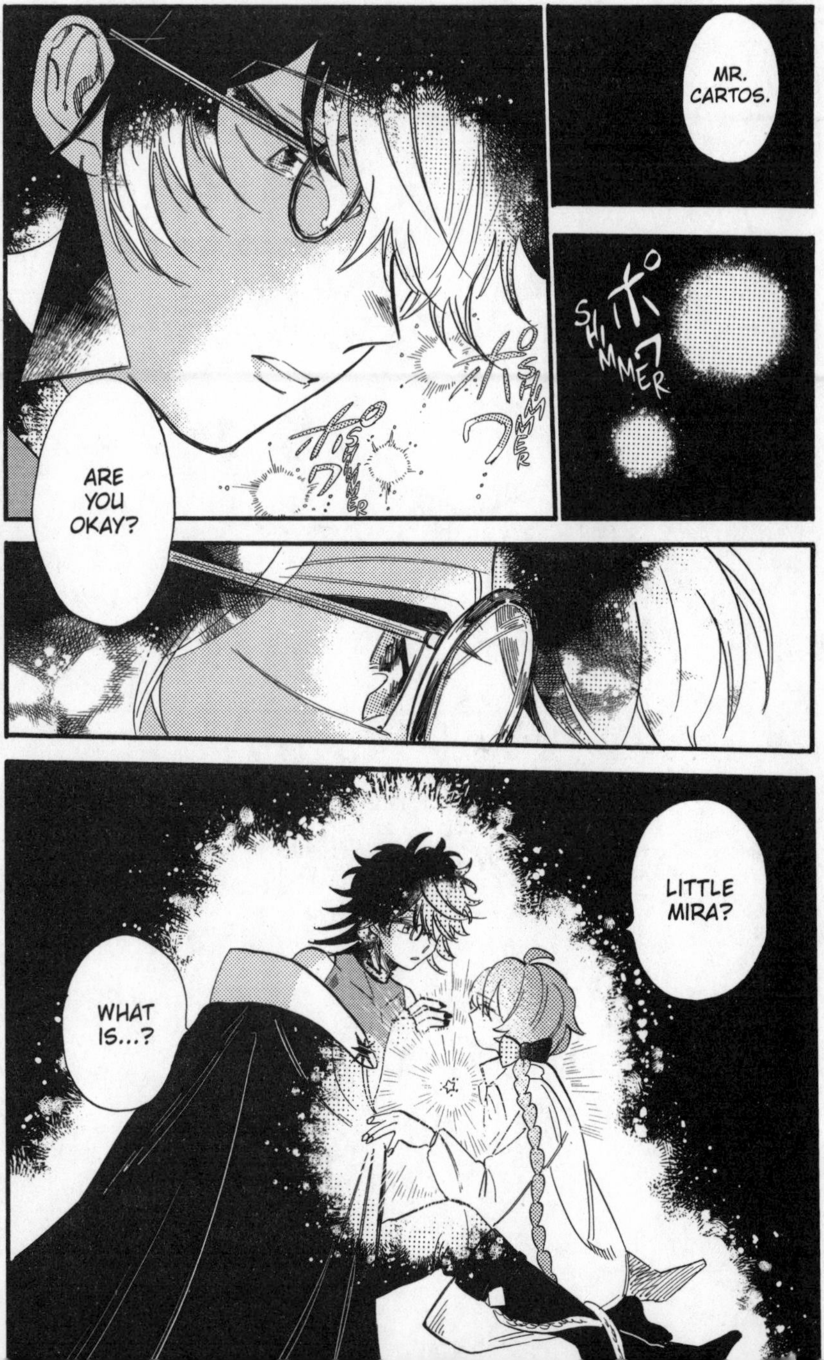
MR. CARTOS.
SHIMMER
SHIMMER
SHIMMER
ARE YOU OKAY?
LITTLE MIRA?
WHAT IS...?

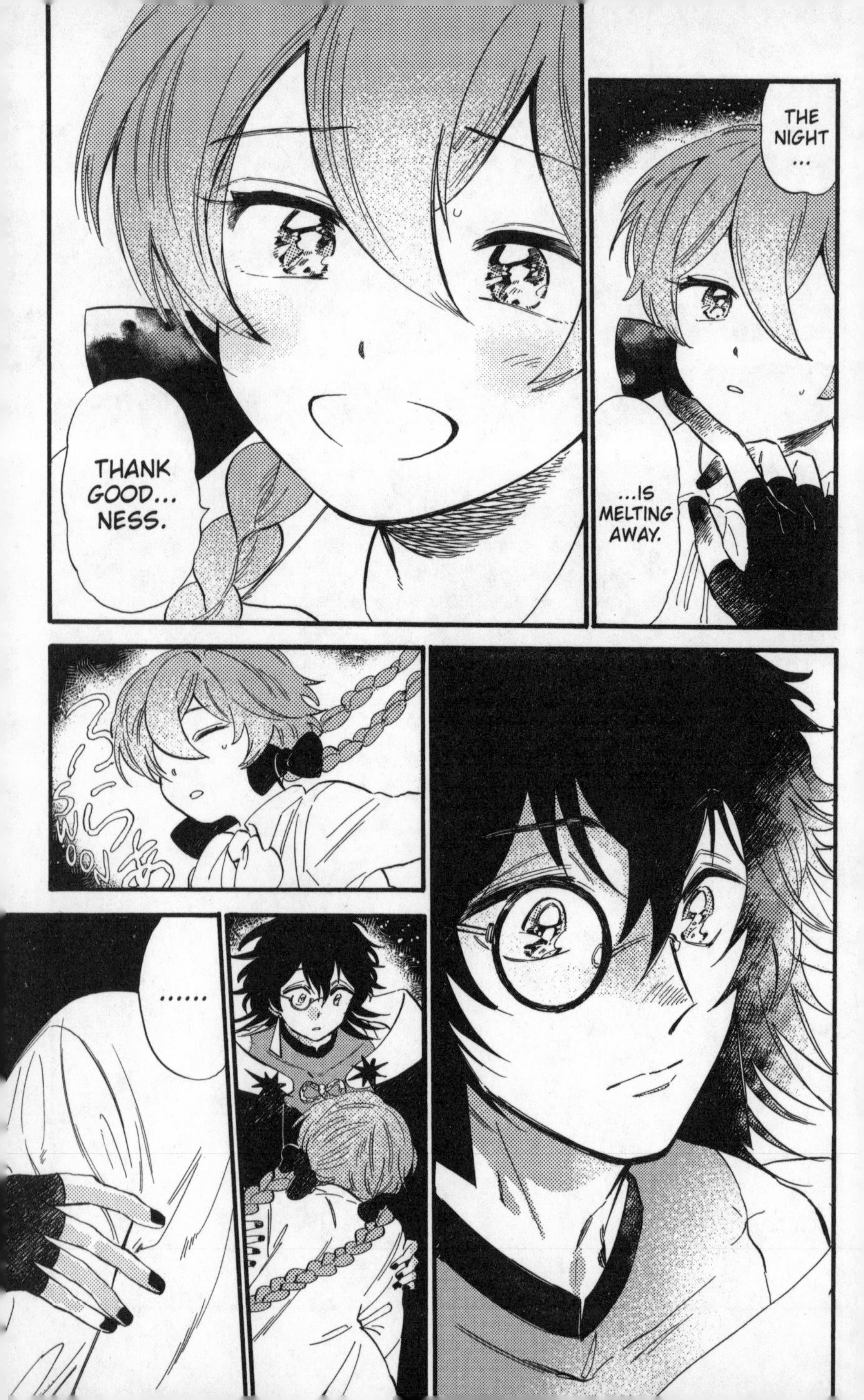
THE NIGHT...
...IS MELTING AWAY.
THANK GOOD... NESS.
......

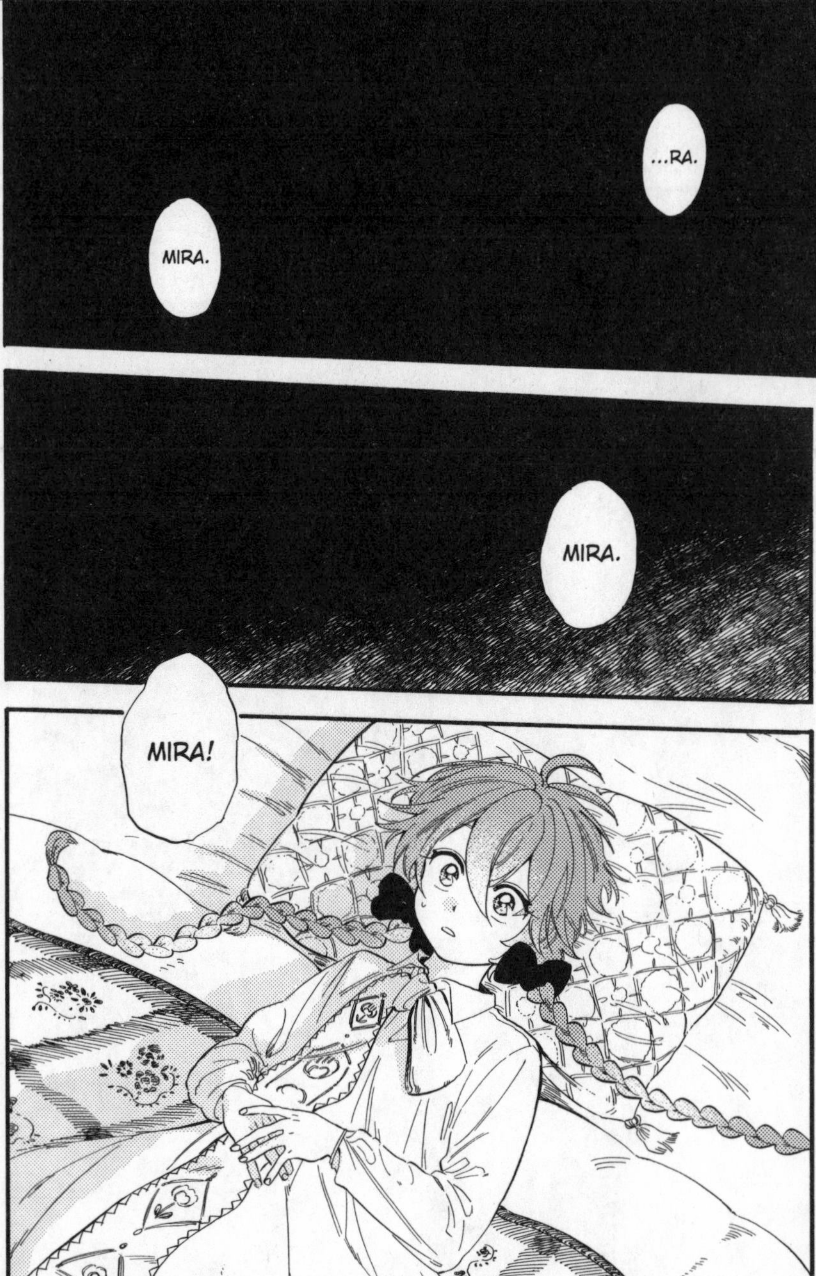
...RA.
MIRA.
MIRA.
MIRA!

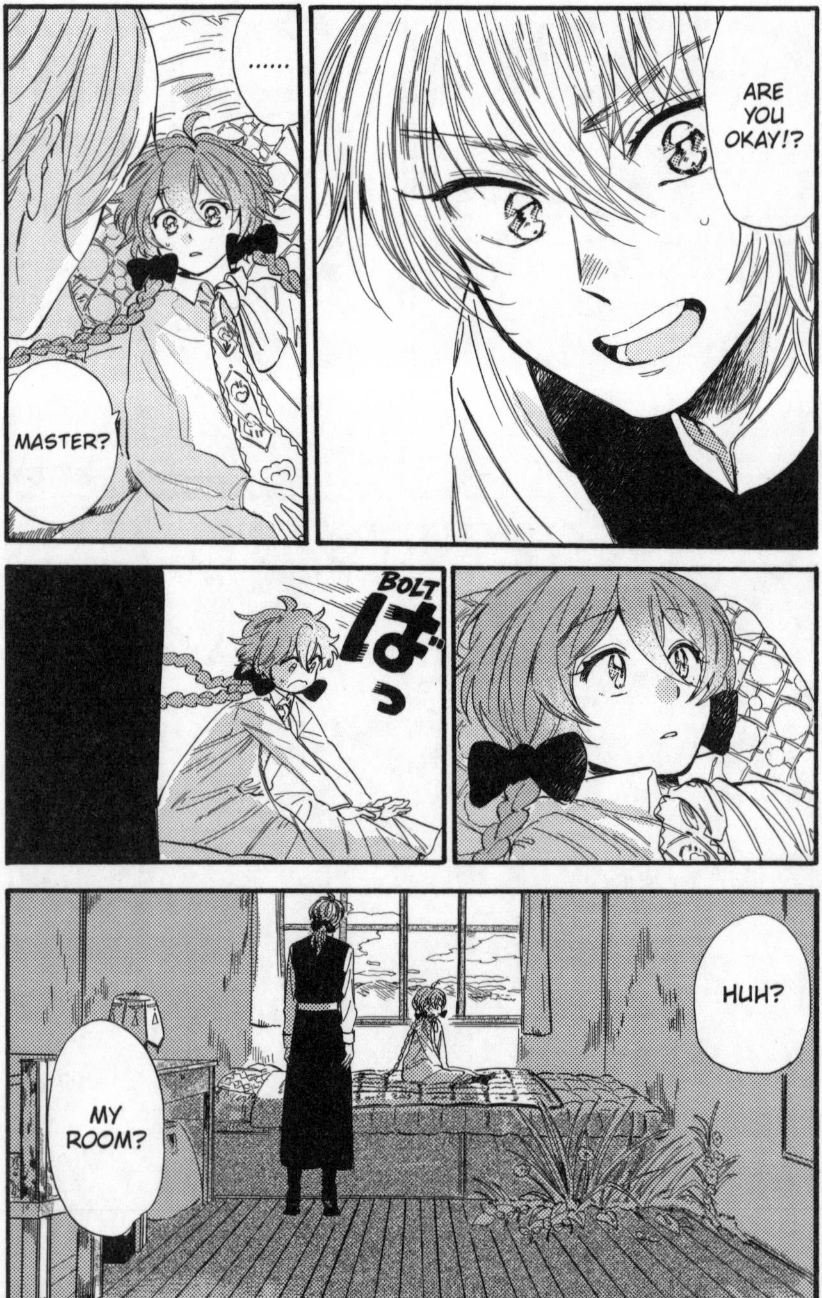
ARE YOU OKAY!?
......
MASTER?
BOLT
ばっ
HUH?
MY ROOM?

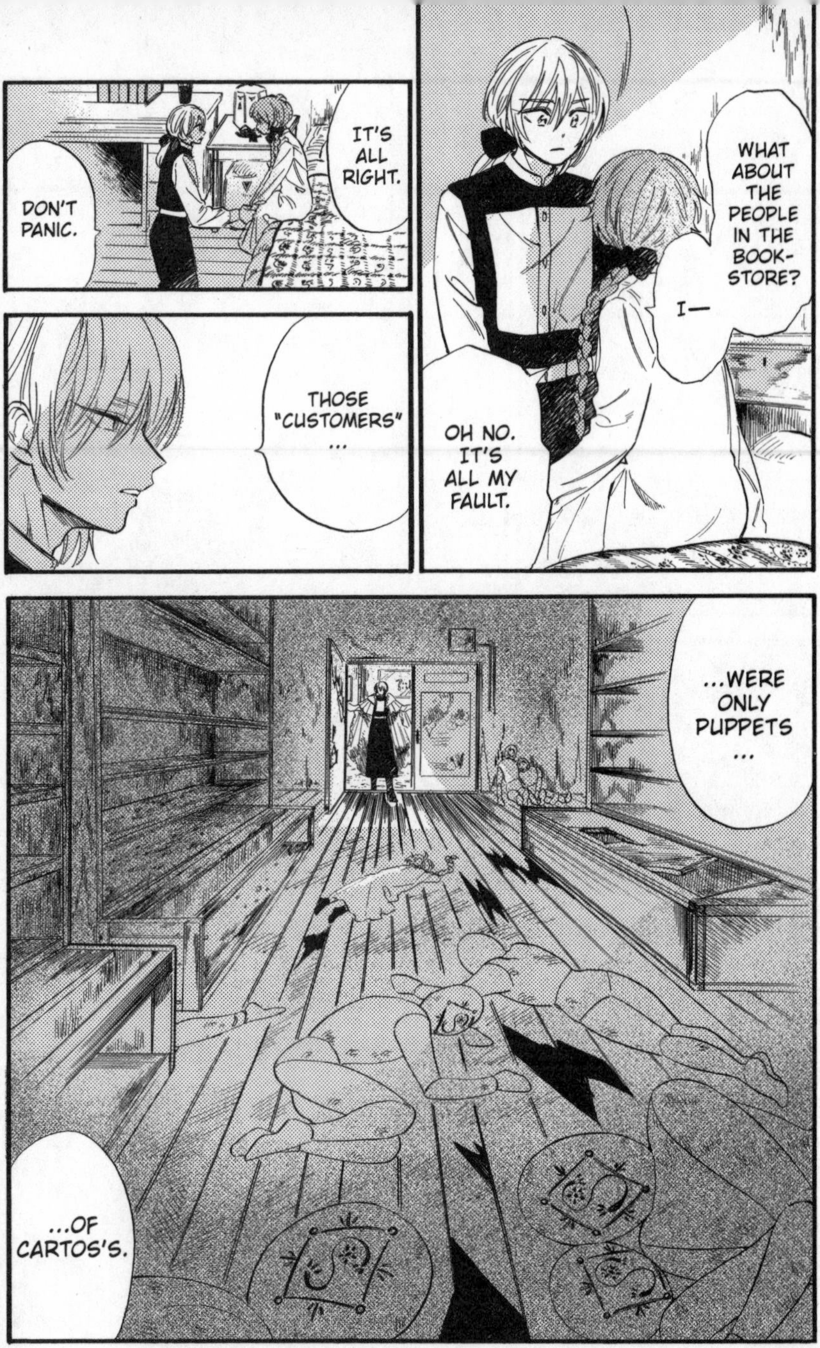

WHAT ABOUT THE PEOPLE IN THE BOOK-STORE?
I—
OH NO. IT'S ALL MY FAULT.
IT'S ALL RIGHT.
DON'T PANIC.
THOSE "CUSTOMERS"...
...WERE ONLY PUPPETS...
...OF CARTOS'S.

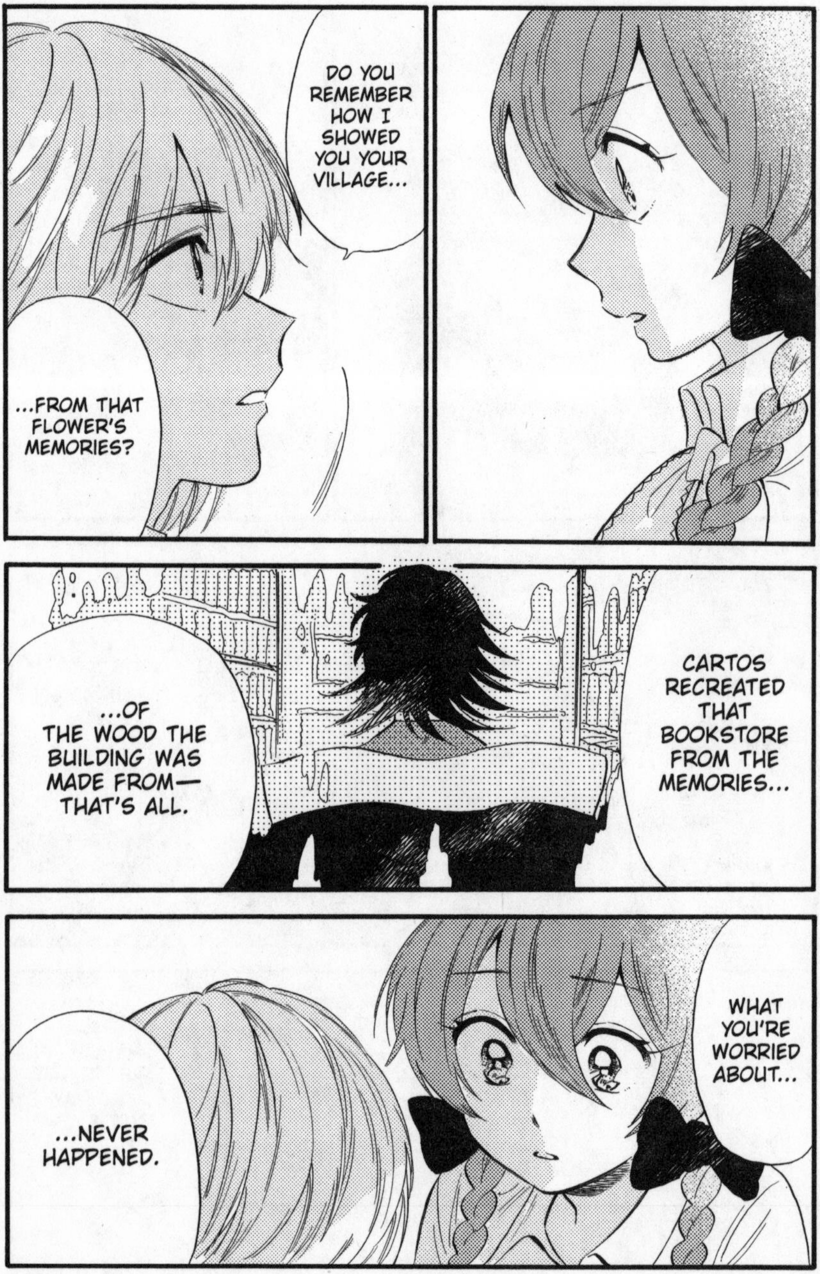
DO YOU REMEMBER HOW I SHOWED YOU YOUR VILLAGE...
...FROM THAT FLOWER'S MEMORIES?
CARTOS RECREATED THAT BOOKSTORE FROM THE MEMORIES...
...OF THE WOOD THE BUILDING WAS MADE FROM—THAT'S ALL.
WHAT YOU'RE WORRIED ABOUT...
...NEVER HAPPENED.

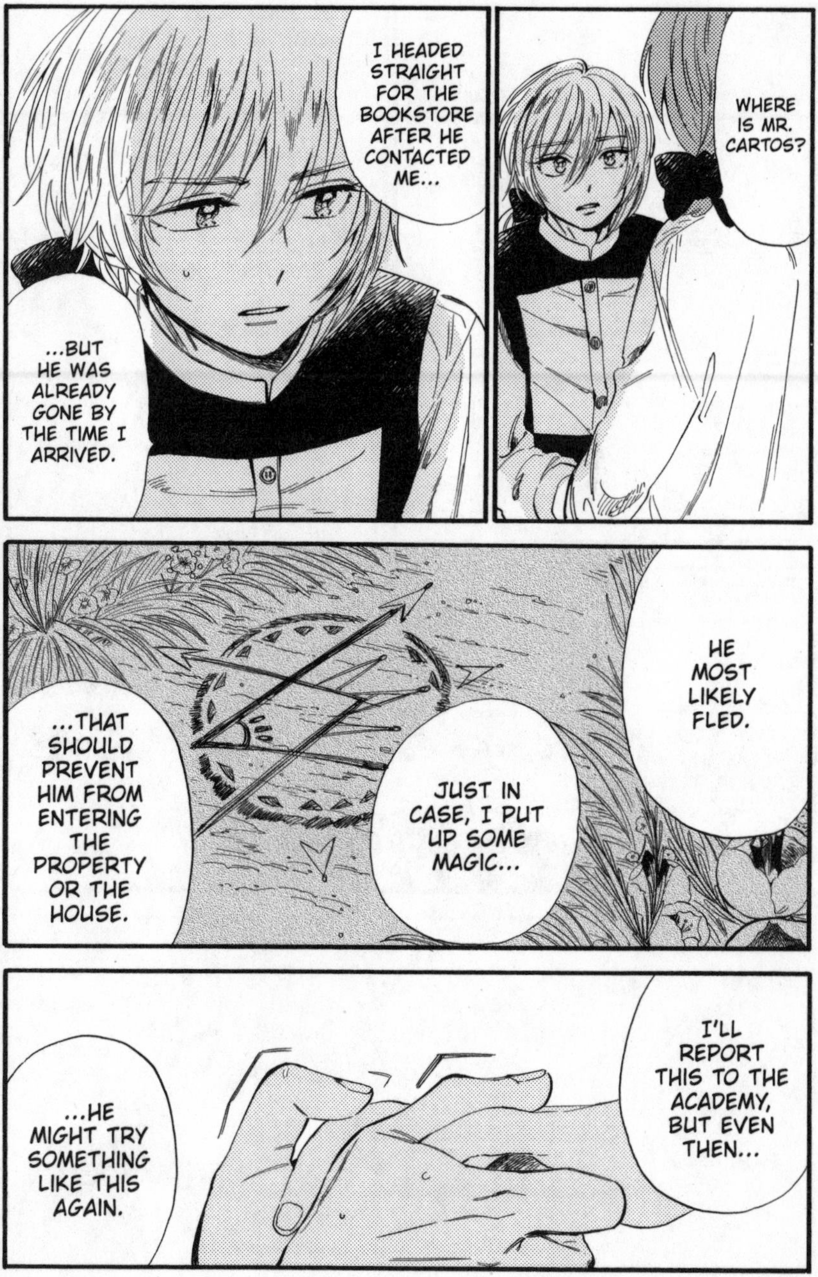
WHERE IS MR. CARTOS?
I HEADED STRAIGHT FOR THE BOOKSTORE AFTER HE CONTACTED ME...
...BUT HE WAS ALREADY GONE BY THE TIME I ARRIVED.
HE MOST LIKELY FLED.
JUST IN CASE, I PUT UP SOME MAGIC...
...THAT SHOULD PREVENT HIM FROM ENTERING THE PROPERTY OR THE HOUSE.
I'LL REPORT THIS TO THE ACADEMY, BUT EVEN THEN...
...HE MIGHT TRY SOMETHING LIKE THIS AGAIN.

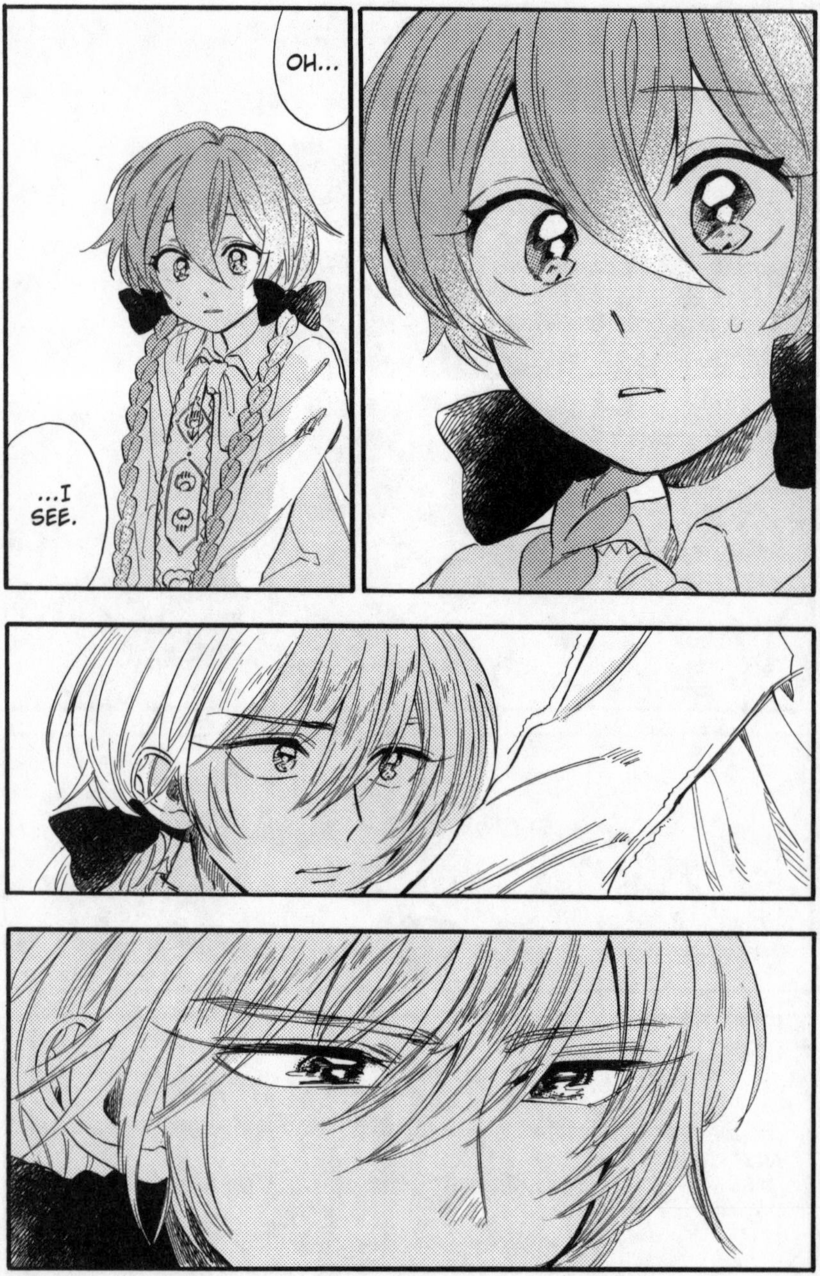
OH...
...I SEE.

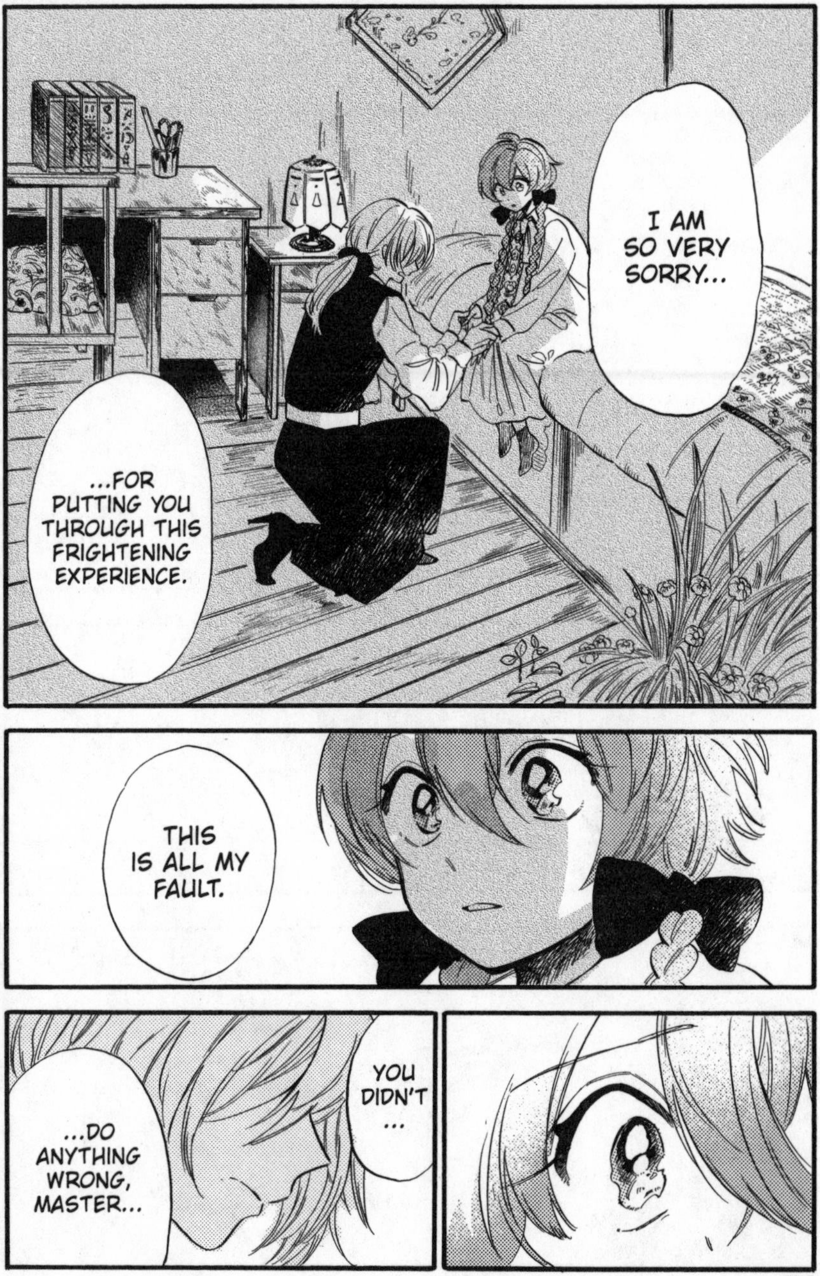
I AM SO VERY SORRY...
...FOR PUTTING YOU THROUGH THIS FRIGHTENING EXPERIENCE.
THIS IS ALL MY FAULT.
YOU DIDN'T ...
...DO ANYTHING WRONG, MASTER...

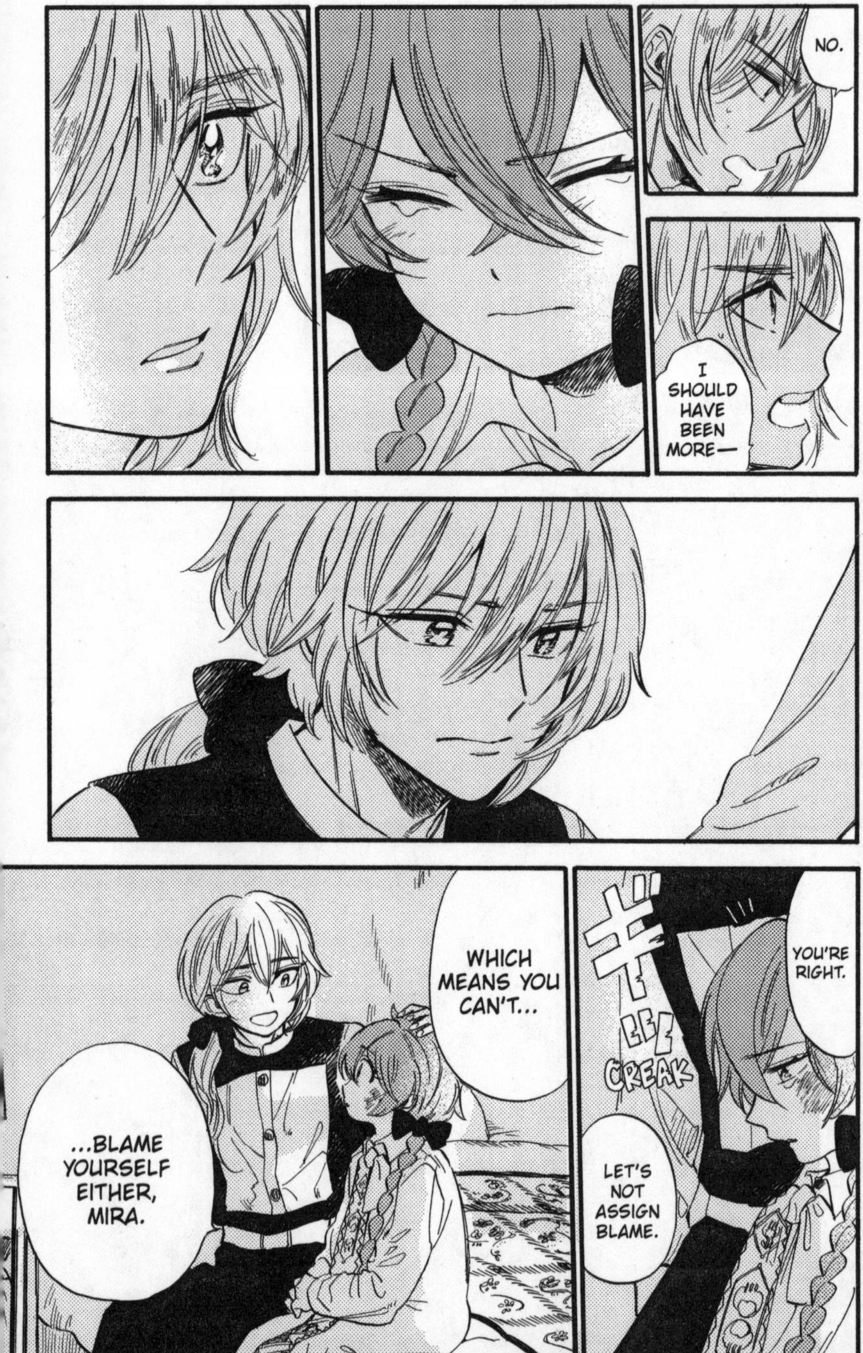
NO.
I SHOULD HAVE BEEN MORE—
YOU'RE RIGHT.
CREAK
LET'S NOT ASSIGN BLAME.
WHICH MEANS YOU CAN'T...
...BLAME YOURSELF EITHER, MIRA.

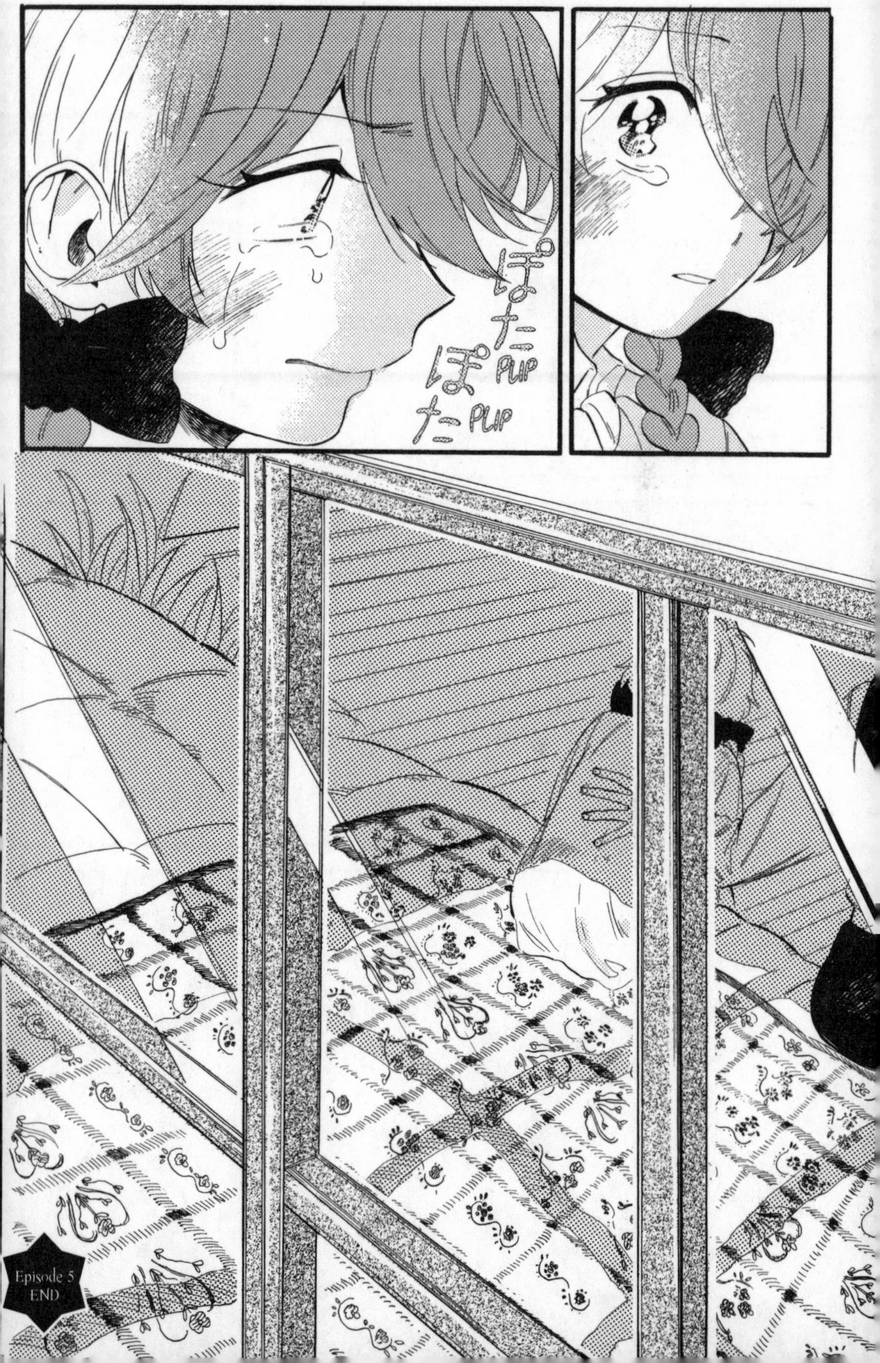
ぽた PLIP
ぽた PLIP
Episode 5 END

Call the Name of the Night

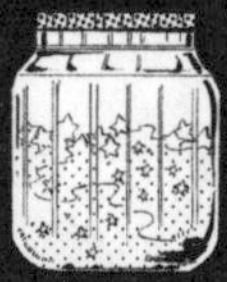

Call the Name of the Night

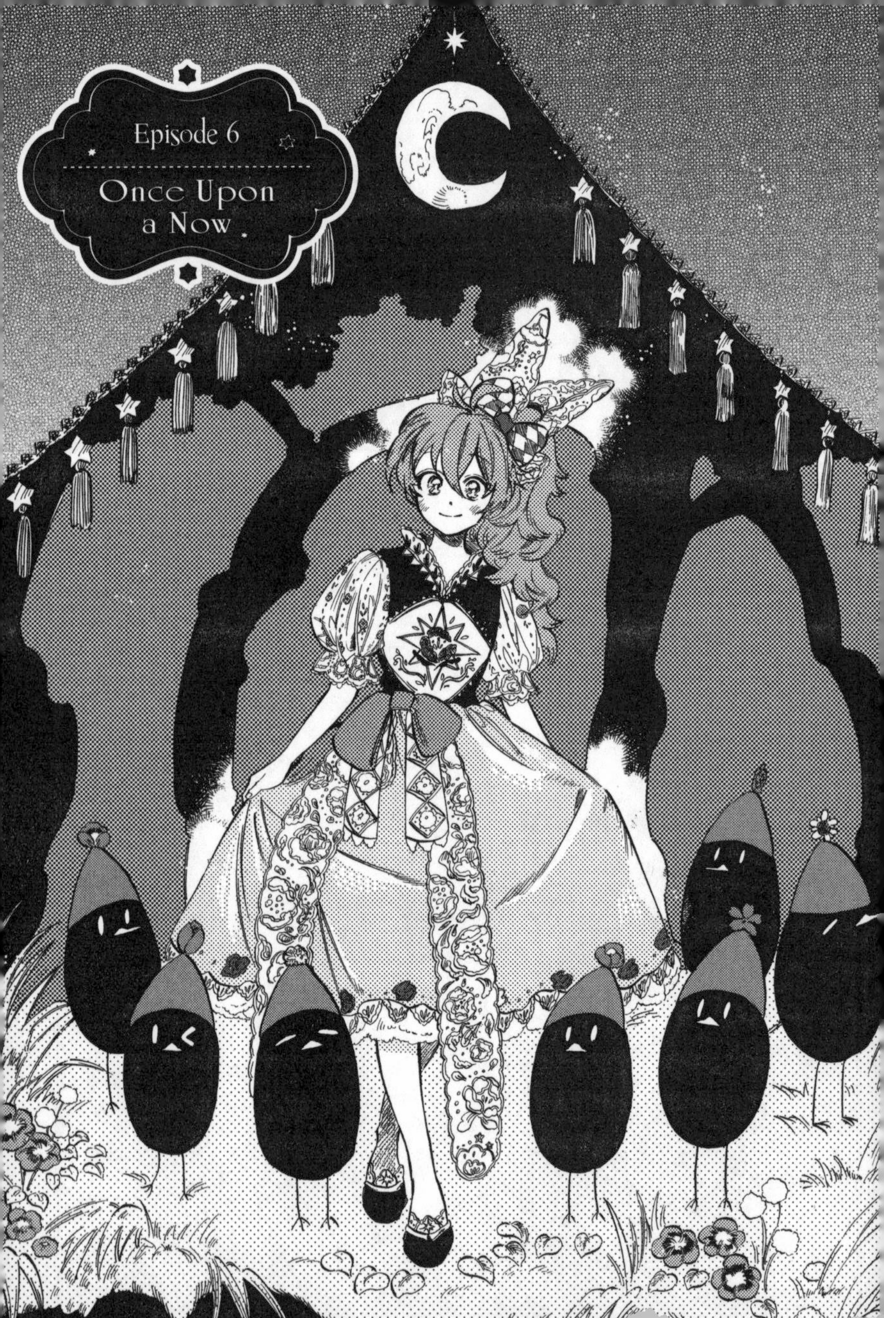
Episode 6
Once Upon a Now

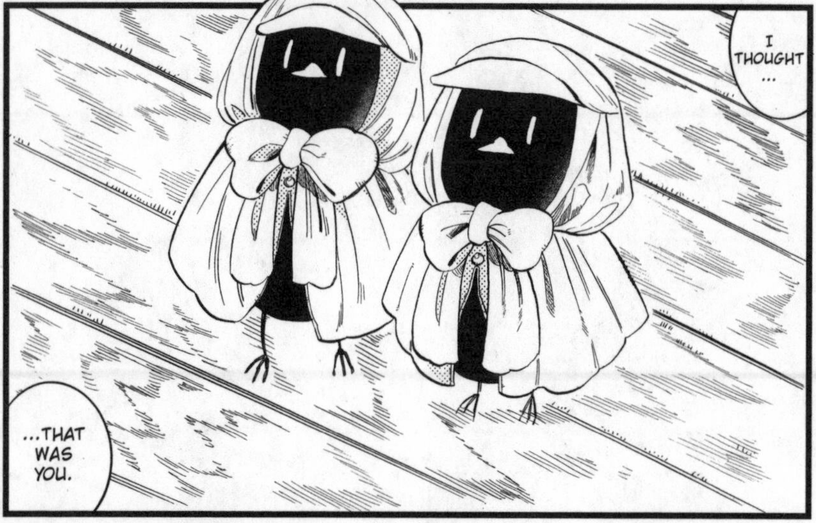
I THOUGHT...
...THAT WAS YOU.

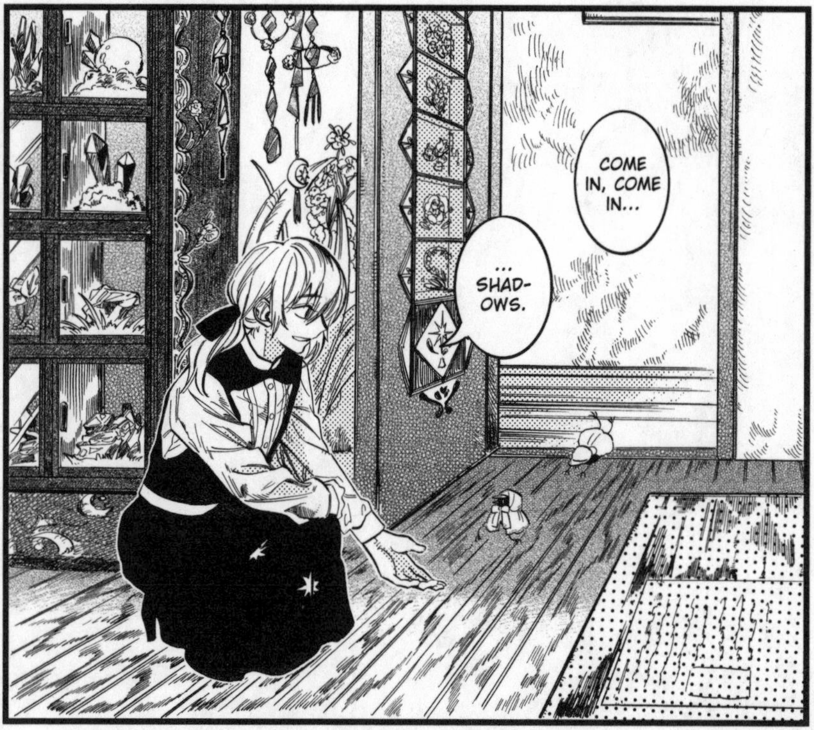
COME IN, COME IN...
...SHADOWS.

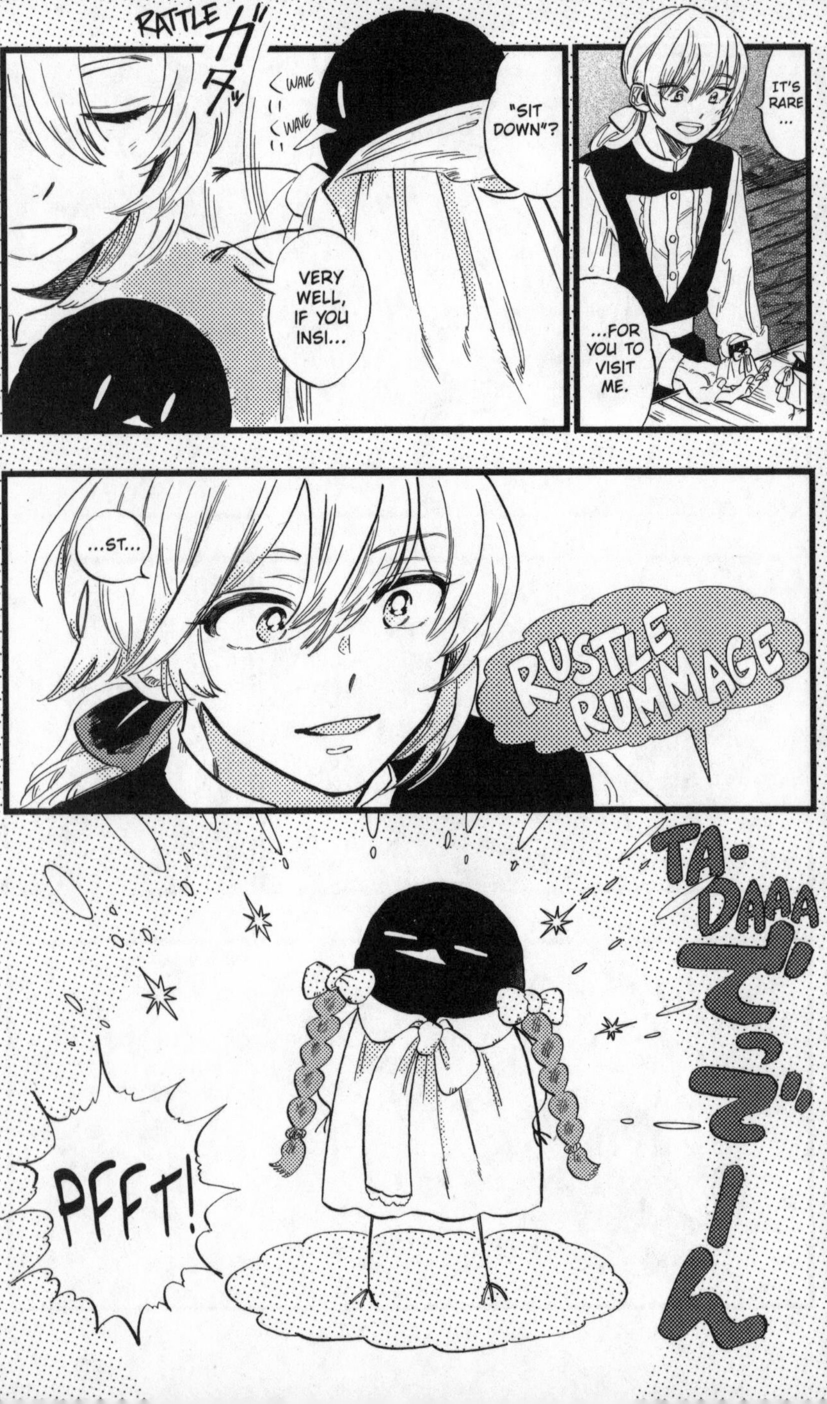
IT'S RARE...
...FOR YOU TO VISIT ME.
"SIT DOWN"?
WAVE
WAVE
RATTLE ガタッ
VERY WELL, IF YOU INSI...
RUSTLE RUMMAGE
...ST...
TA-DAAA
PFFT!

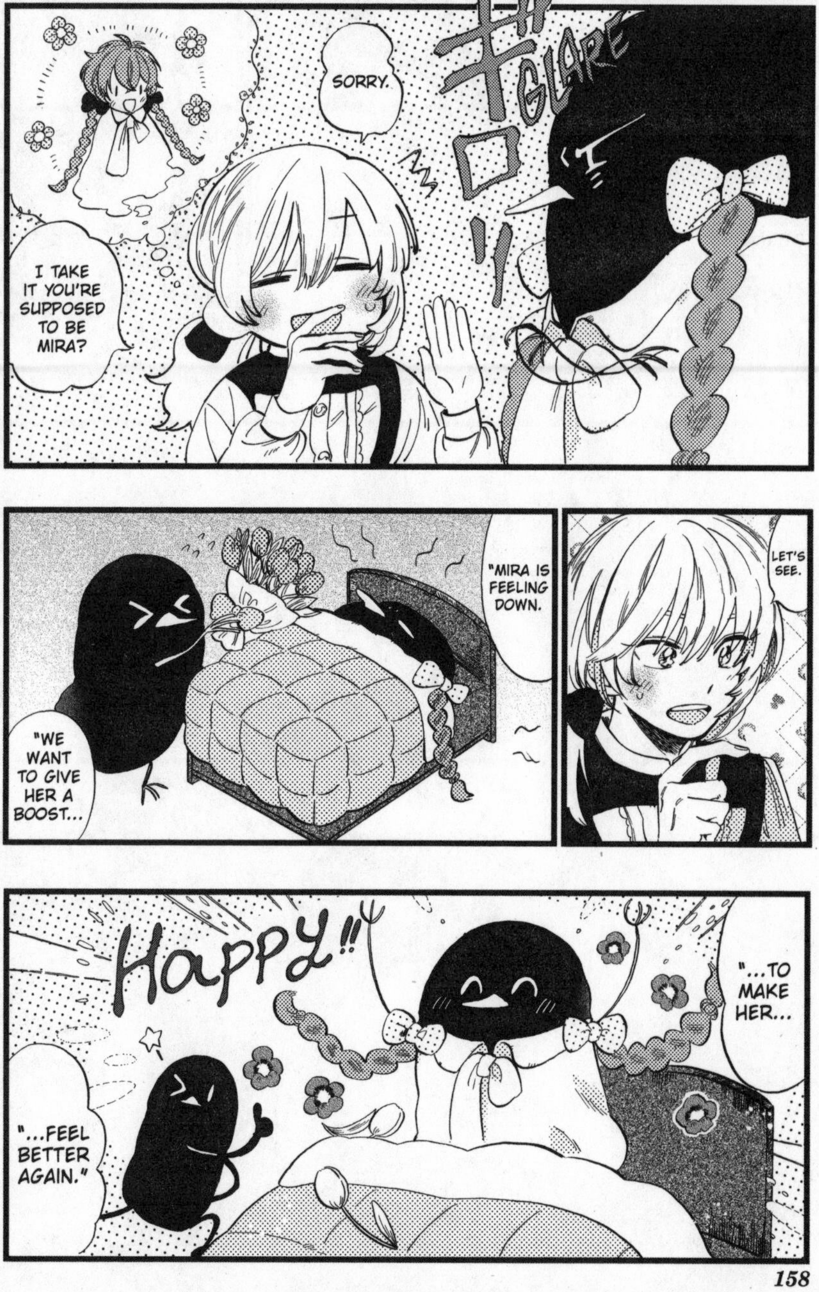
GLARE
SORRY.
I TAKE IT YOU'RE SUPPOSED TO BE MIRA?
LET'S SEE.
"MIRA IS FEELING DOWN.
"WE WANT TO GIVE HER A BOOST...
"...TO MAKE HER...
HAPPY!!
"...FEEL BETTER AGAIN."

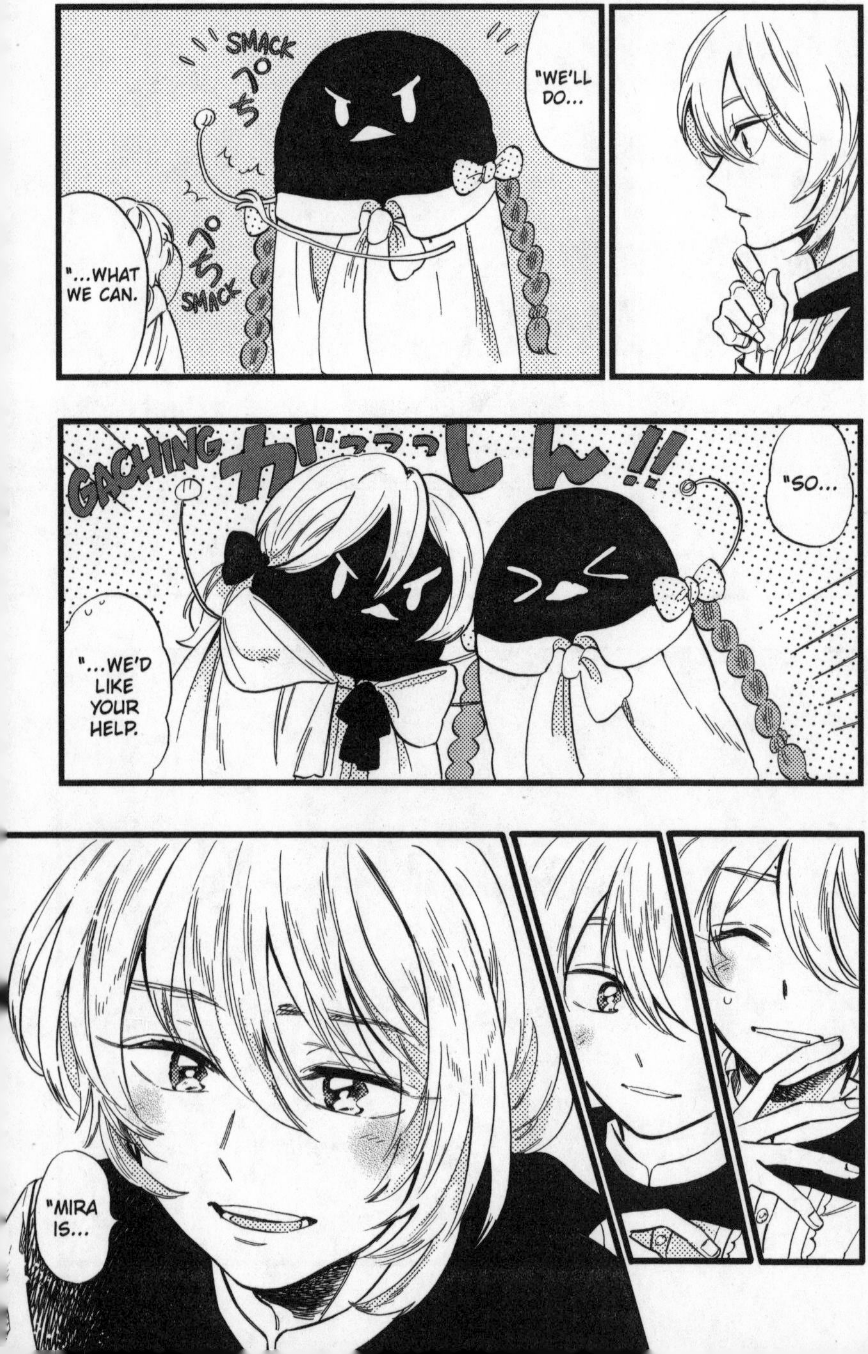
"WE'LL DO...
SMACK
ぺち
ぺち
SMACK
"...WHAT WE CAN.
"SO...
GACHING
がっっっしん!!
"...WE'D LIKE YOUR HELP.
"MIRA IS...

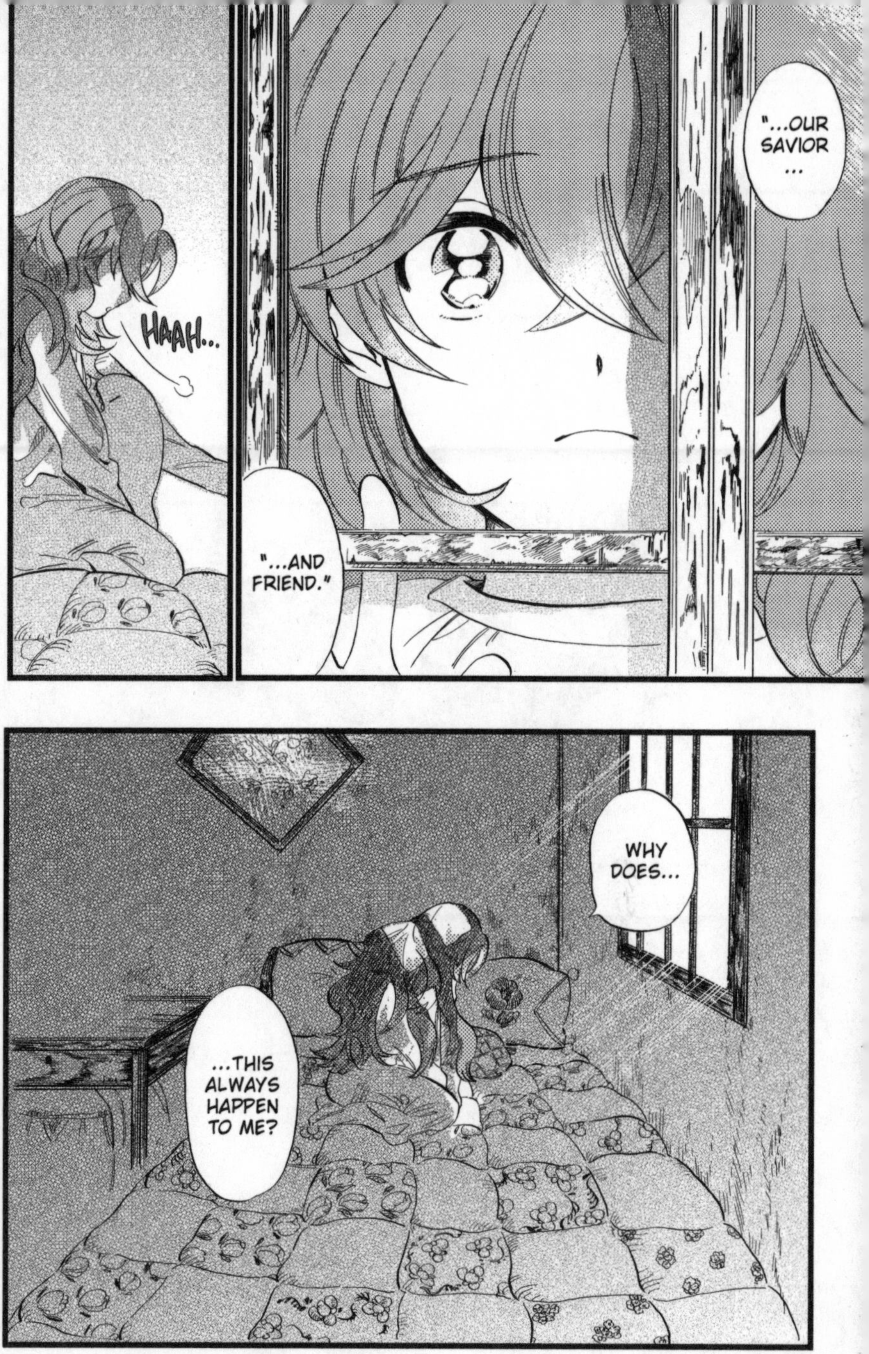
"...OUR SAVIOR ...
"...AND FRIEND."
HAAH...
WHY DOES...
...THIS ALWAYS HAPPEN TO ME?

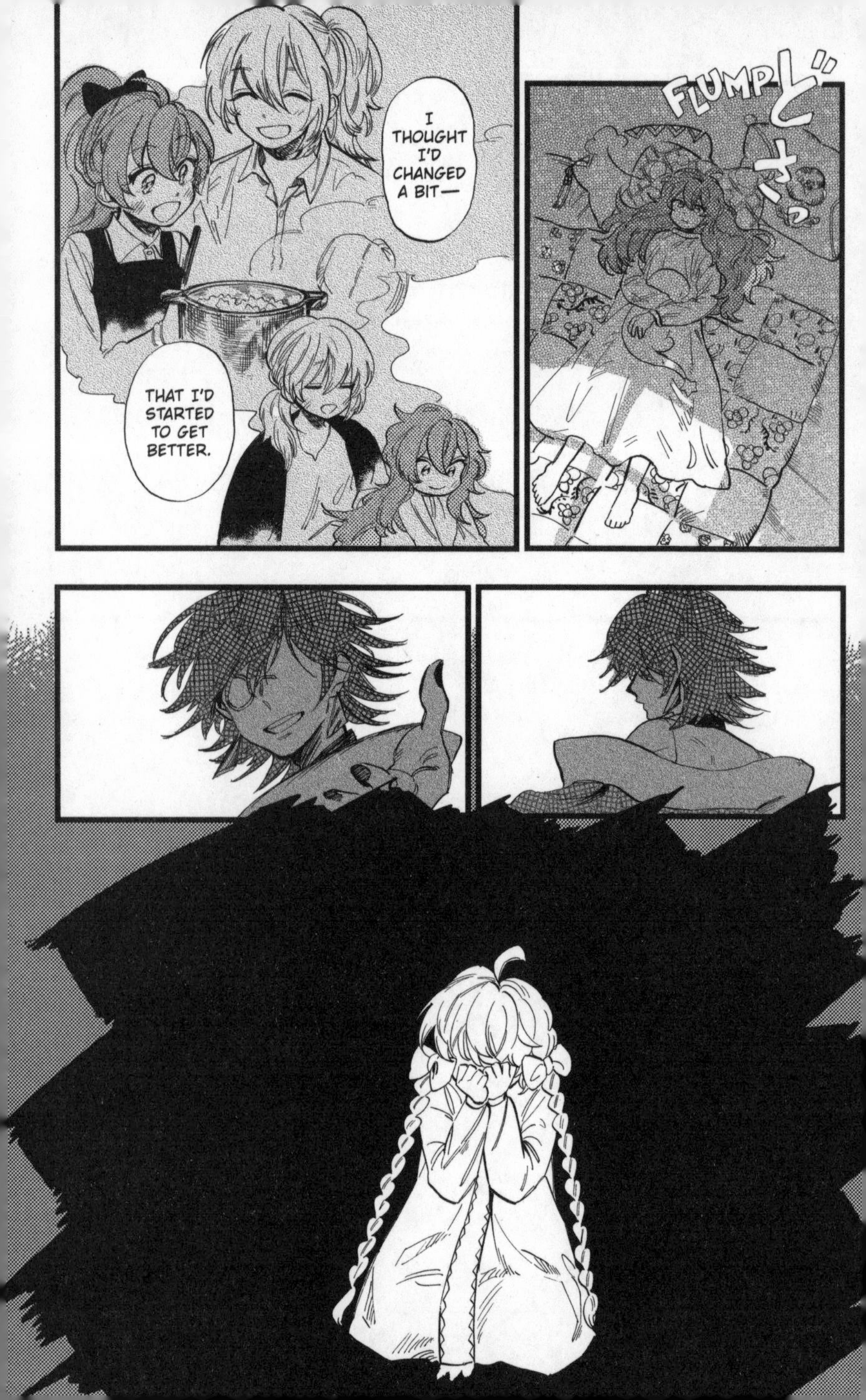
FLUMP
どさっ
I THOUGHT I'D CHANGED A BIT—
THAT I'D STARTED TO GET BETTER.

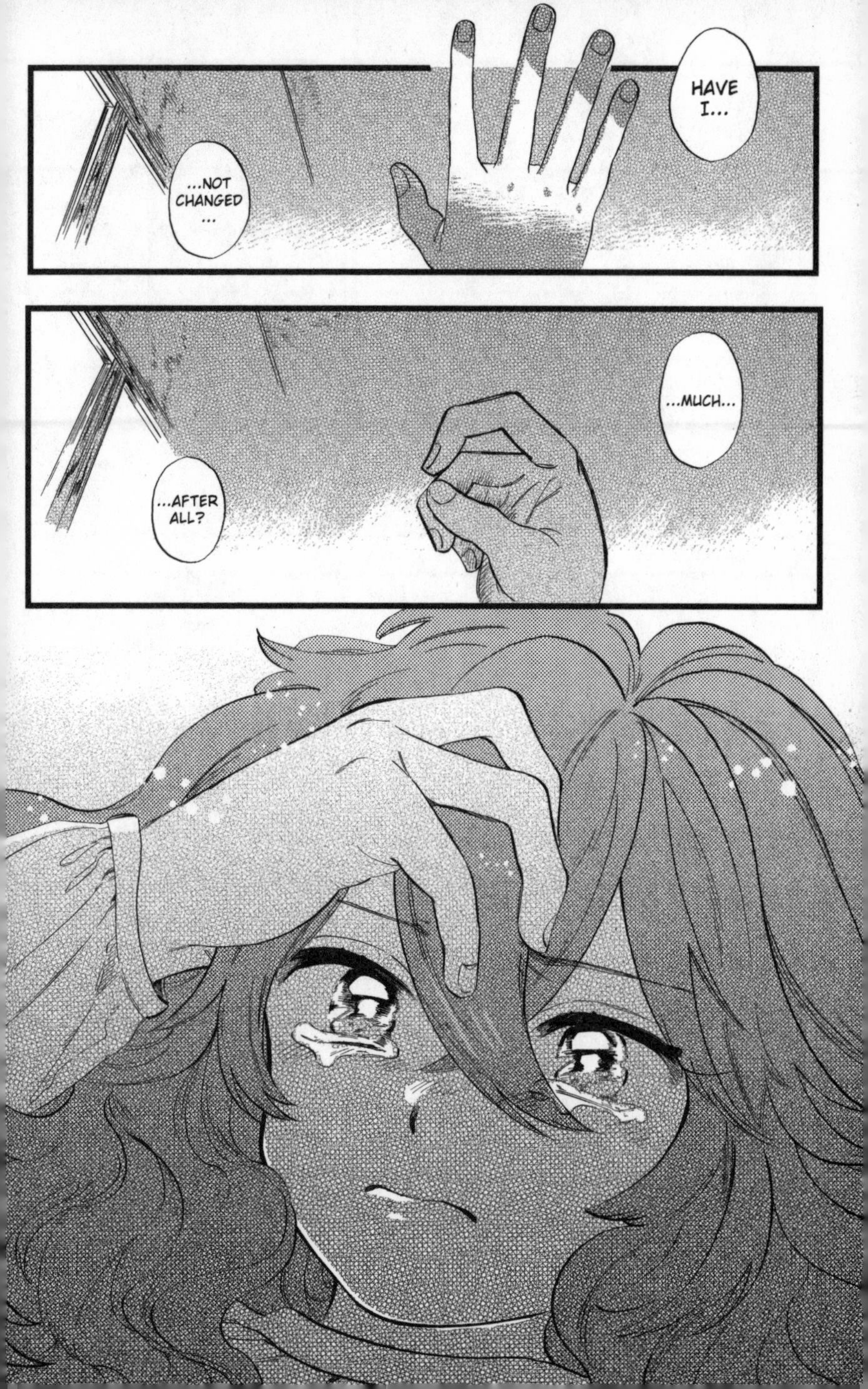
HAVE I...
...NOT CHANGED ...
...MUCH...
...AFTER ALL?

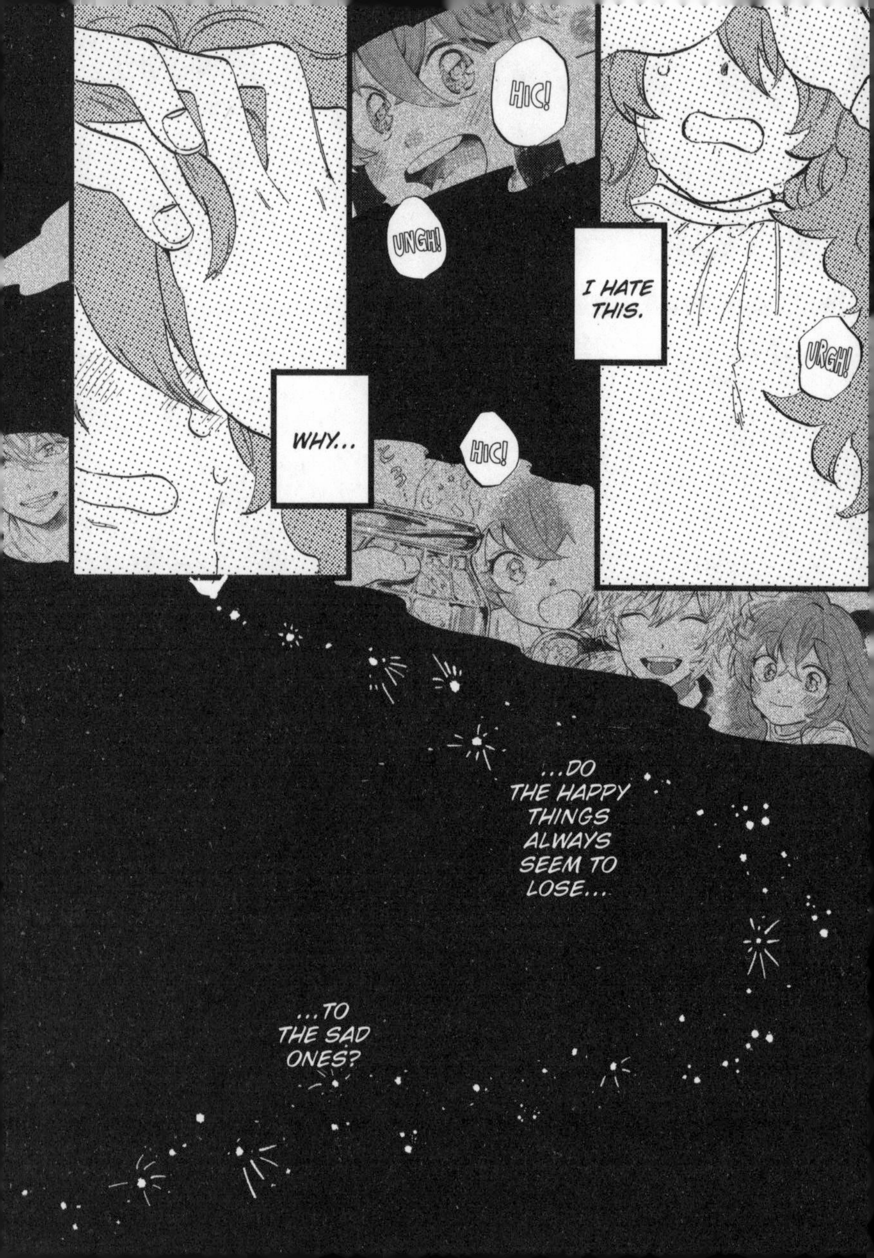
I HATE THIS.
URGH!
HIC!
UNGH!
WHY...
HIC!
...DO THE HAPPY THINGS ALWAYS SEEM TO LOSE...
...TO THE SAD ONES?

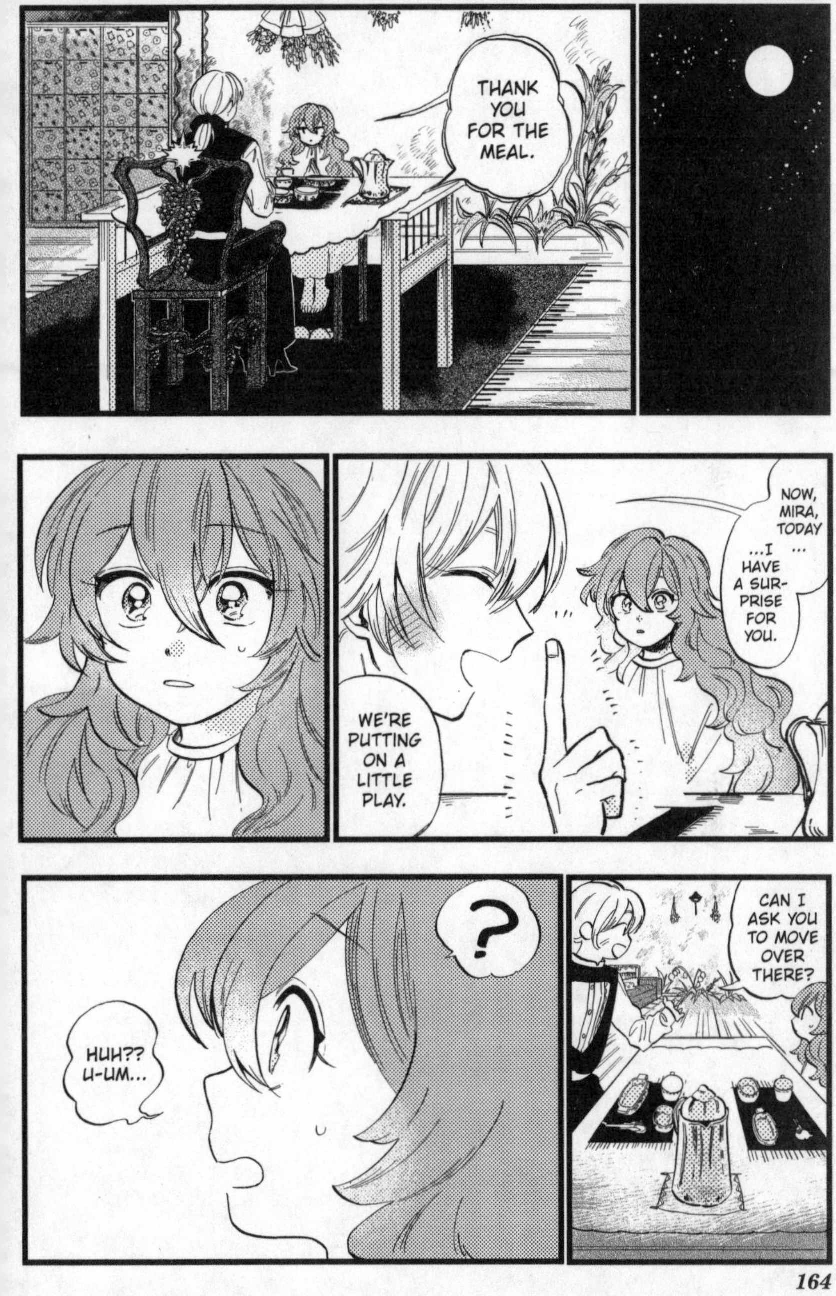
THANK YOU FOR THE MEAL.
NOW, MIRA, TODAY ...
...I HAVE A SURPRISE FOR YOU.
WE'RE PUTTING ON A LITTLE PLAY.
CAN I ASK YOU TO MOVE OVER THERE?
?
HUH?? U-UM...

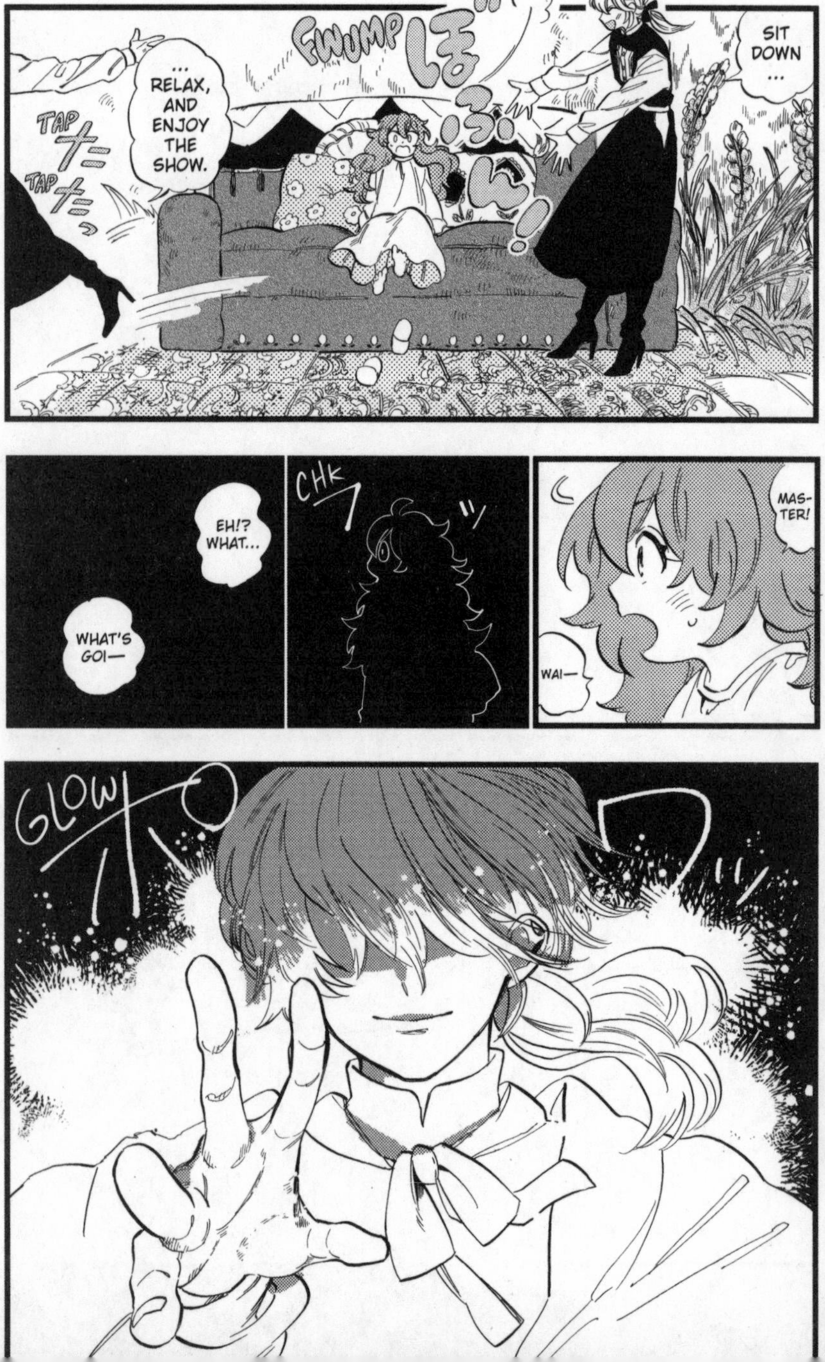
SIT DOWN ...
FWUMP
... RELAX, AND ENJOY THE SHOW.
TAP
TAP
MAS-TER!
WAI—
CHK
EH!? WHAT...
WHAT'S GOI—
GLOW

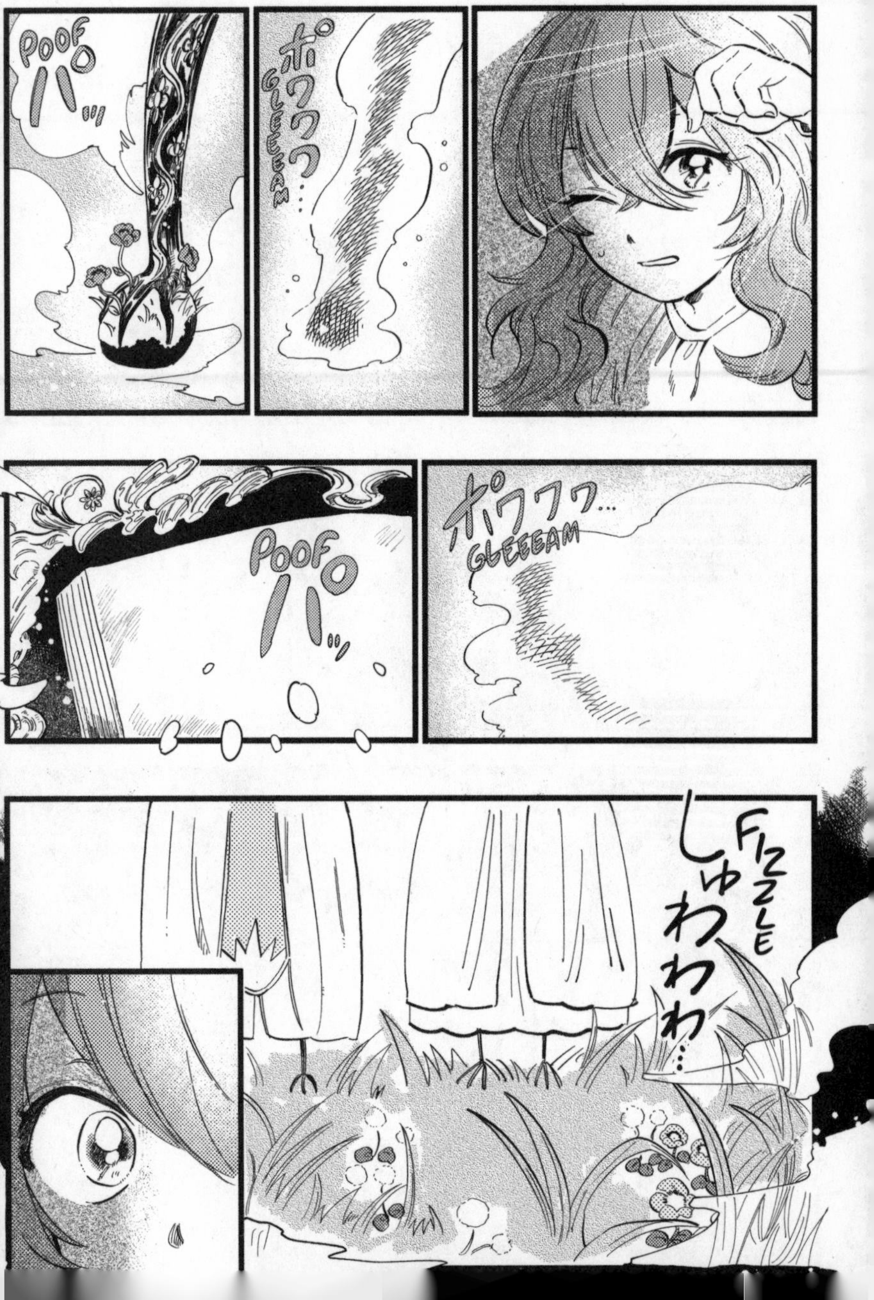
ポワワワ…
GLEEEAM
POOF
パッ
ポワワワ…
GLEEEAM
POOF
パッ
FIZZLE
しゅわわわ…

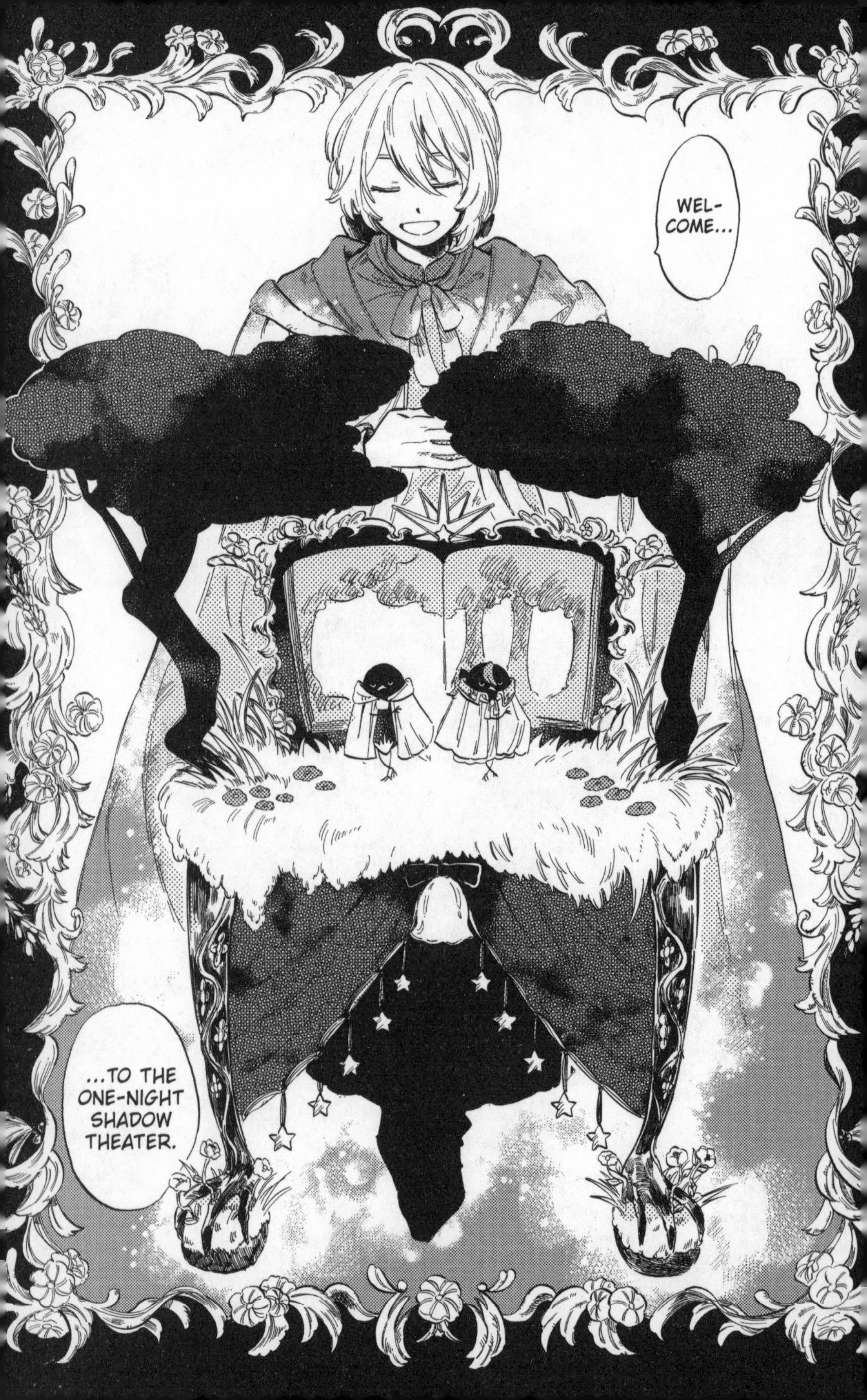
WEL-COME...
...TO THE ONE-NIGHT SHADOW THEATER.

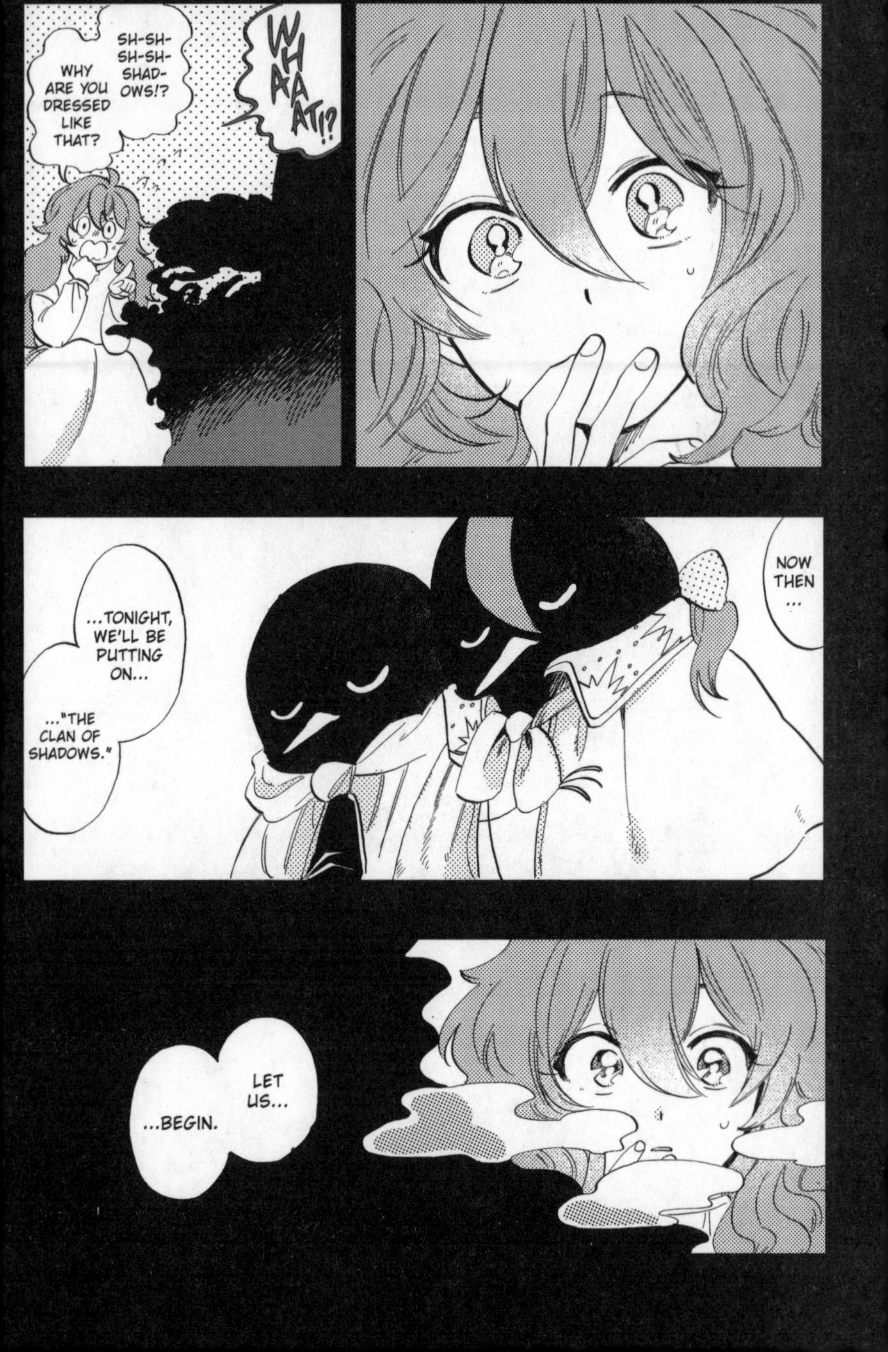
WHAAAT!?
SH-SH-SH-SH-SHADOWS!?
WHY ARE YOU DRESSED LIKE THAT?
NOW THEN...
...TONIGHT, WE'LL BE PUTTING ON...
..."THE CLAN OF SHADOWS."
LET US...
...BEGIN.

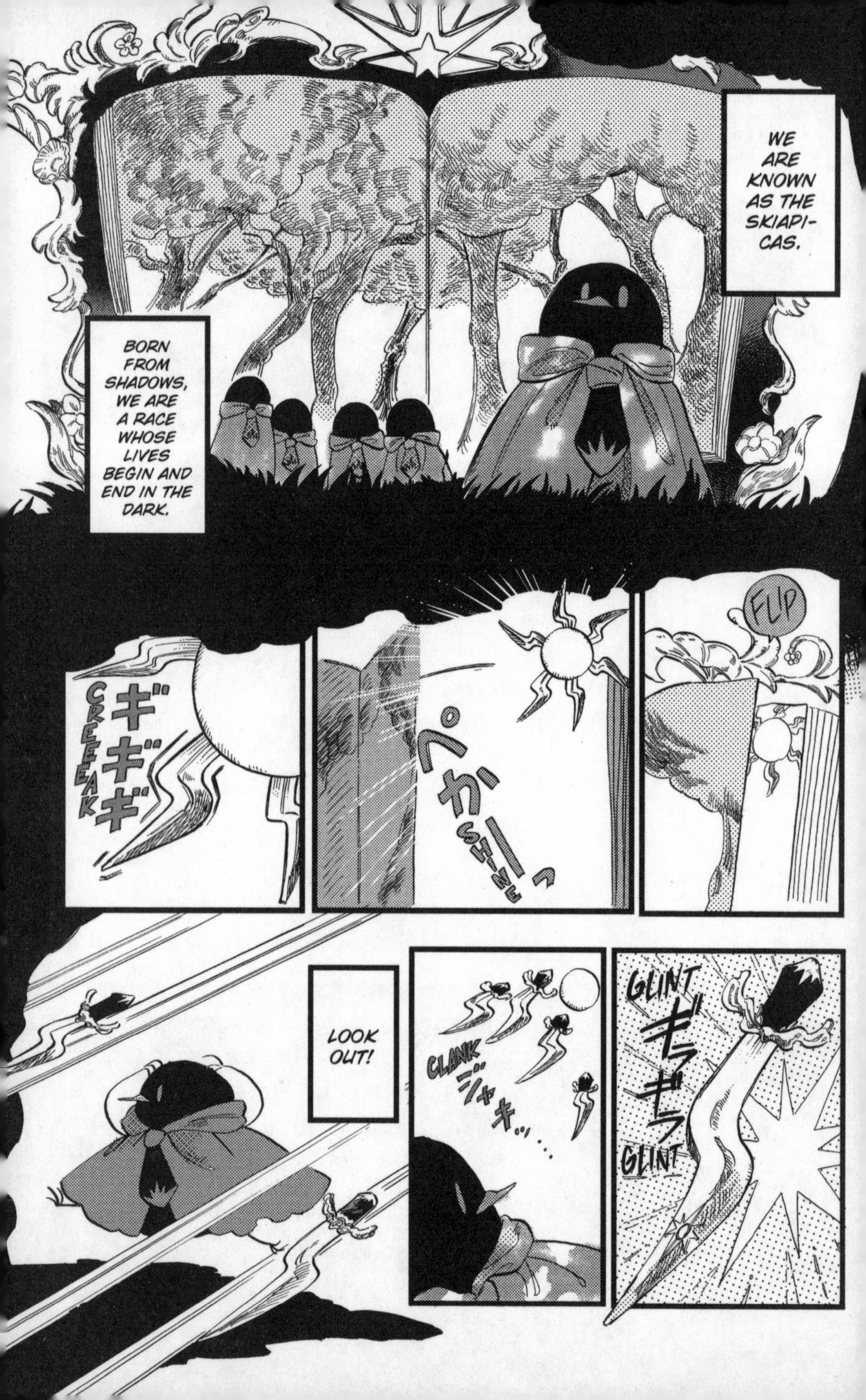
WE ARE KNOWN AS THE SKIAPI-CAS.
BORN FROM SHADOWS, WE ARE A RACE WHOSE LIVES BEGIN AND END IN THE DARK.
FLIP
ぺかー
SHI-NE
CREEEAK
ギギギ
GLINT
ぎらぎら
GLINT
CLANK
ジャキ…
LOOK OUT!

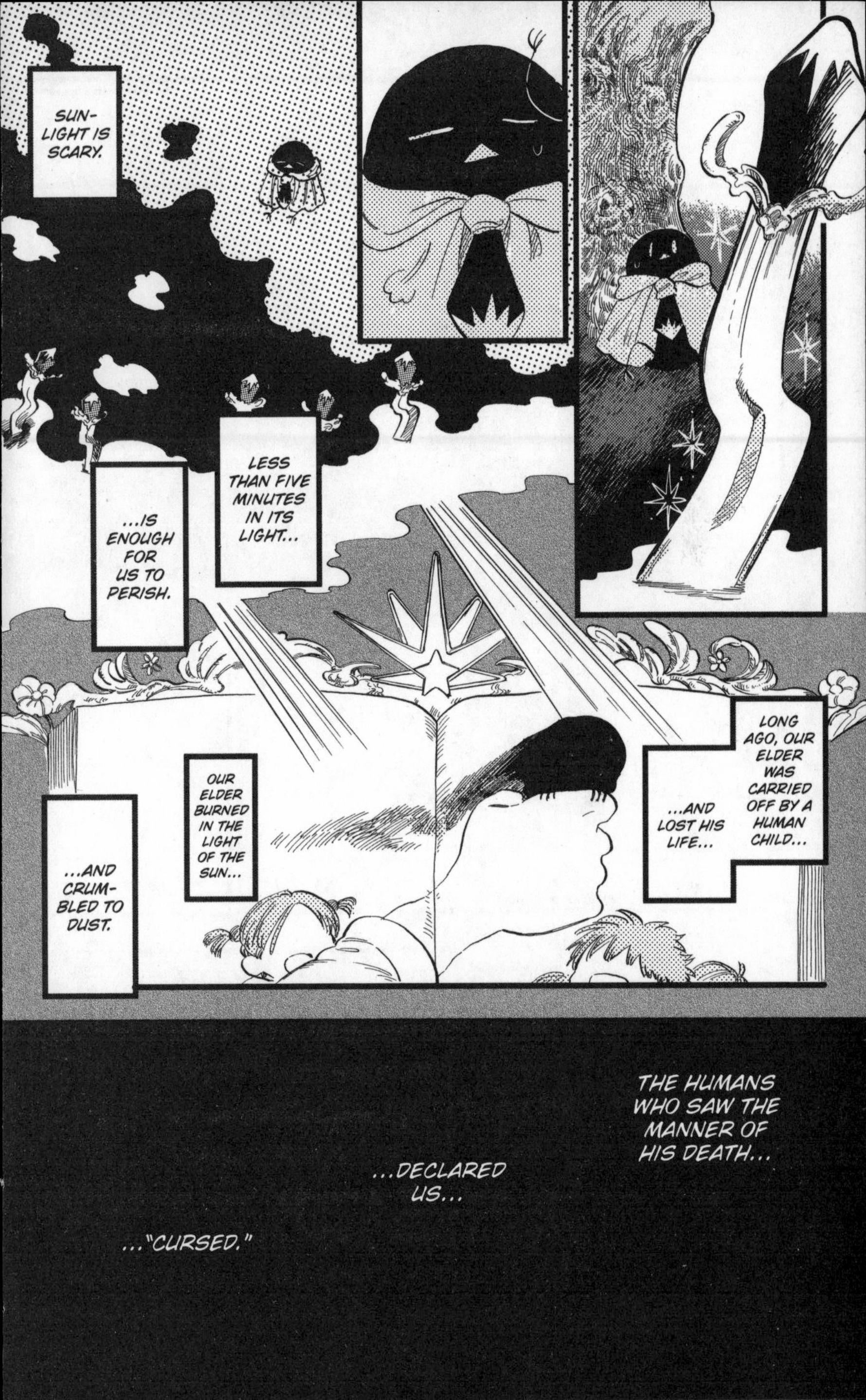
SUN-LIGHT IS SCARY.
LESS THAN FIVE MINUTES IN ITS LIGHT...
...IS ENOUGH FOR US TO PERISH.
LONG AGO, OUR ELDER WAS CARRIED OFF BY A HUMAN CHILD...
...AND LOST HIS LIFE...
OUR ELDER BURNED IN THE LIGHT OF THE SUN...
...AND CRUM-BLED TO DUST.
THE HUMANS WHO SAW THE MANNER OF HIS DEATH...
...DECLARED US...
..."CURSED."

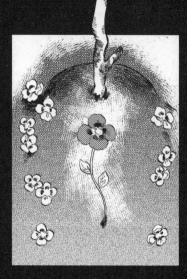

EACH TIME WE VISIT THE ELDER'S GRAVE, WE MAKE A VOW.
WE WILL STAY AWAY FROM HUMANS.
WE WILL REMAIN IN THE DEEP FOREST FOR THE REST OF OUR LIVES.
WE WILL NEVER ALLOW SUCH A TRAGEDY TO OCCUR AGAIN.
ザッ ZOOSH
ザッ ZOOSH
THEN, ONE DAY...
...THERE WAS...
...A HUMAN CHILD IN OUR FOREST.

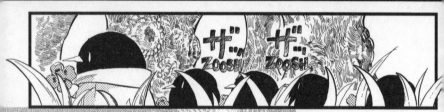

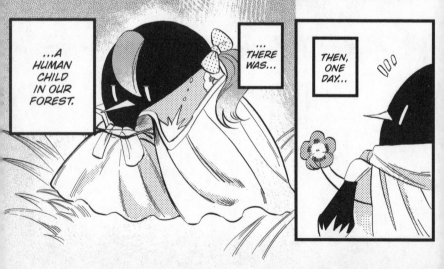

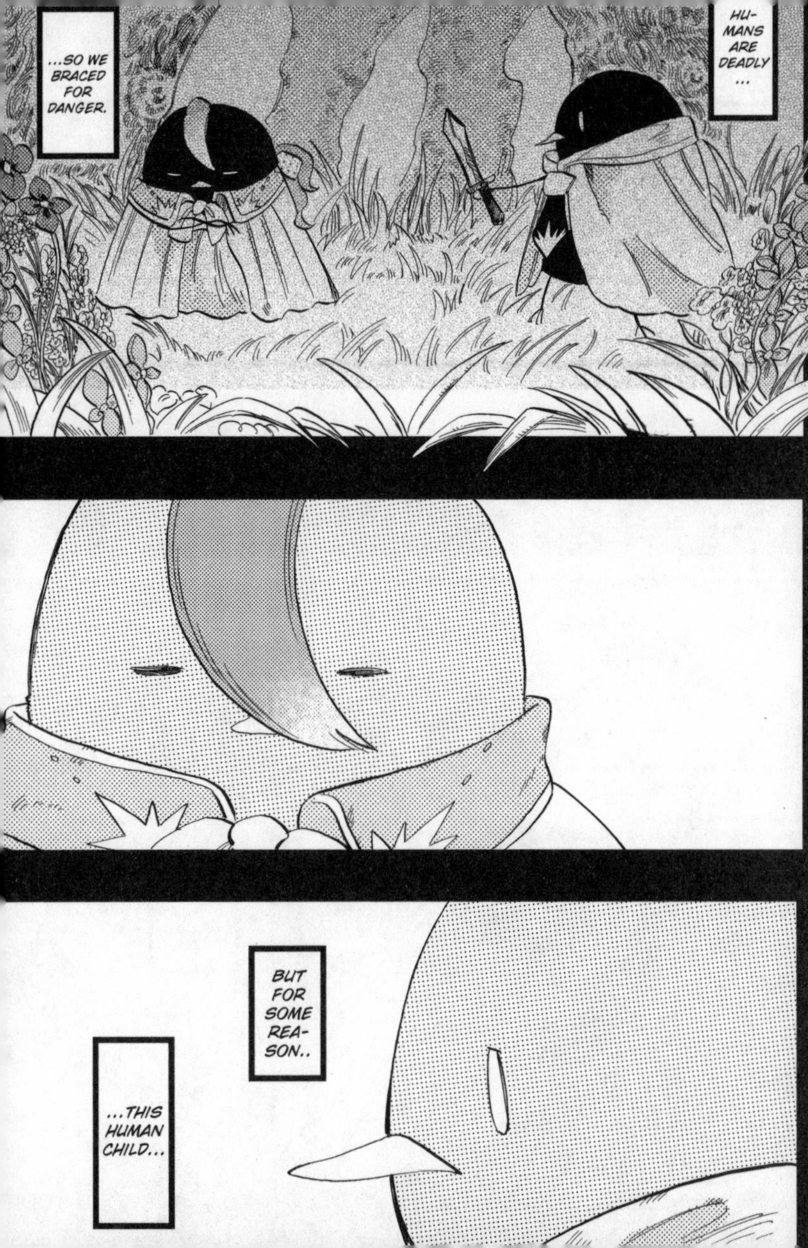
HU-MANS ARE DEADLY...
...SO WE BRACED FOR DANGER.
BUT FOR SOME REA-SON..
...THIS HUMAN CHILD...

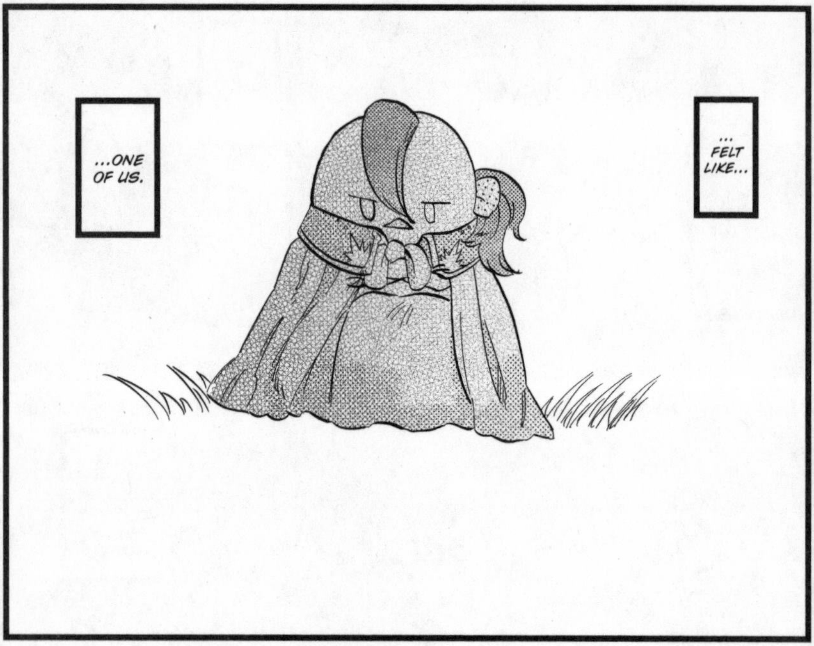
...FELT LIKE...
...ONE OF US.

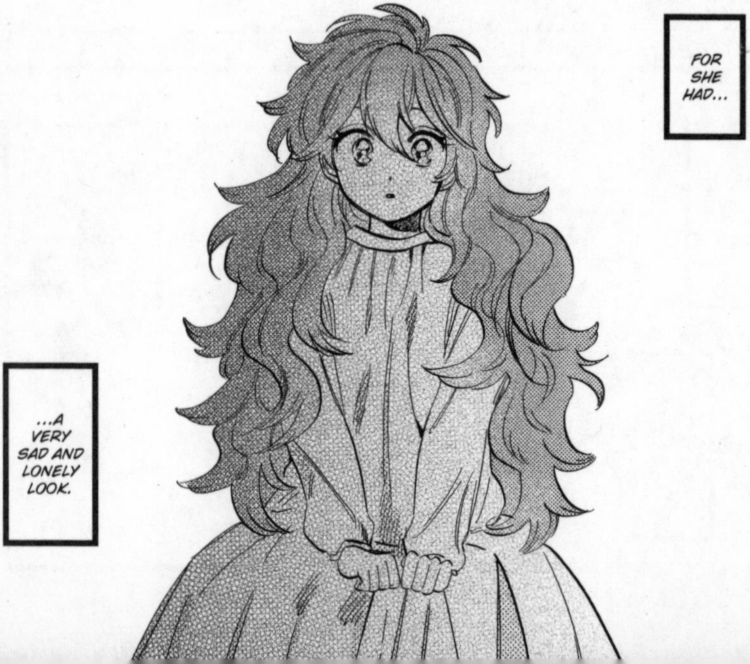
FOR SHE HAD...
...A VERY SAD AND LONELY LOOK.

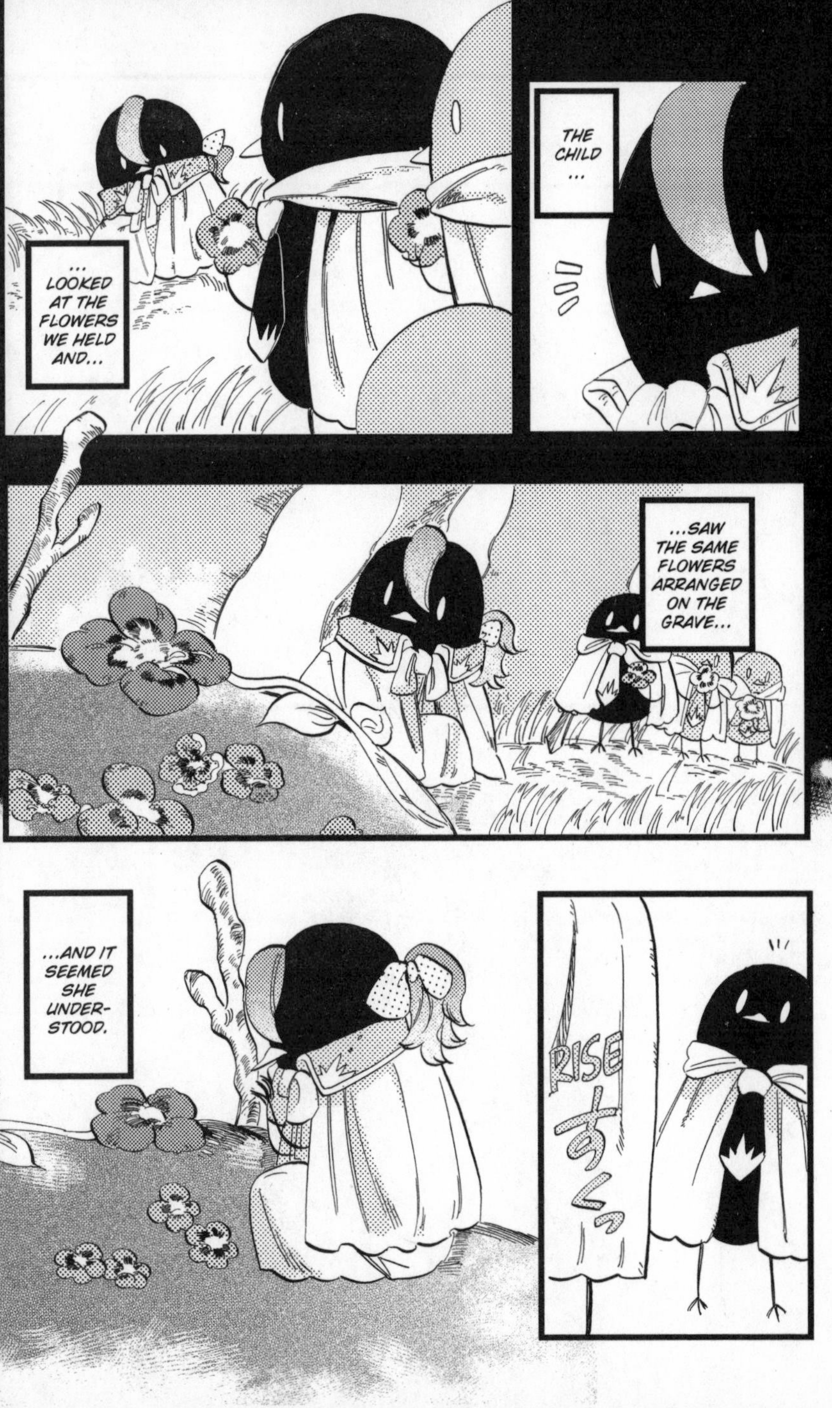
THE CHILD ...
... LOOKED AT THE FLOWERS WE HELD AND...
...SAW THE SAME FLOWERS ARRANGED ON THE GRAVE...
RISE
すっく
...AND IT SEEMED SHE UNDERSTOOD.

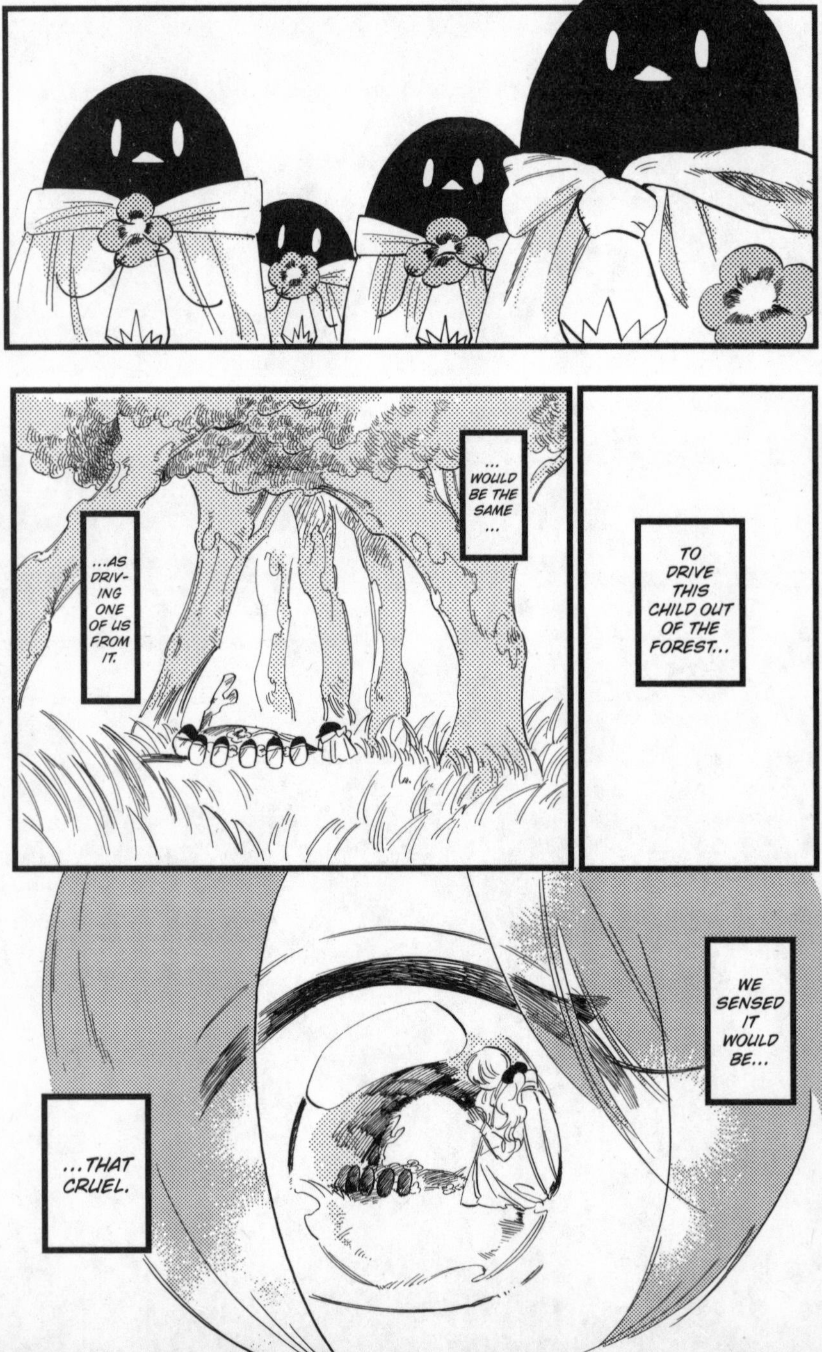
TO DRIVE THIS CHILD OUT OF THE FOREST...
...WOULD BE THE SAME...
...AS DRIVING ONE OF US FROM IT.
WE SENSED IT WOULD BE...
...THAT CRUEL.

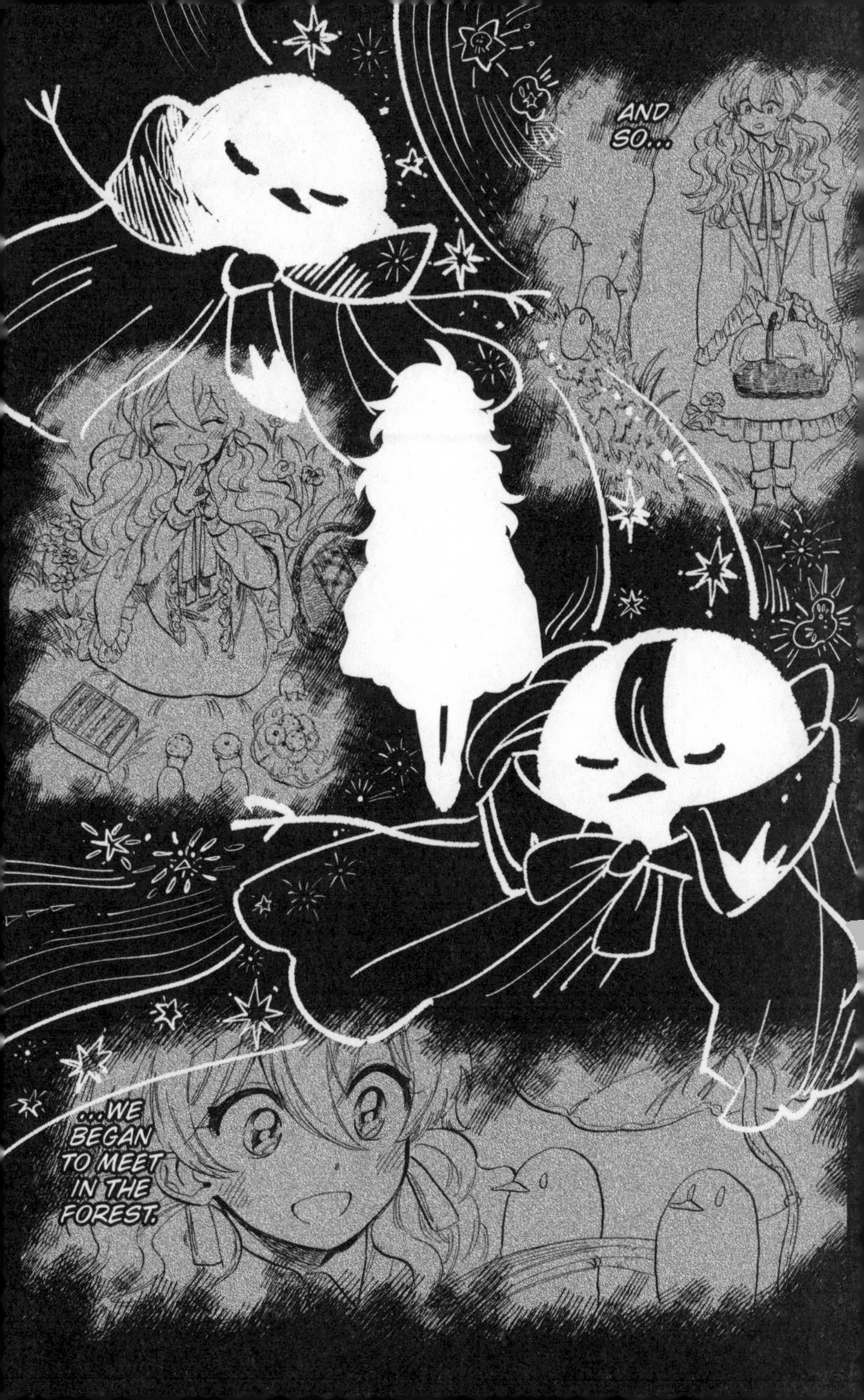
AND SO...
...WE BEGAN TO MEET IN THE FOREST.

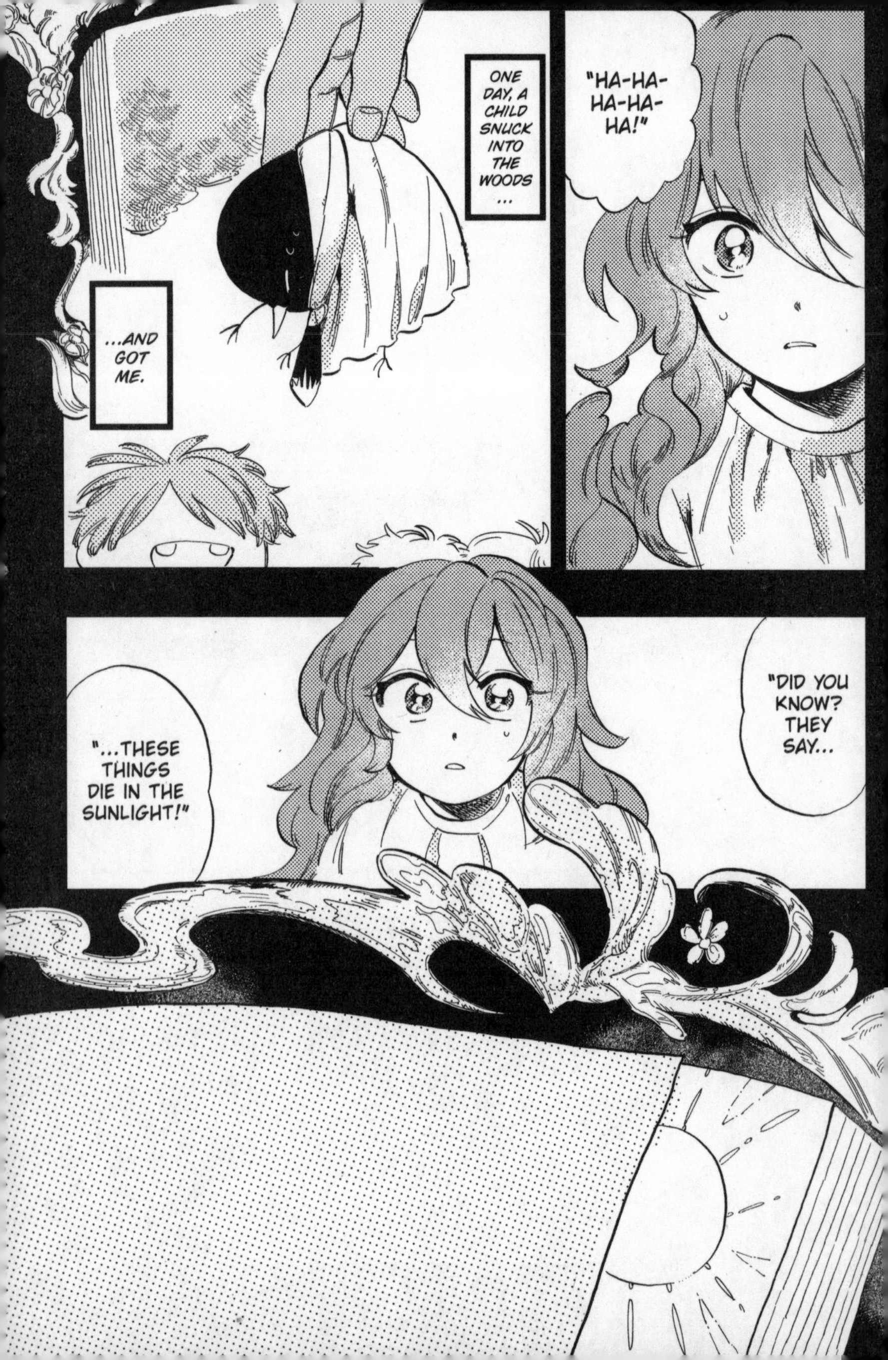
"HA-HA-HA-HA-HA!"
ONE DAY, A CHILD SNUCK INTO THE WOODS ...
...AND GOT ME.
"DID YOU KNOW? THEY SAY...
"...THESE THINGS DIE IN THE SUNLIGHT!"

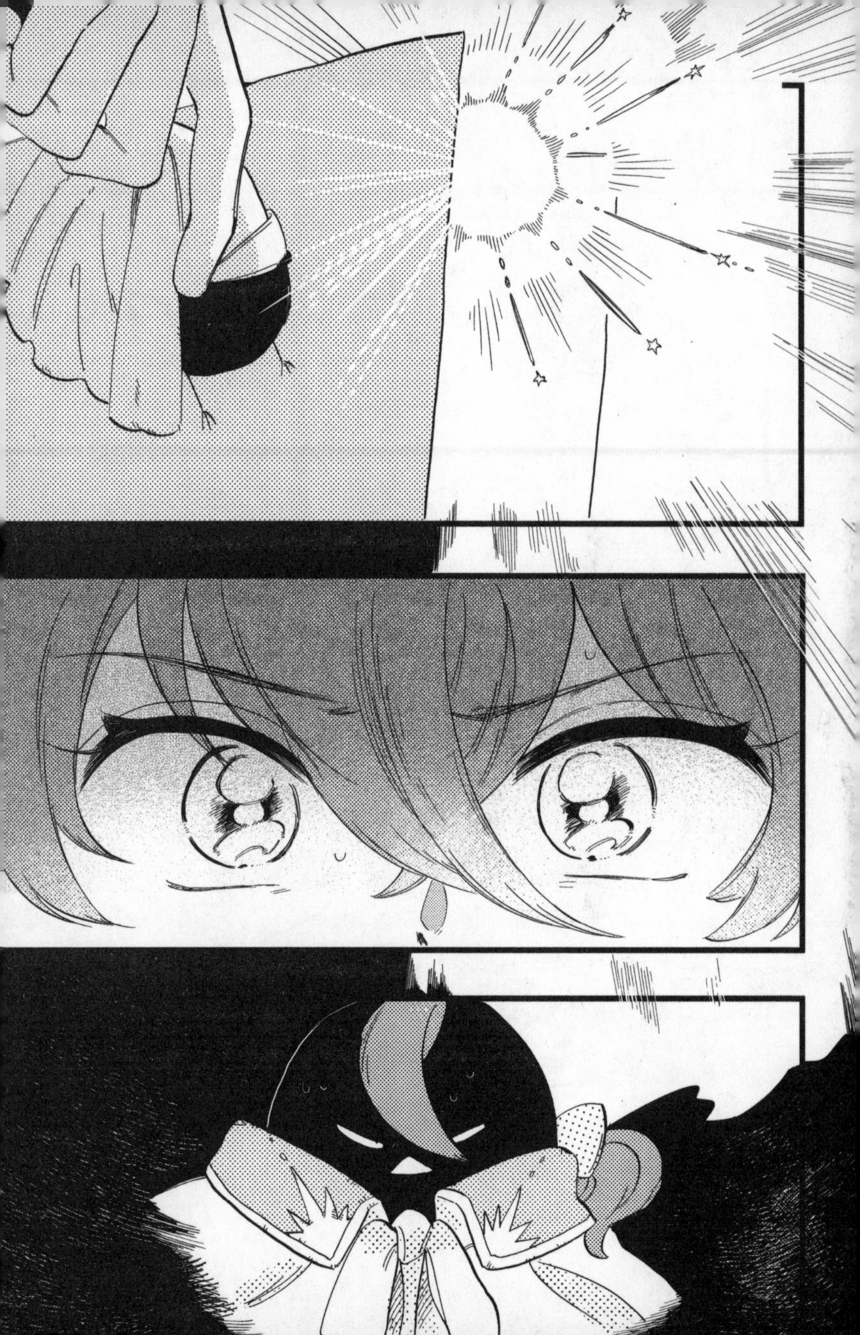

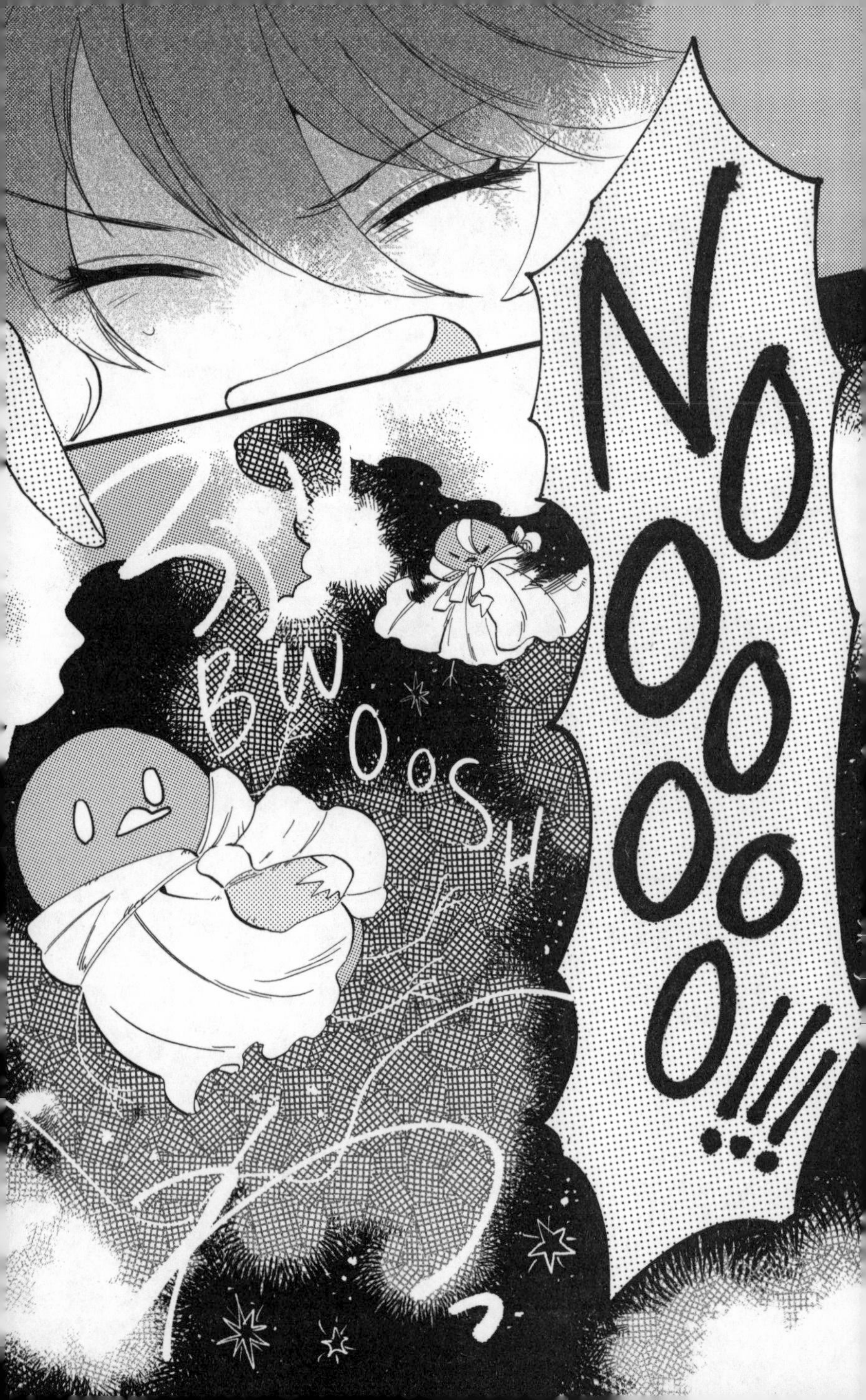
NOOOOOO!!!...
BWOOSH

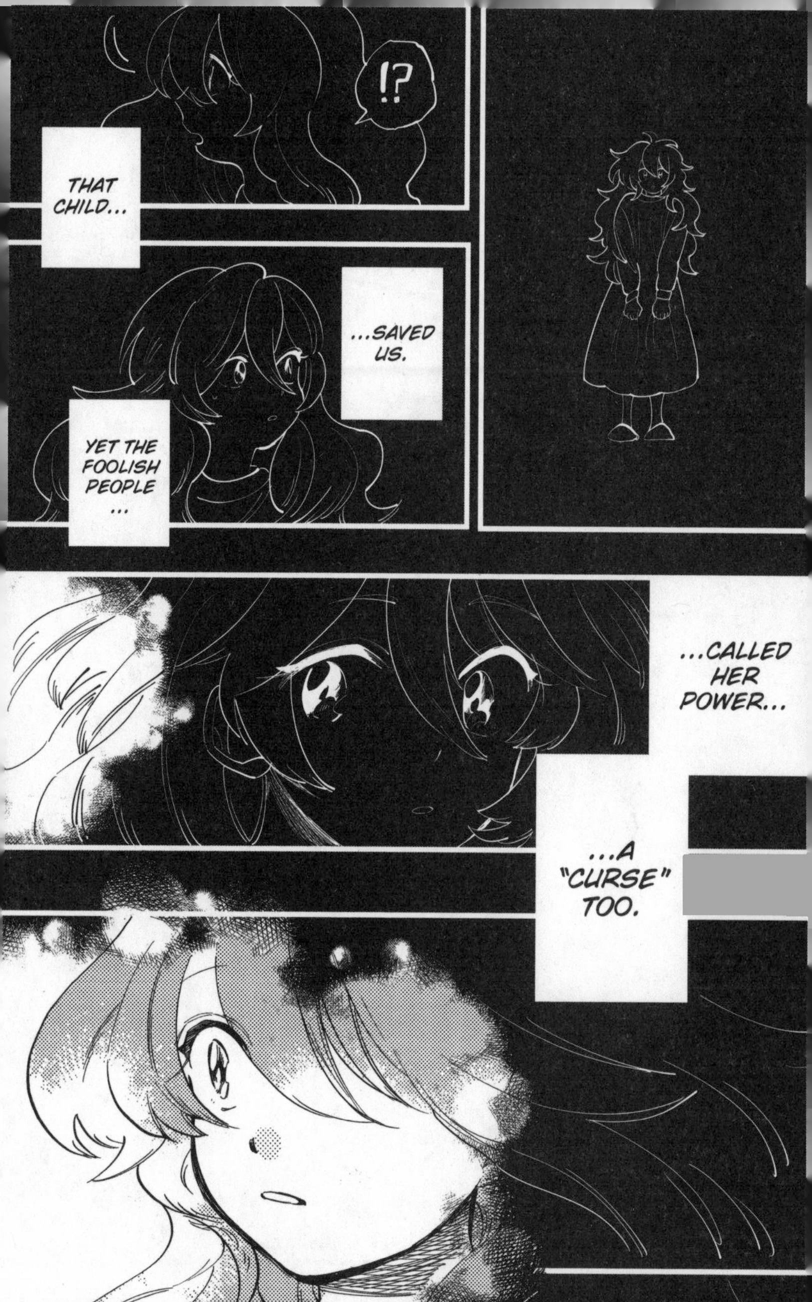
!?
THAT CHILD...
...SAVED US.
YET THE FOOLISH PEOPLE ...
...CALLED HER POWER...
...A "CURSE" TOO.

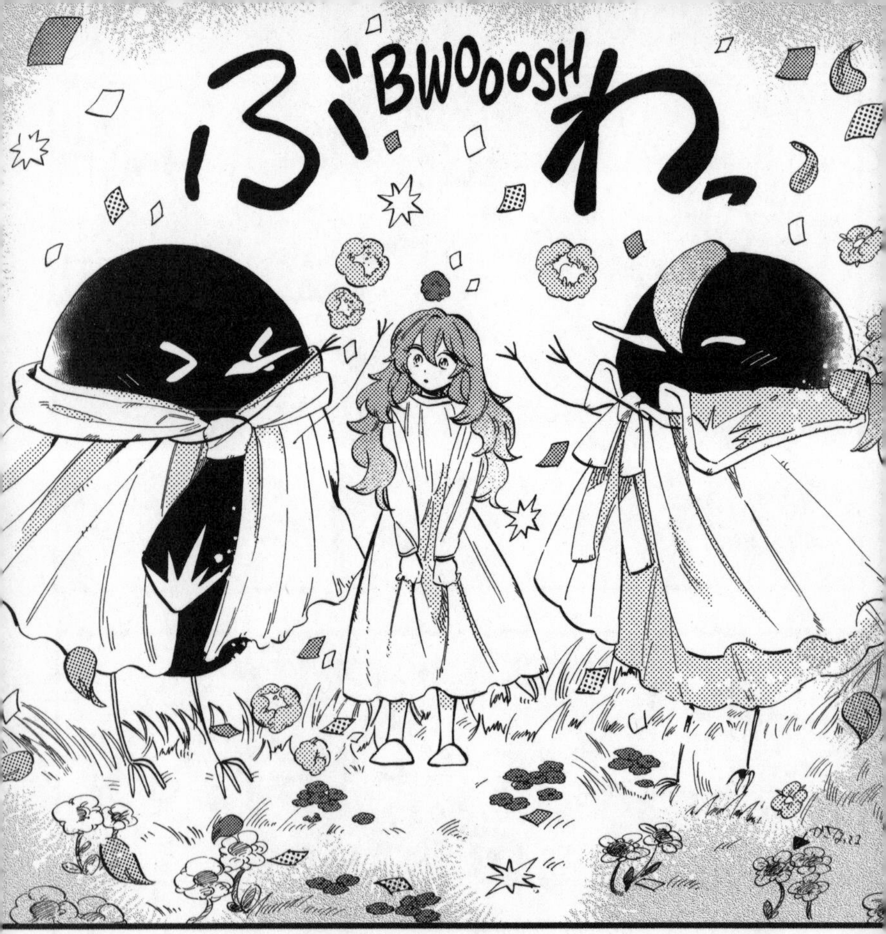
ぶわっ
BWOOOSH

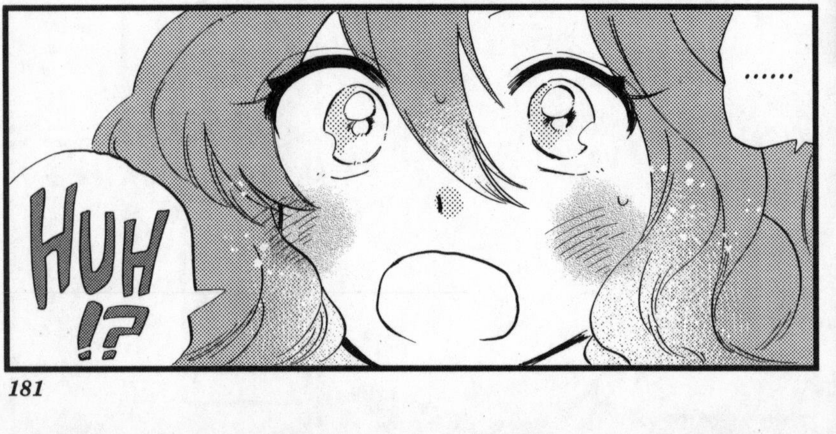
......
HUH!?

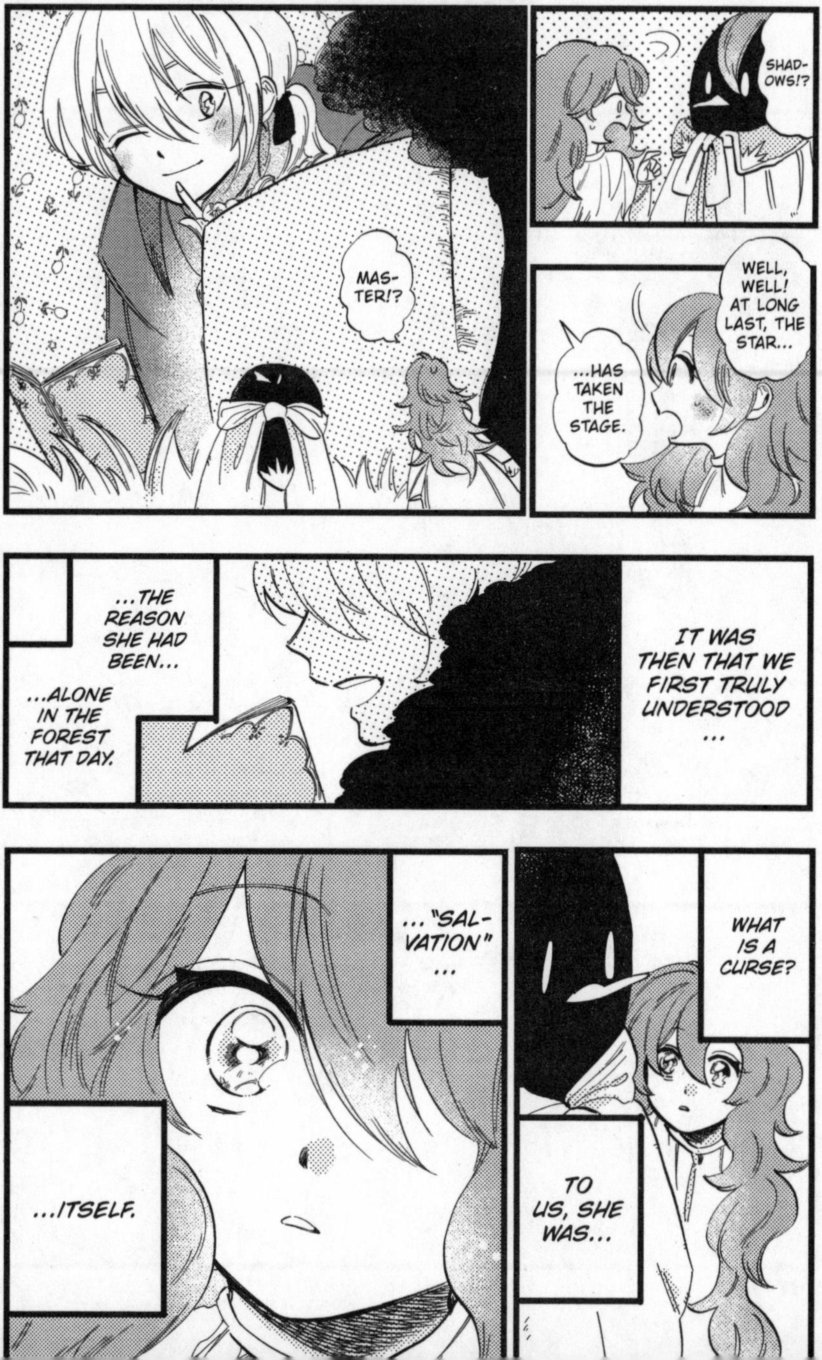
SHADOWS!?
WELL, WELL! AT LONG LAST, THE STAR...
...HAS TAKEN THE STAGE.
MASTER!?
IT WAS THEN THAT WE FIRST TRULY UNDERSTOOD...
...THE REASON SHE HAD BEEN...
...ALONE IN THE FOREST THAT DAY.
WHAT IS A CURSE?
TO US, SHE WAS...
..."SALVATION"...
...ITSELF.

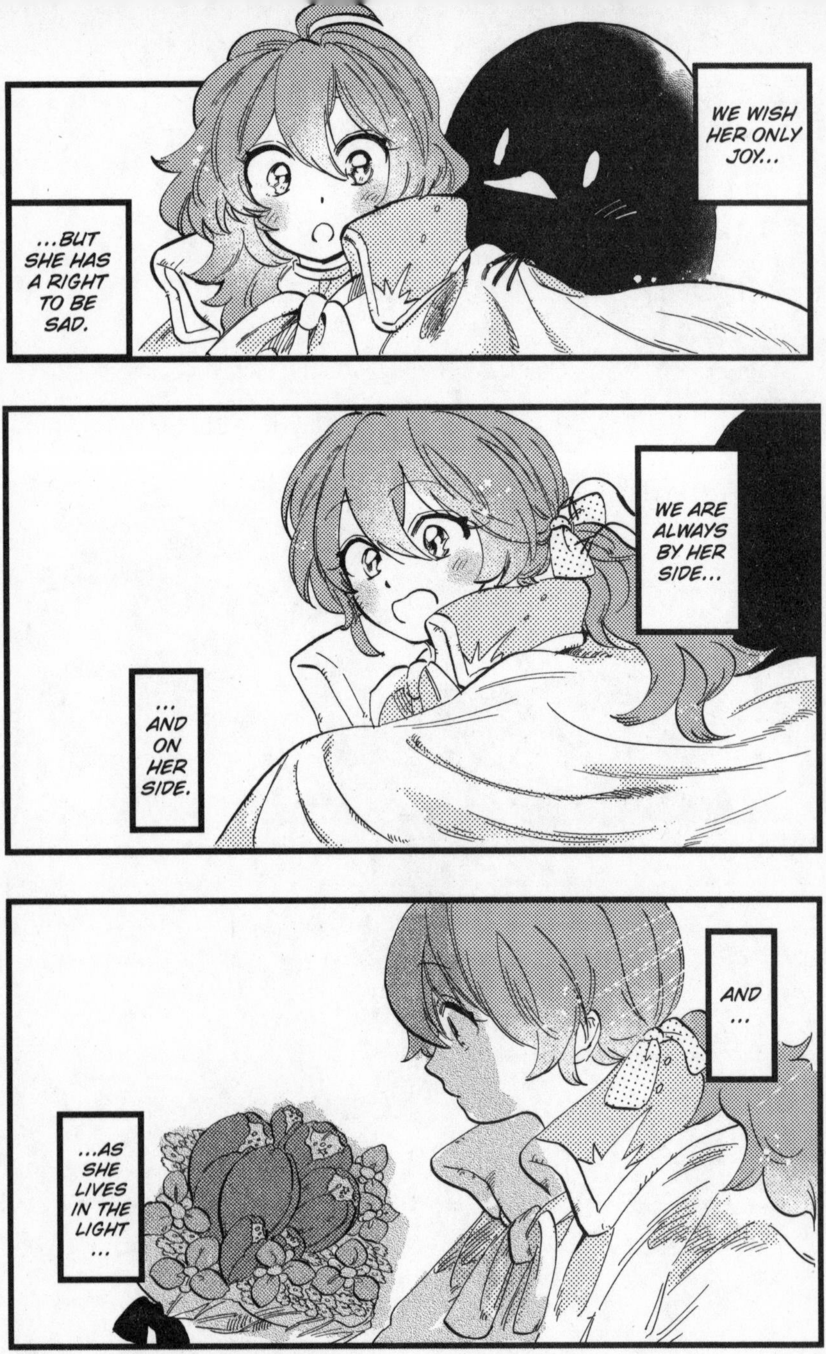
WE WISH HER ONLY JOY...
...BUT SHE HAS A RIGHT TO BE SAD.
WE ARE ALWAYS BY HER SIDE...
... AND ON HER SIDE.
AND ...
...AS SHE LIVES IN THE LIGHT ...

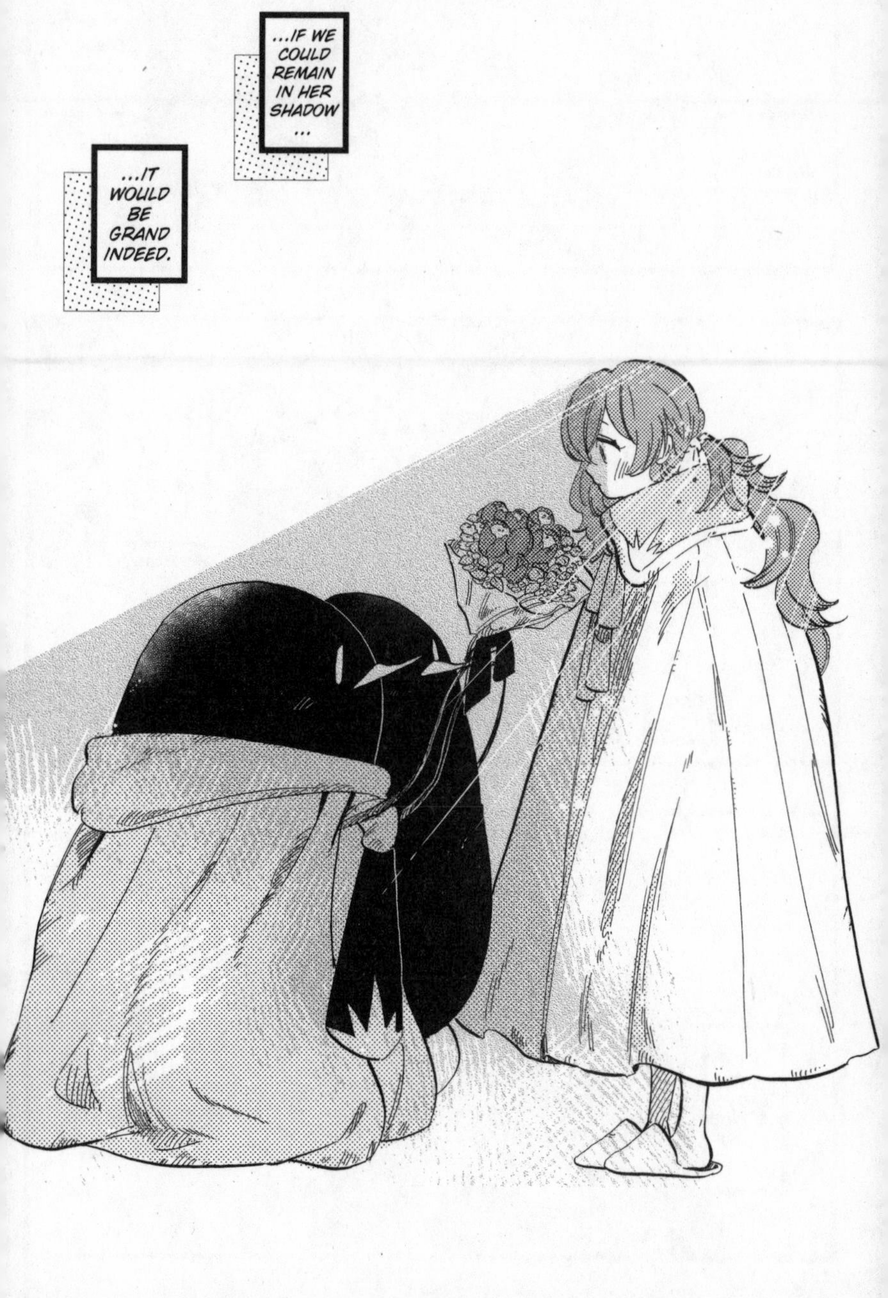
...IF WE COULD REMAIN IN HER SHADOW...
...IT WOULD BE GRAND INDEED.

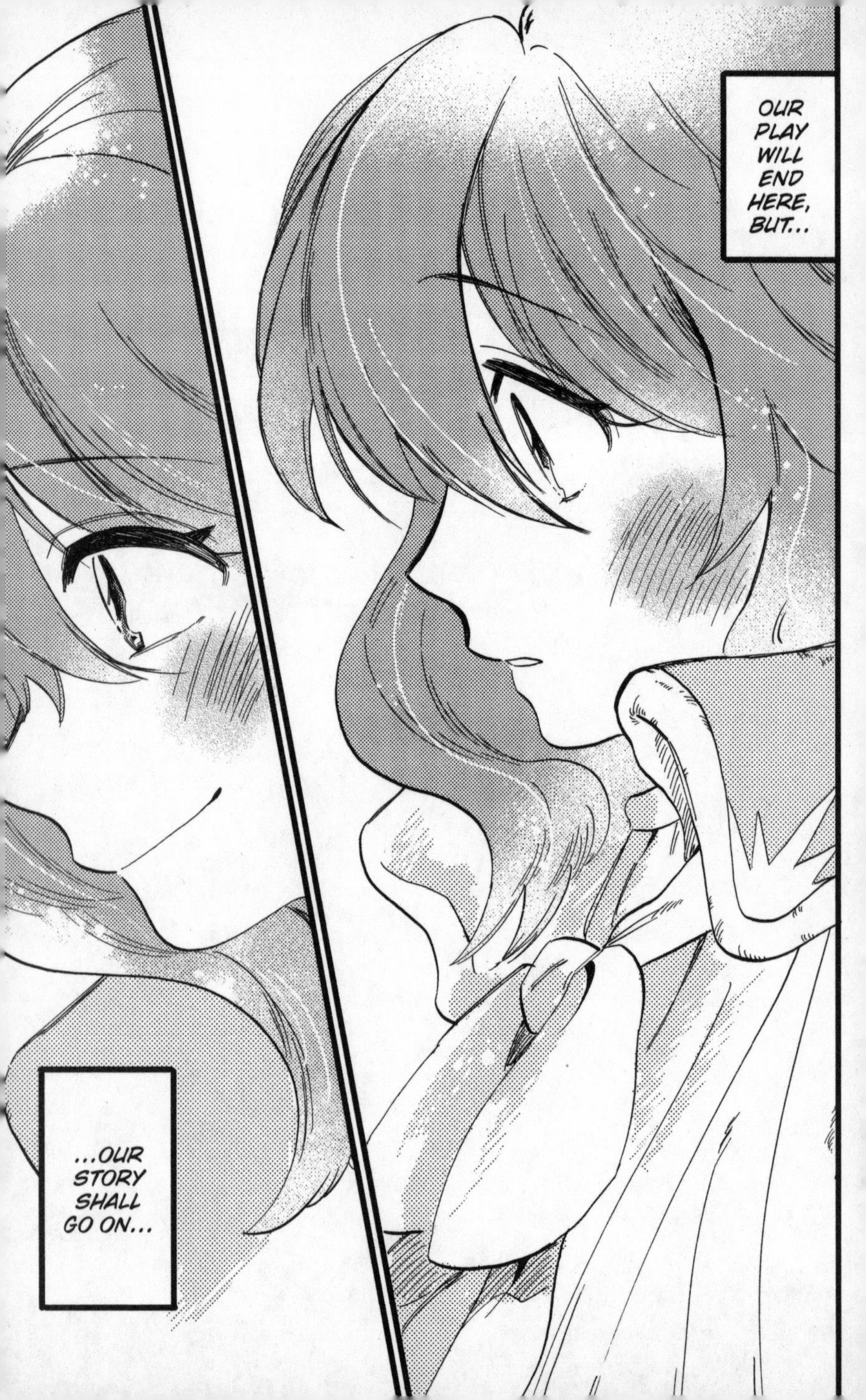
OUR PLAY WILL END HERE, BUT...
...OUR STORY SHALL GO ON...

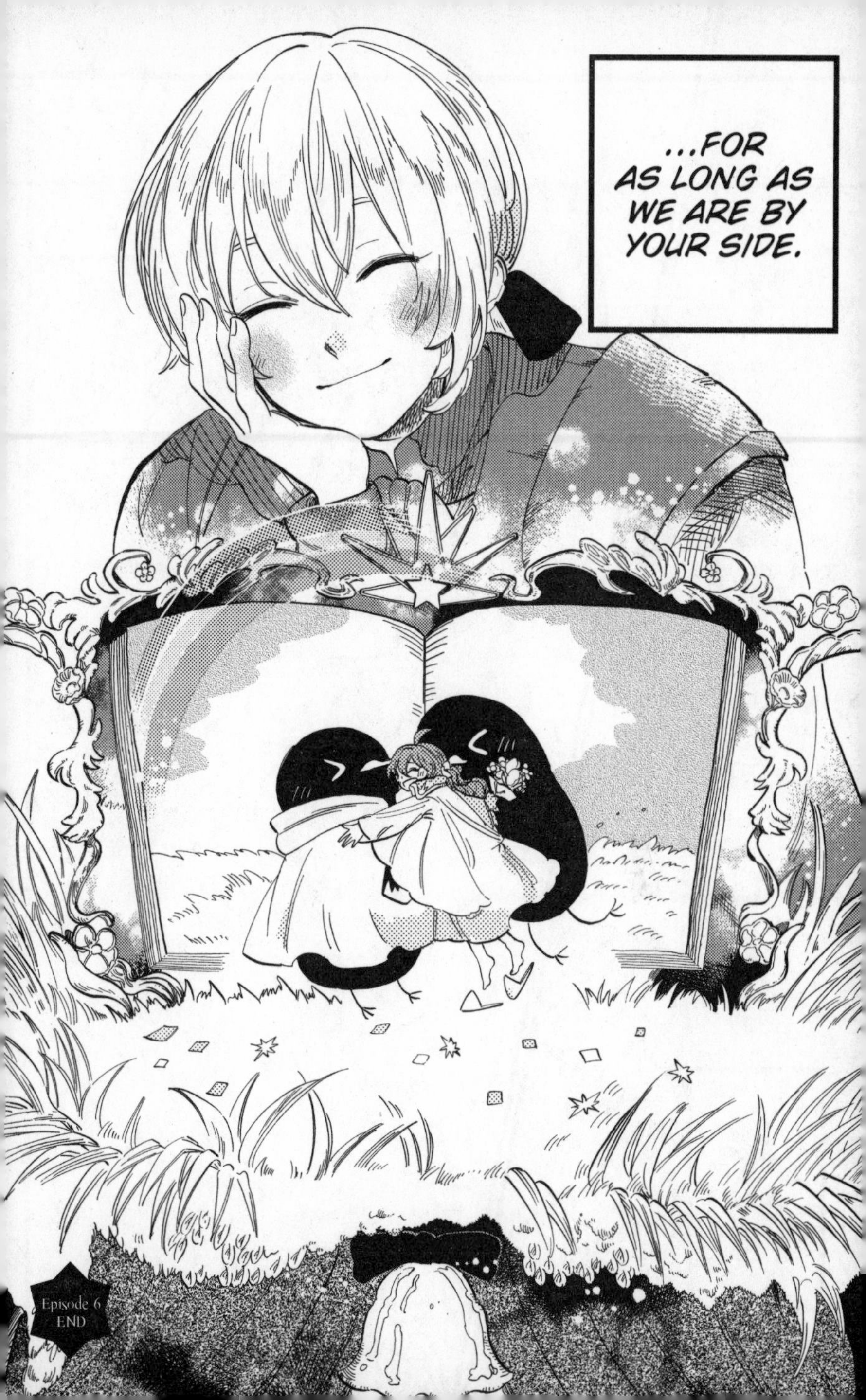
...FOR AS LONG AS WE ARE BY YOUR SIDE.
Episode 6 END

Call the Name of the Night

COMING SOON

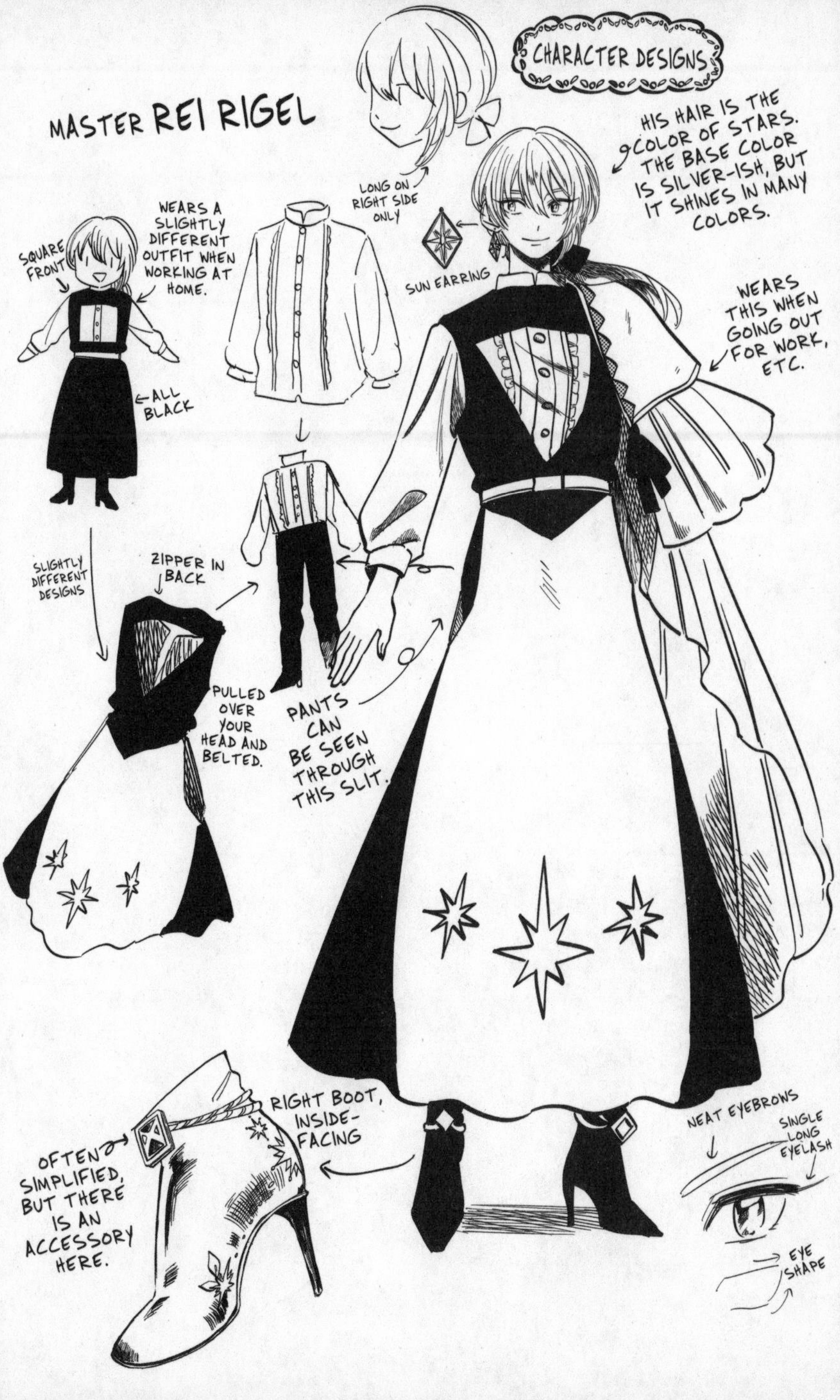
CHARACTER DESIGNS
MASTER REI RIGEL
HIS HAIR IS THE COLOR OF STARS. THE BASE COLOR IS SILVER-ISH, BUT IT SHINES IN MANY COLORS.
LONG ON RIGHT SIDE ONLY
SUN EARRING
WEARS A SLIGHTLY DIFFERENT OUTFIT WHEN WORKING AT HOME.
SQUARE FRONT
ALL BLACK
WEARS THIS WHEN GOING OUT FOR WORK, ETC.
SLIGHTLY DIFFERENT DESIGNS
ZIPPER IN BACK
PULLED OVER YOUR HEAD AND BELTED.
PANTS CAN BE SEEN THROUGH THIS SLIT.
RIGHT BOOT, INSIDE-FACING
OFTEN SIMPLIFIED, BUT THERE IS AN ACCESSORY HERE.
NEAT EYEBROWS
SINGLE LONG EYELASH
EYE SHAPE

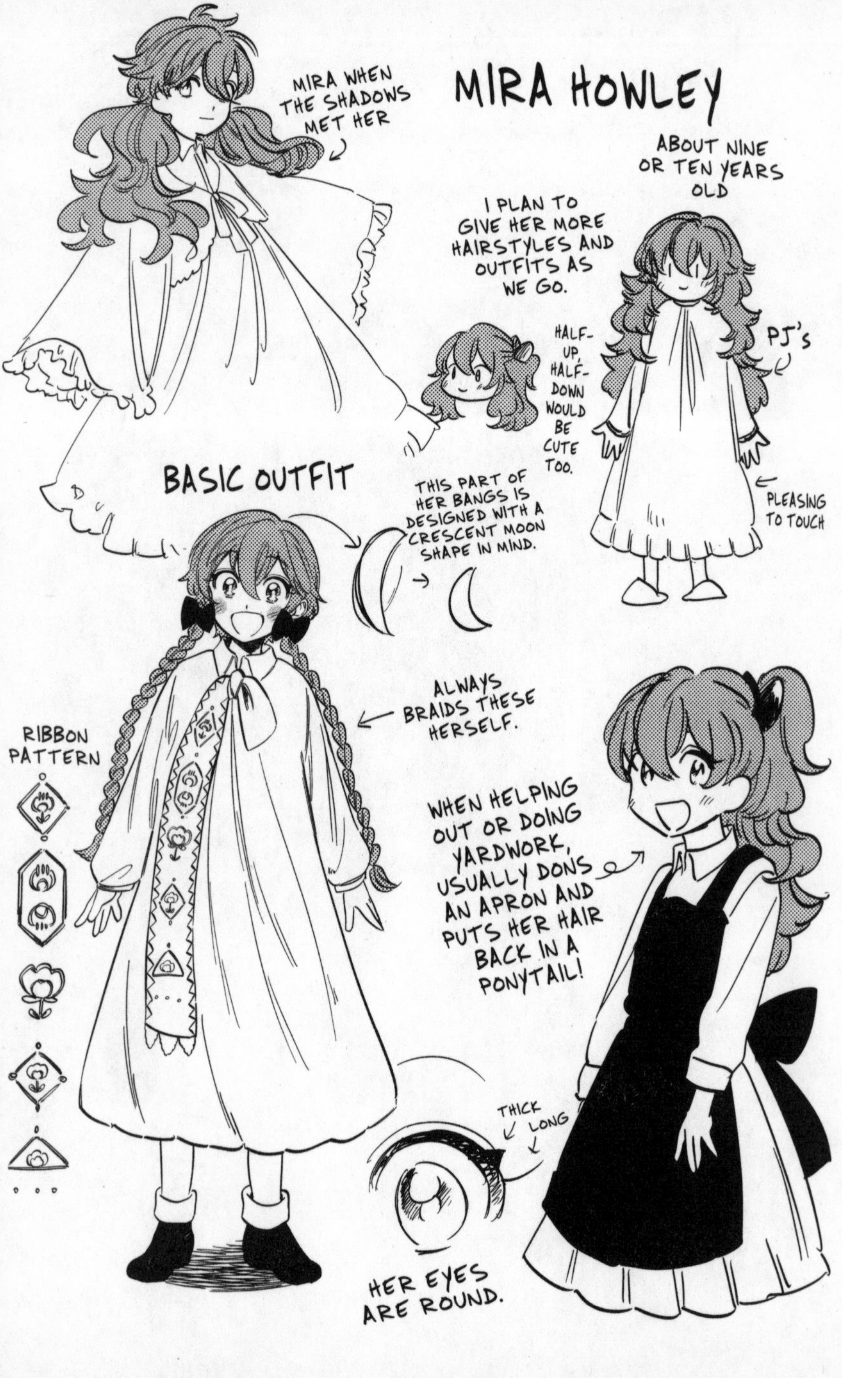
MIRA HOWLEY
MIRA WHEN THE SHADOWS MET HER
ABOUT NINE OR TEN YEARS OLD
I PLAN TO GIVE HER MORE HAIRSTYLES AND OUTFITS AS WE GO.
HALF-UP, HALF-DOWN WOULD BE CUTE TOO.
PJ'S
PLEASING TO TOUCH
BASIC OUTFIT
THIS PART OF HER BANGS IS DESIGNED WITH A CRESCENT MOON SHAPE IN MIND.
ALWAYS BRAIDS THESE HERSELF.
RIBBON PATTERN
WHEN HELPING OUT OR DOING YARDWORK, USUALLY DONS AN APRON AND PUTS HER HAIR BACK IN A PONYTAIL!
THICK
LONG
HER EYES ARE ROUND.

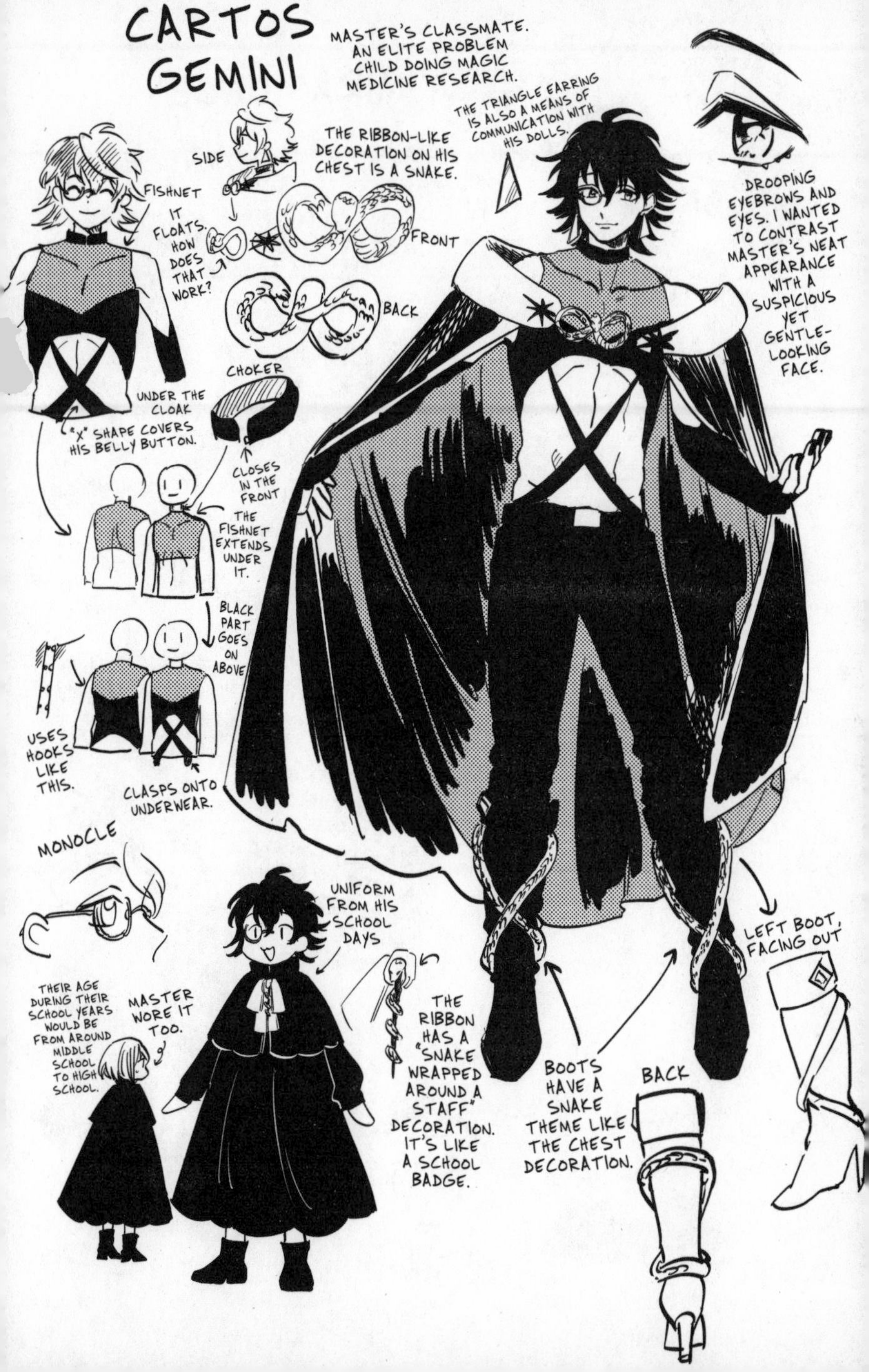

CARTOS GEMINI
MASTER'S CLASSMATE. AN ELITE PROBLEM CHILD DOING MAGIC MEDICINE RESEARCH.
THE TRIANGLE EARRING IS ALSO A MEANS OF COMMUNICATION WITH HIS DOLLS.
THE RIBBON-LIKE DECORATION ON HIS CHEST IS A SNAKE.
SIDE
FISHNET
IT FLOATS. HOW DOES THAT WORK?
FRONT
BACK
DROOPING EYEBROWS AND EYES. I WANTED TO CONTRAST MASTER'S NEAT APPEARANCE WITH A SUSPICIOUS YET GENTLE-LOOKING FACE.
CHOKER
UNDER THE CLOAK
"X" SHAPE COVERS HIS BELLY BUTTON.
CLOSES IN THE FRONT
THE FISHNET EXTENDS UNDER IT.
BLACK PART GOES ON ABOVE
USES HOOKS LIKE THIS.
CLASPS ONTO UNDERWEAR.
MONOCLE
UNIFORM FROM HIS SCHOOL DAYS
THEIR AGE DURING THEIR SCHOOL YEARS WOULD BE FROM AROUND MIDDLE SCHOOL TO HIGH SCHOOL.
MASTER WORE IT TOO.
THE RIBBON HAS A "SNAKE WRAPPED AROUND A STAFF" DECORATION. IT'S LIKE A SCHOOL BADGE.
BOOTS HAVE A SNAKE THEME LIKE THE CHEST DECORATION.
BACK
LEFT BOOT, FACING OUT

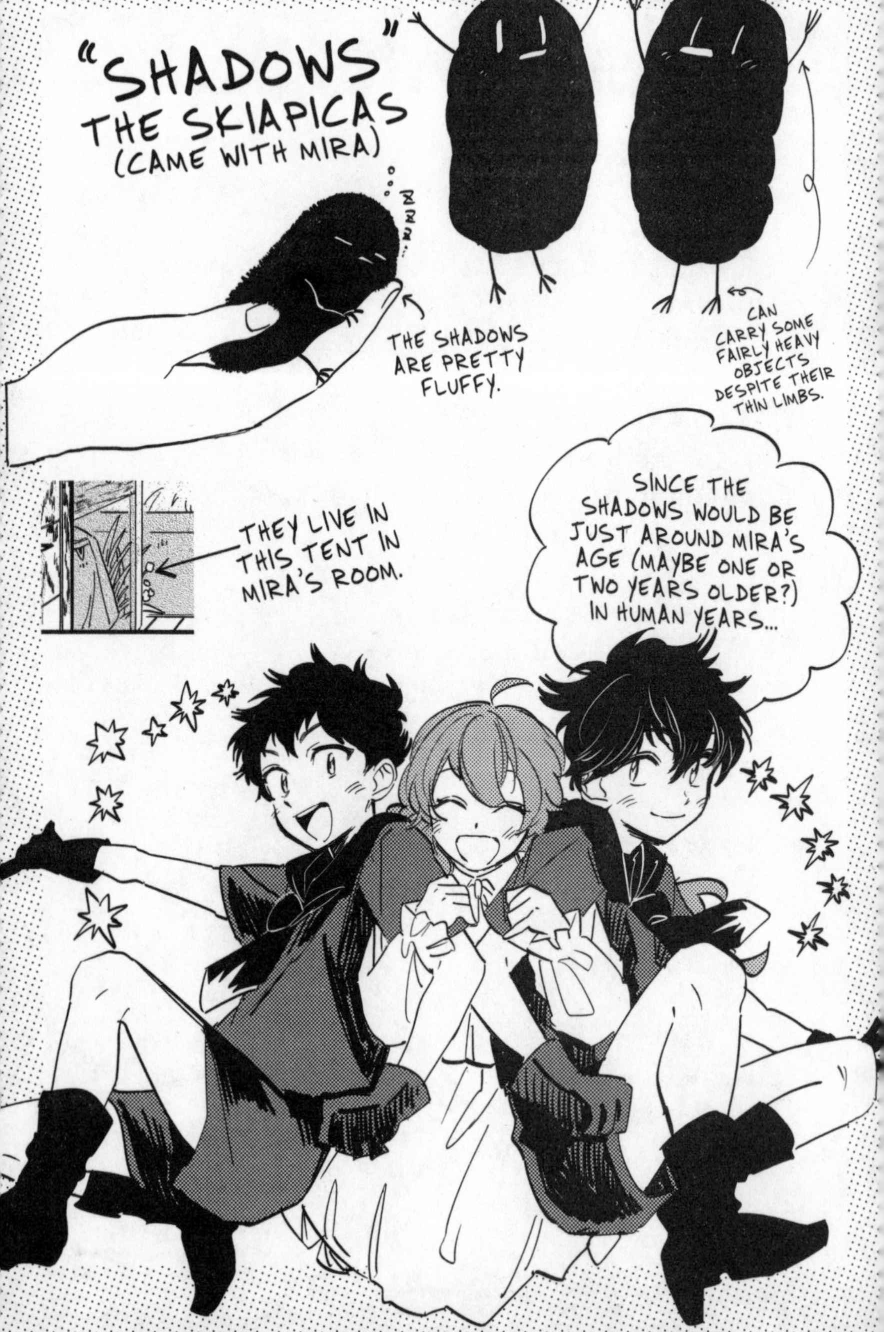
"SHADOWS"
THE SKIAPICAS
(CAME WITH MIRA)
ZZZ...
CAN CARRY SOME FAIRLY HEAVY OBJECTS DESPITE THEIR THIN LIMBS.
THE SHADOWS ARE PRETTY FLUFFY.
SINCE THE SHADOWS WOULD BE JUST AROUND MIRA'S AGE (MAYBE ONE OR TWO YEARS OLDER?) IN HUMAN YEARS...
THEY LIVE IN THIS TENT IN MIRA'S ROOM.

AFTERWORD

Pleased to meet you.
I'm Tama Mitsuboshi
This is *Call the Name of the Night* volume 1.
Thank you very (Soooo much!) much for picking it up!! (I'm tickled pink!!)

The star jam chapter was inspired by memories of the raspberry jam my grandmother would sometimes make.

I feel a renewed sense that I've lived along with many different kinds of time that someone else gave me.

I expect Mira and friends will also give and be given lots of time.

It would make me happy if you could watch over them.

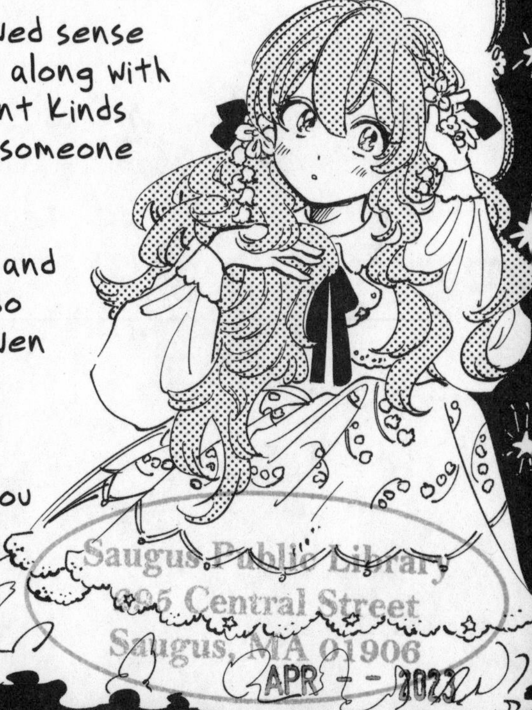

みつぼしたま
Tama Mitsuboshi

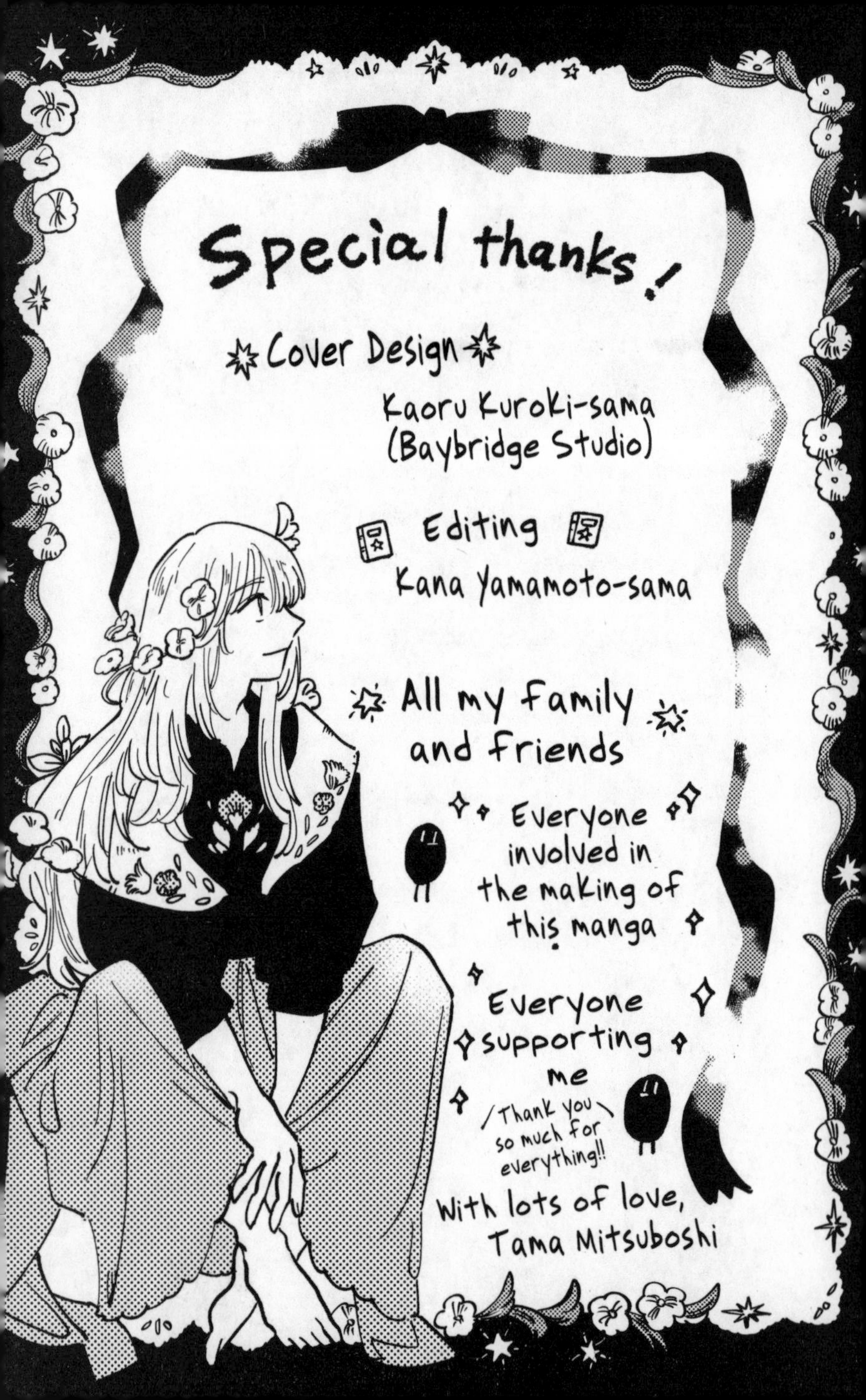
Special thanks!
Cover Design
Kaoru Kuroki-sama
(Baybridge Studio)
Editing
Kana Yamamoto-sama
All my family and friends
Everyone involved in the making of this manga
Everyone supporting me
Thank you so much for everything!!
With lots of love,
Tama Mitsuboshi

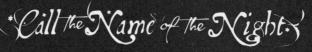

Call the Name of the Night

Tama Mitsuboshi

1

Translation: AMANDA HALEY ✳ Lettering: LYS BLAKESLEE

YORU NO NAMAE O YONDE Vol. 1

First published in Japan in 2021 by KADOKAWA CORPORATION, Tokyo.
English translation rights arranged with KADOKAWA CORPORATION, Tokyo, through Tuttle-Mori Agency, Inc., Tokyo.

Yen Press
150 West 30th Street, 19th Floor
New York, NY 10001

Visit us at yenpress.com ✳ facebook.com/yenpress ✳ twitter.com/yenpress
yenpress.tumblr.com ✳ instagram.com/yenpress

First Yen Press Edition: March 2023

Edited by Yen Press Editorial: Danielle Niederkorn, JuYoun Lee
Designed by Yen Press Design: Wendy Chan

Yen Press is an imprint of Yen Press, LLC.
The Yen Press name and logo are trademarks of Yen Press, LLC.
The publisher is not responsible for websites (or their content) that are not owned by the publisher.

Library of Congress Control Number: 2022950357

ISBNs: 978-1-9753-5200-4 (paperback)
978-1-9753-5201-1 (ebook)

1 3 5 7 9 10 8 6 4 2

WOR

Printed in the United States of America